THE HIDDEN PLACES OF
YORKSHIRE

By David Gerrard

Published by:
Travel Publishing Ltd
Airport Business Centre, 10 Thornbury Road,
Estover, Plymouth PL6 7PP

ISBN13 9781904434955

First Published: 1990   Second Edition: 1993
Third Edition: 1995   Fourth Edition: 1998
Fifth Edition: 2000   Sixth Edition: 2002
Seventh Edition: 2004   Eighth Edition: 2006
Ninth Edition: 2008   Tenth Edition: 2010

Please Note:

All advertisements in this publication have been accepted in
good faith by Travel Publishing.

All information is included by the publishers in good faith and
is believed to be correct at the time of going to press. No
responsibility can be accepted for errors.

Editor: David Gerrard

Printing by: Latimer Trend, Plymouth

Location Maps: © Maps in Minutes ™ (2010)
                   © Collins Bartholomews 2010 All rights reserved.

Cover Photo: Whitby Abbey, Whitby, Yorkshire
                   © www.britainonview.co.uk

Text Photos: See page 311

Foreword

This is the 10th edition of the *Hidden Places of Yorkshire* which has an attractive new cover and redesigned page layouts. The changes will significantly improve the usefulness, accessibility and appeal of the guide. We do hope you like the new look.

Editorially, the new style will continue Travel Publishing's commitment to exploring the more interesting, unusual or unique places of interest in Yorkshire. In this respect we would like to thank the Tourist Information Centres in Yorkshire for helping us update the editorial content of the book.

The county of Yorkshire is full of scenic, historical and cultural diversity. In the northwest are the picturesque Dales with their varied scenery of peat moorland, green pastureland and scattered woods intersected by numerous brooks, streams and rivers. To the northeast are the imposing Yorkshire Moors, the rich agricultural Vale of York, the chalky hills of the Wolds and the dramatic storm-tossed coastline. In the south and west are the industrial and commercial cities and towns, which have made such a major contribution to our industrial and cultural heritage

The Hidden Places of Yorkshire contains a wealth of interesting information on the history, the countryside, the cities, towns and villages of England's largest county. But it also promotes the more secluded and little known visitor attractions and advertises places to stay, eat and drink many of which are easy to miss unless you know exactly where you are going. These are cross-referenced to more detailed information contained in a separate, easy-to-use section to the rear of the book. This section is also available as a free supplement from the local Tourist Information Offices.

We include hotels, bed & breakfasts, restaurants, pubs, bars, teashops and cafes as well as historic houses, museums, gardens and many other attractions throughout Yorkshire, all of which are comprehensively indexed. Many places are accompanied by an attractive photograph and are easily located by using the map at the beginning of each chapter. We do not award merit marks or rankings but concentrate on describing the more interesting, unusual or unique features of each place with the aim of making the reader's stay in the local area an enjoyable and stimulating experience.

Whether you are travelling around Yorkshire on business or for pleasure we do hope that you enjoy reading and using this book. We are always interested in what readers think of places covered (or not covered) in our guides so please do not hesitate to use the reader reaction form provided to give us your considered comments. We also welcome any general comments which will help us improve the guides themselves. Finally if you are planning to visit any other corner of the British Isles we would like to refer you to the list of other *Hidden Places* titles to be found to the rear of the book and to the Travel Publishing website.

Travel Publishing

Did you know that you can also search our website for details of thousands of places to see, stay, eat or drink throughout Britain and Ireland? Our site has become increasingly popular and now receives hundreds of thousands of visits. Try it!

website: www.findsomewhere.co.uk

Location Map

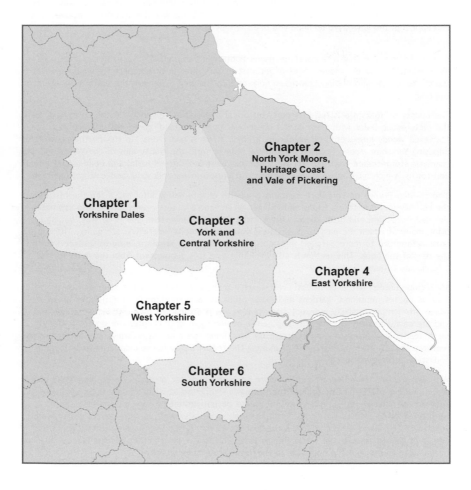

Chapter 2
North York Moors,
Heritage Coast
and Vale of Pickering

Chapter 1
Yorkshire Dales

Chapter 3
York and
Central Yorkshire

Chapter 4
East Yorkshire

Chapter 5
West Yorkshire

Chapter 6
South Yorkshire

Contents

LOCATION MAP

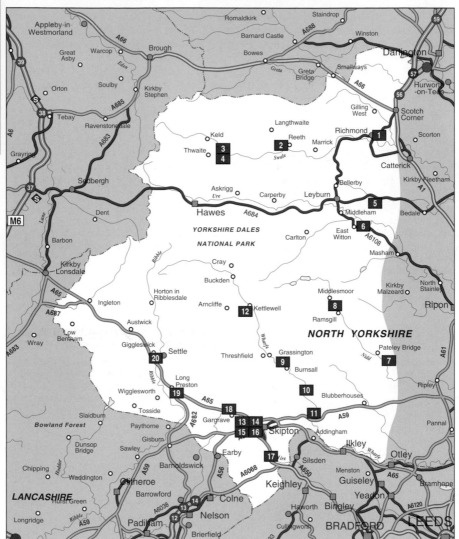

YORKSHIRE DALES

With most of this extensive region protected from unsuitable development by its status as a National Park, the Yorkshire Dales look set to enjoy many more years of unspoilt scenic glory. Within the 680 square miles of the Park, those glories vary from dale to dale. Swaledale has a rugged beauty that is in contrast to the pretty and busier Wensleydale to the south. One of the longer dales, Wensleydale is a place of green pastureland grazed by flocks of Wensleydale sheep, lines of drystone walls and, of course, this is where the famous cheese is made. Further south again, is Wharfedale, a spectacular valley that is home to one of the National Park's most famous features, the Strid, where the River Wharfe charges through a narrow gorge just to the north of Bolton Abbey.

To the east lies Nidderdale, a charming valley that was dubbed 'Little Switzerland' by the Victorians as its upper reaches are steep and wooded with the River Nidd flowing through narrow gorges. To the west is Ribblesdale, overlooked by the famous Three Peaks of Whernside, Ingleborough and Pen-ghent. It also contains a spectacular stretch of the famous Settle-Carlisle Railway. Finally, there is Airedale, the valley of the River Aire. The most notable natural feature here is the extraordinary limestone landscape around Malham Tarn. Further downstream lies Skipton, an ancient market town and 'Gateway to the Dales' that is often many people's first experience of this glorious region of Britain.

Accommodation

Food & Drink

Food & Drink

Places of Interest

SWALEDALE

For many, Swaledale is the loveliest of the Yorkshire Dales. From historic Richmond it runs westwards through countryside that ranges from the dramatic lower dale with its steep-sided wooded hills to austere upper reaches – a terrain where your nearest neighbour could be several miles away. Its rugged beauty makes quite a contrast to pretty and busier Wensleydale just to the south. There are several other noticeable differences: the villages in Swaledale all have harsher, Nordic sounding names, the dale is much less populated, and the rivers and becks are fast-flowing mountain streams.

River Swale, Swaledale

At one time Swaledale was a hive of activity and enjoyed a prosperous century and more when the lead-mining industry flourished here. The valley of the River Swale still bears many of the scars left behind since the mining declined and the dale once again became a remote and under-populated place. The attractive market town of Richmond, first settled by the Romans, has for many years been the major focal point of this northerly region of Yorkshire. With several interesting museums, a fine Norman castle and good shopping facilities, Richmond is still the key town in the northern dales.

There are several side dales to Swaledale: the small, thriving market town of Reeth lies at the junction of Arkengarthdale and the valley of the River Swale. First settled by Norsemen who preferred wild and remote countryside, the valley of Arkle Beck was not considered important enough to gain an entry in the *Domesday Book*. There is much evidence of the old lead-mining days although the dale is now chiefly populated by hardy Swaledale sheep. At the head of this rather bleak and barren dale stands England's highest inn, Tan Hill. Though only a short section of the River Tees flows through Yorkshire, the part of Teesdale around Piercebridge is particularly charming and well worth a visit.

RICHMOND

Named the UK's "Great Town of the Year 2009" by the Academy of Urbanism, Richmond was also commended by the architectural guru Nikolaus Pevsner it as 'one of the most visually enjoyable small towns in England'. Another visitor described it as "a town to savour like old wine".

The former county of Richmondshire (which still survives as a parliamentary constituency) once occupied a third of the North Riding of Yorkshire. Today, Richmond is an appealing small town with a cobbled Market Place. Surrounded by fine Georgian buildings, it is said to be one of the largest in England. It has even been compared (by the Prince of Wales) to the sweeping market area in Siena. The outdoor market takes place on Saturdays and is joined on the 3rd Saturday of the month by a Farmer's Market.

Dominating the town centre is the mighty Keep of **Richmond Castle** (English Heritage), built by Alan Rufus, the 1st Earl of Richmond, in 1071. He selected an impregnable site, 100 feet up on a rocky promontory with the River Swale passing below. The keep rises to 109 feet with walls

---

1 SIP COFFEE

Richmond

A popular coffee shop which serves an excellent choice of coffees, refreshments and freshly baked paninis.

See entry on page 172

Richmond Parish Church

11 feet thick, while the other side is afforded an unassailable defence by means of the cliff and the river. Richmond Castle was the first Norman castle in the country to be built, right from the foundations, in stone. Additions were made over subsequent years but it reached its final form in the 14th century. Since then it has fallen into ruin though a considerable amount of the original Norman stonework remains intact.

With such an inspiring setting, it is hardly surprising that there is a legend suggesting that King Arthur himself is buried here, reputedly in a cave beneath the castle. The story goes that a simple potter called Thompson stumbled across an underground passage which led to a chamber where he discovered the king and his knights lying in an enchanted sleep, surrounded by priceless treasures. A voice warned him not to disturb the sleepers and he fled. Predictably, he was unable to locate the passage again.

Another legend associated with the castle tells how a drummer boy was sent down the passageway. Beating his drum as he walked, the boy's progress was followed by the soldiers on the surface until, suddenly, the drumming stopped. Though the passageway was searched the boy was never seen again but, it is said, his drumming can still be heard. The mile-long **Drummer Boy Walk** takes a scenic route along the banks of the River Swale to Easby Abbey.

The **Green Howards Museum**, the regimental museum of the North Riding's infantry, is based in the former Holy Trinity Church in the centre of the cobbled market square. The regiment dates back to 1688 and

the displays and collections illustrate its history with war relics, weapons, uniforms, medals, and regimental silver. Also housed in the museum is the town's silver. The church itself was founded in 1135 and, though it has been altered and rebuilt on more than one occasion, the original Norman tower and some other masonry have survived.

Just a few yards from the museum, the **Town Hall,** built in 1756, has a superbly restored Georgian Court which is open to the public on weekday mornings.

Located at the bottom of the Market Place, **Millgate House Garden** was described by the Sunday Times as "one of the most fascinating gardens in the North of England. Perched high above the River Swale, this small walled garden has richly scented roses interwoven with a tapestry of flowering shrubs.

Just down from the Market Place is the **Richmondshire Museum** traces the history of this ancient place and its county. There is also a reconstruction of James Herriot's veterinary surgery taken from the popular television series *All Creatures Great and Small,* as well as other period costumes and displays.

One of the grandest buildings in the town is the **Culloden Tower,** just off the town green. It was erected in 1747 by the Yorke family, one of whose members had fought at the Battle of Culloden the previous year. Unlike most follies, the interior of the three storey tower is elaborately decorated in the rococo style and since it is now in the care of the Landmark Trust it is possible to stay there.

Richmond is also home to England's oldest theatre, the **Georgian Theatre Royal,** which originally formed part of a circuit that

Richmond Castle

included Northallerton, Ripon, and Harrogate. Built in 1788 by the actor and manager Samuel Butler, it had at that time an audience capacity of 400. The connection with the theatrical Butler family ended in 1830 and from then until 1848 it was used, infrequently, by travelling companies. After the mid-19th century and right up until the 1960s, the theatre saw a variety of uses, as a wine cellar and a corn chandler's among others, and it did not re-open as a theatre until 1963 and only then after much restoration work had been carried out. Guided tours are available. The **Georgian Theatre Royal Museum** was also opened and it contains a unique collection of original playbills as well as the oldest and largest complete set of painted scenery in Britain.

A few yards from the museum. **The Friary Tower and Gardens,** with its picturesque ruined Franciscan bell tower, provides a pleasant setting in which to relax.

A fairly recent addition to the town's amenities is the former **Richmond Railway Station,** a fine old Victorian building which now contains a top-quality café/restaurant, an art gallery, a two-screen cinema, a heritage room, a micro-brewery, an ice-cream maker, a cheese-maker, a craft bakery, and a range of rooms for community use, private or corporate hire.

From the station, the trackbed of the old railway provides an easy one-mile walk to the striking ruins of **Easby Abbey**, founded in 1152. The best-preserved part of the abbey is the Refectory of around 1300. Within the precinct is the still-active parish Church of St Agatha which is notable for its fine 13th century wall paintings and for its

facsimile richly carved 9th century Cross, the original of which is in London's Victoria and Albert Museum.

AROUND RICHMOND

HUDSWELL

2 miles W of Richmond off the A6136

This ancient village, which was well established by the time it was recorded in the *Domesday Book*, stands high above the River Swale and over the years the village has gravitated to a more sheltered spot. The present St Michael's Church was built in the late 19th century on the site of an older building and the view from the churchyard is considered to be one of the finest in Richmondshire.

The walk from the village down to the river leads through pleasant woodland and also takes in some 365 steps. About half way down, below a path leading off to an old lime kiln, can be found **King Arthur's Oven**, a horizontal crack in the limestone which, it is claimed, has connections with Richmond Castle and the legend of King Arthur.

KIRBY HILL

4 miles NW of Richmond off the A66

This quiet hamlet lies midway between London and Edinburgh on the old Great North Road and in the days of the stagecoach it was a busy stopping place. The cellar of the Blue Bell Inn still retains the rings to which prisoners travelling between the two capitals were tethered overnight.

REETH

11 miles W of Richmond on the B6270

Considered the capital of Upper Swaledale, this popular hill-top town is scattered around a spacious village green above the junction of the River Swale and its main tributary, Arkle Beck. The town was recorded in the *Domesday Book*, while everything else in the area was written off as untaxable wasteland.

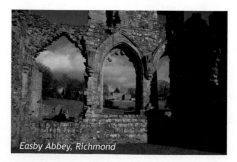
Easby Abbey, Richmond

Along the top of the green is High Row, with its inns and shops and outstanding Georgian architecture, reflecting the affluence of the town in the 18th century when the trade in wool and lead was booming. The volunteer-run **Swaledale Museum**, housed in the old Methodist Sunday School of 1836, contains more than 500 exhibits of local farming methods, crafts, and mining skills, as well as displays on local pastimes, the impact of Wesleyan Methodism, and the exodus of the population to the industrial areas of the south Pennines and America when the lead mines closed. The museum has its own shop and a tearoom.

This little town is noted for its variety of craft shops. There's a cluster of them at the **Reeth Dales Centre** near the green. Here you'll find a cabinet maker, a furniture maker, a guitar maker, a pottery shop, a clock maker and restorer, a sculptor, a silversmith, a photographer, a fused glass artist and Stef's Models where visitors can see the production of beautifully crafted animal models. Paintings are also on sale here.

A good time to visit Reeth is on the last Wednesday in August when the town hosts the annual **Agricultural Show** which attracts not just tourists but working farmers from the length of the dale. Entertainments, trade stands, fell racing and a chance to see some of the best livestock on display make the event a great day out for the family.

GRINTON

1 mile S of Reeth on the B6270

Just to the south of Reeth is the quiet village of Grinton whose fine parish **Church of St Andrew** served the whole of the dale for centuries. The building dates back to the 13th

Church of St Andrew, Grinton

and 15th centuries, though there are still some Norman remains as well as a Leper's Squint (a small hole through which those afflicted by the disease could follow the service within). For those people living in the upper reaches of Swaledale who died, there was a long journey down the track to Grinton which became known as the **Corpse Way**.

HEALAUGH

2 miles W of Reeth on the B6270

In the 12th century an Augustinian Priory was founded here but none of the remaining fragments date from earlier than the 15th century. However, the village Church of St Helen and St John, which dates from around 1150, not only has outstanding views over the dale to the Pennines but also has a bullet hole which, it is alleged, was made by a Cromwellian trooper on his way to Marsden Moor.

LANGTHWAITE

3 miles NW of Reeth off the B6270

Langthwaite, the main village of Arkengarthdale, will seem familiar to many who have never been here before as its bridge featured in the title sequence of the popular television series *All Creatures Great and Small*. Just outside this beautiful place stands the cryptically named CB Hotel – named after Charles Bathurst, an 18th-century lord of the manor who was responsible for the development of the lead-mining industry in the dale. His grandfather, Dr John Bathurst, physician to Oliver Cromwell, had purchased the land here in

---

2 **SWALEDALE FOLK MUSEUM**

Reeth

The **Swaledale Folk Museum** was opened in 1974, and is based in the old Methodist School, which took its first pupils in 1836.

See entry on page 172

1659 with the exploitation of its mineral wealth in mind.

In a field just up the hill from Langthwaite, where the Barnard Castle road goes off to the right, stands a curious 6-sided building, very solidly constructed. It needed to be since it served as a **Powderhouse** providing storage for the gunpowder used to blast tunnels through the hillsides for the lead mines.

LOW ROW

4 miles W of Reeth on the B6270

In medieval times the track along the hillside above Low Row formed part of the Corpse Way along which relays of bearers would carry the deceased in a large wicker basket on journeys that could take two days to complete. Along their route, you can still see the large stone slabs where they rested their burden. Even more convenient was the 'Dead Barn' above Low Row where the carriers could deposit the body and scramble downhill for a convivial evening at the Punch Bowl Inn.

Located on the edge of the village, **Hazel Brow Organic Farm & Visitor Centre** provides a popular family day out. Set in glorious Swaledale countryside the 200-acre traditional family-run farm offers children the opportunity of bottle feeding lambs, riding a pony or helping to feed the calves, sheep and pigs. The farm also has a tea room, children's play area and gift shop, and hosts various demonstrations of farming activities throughout the year.

GUNNERSIDE

6 miles W of Reeth on the B6270

This charming Dales village in the heart of Swaledale was, until the late 19th century, a thriving lead-mining village. Gunnerside became known as the Klondyke of Swaledale and the Old Gang Mines are the most famous in Yorkshire. The paths and trackways here are mainly those trodden by the many miners travelling to their work and the valley's sides still show the signs of the mine workings. In the village, one can visit tearooms that offer such delights as 'Lead Miners' Bait' and the delicious 'Gunnerside Cheese Cake' made

from a recipe handed down from mining days.

After the closure of the mines, many families left the village to find work elsewhere in northern England while others emigrated to America and even as far afield as Australia. For many years afterwards one of the village's most important days was Midsummer Sunday when those who had left would, if able, return and catch up with their families and friends.

Gunnerside's most impressive building is its **Methodist Chapel,** a classically elegant building, wonderfully light and airy. The indefatigable John Wesley visited Gunnerside in 1761 and found the local congregation 'earnest, loving and simple people'.

What makes **The Old Working Smithy & Museum** rather special is the fact that nothing has been bought in – all the artefacts on show are from the smithy itself, indeed many of them were actually made here. The smithy was established in 1795 and over the years little has been thrown away. Cartwheels, cobblers' tools, horseshoes, fireside implements and a miner's 'tub' (railway wagon) from a lead mine are just some of the vintage articles on show. This is still a working smithy. Stephen Calvert is the 6th generation of his family to pursue the trade of blacksmith and he still uses the original forge and hand bellows to create a wide range of wrought ironwork.

Gunnerside's picturesque hump-backed bridge over the Swale is reputed to be haunted by a headless ghost. Oddly, no gruesome tale has grown up around this unfortunate spirit.

IVELET

7 miles W of Reeth off the B6270

Just a few hundred yards off the B6270, the 14th-century **Packhorse bridge** at Ivelet is regarded as one of the finest in Yorkshire. It's a very picturesque spot and you can also join a delightful riverside walk here.

MUKER

8 miles W of Reeth on the B6270

An old stone bridge leads into this engaging

village which consists of a collection of beige-coloured stone cottages overlooked by the **Church of St Mary** which dates back to the time of Elizabeth I – one of the very few to be built in England during her reign. Most church builders until that time had spared no expense in glorifying the house of God. At Muker they were more economical: the church roof was covered in thatch, its floor in rushes. No seating was provided. Despite such penny-pinching measures, the new church of 1580 was warmly welcomed since it brought to an end the tedious journey for bereaved relatives along the Corpse Way to the dale's mother church at Grinton, some eight miles further to the east.

On the gravestones in the churchyard local family names, such as Harker, Alderson, and Fawcett feature prominently as they do among the villagers still living here.

Close by the church is a quaint little building identified as the Literary Institute from whence you may hear the strains of a brass band rehearsing. In Victorian times, most of the Dales villages had their own brass band – Muker's is the only survivor and is in great demand at various events throughout the year.

Swaledale cuisine is equally durable: specialities on offer in the local tearooms include Swaledale Curd Tart, Yorkshire Rarebit, and Deep Apple Pie with Wensleydale cheese. And the main crafts still revolve around the wool provided by the hardy Swaledale sheep, in great demand by carpet manufacturers and for jumpers worn by fell walkers, climbers, and anyone else trying to defeat the British weather.

You'll find many of these items on sale at **Swaledale Woollens** which was founded in Muker almost 40 years ago by villagers reviving the old cottage industry of knitting. Today there are more than 30 people knitting from their homes and producing a unique range of quality woollen knitwear using Swaledale, Wensleydale and Welsh hill sheep wool. The shop stocks a wide range of high quality knitwear, including sweaters, cardigans, hats, gloves, rugs, hangings, shawls, scarves, slippers and socks. It also stocks sheepskin slippers, gloves and rugs.

THWAITE

10 miles W of Reeth on the B6270

Surrounded by dramatic countryside which includes Kisdon Hill, Great Shunnor, High Seat, and Lovely Seat, this is a tiny village of ancient origins. Like so many places in the area the name comes from the Nordic language, in this case *thveit*, meaning a clearing in the wood. The woodlands which once provided shelter and fuel for the Viking settlers have long since gone.

The surrounding hills and moors are rich in wildlife. It's easy to understand why the brothers Richard and Cherry Kearton, who were born at Thwaite in the late 1800s, developed an early enthusiasm for studying

3 SWALEDALE WOOLLENS

Muker

Quality hand-crafted woollen garments and accessories from Swaledale, Wensleydale and Welsh wools.

See entry on page 173

4 MUKER VILLAGE STORE AND TEASHOP

Muker

A local couple offer a convenience store stocking great locally made produce alongside their charming tearoom with four star accommodation above.

See entry on page 174

Thwaite, Swaledale

nature. They went on to become the David Attenboroughs of their day. Pioneers in wildlife photography, their work took them all over the world. The small house where they were born, set back from the main road, has a stone lintel decorated with carvings of birds and animals, together with the initials RK and CK and their dates of birth.

To the southwest of the village runs **Buttertubs Pass**, one of the highest and most forbidding mountain passes in the county. The Buttertubs themselves are a curious natural feature of closely packed vertical stone stacks rising from some unseen, underground base to the level of the road. A local Victorian guide to the Buttertubs, perhaps aware that the view from above was not all that impressive, solemnly assured his client that 'some of the Buttertubs had no bottom, and some were deeper than that'. No one is quite sure where the Buttertubs name came from. The most plausible explanation is that farmers used its deep-chilled shelves as a convenient refrigerator for the butter they couldn't sell immediately. Unusually, these potholes are not linked by a series of passages as most are, but are free-standing and bear only a slight resemblance to the objects after which they are named.

The narrow road from Thwaite across the Buttertubs Pass is not for the faint-hearted driver. Only a flimsy post and wire fence separates the road from a sheer drop of Alpine proportions. In any case, it's much more satisfying to cross the pass from the other direction, from Hawes: from the south, as you crest the summit you will be rewarded with a stupendous view of Swaledale stretching for miles.

Catrake Force, Keld

KELD

10 miles W of Reeth on the B6270

The little cluster of stone buildings that make up this village stand beside the early stages of the River Swale. The place is alive with the sound of rushing water and it comes as no surprise that the word *keld* is Nordic for 'spring'.

Wain Wath Force, with rugged Cotterby Scar providing a fine backdrop, can be found alongside the Birkdale road. **Catrake Force**, with its stepped formation, can be reached from the cottages on the left at the bottom of the street in the village. Though on private land the falls and, beside them, the entrance to an old lead mine can still be seen. For less adventurous pedestrians Kisdon Force, the most impressive waterfall in Swaledale, can be reached by a gentle stroll of less than a mile from the village along a well-trodden path.

TAN HILL

10 miles NW of Reeth off the B6270

Standing at the head of Arkengarthdale on the border with County Durham, 1732 feet above sea level, stands England's highest pub, the **Tan Hill Inn**. Why on earth should there be a pub here, in one of the most remote and barren stretches of the north Pennines, frequently cut off and often in total isolation during the winter? A century ago, the inn's patrons didn't need to ask. Most of them were workers from the Tan Hill coal mines; others were drivers waiting for their horse-drawn carts to be filled with coal. The coal mines have long since closed but an open coal fire still burns in the inn 365 days a year and some 50,000 visitors a year still find their way to Tan Hill. Many of them are walkers who stagger in from one of the most gruelling stretches of the Pennine Way Walk and, clutching a pint of Theakston's 'Old Peculier', collapse on the nearest settle.

Before the present series of mild winters, the moorland roads often disappeared under 12-feet deep snowdrifts. Despite cellar walls three feet thick, the pub's beer-pumps have frozen, and trade tends to fall off a bit. There was a brief return of those Arctic conditions over the New Year's Day period in 2010 when 30 students and teachers from Leeds University's cross-country club were cut off for two days amid 7ft drifts..

The most significant event in the Tan Hill calendar occurs on the last Thursday in May. This is when the **Tan Hill Sheep Fair** takes place and, if only for a day, Tan Hill Inn becomes the centre of agricultural Yorkshire. 'It's the Royal Show for Swaledale Sheep is Tan Hill,' said one proud farmer scrutinising his flock, 'and I've got some princes and princesses here.' In cash terms the value of the prizes awarded at the Fair is negligible – just a few pounds for even a first class rosette. But at the auction that follows it's a different story. In 1990 one particularly prized Tupp Hogg (a young ram) was sold for £30,000.

WENSLEYDALE

Wensleydale, perhaps above all the others, is the dale most people associate with the Yorkshire Dales. Charles Kingsley once described it as 'the richest spot in all England ... a beautiful oasis in the mountains'. At some 40 miles long it is certainly the longest dale and it is also softer and greener than many of its neighbours. The pasture land, grazed by flocks of Wensleydale sheep, is only broken by the long lines of dry stone walls and the occasional field barn. The dale is, of course, famous for its cheese whose fortunes were given an additional boost by Wallace and Gromit when they

declared it to be their favourite!

Wensleydale is the only major dale not to be named after its river, the Ure, although until fairly recent years most locals still referred to the area as Yoredale, or Uredale. The dale's name comes from the once important town of Wensley where the lucrative trade in cheese began in the 13th century. Wensley prospered for many years until 1563 when the Black Death annihilated most of its people. Nearby Leyburn assumed its role as the trading centre of the lower dale.

At the western end of the dale is Hawes, derived from the Norse word *hals* meaning neck and, indeed, the town does lies on a neck of land between two hills. Home of the Dales Countryside Museum and the Wensleydale Creamery, Hawes is an ideal starting point for exploring the dale. It is widely believed that the medieval monks of Jervaulx Abbey were responsible for introducing the manufacture of cheese to the dale some 700 years ago (they were of French origin). It was first made from ewe's milk but by the 1600s the milk of shorthorn cows was used instead since the sheep were becoming increasingly important for their wool and mutton. Originally just a summer occupation and mainly the task of the farmer's wife, the production of Wensleydale cheese was put on a commercial footing when the first cheese factory was established at Gayle Beck, near Hawes, in 1897.

As it flows down the dale, the Ure is fed by a series of smaller rivers and becks, many of which have their own charming dale. Among the better-known are Coverdale, the home of some of England's finest racehorse stables, and peaceful Bishopdale with its

Wensleydale

ancient farmhouses. Remote Cotterdale, with its striking waterfall, and the narrow valley of the River Waldern are also well worth exploring.

LEYBURN

The main market town and trading centre of mid-Wensleydale, Leyburn is an attractive town with a broad cobbled marketplace (plus two other squares) lined by handsome late-Georgian and Victorian stone buildings. Friday is market day when the little town is even busier than usual. There's an interesting mix of traditional family-run shops and surprisingly large supermarkets behind deceptively small frontages.

A fairly recent addition to Leyburn's attractions is **Beech End Model Village** in Commercial Square. Unique among model villages, this one is indoors. The scenery is finely detailed and there's plenty of hands-on fun to be had controlling the working models.

The town has several interesting connections with famous people. Lord Nelson's surgeon, Peter Goldsmith, once lived in the Secret Garden House on Grove Square (and is buried in Wensley church, just a mile up the road). Flight Lieutenant Alan Broadley DSO, DFC, DFM, of Dam Busters fame, is named on the War Memorial in the main square, and just a few yards away is the birthplace of the 'Sweet Lass' of Richmond Hill. Many believe that the popular song refers to Richmond Hill in Surrey rather than Richmond, North Yorkshire. Not so. Frances l'Anson was born in her grandfather's house on Leyburn High Street and his initials, WIA, can still be seen above the door of what is now an interior decorator's shop. It was her husband-to-be, Leonard McNally, who composed the immortal song.

On the eastern edge of the town is Leyburn Station. Until recently you would have had a long wait here for a train – the last passenger train left in 1954. But an energetic group of railway enthusiasts have laboured for years to get the line re-opened and on July 4th, 2003 their efforts were finally successful. The **Wensleydale Railway**

now offers regular services to Bedale and Leeming Bar, a 12-mile route through pretty countryside. Normally, the train is driven by a vintage diesel locomotive but there are special steam train days. Passengers can connect with a vintage bus at Redmire station to travel on to Hawes. The Wensleydale Railway Company hopes to extend the service to the main line station at Northallerton and, even more ambitiously, to extend westwards to meet up with the Settle and Carlisle railway.

The Shawl, to the west of the town, is a mile-long limestone scarp along which runs a footpath offering lovely panoramic views of the dale. A popular legend suggests that it gained its unusual name when Mary, Queen of Scots dropped her shawl here during her unsuccessful attempt to escape from nearby Bolton Castle. However, a more likely explanation is that Shawl is a corruption of the Nordic name given to the ancient settlement here.

Leyburn Business Park is home to **The Violin Making Workshop.** Little has changed in the art of violin making over the centuries and the traditional tools and methods used by such master craftsmen as Stradivari are still employed today. Repairs and commissions are undertaken.

Close by, at **The Teapottery**, you can see other craftspeople at work – in this case creating a whole range of witty and unusual teapots, anything from a grand piano to a bathtub complete with yellow duck. The finished pots can be purchased in the showroom where there's also a tea room where your tea is served, naturally, in one of the astonishing teapots produced here.

Leyburn Shawl

Within the same business park are Tennant's of Yorkshire, the only major provincial auction house in England which holds regular auctions throughout the year, and the **Little Chocolate Shop** where visitors can watch hand-made chocolates being crafted and choose from more than 200 varieties of chocolates and confectionery.

About three miles east of Leyburn, off the A684, the **Longwool Sheepshop** at Cross Lanes Farm in Garriston is a treat for anyone who appreciates good knitwear. Garments can be specially knitted to the customer's requirements. You can see the raw material grazing in the surrounding fields – rare Wensleydale longwool sheep. The Sheepshop also stocks an extensive range of hand knitting yarns and patterns for the enthusiast.

AROUND LEYBURN

CONSTABLE BURTON

4 miles E of Leyburn on the A684

Surrounded by walled and wooded parkland **Constable Burton Hall** is famous for its gardens (open March to October) and in particular its spacious, romantic terraces. The house itself, designed by John Carr, is not open to the public but its stately Georgian architecture provides a magnificent backdrop to the fine gardens, noble trees and colourful borders.

SPENNITHORNE

2 miles SE of Leyburn off the A684

This pleasant little village dates back many years. The present Church of St Michael and

All Angels stands on the site of a Saxon church although the only remains of the ancient building to be seen are two ornamental stones set into the walls of the chancels and a Saxon monument in the vestry.

Two of Spennithorne's earlier residents are worth mentioning. John Hutchinson was born here in 1675 and went on to become steward to the 6th Duke of Somerset – and a rather controversial philosopher. He vehemently disagreed with Sir Isaac Newton's theory of gravity and was equally ardent in asserting that the earth was neither flat, nor a sphere, but a cube. Though there are no records mentioning that Hutchinson was ever considered as of unsound mind, another resident of Spennithorne, Richard Hatfield, was officially declared insane after he fired a gun at George III.

MIDDLEHAM

2 miles SE of Leyburn on the A6108

Middleham is an enchanting little town which, despite having a population of fewer than 800, boasts its own Mayor, Corporation and quaint Town Hall. It is also the site of one of Yorkshire's most historic castles, 12 of England's most successful racing stables and not just one, but two, marketplaces. It is almost totally unspoilt, with a wealth of handsome Georgian houses and hostelries huddled together in perfect architectural harmony.

Rising high above the town are the magnificent ruins of **Middleham Castle** (English Heritage), a once-mighty fortress whose most glorious days came in the 15th century when most of northern England was ruled from here by the Neville family. The castle's most famous resident was the 'evil' Richard III who was sent here as a lad of 13 to be trained in the 'arts of nobilitie'. Whatever crimes he committed later down in London, Richard was popular locally, ensuring the town's prosperity by granting it a fair and a twice-yearly market. The people of Middleham had good reason to mourn his death at the Battle of Bosworth in 1485.

Middleham is often referred to as the "Newmarket of the North", a term you'll

5 THE QUEEN'S HEAD

Finghall

Embodying all that a four star country inn should, real fires, 17th century features, fine real ales and mouth-watering cuisine.

See entry on page 175

understand when you see the strings of thoroughbred racehorses clip-clopping through the town on their way to the training runs on Low Moor. It was the monks of Jervaulx Abbey who founded this key industry. By the late 18th century, races were being run across the moorland and the first stables established. Since then the local stables have produced a succession of classic race winners with one local trainer, Neville Crump, having three Grand National winners to his credit within the space of 12 years. Some of the stables offer guided tours.

EAST WITTON
4 miles SE of Leyburn on the A6108

An attractive village set beside the confluence of the rivers Cover and Ure, East Witton was almost entirely rebuilt after a great fire in 1796. The new buildings included the well-proportioned Church of St John although the old churchyard with its many interesting gravestones remains. Some two decades after that conflagration the village was struck by another calamity. In 1820, 20 miners perished in a coal mine accident at Witton Fell. They were all buried together in one grave in the new churchyard.

Just to the west of the village is **Jervaulx Abbey**, one of the great Cistercian sister houses to Fountains Abbey. The name Jervaulx is a French derivation of Yore (or Ure), and Vale, just as Rievaulx is of Rye Vale. Before the Dissolution, the monks of Jervaulx Abbey owned huge tracts of Wensleydale and this now-solitary spot was once a busy trading and administrative centre. Despite its ruination, Jervaulx is among the most evocative of Yorkshire's many fine abbeys. The grounds have been

6 JERVAULX ABBEY

Jervaulx

This beautiful ruin is the second largest Cistercian abbey in the UK, offering tranquillity and history with nearby tea rooms and accommodation.

See entry on page 176

transformed into beautiful gardens with the crumbling walls providing interesting backdrops for the sculptured trees and colourful plants and shrubs.

COVERHAM
4 miles S of Leyburn off the A6108

Lying beside the River Cover in little-visited Coverdale, this village is perhaps best known for the remains of Coverham Abbey (private). Built in the late 1200s, only some decorated arches remain, along with a Norman gateway. The nearby 17th-century manor house, **Braithwaite Hall** (National Trust), as well as other surrounding buildings, have clearly used the Abbey's stones in their construction – in some of the walls effigies from the old building can clearly be seen. The Hall can be visited by prior arrangement.

Just outside the village, on the Tupgill Park Estate is the delightful walled **Forbidden Garden,** a series of follies created by Colin Armstrong, an eccentric millionaire and former ambassador to Ecuador. Strange and exotic buildings are scattered around the park, including a grotto with an underground labyrinth of chambers and passages. Visitors are given a list and then discover these fantastic constructions by themselves. "In parts you might find your heart's delight" says the brochure, "In others you'll tremble with fear". There's also a shop and refreshment room. Admission is by pre-booked tickets only which can be obtained from the Leyburn Tourist Information Centre.

WENSLEY
1 mile W of Leyburn on the A684

Set beside the River Ure this peaceful little village was once the main settlement in mid-Wensleydale and such was its importance it gave its name to the dale. However, in 1563, the town was struck by plague and those whom the pestilence had not struck down fled up the hill to Leyburn which was thought to be a healthier place.

The stately **Church of the Holy Trinity** is one of only two surviving medieval structures in Wensley - the other is the graceful bridge nearby. Inside can be seen the unusual Bolton family pews which are actually a pair of opera boxes that were brought here from London during the 1700s when a theatre was being refurbished. The Bolton family still live at nearby Bolton Hall, a massive 18th-century house which is closed to the public although its splendid gardens are occasionally open during the summer months.

'Purveyors to the Military, Colonies, Overseas Missions, Churches and the Cinematograph Industries' runs the proud claim in the brochure for the **White Rose Candles Workshop**. 'Patronised by the Nobility and Gentry' it continues; 'Cathedrals supplied include Ripon and Norwich'. One of Wensleydale's most popular attractions, the workshop is housed in a 19th-century water mill – the water wheel still exists and mills have been recorded on this site since 1203.

WEST WITTON

4 miles W of Leyburn on the A684

Recorded in the *Domesday Book* as 'Witun', this village was then the largest in Wensleydale and exceptional in having stone rather than wooden houses. West Witton is well known for its annual feast of St Bartholomew, patron saint of the parish church. The festival takes place on August 24th when an effigy of a man, known as the Bartle, is carried through the village. According to legend, Bartle was an 18th-century swine that was hunted over the surrounding fells before being captured and killed. The culmination of the three days of celebration is the burning of the effigy at Grassgill End.

CARLTON-IN-COVERDALE

4 miles SW of Leyburn off the A684

Unspoilt Coverdale is known as the 'Forgotten Dale'. Carlton is the dale's principal village – with a population of less than 100. Nevertheless, it has its own pub and provides a wonderfully peaceful base for walking, hiking, fishing or touring the Dales National Park.

REDMIRE

4 miles W of Leyburn off the A684

Until 2003, the station at Redmire had not seen a passenger train since 1954. It now has regular services on the Wensleydale Railway which runs from here to Leyburn, Bedale and Leeming Bar.

On the peaceful village green stands an old oak tree, supported by props, which is estimated to be at least 300 years old. When John Wesley preached in the village during his two visits in 1744 and 1774 it is believed that he stood in the shade of this very tree.

CASTLE BOLTON

5 miles W of Leyburn off the A684

Bolton Castle has dominated mid-Wensleydale for more than six centuries and is one of the major tourist attractions of the area. In 1379 the lord of the manor, Richard le Scrope, Lord Chancellor of England in the reign of Richard II, was granted permission to fortify his manor house and, using stone from a nearby quarry and oak beams from Lake District forests, the building was completed some 18 years later. The 14th century state-of-the-art garde-robes (lavatories) were constructed with such sophistication that they were still in use some 500 years later. Today, this fortified manor house remains an impressive sight with its four-square towers acting as a local landmark. The halls and galleries are remarkably well-preserved as are some of the private apartments used by Mary, Queen of Scots when she was a

Bolton Castle

reluctant visitor here for six months between 1568-69. Indeed, modern day visitors can take tea in the grand room where she spent many melancholy days.

Vivid tableaux help bring history to life – the castle chaplain, the miller at work, the blacksmith at his forge – and there are regular living history events during the summer. If you climb to the battlements you will be rewarded with some breathtaking views along the dale.

The owner, Lord Bolton, has recently restored two of the castle gardens as they would have been in medieval times – a Herb Garden and a Walled Garden. Other recent additions are a medieval nursery with some authentic toys and games, and a costume store so that visitors can really get into the medieval mood by adopting the proper garb.

THORALBY

8 miles W of Leyburn off the A684

Situated on the north slope of Bishopdale, opposite its sister village Newbiggin, Thoralby was once a centre for lead-mining and although lead is no longer extracted here, the mine can still be found on maps of the area. A side dale of Wensleydale, Bishopdale was once covered by a glacial lake that has given rise to its distinctive wide valley base. Here can be found many of Wensleydale's oldest houses.

NEWBIGGIN-IN-BISHOPDALE

9 miles SW of Leyburn on the B6160

As might be supposed, the name of this Bishopdale village means 'new buildings' and it is indeed a relatively new settlement having been first mentioned in 1230! There is only one road along Bishopdale, a beautiful unspoilt valley with hay meadows, stone barns, traditional Dales long houses and a fine old coaching inn.

WEST BURTON

7 miles SW of Leyburn off the B6160

One of the most picturesque villages in Wensleydale, West Burton developed around its large central green where a busy weekly market used to take place. A distinctive feature of the green is its market 'cross'- actually a modestly sized pyramid erected here in 1820. Just to the east of the village a path leads across a small packhorse bridge to **Mill Force**, perhaps the most photogenic of the Wensleydale waterfalls.

Cat lovers will enjoy the wide variety of felines on display at the **Cat Pottery**, overlooking the village green. The Nichols family has been making their Moorside Cats since 1982 and their original collection of cats in ceramics and metallic or granite resin includes life-size stone cats for house or garden.

West Burton lies at the bottom of Walden, a narrow, steep-sided valley that provides a complete contrast to neighbouring Bishopdale. Secluded and with a minimal scattering of houses and farms, Walden was one of the last places in Yorkshire where wild red deer were seen.

CARPERBY

7 miles W of Leyburn off the A684

This ancient village reflects its typical Danish layout with a long straggling street and a small green at one end. In some of the nearby fields, grassy terraces indicate the old ploughed strips left by both pre-Norman Conquest and medieval farming methods. Carperby was one of the first villages to have a market - the charter was granted in 1305. The village's market cross dates from 1674 and it was from its steps that George Fox, the founder of the Quaker Movement, preached in the 17th century.

AYSGARTH

7 miles W of Leyburn on the A684

The village is famous for the spectacular **Aysgarth Falls** where the River Ure thunders through a rocky gorge and drops some 200 feet over three huge slabs of limestone which divide this wonderful natural feature into the Upper, Middle and Lower Falls. So cinematic are they that they were deemed to be the perfect location for the battle between Robin

Aysgarth Falls

Hood and Little John in Kevin Costner's film *Robin Hood, Prince of Thieves*.

Close to the falls stands the **Church of St Andrew**, home of the Jervaulx Treasures – a vicar's stall that is made from the beautifully carved bench ends salvaged from Jervaulx Abbey. During the Middle Ages, Aysgarth enjoyed the distinction of being the largest parish in England though the parish has since been subdivided into more manageable areas. But it still has the largest churchyard in England.

The Dales National Park has a Visitor Information Centre here, with a spacious car park and café located close to the Church and Falls.

The **Aysgarth Edwardian Rock Garden,** originally designed by James Backhouse in 1906 and restored in 2003, is one of the few examples of a Backhouse rock garden remaining in the UK. The garden is visited and admired by many alpine gardeners each year and has recently been the subject of many magazine articles. Guided tours are available by arrangement.

St Andrews Church, Aysgarth

ASKRIGG

10½ miles W of Leyburn off the A684

With its tall houses and narrow cobbled streets clustered around St Oswald's Church, this once-important market town became better known to TV viewers as Darrowby, a major location for the long-running series *All Creatures Great and Small*. The 18th-century Kings Arms Hotel often featured as 'The Drovers Arms', and the exterior of Cringley House (private) doubled as 'Skeldale House', the fictional home of the TV vets.

Although recorded in the *Domesday Book* as 'Ascric', it wasn't until the 18th century that Askrigg became a thriving town with several prosperous industries. Cotton was spun in a nearby mill, dyeing and brewing took place here and it was also a centre for hand-knitting. However, the town is particularly famous for clock-making, introduced by John Ogden in 1681.

The village has been popular with tourists since the days of Turner and Wordsworth when the chief attractions here were the two waterfalls, Whitfield Force and Mill Gill. Despite its olde worlde atmosphere Askrigg was one of the first places in the dales to be supplied with electricity. That was in 1908 when the local miller harnessed the power of Mill Gill Beck.

Askrigg is bountifully supplied with footpaths radiating out to other villages, river crossings and farmsteads. One of the most scenic takes little more than an hour and takes in the two impressive waterfalls. The route is waymarked from Mill Lane alongside the church.

BAINBRIDGE

11½ miles W of Leyburn on the A684

Ancient stocks are still in place on the spacious village green and on the eastern edge of the village, the River Bain, officially the shortest river in England at less than 2 miles long, rushes over a small waterfall as it makes its way down from Semer Water.

Back in the Middle Ages this area of Upper Wensleydale was a hunting forest, known as the Forest and Manor of Bainbridge. The

Hidden Places of Yorkshire   Yorkshire Dales

village itself was established around the 12th century as a home for the foresters. One of their duties was to show travellers the way through the forest. If anyone was still out by nightfall, a horn was blown to guide them home. The custom is still continued between the Feast of Holy Rood (September 27th) and Shrove Tuesday when the present horn is blown at 10pm. The horn is kept on display in the Rose & Crown pub.

Just to the east of Bainbridge is Brough Hill (private) where the Romans built a succession of forts known collectively as *Virosidum*. First excavated in the late 1920s, they now appear as overgrown grassy hummocks. Much easier to see is the Roman road that strikes south-westwards from Bainbridge, part of the trans-Pennine route to Lancaster. It passes close to the isolated lake of **Semer Water**, one of Yorkshire's only two natural lakes. (The other is Lake Gormire, near Thirsk.) Semer Water stretches half a mile in length and teems with wild fowl.

An enduring legend claims that a town lies beneath the depths of Semer Water, cast under water by a curse. A poor traveller once sought shelter in the town but was turned away by the affluent inhabitants. The next day he stood on the hill above the town, pronounced a curse, and a great flood engulfed the town immediately. There's an intriguing postscript to this tale. During a severe drought, the level of the lake dropped to reveal the remains of a Bronze Age town.

GAYLE

15½ miles W of Leyburn off the A684

Set beside the Gayle Beck, the village has some pleasant riverside walks that pass close to **Gayle Mill**, a late 18th-century structure built originally to support cotton spinning but then changing to wool to supply local hand-knitters. In 1870 the old waterwheel was replaced by a turbine. This, in turn, gave the village electric street lights as early as 1917. The turbine is still in operation and is believed to be the world's oldest still working. The Mill eventually fell into disuse in the 1980s but thanks to its appearance in the television series *Restoration* in 2004 has

Gayle Mill

been renovated, its water-power systems reinstated and the Victorian wood-working machinery returned to working order. Tickets must be bought in advance at the Dales Countryside Museum in Hawes.

HAWES

15½ miles W of Leyburn off the A684

At 850 feet above sea level, Hawes is the highest market town in Yorkshire. The present town expanded greatly in the 1870s after the arrival of the railways but there's still plenty of evidence of the earlier settlement in street names relating to ancient trades: Dyer's Garth, Hatter's Yard and Printer's Square. Now the commercial and market centre of the upper dale, Hawes offers a good range of shops, inns, accommodation and visitor attractions.

The most picturesque corner of the town is by the bridge over Gayle Beck where the stream tumbles over a sheer drop by the old mill. It's just a short step from the bridge to the **Dales Countryside Museum**, housed in the former railway station. The museum tells the story of how man's activities have helped to shape the Dales' landscape. Providing fascinating historical details on domestic life, the lead-mining industry, hand-knitting and other trades as well as archaeological material, the museum covers many aspects of Dales' life from as far back as 10,000BC. Children visit free.

One of those local industries was rope-making and at **The Hawes Ropeworkers**, adjacent to the museum, visitors can still see it in operation, with experienced ropers twisting cotton and man-made fibres to make halters, hawsers, picture cords, dog leads, clothes lines and other 'rope' items. The gift shop here stocks a comprehensive range of rope-related items along with an extensive choice of other souvenirs of the dale.

Wensleydale's most famous product (after its sheep), is its soft, mild cheese. At the **Wensleydale Creamery**, on the western edge of the town, you can sample this delicacy and also learn about its history through a series of interesting displays. With a museum, viewing gallery of the production area, cheese shop, gift shop and licensed restaurant, there's plenty here for the cheese lover to enjoy.

HARDRAW

15½ miles W of Leyburn off the A684

Located in a natural amphitheatre of limestone crags, **Hardraw Force** is the highest, unbroken waterfall in England above ground, a breathtaking cascade 98 feet high. The top ledge of hard rock projects so far beyond the softer stone beneath that it used to be possible to walk behind the falling water as JMW Turner and Wordsworth did. Sadly, for safety reasons this is no longer possible. The waterfall shows at its best after heavy rain as, generally, the quantity of water tumbling over the rocks is not great. On two separate occasions, in 1739 and 1881, the falls froze solid into a 100-feet icicle. In the 1870s, the French stuntman Blondin astounded spectators when, not content with

crossing the falls on a tightrope, he paused halfway to cook an omelette.

The amphitheatre here provides superb acoustics, a feature which has been put to great effect in the annual brass band competitions which began here in 1885 and have recently resumed. Access to Hardraw Force is through the Green Dragon pub where a small fee is payable. The inn itself is pretty venerable with records of a hostelry on this site since at least the mid-13th century. At that time the land here was a grange belonging to the monks of Fountains Abbey who grazed their sheep nearby.

COTTERDALE

18 miles W of Leyburn off the A684

The small valley of Cotter Beck lies below the vast bulk of Great Shunner Fell which separates the head of Wensleydale from Swaledale. **Cotter Force**, although smaller than Hardraw, is extremely attractive though often neglected in favour of its more famous neighbour.

NIDDERDALE

Designated an Area of Outstanding Natural Beauty, Nidderdale is a typical Yorkshire dale with a lattice-work of dry stone walls, green fields, and pretty stone villages. The Victorians christened the dale 'Little Switzerland' and the upper reaches of the valley of the River Nidd are indeed steep and wooded, with the river running through gorges. With a covering of snow in winter it is easy to see the resemblance.

The history of the dale is similar to that of its neighbours. The Romans and Norsemen both settled here and there are also reminders that the dale was populated in prehistoric times. It was the all powerful Cistercian monks of Fountains and Byland Abbeys who began the business-like cultivation of the countryside to provide grazing for cattle and

Hadraw Force

sheep and the space to grow food. This great farming tradition has survived and, though prosperity came and went with lead-mining, a few of the textile mills established in the golden age of the Industrial Revolution can still be found.

Best explored from Pateley Bridge, keen walkers will delight in the wide variety of landscape that can be covered within a reasonable amount of time. High up on the moorland, famed for its brilliant colour in late summer, there are several reservoirs, built to provide water for the growing population and industry in Bradford. This area is a must for bird watchers as there are excellent opportunities for spotting a number of species of duck as well as brent geese and whooper swans. Further down the valley, in the rich woodland, wildlife again abounds and the well-signposted footpaths help visitors reach the most spectacular sights.

PATELEY BRIDGE

Considered one of the prettiest towns in the Dales, Pateley Bridge straggles up the hillside from its elegant 18th-century bridge over the Nidd. Considering its compact size, the town is remarkably well connected by roads which have been here since the monastic orders established trade routes through the town for transporting their goods. A street market, whose charter was granted in the 14th century, has however, been abandoned for some time although sheep fairs and agricultural shows still take place here.

Much of the Pateley Bridge seen today was built in the 1800s hwen the town was prospering from industries such as flax-spinning and lead mining. Amongst many quaint and pretty buildings, the oldest is St Mary's Church, a lovely ruin dating from 1320 from which there are some fine panoramic views. Another excellent vista can be viewed from the aptly named **Panorama Walk**, part of the main medieval route from Ripon to Skipton. The **Nidderdale Museum**, a winner of the National Heritage Museum of the Year award, is housed in one of the town's original

Victorian workhouses and presents a fascinating record of local folk history. The exhibits include a complete cobbler's shop, general store, Victorian parlour, kitchen and schoolroom, chemist's, haberdasher's, joiner's shop, solicitor's office as well as an agricultural, transport and industrial display.

Those with a sweet tooth might like to pay a visit to the Oldest Sweet Shop in England, established in 1827, which stocks a toothsome array of old-fashioned sweets in traditional square bottles.

AROUND PATELEY BRIDGE

WILSILL

1 mile E of Pateley Bridge on the B6165

About two miles east of Wilsill are **Brimham Rocks** (National Trust), an extraordinary natural sculpture park. Formed into fantastic shapes by years of erosion, these great millstone grit boulders lie atop a steep hill amidst some 400 acres of heathland. Some of the shapes really do resemble their names – the 'Dancing Bear' in particular, but perhaps the most awe-inspiring is 'Idol Rock', a huge boulder weighing several tons which rests on a base just one foot in diameter. The National Trust has provided large scale maps showing suggested itineraries and the positions and names of the major formations.

GLASSHOUSES

1 mile SE of Pateley Bridge off the B6265

From Pateley Bridge a riverside walk leads to Glasshouses and **Yorkshire Country Wines** where fruit wines, produced in the

7 THE BIRCH TREE INN

Wilsill

A fine old country inn providing a diverse menu, well kept ales and attentive hosts.

See entry on page 177

vaulted cellars of a 19th century flax mill are on sale. Tours and tastings are available on Fridays and Saturdays at 11.45am. A former Steam Engine Room on the site is now a tearoom.

BEWERLEY

1 mile SW of Pateley Bridge on the B6265

Recorded as *Bevrelie* (a clearing inhabited by badgers) in the *Domesday Book*, this is Nidderdale's oldest settlement. It was also the site of the earliest and most important of Fountains Abbey's many granges. Not only were they farming here but lead was being extracted from the nearby moor. The recently restored Chapel, built here by one of the last abbots, Marmaduke Huby, acted for many years as the village school.

In the 17th century the Yorke family moved to the embellished hall at Bewerley following their purchase of the former lands of Byland Abbey in Nidderdale. During the subsequent years, the family laid out the parkland as well as rebuilding some of the village and, though the estate was sold in the 1920s and the hall demolished, the park remains and plays host to the annual Nidderdale Show. The name of the village's most influential family, however, is not lost to the village as Yorke's Folly, two stone stoops, still stands on the hillside overlooking Bewerley.

RAMSGILL

5 miles NW of Pateley Bridge off the B6265

This pleasant village, clustered around a well kept green, was the birthplace of Eugene Aram in 1704. The son of a gardener at Newby Hall, Aram was arrested in 1758 in Kings Lynn for the murder of Daniel Clark in Knaresborough 13 years before. The trial took place in York and Aram caused a stir by conducting his own defence. However, he was convicted and later executed. His body was then taken to Knaresborough where it was hung from a gibbet. The gruesome story has been the centre of many tales and songs including a very romantic version by Sir Bulwer Lytton.

LOFTHOUSE

7 miles NW of Pateley Bridge off the B6265

This is a small dales' village lying in the upper valley of the River Nidd and, unlike neighbouring Wharfedale, the stone walls and rocky outcrops are of millstone grit though the valley bottom consists of limestone. As a result, only in excessive weather is there water under the bridge here as, in normal conditions, the river drops down two sumps: Manchester Hole and Goydon Pot.

Nearby **How Stean Gorge**, in the heart of Nidderdale, is often called Yorkshire's Little Switzerland and for good reason. This spectacular limestone gorge, which is up to 80 feet deep in places, through which the Stean Beck flows, is a popular tourist attraction. A narrow path with footbridges guide the visitor along the gorge where the waters rush over the large boulders below. There are also many sheltered areas of calm water where fish hide under the rocks. As well as taking a stroll up this fascinating path, visitors can also step inside Tom Taylor's Cave and, along the walk, marvel at the wide variety of plant life that grows in this steep ravine.

MIDDLESMOOR

8 miles NW of Pateley Bridge off the B6265

This tucked away village of stone built cottages and houses lies at the head of Upper Nidderdale and is reached by a single, winding road. The existence of ancient settlers can be seen in the present 19th-century Church of St Chad where an early 10th- or 11th-century preaching cross, bearing the inscription *Cross of St Ceadda* can be seen.

8 HOW STEAN GORGE

Lofthouse

Adrenaline packed ways to experience the thrill of nature are all offered at this stunning gorge in the heart of Nidderdale.

See entry on page 177

WHARFEDALE

Wharfedale is the longest of the Yorkshire Dales, following the River Wharfe from its origins on Cam Fell for more than 70 miles to Cawood, where it joins the River Ouse. At its source, almost 2000 feet above sea level, the river is nothing more than a moorland stream and, even in mid-Wharfedale, it is little more than a mountain river, broad, shallow, and peat brown in colour. The Romans named a local Goddess, *Verbeia*, after the river, and those who visit will understand why since the goddess was known for her treachery as well as her beauty. Wharfedale is one of the most spectacular and most varied of the Yorkshire dales. No one who sees the river charging through the narrow gorge at The Strid, near Bolton Abbey, will deny that the power of the river is to be respected.

Over the years, Wharfedale has inspired many poets, writers and painters. Colderidge and Wordsworth were captivated by its beauty and, in Wordsworth's case, with the local stories and legends. Ruskin enthused about its contrasts and Turner painted several scenes that capture the dale's history and mystery.

GRASSINGTON

One of the best loved villages within the Yorkshire Dales National Park, Grassington in many ways typifies the dales' settlement with its characteristic cobbled market square where a farmer's market is hled on the third Sunday of each month. Known as the capital of Upper Wharfedale, the historically important valley roads meet here and the ancient monastic route from Malham to Fountains Abbey passes through the village.

Grassington's origins are rooted in ancient history; there was certainly a Bronze Age settlement here, the remains of an Iron Age village have been found, a Celtic field system can be seen on nearby Lea Green, and the village was mentioned in the *Domesday Book*. Having passed through various families, the village is now part of the estate of the Dukes of Devonshire. With its narrow streets lined with attractive Georgian buildings, Grassington is a delightful place to wander around. It is also home to the National Park Dale Visitor Centre.

The **Grassington Folk Museum** came into being in 1975 when a group of local people spent their winter evenings making a large-scale relief map of Grassington Parish taken from a 19th century tithe map. When it was put on display, other villages offered enough old items of local interest to establish a small museum. Housed in two 18th-century lead miners' cottages, the museum today contains many exhibits and displays relating to the lives of those who have lived in the dale. It also has an exhibit featuring the Yorkshire Dales Railway that ran from Grassington to Skipton from 1902 to 1969.

In October, the museum hosts the Feast Sports. Among the many traditional events it features is a teacake eating race in which children have to eat a teacake then race to the other end of the field. The winner is the first child to then whistle a tune.

Two annual events which attract many visitors are the Grassington Festival of Music and Arts, which is held over the last two weeks of June, and the Grassington Dickensian Festival - a lively market, with street entertainment, dancing and music - held just before Christmas.

AROUND GRASSINGTON

HEBDEN

3 miles E of Grassington on the B6265

From this quiet hamlet it is only a short distance to the wonderful 500,000-year-old

9   OLD SCHOOL TEA ROOM

Hebden

A quaint tea room offering hearty meals, freshly baked scones and homemade cakes.

See entry on page 178

caves at **Stump Cross Caverns**. The caves ere discovered in 1860 by miners looking for lead. they didn't find any lead and didn't see any commercial value in the caves. It was a man named William Newbould who had the vision to see that they could be a profitable enterprise. He opened the caves to the public at a cost of 1 shilling (5p) per visit. The large show cave holds a fantastic collection of stalactites and stalagmites which make it one of the most visited underground attractions in the area. During excavations, remains of wolverines, a giant member of the weasel family were discovered . It is thought that these animals entered the caves looking for food such as reindeer and bison, the remains of which have also been found. The wolverine remains are on display in the visitor's centre where there is a gift shop, tea room and a lecture room where a 20-minute video of the caves is shown.

BURNSALL

2 miles S of Grassington on the B6160

The site of the quintessential village fête featured in the 2003 film *Calendar Girls*, Burnsall can claim to be the most photographed village in England. It is dramatically situated on a bend in the River Wharfe with the slopes of Burnsall Fell as a backdrop. It is thought that, sometime prior to the 8th century, Wilfrid Bishop of York, founded a wooden church here. Its site is now occupied by the village's 12th-century church. The only remnant of Wilfrid's building is the font which can still be seen at the back of **St Wilfrid's Church**. The churchyard is entered via a unique lychgate and here can be seen two hogback tombstones and various other fragments which date back to the times of the Anglo-Saxons and the Danes.

However, it is not this sturdy dales' church which draws visitors to Burnsall but its bridge. Today, this typical dales' bridge of five stone arches is the start of the annual Classic Fell Race which takes place on a Saturday towards the end of August. Over the years, the flood waters of the River Wharfe have washed away the arches on several occasions but the villagers have always

replaced them as this is the only crossing point for three miles in each direction.

APPLETREEWICK

4 miles SE of Grassington off the B6160

This peaceful village, which is known locally as Aptrick, lies between the banks of the River Wharfe and the bleak moorland and is overlooked by the craggy expanse of **Simon's Seat**, one of Wharfedale's best-loved hilltops. The village was once the home of William Craven, a Lord Mayor of London, who returned to spend much of his amassed wealth on improvements and additions to Appletreewick's fine old buildings. Known as the Dick Whittington of the Dale, Craven was born in 1548 and moved to London when he became apprenticed to a mercer (a dealer in textiles and fine fabrics).

A little further down river is the stately ruin of **Barden Tower**, a former residence of Lord Henry Clifford, owner of Skipton Castle. It was built in the 15th century but allowed to fall into decay and, despite repair in 1657, it is once more a ruin. Nearby is the attractive Barden Bridge, a 17th-century arch now designated as an ancient monument.

Just to the north of Appletreewick, at Skyreholme, lie **Parcevall Hall Gardens,** a wonderful woodland garden which contains many varieties of unusual plants and shrubs. Though the 16-acre gardens are high above sea level - which provides the visitor with some splendid views - many plants still flourish. The gardens have a special quality of peace and tranquillity - appropriately enough since the lovely old Hall is now a Bradford Diocesan Retreat and Conference Centre.

---

10 **HOWGILL LODGE**

Barden

In seven acres of magnificent countryside in the Yorkshire Dales National Park holiday makers can choose from B&B, caravan or tent and touring sites at this family run park.

See entry on page 178

BOLTON ABBEY

7 miles S of Grassington on the B6160

The village is actually a collection of small hamlets which have all been part of the estate of the Dukes of Devonshire since 1748. Bolton Abbey itself stands on the banks of the River Wharfe while the hamlets of Storiths, Hazelwood, Deerstones, and Halton East lie higher up.

The main attraction in the village is the substantial ruin of **Bolton Priory**, an Augustinian house that was founded in 1155 by monks from Embsay. Occupying an idyllic situation on the bank of the River Wharfe, the ruins are well preserved while the nave of the priory church, first built in 1220, now serves as the parish church.

After the Dissolution of the Monasteries the priory was sold to the 2nd Earl of Cumberland, Henry Clifford, and it has since passed into the hands of the Cavendish family, Dukes of Devonshire. An attractive option when visiting the priory is to travel on the Embsay and Bolton Abbey Steam Railway whose station is about half a mile away, reached by a pleasant riverside footpath.

In and around this beautiful village there are some 80 miles of footpaths and nature trails, skirting the riverbanks and climbing up onto the high moorland. Upstream from the priory lies one of the most visited natural features in Wharfedale, a point where the wide river suddenly narrows into a confined channel of black rock through which the water thunders. This spectacular gorge is known as **The Strid** because, over the centuries, many heroic (or foolhardy) types have attempted to leap across it as a test of bravery.

---

11 BOLTON ABBEY

Bolton Abbey, Skipton

Visitors flock to the Yorkshire Estate of the Duke and Duchess of Devonshire, to enjoy the magnificent scenery and superb facilities.

See entry on page 179

Located within the Bolton Abbey estate, **Hesketh Farm Park** is a 600-acre working beef and sheep farm. Voted National Farm Attraction of the Year, 2006, the farm encourages visitors to interact with the many animals within the site. Tractor and trailer tours are available, there are outdoor and indoor play areas, and a pedal go-kart course.

LINTON

1 mile SW of Grassington off the B6160

This delightful and unspoilt village, that is more correctly called Linton-in-Craven, has grown up around its village green through

Linton-in-Craven

which runs a small beck.

The **Church of St Michael and All Angels** is a fine example of rural medieval architecture. Believed to have been built on the site of a pagan shrine, the church lies some way from the village centre though its handsome bell-cote is a suitable landmark. Among the 14th-century roof bosses can be seen the Green Man, an ancient fertility symbol of a man's head protruding through foliage.

Spanning Linton Beck is a graceful 14th-century packhorse bridge that was repaired by Dame Elizabeth Redmayne in the late 17th century. During the repair work, Dame Elizabeth had a narrow parapet added to the bridge to prevent carts from crossing because, so it is said, the local farmers refused to contribute to the cost of the repairs.

CRACOE

3 miles SW of Grassington on the B6265

The village contains several 17th-century houses that are typical examples of the building style of that time. Constructed from stone quarried on nearby Cracoe and Rylstone Fell, the cavity between the three feet thick walls was filled with rubble.

RYLSTONE

4 miles SW of Grassington on the B6265

In the early 1800s, when Wordsworth was touring the area, he heard a local legend which became the basis for his poem *The White Doe of Rylstone*, published in 1815. The story is set in the 16th century and concerns the local Norton family. Francis Norton gave his sister Emily a white doe before he went off to battle. He survived the conflict but after his return to Rylstone was murdered in Norton Tower. Emily was inconsolable but found some comfort from the same white doe which had returned from the wild. It used to accompany Emily when she visited her brother's grave and long after her death, a white doe was often seen lying on Francis's grave.

On Rylstone Fell, above this Pennine village, stands **Rylstone Cross** which was, originally, a large stone that looked rather like a man. In 1885, a wooden cross was erected on top of the stone to commemorate peace with France and the initials DD and TB, carved on the back of the cross, refer to the Duke of Devonshire and his land agent, Mr T Broughton.

THRESHFIELD

1 mile W of Grassington on the B6160

Across the river from Grassington, Threshfield has at its heart a small village green called the Park, complete with the original village stocks and surrounded by charming 17th-century houses. Perhaps the most striking building is the Free Grammar School built in 1674. According to local people its porch is haunted by a fairy known as Old Pam the Fiddler. Threshfield was once known

he production of *besoms* (birch brooms) but the last family to make them, the Ibbotsons, died out in the 1920s.

CONISTONE

2½ miles NW of Grassington off the B6160

This ancient settlement clusters around its maypole and village green. The village Church of St Mary is thought to have been founded in Saxon times and there are certainly two well-preserved Norman arches to be seen. The land surrounding Conistone is unusually flat as it was once the bottom of a lake formed by the melt water from the glacier that carved out Kilnsey Crag.

KILNSEY

3 miles NW of Grassington on the B6160

This quiet and peaceful place on the opposite bank of the River Wharfe from Conistone, is overlooked by the now uninhabited Old Hall which was originally built as a grange for the monks of Fountains Abbey.

Noted for its resident troop of red squirrels, **Kilnsey Park and Trout Farm** is a popular place for family outings. Under-12s can enjoy their first experience of trout fishing, with all the tackle provided. Pony trekking is available, there's an estate shop selling dales' produce and fresh Kilnsey trout, a restaurant and children's adventure centre. Visitors can also wander around the farm. Fly fishing, for those who like to indulge, is available in two well-stocked lakes.

The striking outline of **Kilnsey Crag** is unmistakable as one side of this limestone hill was gouged out by a passing glacier during the Ice Age. One of the most spectacular natural features in the dales, the crag has a huge 'lip' or overhang which presents an irresistible challenge to adventurous climbers.

KETTLEWELL

"The village seems the peculiar abode of peace and quiet beauty; its limestone terraces, with their fringes of hazel and rowan coppices give to the district a characteristic beauty... the eye which delights in the flow and ripple of sky line there is a beauty in Kettlewell which is all its own." So wrote a Professor Moorman almost one hundred years ago and the description still holds.

Dowber Gill Beck Waterfall

This was written nearly one hundred years ago by Professor Moorman but is as true today as it was then. A popular centre for walkers, Kettlewell is surrounded by the beautiful countryside of Upper Wharfedale, It stands at the meeting point of several old packhorse routes which now serve as footpaths and bridleways. At one time the village was a busy market centre, boasting no fewer than 13 public houses. Today, however, Kettlewell is a conservation area, a charming place of chiefly 17th- and 18th-century houses and cottages. Keen cinemagoers will know that Kettlewell provided almost all the locations for the enormously successful 2003 film *Calendar Girls* based on the true story of a local Women's Institute that produced a calendar of discreetly naked ladies to raise funds for leukaemia research.

---

12 BLUE BELL INN

Kettlewell

Letting rooms, good food, great hospitality and real ales are all available at this pub located at the heart of the Yorkshire Dales National Park.

See entry on page 179

AROUND KETTLEWELL

BUCKDEN

4 miles N of Kettlewell on the B6160

Marking the beginning of Wharfedale proper, Buckden is the first full-sized village of the dale and proudly boasts that it is also home to Wharfedale's first shop. Unusually for this area, the village was not settled by the Anglo-Saxons but by the Normans. As the forest was cleared to make way for agriculture, Buckden became an important market town serving a large part of the surrounding area. Wool was one of the important sources of income for the dalesfolk and the local inn here still has some of the old weighing equipment from the days when the trade was conducted on the premises. The village is an excellent starting point for those wanting to climb Buckden Pike (2302 feet), which lies to the east. The route to the summit takes in superb views and several waterfalls.

Designated in Norman times as one of the feudal hunting forests, **Langstrothdale Chase** was governed by the strict forest laws. Just to the south of the village, which lies on the edge of the Chase, can be seen an old stone cross which was used to mark the forest boundary. Buckden's name means the 'valley of the bucks' but its last deer was hunted and killed here in the 17th century.

HUBBERHOLME

5 miles N of Kettlewell off the B6160

This small village appears on very few maps but is definitely worth a visit. It stands where Wharfedale and Langstrothdale come together, at the centre of a triangle formed by Buckden Pike, Pen-y-Ghent and Dodd Fell, all of them over 2000 feet. The Wharfe is only a short way along its journey at this point, but is still powerful enough at times to have flooded the church well above it. The church, St Michael's and All Angels, is a simple, low building with a sturdy tower has a notable 16th century rood loft and oaken pews hand-carved by Robert Thompson "The Mouseman" who left his signature mouse carvings on them. The church was a favourite of JB Priestley - his ashes were scattered in the graveyard. Priestley also favoured the George Inn in the village, an authentic village hostelry with an open fire; real ales; mullioned windows and flagged floors. Each year, on New Year's Day, the villagers gather at the local pub for the **Hubberholme Parliament**. For that night, the public bar becomes the House of Commons, where the farmers congregate, while the room where the vicar and churchwardens meet is the House of Lords. A candle is lit and bidding then takes place between the farmers for the rent of a field behind the church. Encouraged by the vicar, the highest bid when the candle expires takes the land.

YOCKENTHWAITE

6 miles NW of Kettlewell off the B6160

The unusual name of this small village is Viking in origin. Though once a prosperous place, Yockenthwaite is now a collection of old stone farms. On the surrounding fells stands a well-preserved Bronze Age stone circle and **Giant's Grave**, the remains of an Iron Age settlement.

ARNCLIFFE

3 miles W of Kettlewell off the B6160

The village name dates back to Saxon times when the valley was referred to as Amerdale. This is a quiet, tranquil dale and life has remained the same here for many years. Many of the buildings around the central village green are listed and, in its early years, the long running TV series *Emmerdale* was filmed here. Strongly recommended is a visit to the Falcon Inn, run by the Miller family for four generations, where almost nothing has changed in more than half a century.

AIREDALE

The most impressive natural features in Airedale are the beautiful limestone formations found to the north of Malham. The spectacular and enormous curved cliff of Malham Cove, created by glacial action during the last Ice Age, the limestone pavements above the cove, the deep gorge of Gordale Scar, and the remote natural lake, Malham Tarn, are all well worth a visit.

This dramatic scenic area has been designated a Site of Special Scientific Interest as the area supports a wide range of animals, birds, and plant life. As there is a variety of terrain, from bleak, bracken-strewn moorland to coniferous plantations, there is also a wide variety of flora and fauna. Birdwatchers, particularly, will delight in the opportunity to catch sight of red grouse and short-eared owls on the moors while also having the chance to view the many wading birds which populate the lakes and reservoirs of the area.

The 'Gateway to the Dales', Skipton, has long been a starting-point for any tour of the Yorkshire Dales and the town's old industries have given way, to a large degree, to tourism. The source of the River Aire lies in Malhamdale, just to the north of Malham, and it flows through both dales before finally joining the River Ouse. For some of its length, in Airedale, the river flows side-by-side with the Leeds and Liverpool Canal. The construction of a navigable waterway, linking the two great industrial areas of Lancashire and Yorkshire, changed the lives of many living in the dales and certainly played a major part in establishing the textile mills in the area.

However, the importance of farming has never been lost and market day is a key event in the daily lives of the dalesfolk. As well as the sheep, other constant features of the countryside are the dry stone walls- a familiar sight to all those visiting the Yorkshire Dales.

SKIPTON

A good introduction to Skipton is to follow the **Millennium Walk** which links many of the town's attractions. Skipton, mercifully, escaped the 'development' mania of the 1960s when so many old towns had their hearts ripped out. Visitors can still wander down the many alleyways, known here as 'ginnels', explore the side streets with their independent shops, bars and restaurants, or visit the canal area with its boats, footpaths and picnic areas. A leaflet guide to the 2-hour promenade is available at the Tourist Information Centre on the High Street. Included in the walk is the Town Hall which is now also the home of the **Craven Museum & Gallery**. Dedicated to the surrounding area, it contains many interesting displays relating to the geological and archaeological treasures that have been found locally, including a piece of Bronze Age cloth which is considered the oldest textile fragment in the country. Closer to the present day, there are displays of furniture illustrating the fine craftsmanship that went into even the most mundane household item. Also on show are farming exhibits which reflect the changing lives of many of the people who lived off the surrounding countryside.

Almost opposite the Town Hall, on the High Street, are the premises of the **Craven Herald**, a newspaper that was established in 1874 although the publication was produced for a short time in the 1850s. The building is fortunate in having retained its late-Victorian shop front, as well as the passageway to one side. Close to the newspaper's offices is the **Public Library** which opened in 1910 and was funded by Andrew Carnegie. A large, ornate building, it is in contrast to the town's older buildings and stands as a reminder of the change in character which Skipton underwent in the late 19th century.

It was King John who granted the town its market rights, way back in 1204. Today, the market is held on the High Street four days a week (Monday, Wednesday, Friday and Saturday) when more than 50 independent traders set up their stalls. For cattle or sheep there is the Skipton Auction Mart. The Yuletide Festival and Market takes place on first two Sundays in December.

The town's most imposing building is **Skipton Castle,** one of the best-preserved and most complete medieval castles in England, despite enduring a 3-year siege during the Civil War. Built to guard the entrance to Airedale, the powerful stone structure seen today was devised in 1310 by Robert de Clifford, the 1st Earl of Skipton. It is thanks to one of his descendants, Lady Anne Clifford, that visitors to Skipton can marvel at the castle buildings. Following the ravages of the Civil War, Lady Anne undertook a comprehensive restoration programme. As well as an enormous

---

13 **HEMMINGWAYS TEA ROOMS**

Skipton

This is one of Yorkshire's finest tea rooms serving a wide range of delicious homemade delights.

See entry on page 180

---

14 **THE CRAVEN MUSEUM**

Skipton

Crammed full of fascinating exhibits, the **Craven Museum** is a great place to explore the history of Skipton and the Craven

See entry on page 181

---

15 **SPENCER'S CAFE & BISTRO**

Skipton

This cafe is a magnet for lovers of fine cuisine. It is an ideal to relax after a hard day's work or shopping trip

See entry on page 182

---

16 **SKIPTON CASTLE**

Skipton

Guardian of the gateway to the Yorkshire Dales for over 900 years, this unique fortress is one of the most complete and well-preserved medieval castles in England.

See entry on page 181

Skipton Castle Gateway

banqueting hall, a series of kitchens still remain with some of their original fittings. There is also a rather unusually decorated room whose walls are lined with shells that were collected by George Clifford in the 19th century while he was travelling in the South Seas. A beautiful Tudor courtyard has survived, complete with a yew tree planted in 1659 by Lady Anne. However, the most striking feature of the castle is the impressive 14th-century gateway, which is visible from the High Street, and carries the Clifford family motto *Desormais* meaning 'Henceforth'. Visitor amenities at the castle include a licensed tea room, a bookshop and the peaceful Chapel Terrace picnic area. Throughout the year, the castle hosts a wide variety of events, including the Clog Dancing Festival in mid-July.

Many members of the Clifford family are buried in the parish **Church of the Holy Trinity** which stands adjacent to the castle. The most impressive memorial is that of the 3rd earl, George Clifford. Dating back to the 14th century, the church also suffered damage during the Civil War. Once again, Lady Anne Clifford came to the rescue, restoring the interior and rebuilding the steeple in 1655. Inside the church, among the many tombstones, is that of the Longfellow family, which included the uncle of the American poet, Henry Wadsworth Longfellow.

The **Leeds and Liverpool Canal**, which flows through the town, provided a cheap form of transport as well as linking Skipton with the major industrial centres of Yorkshire and Lancashire. The first of three trans-Pennine routes, the 127-mile canal has 91 locks along the full length as well as two tunnels, one of which is over a mile long. The towpath provides a number of pleasant walks, including a stretch along the cul-de-sac Spring Branch beside the castle walls. Boat trips are also available.

It seems fitting that, in a town which over many years has been dedicated to trade and commerce, Thomas Spencer, co-founder of Marks and Spencer, should have been born here in 1851. Skipton, too, was the home of Sir Winston Churchill's physician, Lord Moran, who grew up here as the son of the local doctor.

As with many historic market towns, Skipton has its fair share of inns and public houses. The **Black Horse Inn** is one such pub and its date stone of 1676 is well worth a second look as it is carved with symbols of the butcher's trade: axes, animal heads, and twisted fleeces. Originally called The King's Head, the inn was built by, not surprisingly, a butcher, Robert Goodgion. The Black Horse commands splendid views over the canal and a mounting block for horsemen still stands outside the front door.

AROUND SKIPTON

EMBSAY

1 mile N of Skipton off the A59

Embsay is the western terminus of the **Embsay Steam Railway** which follows a picturesque 4.5 mile route to the award-winning station at Bolton Abbey. There are more than 20 locomotives, both steam and diesel, on display together with railway carriages. During the summer months, trains run 7 days a week with 'Stately Trains' on scheduled Sundays using carriages from the historic Stately Trains collection such as those built to haul first class passengers on the Great North of Scotland Railway. Refreshments are available in the tearooms at Bolton Abbey and Embsay stations. Both have gift shops, including the famous bookshop at Embsay station. Special events are arranged throughout the year.

Those choosing to walk over the moor to the north of the village should take care as the area is peppered with old coal pits and disused shafts. However, the view from **Embsay Crag** (1217 feet high) is well worth the effort of climbing.

KILDWICK

3 miles S of Skipton off the A629

This picturesque little village, on the north bank of the River Aire, is approached over a bridge that was built in the early 14th century by the canons of Bolton Priory. The village **Church of St Andrew** was also rebuilt around the 14th and 15th centuries, though the choir was extended to its unusually long length sometime later and gives the church its local name of Lang Kirk o'Craven.

The River Aire is not the only waterway which passes through the village as it also lies on the banks of the Leeds and Liverpool Canal. The canal, which until the 1930s was still in commercial use, is now the preserve of pleasure craft and Kildwick is a popular overnight mooring.

LOTHERSDALE

4 miles SW of Skipton off the A629

A dramatic stretch of the Pennine Way passes through this village set in a deep valley in the heart of the moors. Charlotte Brontë knew the village well and in *Jane Eyre* the house she calls Gateshead is modelled on Lothersdale's Stonegappe, up on the hillside near the church.

THORNTON-IN-CRAVEN

5 miles SW of Skipton on the A56

This attractive village stands on the Pennine

17 **THE SLATERS ARMS**

Bradley, nr Skipton

Commanding stunning views across the canal and the Aire Valley, this historic pub also offers great real ales, delicious homemade food and friendly service.

See entry on page 183

Way and from here there are magnificent views of Airedale and Pendle Forest in Lancashire. To the west of the village and winner of the National Farm Attraction of the Year, 2008, **Thornton Hall Farm Country Park** promises "Animal encounters, glorious countryside and family fun come rain or shine!" Visitors can meet llamas and lambs, hens and horses, pigs and poultry, and wallabies and deer. They can also watch the sheep dogs in action, hitch a ride on the giant caterpillar, feed the friendly inhabitants, or have fun in the giant sand pit in the all-weather barn.

EARBY

6 miles SW of Skipton on the A56

Though the Yorkshire Dales are thought of as a once thriving textile producer, lead-mining was also a key industry for many centuries. Housed in an old grammar school, founded in the 1590s by Robert Windle, is the **Yorkshire Dales Mining Museum** which re-opened in 2006 after a 4-year programme of extension and renovation. The large collection, as well as the substantial documentation and indexing, has been put together by several local interest groups who began their work in 1945 when the Earby Mines Research Group was formed within the Earby Pothole Club. The museum, which has limited opening times, has many excellent displays including mine tubs, photographs, mine plans, small implements, mining machinery, and miners' personal belongings.

BROUGHTON

4 miles W of Skipton on the A59

The Tempest family has been associated with this farming community for the past 800 years and their family home, **Broughton Hall**, dates back to 1597, with additions made in the 18th and 19th centuries. The building itself may well seem familiar since it, as well as the grounds, have been used frequently by film crews as an historic location. The Hall is only open on Bank Holiday Mondays or by prior arrangement. However, the grounds are open on the last Sunday in June when the

Broughton Hall Game Fair takes place. This well-attended event covers all manner of country sports and pursuits. The Broughton estate covers 3000 acres, part of which is home to a business park where many small businesses thrive.

GARGRAVE

5 miles NW of Skipton on the A65

This picturesque small village in Upper Airedale was once a thriving market town and it also became a busy transport centre after the Leeds and Liverpool Canal was built. Lead from the nearby mines was loaded on to the barges at the five wharves here, while other goods were unloaded ready for distribution to the surrounding area. The village also played a part in the textile boom and there were two cotton mills in the village. Now no longer in commercial use, like the canal, some of the mills have been turned into residential accommodation while the canal is very much alive with pleasure boats.

To the south of the village, at **Kirk Sink**, is the site of a Roman villa that was excavated in the 1970s. Relics recovered from the building can be seen in Skipton and Cliffe Castle Museums; the site itself has since been re-covered.

CONISTON COLD

7 miles NW of Skipton on the A65

Set midway between Skipton and Settle, this small village lies on the old route to the Lake District. Like most places situated on once busy routes, the village had its share of coaching inns and one in particular was the Punch Bowl Inn which has an unusual circular indentation on the front outside wall. In days

gone by the inn's patrons would stand a few yards from the wall and try to kick a ball to this mark.

AIRTON

8 miles NW of Skipton off the A65

This charming Airedale village is well known to long-distance walkers as it lies on the Pennine Way. At the beginning of the 18th century Airton became a Quaker community and the **Meeting House**, which was built on land donated by the well-known Quaker weavers William and Alice Ellis, can still be seen by the village green. Another legacy of the village's Quaker community is the absence of a public house as the drinking of alcohol was strictly forbidden by the Friends.

Also overlooking the village green is a 17th-century Squatter's Cottage – so-called because, according to the law, any person building a house and having smoke rising from the chimney within 24 hours was granted the freehold of the property including the land within a stone's throw of the front door.

MALHAM

11 miles NW of Skipton off the A65

"I won't know for sure if Malhamdale is the finest place there is until I have died and seen heaven (assuming they let me at least have a glance), but until that day comes, it will certainly do." Such was the considered view of the author Bill Bryson who lived in Malhamdale for several years. The focal point of Malham is the village green where the annual sheep fairs were held. This pretty village of farms and cottages is one of the most visited places in the Yorkshire Dales though it is not so much the charming stone built dwellings which visitors come to admire but the spectacular limestone scenery which lies just to the north. However, the two ancient stone bridges in the village centre are also worth a second glance. The New Bridge, which is also known as the Monks' Bridge, was built in the 17th century while the Wash-Dub Bridge dates from the 16th century and is of a clapper design (limestone

---

18 THE OLD SWAN INN

Gargrave

With a fascinating history, this inn also serves up delicious home cooked food with plenty of real ale and guest accommodation for all.

See entry on page 184

31

Malham Tarn

slabs placed on stone supports).

To the north of the village rises the ancient glacial grandeur of **Malham Cove**. Access is from the Langcliffe road beyond the last buildings of the village, down a path alongside the beck that leads through a scattering of trees. The 300-ft limestone amphitheatre is the most spectacular section of the mid-Craven fault and, as recently as the 1700s, a massive waterfall that was higher than Niagara Falls cascaded over its edge. A steep path leads to the limestone pavement at the top, with its characteristic clints and grykes, where water has carved a distinctive natural sculpture through the weaknesses in the limestone.

From here it is not too far to reach the equally inspiring **Gordale Scar**, a huge gorge carved by glacial melt water with an impressive waterfall leaping, in two stages, from a fissure in its face. Further on still is another waterfall known as Janet's Foss. Beside the waterfall is a cave which Janet, a friendly fairy, is reputed to inhabit. Three miles north of the scar is **Malham Tarn**, a glacial lake which by way of an underground stream is the source of the River Aire.

RIBBLESDALE AND THE THREE PEAKS

The River Ribble, the source of which lies high up on bleak moorland to the northeast of Ingleton, flows through several ancient settlements before leaving the county of Yorkshire and flowing on into Lancashire. On opposite banks of the river, lie Settle and Giggleswick, which are overlooked by the towering white limestone cliffs of Castleberg Crag and Langcliffe Scar, parts of the mid-Craven fault.

Further north from these two market towns is one of the most popular tourist centres in the dales, Ingleton, and high above the village are the famous **Three Peaks** of Ingleborough, Pen-y-ghent, and Whernside. The surrounding countryside is dominated by caves, potholes, and waterfalls.

The layer of limestone which lies across this whole area was laid down around 400 million years ago when the shells of dead sea creatures along with mud accumulated at the bottom of the warm sea that covered a huge area of northern England. Much later, the layer of sandstone, known as millstone grit, was formed over the top.

Much is talked about the **Craven Fault** and, though it was formed by a series of mighty earthquakes, this all happened well over 30 million years ago so visitors need not worry about visiting the area. The line of the fault, where the land to the northwest was lifted up and the land to the southeast slipped down, is all too evident today. It was the action of water, seeping into the limestone, which froze during the Ice Age, that has created the many caves and potholes of the area. Erosion, though this time on the surface, near Malham and elsewhere, formed the magnificent limestone pavements while the Three Peaks, as they are capped by millstone grit, have stood the test of time and still stand proud.

This is farming country and the traditional agricultural methods, along with the abundance of limestone, have given this region its own distinctive appeal. The high fells, composed of grits and sandstone, support heather moorlands and here can be found the only bird unique to Britain, the red grouse, and several birds of prey. Meanwhile, the limestone areas support a much more varied plant life, though the woodlands are chiefly of ash. In these shaded places, among the wild garlic and lily of the valley, visitors might be lucky enough to come across roe deer, badgers, and foxes.

SETTLE

This busy market town in the foothills of the Pennines is dominated by one of the huge viaducts from the **Settle to Carlisle Railway** as well as the towering limestone cliffs of **Castleberg Crag** which offers spectacular views over the town. It can be reached by following the Tot Lord Woodland Trail.

Settle is at its most liveliest and colourful on Tuesdays, when the weekly market takes place, an event that dates back to 1249 when Henry III granted Settle a Market Charter. In addition to the open air market, there's also an indoor market in Victoria Hall where the traders specialise in bric-à-brac and curios.

The market place is surrounded by mainly family-owned shops and is dominated by two impressive buildings: the arcaded Shambles, a historic 3-storey building with shops on two levels and houses above, and the French-style Town Hall of 1820. The town's oldest building is the 17th-century **Preston's Folly,** described as "an extravaganza of mullioned windows and Tudor masonry". It is named after the man who created this anomalous fancy and impoverished himself in the process.

Apart from the grander structures on the main streets, there are charming little side streets, lined with Jacobean and Georgian cottages, and criss-crossed with quirky little alleyways and ginnels with hidden courtyards and workshops of a time gone by. Almost as old is **Ye Olde Naked Man** pub in the Market Place. The inn sign depicts a naked man protecting his modesty with a carpenter's plane bearing the date 1663.

Settle is probably best known as the southern terminus of the **Settle to Carlisle Railway,** a proudly preserved survivor of the glorious age of steam travel, although the regular daily services are now provided by diesel locomotives. Built between 1869 and 1872, the route crosses 21 viaducts, of which the Ribblehead Viaduct is the most spectacular, passes through 14 tunnels and over numerous bridges. The 72-mile line is still flanked by charming little stations and signal boxes - the station buildings at Settle are particularly appealing. This attractive railway was built amidst great controversy and even greater cost, in both money and lives, earning it the dubious title of "the line that should never have been built'. In the churchyard at St Leonard's in Chapel-le-Dale, more than 100 railway workers who perished in the construction of the line are buried.

Just outside the town, housed in an old cotton mill dating from the 1820s, is the **Watershed Mill Visitor Centre.** This charming place, on the banks of the River Ribble, offers a unique shopping experience. One of the most popular shops offers real ales from 12 Yorkshire breweries and 3 Scottish breweries along with more than 100 Scottish single malt whiskies, of which over 90 are available for taste every day.

AROUND SETTLE

LANGCLIFFE

1 mile N of Settle on the B6479

As its name suggests, Langcliffe lies in the shelter of the long cliff of the Craven fault where the millstone grit sandstone meets the silver grey of the limestone. Although the majority of the houses and cottages surrounding the central village green are built from the limestone, some sandstone has also been used which gives this pretty village an added charm. The Victorian urn on the top of the

Settle Station

Catrigg Force

Langcliffe Fountain was replaced by a stone cross after the First World War in memory of those villagers who died in the conflict.

STAINFORTH

1 mile N of Settle on the B6479

This sheltered sheep farming village owes its existence to the Cistercian monks who brought those animals to this area. The monks were also responsible for building the 14th-century stone packhorse bridge which carries the road over the local beck, a tributary of the River Ribble. **Catrigg Force**, found along a track known as Goat Scar Lane, is a fine waterfall which drops some 60 feet into a wooded pool, while to the west is **Stainforth Force** flowing over a series of rock shelves.

HORTON IN RIBBLESDALE

6 miles N of Settle on the B6479

The oldest building in Horton is the 12th-century **St Oswald's Church** which still shows signs of its Norman origins in the chevron designs over the south door. Inside, peculiarly, all the pillars lean to the south and, in the west window, there is an ancient

piece of stained glass showing Thomas à Becket wearing his bishop's mitre. This village is the ideal place from which to explore the limestone landscapes and green hills of Upper Ribblesdale. To the east lies **Pen-y-ghent** (2,273 feet high), one of the famous Three Peaks. The whole of this area has been designated as being of Special Scientific Interest, mainly due to the need to conserve the swiftly eroding hillsides and paths. This is an ancient landscape, well worth the efforts to preserve its ash woodlands, primitive earthworks, and rare birdlife such as peregrine falcon, ring ouzel, curlew and golden plover. There are also a great many caves in the area, which add to the sense of romance and adventure one feels in this place.

There are several listed buildings in the area including Lodge Hall, which was formerly known as Ingman Lodge. Before the 20th century, a judge would travel around the countryside on horseback stopping to try cases rather than villagers commuting to major towns for their trials. Here, if anyone was found guilty of a capital crime, they were brought to Ingman Lodge to be hanged.

RATHMELL

2 miles S of Settle off the A65

A small village set beside the River Ribble, Rathmell is home to the **Northern Equine Therapy Centre** which was established in 1991 to provide a unique centre for the treatment of horses and ponies, and to put an edge on the fitness of performance animals. Within the 150 acres of farm land are a hydrotherapy pool, solarium, an all-weather arena for schooling and a farrier's forge. The Visitor Centre was opened in 1998 in response to

---

19 THE BOARS HEAD HOTEL

Long Preston

This magnificent 16th century inn offers guests a traditional Yorkshire menu, real ales, live fires, and great guest accommodation year round.

See entry on page 185

---

public interest in the work done here. Visitors can watch horses swimming in the pool and enjoying the solarium treatment, and cheer on the Racing Miniature Shetlands. The centre is only open on certain days but group visits are welcome if booked in advance.

GIGGLESWICK

1 mile W of Settle off the A65

Now virtually a suburb of Settle, this ancient village is best known for **Giggleswick School** which was granted a Royal Charter in 1553 by Edward VI. The school's fame stems partly from its observatory which was used by the Astronomer Royal in 1927 to observe an eclipse of the sun. The school's chapel, the copper dome of which is a well-known local landmark, was built to commemorate the Diamond Jubilee of Queen Victoria. A former pupil was the late TV celebrity Richard Whiteley whose teacher, Russell Harty, was also to achieve TV fame. In memory of the former the school has established the Richard Whiteley Theatre as a showcase for both school productions and for visiting companies.

Just to the north of Giggleswick can be found the famous Ebbing and Flowing Well, one of many in the area which owe their unusual names to the porous nature of the limestone which causes there sometimes to be water and sometimes not.

AUSTWICK

4 miles NW of Settle off the A65

This ancient village of stone cottages and crofts, dry stone walls, abandoned quarries, and patchwork hills was originally a Norse settlement: the name is Nordic for Eastern Settlement. The mostly 17th-century

buildings, with their elaborately decorated stone lintels, flank what remains of the village green where the ancient cross stands as a reminder of when this was the head of a dozen neighbouring manors and the home of an annual cattle fair.

On the edge of the village is the **Yorkshire Dales Falconry Centre,** home to more than 40 birds of prey from around the world. They include eagles, owls, vultures, falcons and hawks. The centre has been careful to re-create their natural habitats, transporting 350 tons of limestone boulders to provide cliff-faced aviaries. One of the star attractions is 'Vera', the UK's only free-flying Lappet-Faced Vulture, with a wingspan of more than 8 feet. Along with other vultures, eagles and hawks, Vera takes part in the regular free-flying demonstrations. The centre has full educational facilities, an adventure playground, tea room and gift shop.

CLAPHAM

6 miles NW of Settle off the A65

By far the largest building in the village is **Ingleborough Hall,** once the home of the Farrer family and now a centre for outdoor education. One member of the family, Reginald Farrer, was an internationally renowned botanist and he was responsible for introducing many new plant species into the country. Many examples of his finds still exist in the older gardens of the village and in the hall's grounds. From the hall there is a particularly pleasant walk, the **Reginald Farrer Nature Trail,** which leads from Clapham to nearby Ingleborough Cave.

Though the existence of **Ingleborough Cave** was known for centuries, it was not until the 19th century that its exploration was begun. One of the early explorers, geologist Adam Sedgwick, is quoted as saying, 'We were forced to use our abdominal muscles as sledges and our mouths as candlesticks', which gives an excellent indication of the conditions the early pot-holers had to endure. Those visiting the caves today see only a small part of the five miles of caverns and tunnels though, fortunately, this easily accessible portion is spectacular,

---

20 GIGGLESWICK TEA ROOMS AND VILLAGE SHOP

Giggleswick

What this place lacks in size it makes up for in hospitality and delicious food cooked to order.

See entry on page 186

with large natural passages and a veritable wonderland of stalactites and stalagmites. As well as exotic cave formations and illuminated pools there is Eldon Hall Cavern, home to a vast mushroom bed.

This is an area that has a great abundance of natural waterfalls but the waterfall seen near the village church is one of the very few which owes its existence to man. In the 1830s the Farrer family created a large lake, covering some seven acres of land, and the waterfall is the lake's overflow. As well as providing water for the village, a turbine was placed at the bottom of the waterfall and, with the help of the electrical power, Clapham was one of the first villages in the country to have street lighting. This is perhaps not as surprising as it might seem as Michael Faraday, the distinguished 19th-century scientist, was the son of the village blacksmith.

The most peculiar feature of the area surrounding Clapham has to be the **Norber Boulders,** a series of black boulders that stand on limestone pedestals. Despite their contrived appearance, they are a completely natural feature. Another distinctive local feature is the clapper bridge, a medieval structure made from large slabs of rock spanning the local becks.

Also close to Clapham is the gigantic pot-hole known as **Gaping Gill.** Some 360ft deep, the hole is part of the same underground limestone cave system as Ingleborough Cave. The main chamber is similar in size to York Minster. Twice a year, the public can gain access via a bosun's chair on a winch that is operated by local caving clubs.

INGLETON

10 miles NW of Settle off the A65

From as long ago as the late 1700s, Ingleton has been famous for the numerous caves and other splendid scenery that lie within a short distance, though some are harder to find and even harder to reach. Though Ingleton is no longer served by trains, the

village is still dominated by the railway viaduct that spans the River Greta. The river, which is formed here by the meeting of the Rivers Twiss and Doe, is famous for its salmon leaps. There are riverside walks or you can just relax in the Millennium Gardens.

Discovered in 1865 by Joseph Carr, the **Ingleton Waterfalls** were not revealed to the public until 1885 and have been delighting visitors ever since. Along the four miles of scenic walks, the stretch of waterfalls includes those with such interesting names as Pecca Twin Falls, Holly Bush Spout, Thornton Force and Baxengill Gorge.

Many thousands of years old, **White Scar Cave** was only discovered in 1923, by an adventurous student named Christopher Long. Though he saw only by the light of a torch, standing alone in the vast underground cave now known as Battlefield Cavern must have been an awesome experience. The longest Show Cave in Britain, it stretches for more than 330 feet, soaring in places to 100 feet high, with thousands of oddly-shaped stalactites dripping from its roof. The 80-minute guided tour covers one mile and passes cascading waterfalls and curious cave formations such as the Devil's Tongue, the Arum Lily and the remarkably lifelike Judge's Head. The temperature inside the cave stays constant all year round at a cool 8oC (46oF) so don't forget to bring something warm to wear.

Ingleborough, at 2375 feet, is the middle summit of the **Three Peaks**. For more than

Ingleborough Summit

2000 years, the peak has been used as a beacon and a fortress. A distinctive feature of the horizon for miles around, it is made of several layers of rock of differing hardnesses. There are several paths to the summit most of which begin in Ingleton. On top of the peak are the remains of a tower that was built by a local mill owner, Mr Hornby Roughsedge. Though the intended use of the building is not known, its short history is well-documented. A grand opening was arranged on the summit and the celebrations, probably helped by a supply of ale, got a little out of hand when a group of men began tearing down the structure.

At the highest point is a triangulation point while, close by, a cross-shaped shelter has been built which offers protection from the elements whatever their direction. The shelter acts as a reminder that the weather can change quickly in this area and a walk to the summit, however nice the day is at lower levels, should not be undertaken without careful thought as to suitable clothing.

To the east, on the edge of the summit plateau, are the remains of several ancient hut circles and, beyond, the remains of a wall. The Romans are known to have used Ingleborough as a signal station but the wall may have been built by the Brigantes whose settlement on the mountain was called *Rigodunum*.

CHAPEL-LE-DALE

6 miles N of Ingleton on the B6255

Whernside, to the north of the village, is the highest of the Three Peaks, at 2418 feet, and also the least popular of the mountains – consequently there are few paths to the summit. Just below the top are a number of tarns. Here, in 1917, it was noticed that they were frequented by black-headed gulls. Those walking to the top

of the peak today will also see the birds, a reminder that the northwest coast is not so far away.

RIBBLEHEAD

10 miles N of Settle on the B6479

One of the most famous bridges in the world, the **Ribblehead Viaduct** took five years to build, between 1870 and 1875. Its 24 lofty arches carry the Settle to Carlisle Railway over Batty Moss, some 100ft below. The viaduct is 440 yards long and shortly after it the track enters Blea Moor Tunnel, at 2629 yards long the longest tunnel on the line. Because the viaduct is curved, passengers on the train get to see the remarkable stone arches of the viaduct as the train passes over it. Occupying a bleak and exposed site, the viaduct is often battered by strong winds which on occasion can literally stop a train in its tracks. The **Ribblehead Station & Visitor Centre**, housed in former station buildings, presents an interpretive display showing the history of the line with special emphasis on the Ribblehead locality.

A couple of miles south of Ribblehead, the confluence of Gayle Beck and Cam Beck is generally regarded as the beginning of the River Ribble which runs for 75 miles through Yorkshire and Lancashire before emptying into the Irish Sea near Lytham.

Ribblehead Viaduct

LOCATION MAP

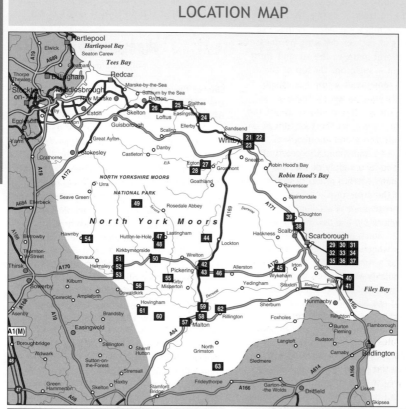

Accommodation

Food & Drink

NORTH YORK MOORS, HERITAGE COAST & VALE OF PICKERING

Established in 1952, the North York Moors National Park covers an area of covers an area of 554 square miles (1.436 square km) extending from Whitby in the east almost to Northallerton in the west; and from Guisborough in the north to Ampleforth in the south. Within its boundaries is the largest expanse of heather moorland in England; a spectacular stretch of coastline, and expanses of ancient woodland. Some of Yorkshire's prettiest villages are here but these settlements are few and far between: indeed, there may have been more people living here in the Bronze Age (1500-500 BC) than there are now to judge by the more than 3000 'howes', or burial mounds, that have been discovered.

Just as the Yorkshire Dales have large areas of moorland, so the North York Moors have many dales – Eskdale, Ryedale, Farndale, more than 100 of them in all. They cut deep into the great upland tracts and are as picturesque, soft and pastoral as anywhere in Yorkshire.

Between Saltburn and Filey runs some of the most striking coastal scenery in the country. Along this stretch of the Heritage Coast you'll find the highest cliffs in the country, a shoreline fretted with rocky coves, with miles of golden sandy beaches, a scattering of picture postcard fishing villages and, at its heart, the historic port of Whitby dramatically set around the mouth of the River Esk. It was at Whitby that one of England's greatest mariners, Captain Cook, learnt his seafaring skills and it was from here that he departed in the tiny bark, *Endeavour*, a mere 370 tons, on his astonishing journeys of exploration.

Further down the coast are the popular resorts of Scarborough (where visitors were frolicking naked in the sea as early as 1735), and Filey, both of them offering long stretches of sandy beach and a huge variety of holiday entertainments.

To the south of the Park, runs the Vale of Pickering which was once a huge lake which has only been drained in comparatively recent times. In parts such as The Carrs near Scarborough, the land is still waterlogged. It was here, in August 2010, that archaeologists discovered the oldest house in Britain dating back some 10,500 years.

GREAT AYTON

The Captain Cook Country Tour is a 70-mile circular trip taking in all the major locations associated with the great seafarer. The appealing small town of Great Ayton, set around the River Leven, is an essential stopping point on this tour. Cook's family moved to Great Ayton when he was eight years old and he attended the little school which is now the **Captain Cook Schoolroom Museum**. The building dates back to 1785 and was built as a school and poorhouse on the site of the original charity school that was built in 1704 by Michael Postgate, a wealthy local landowner. It was at the Postgate School that James received his early education paid for by Thomas Skottowe, his father's employer. The museum first opened in the 1920s and the exhibits here relate to Cook's life and to the 18th-century village in which he lived. The family had moved to Great Ayton in 1736 but the cottage in which they lived was dismantled stone by stone in 1934 and now stands in Fitzroy Park, Melbourne, Australia. In its place is an obelisk chiselled from stone taken from Point Hicks, Australia. It stands within a Memorial Garden.

On High Green a statue commissioned by Hambleton District Council and sculpted by Nicholas Dimbleby portrays Cook at the age of 18 when he left the village for Staithes.

On Easby Moor above the village stands an impressive 60 feet obelisk to Cook's memory

erected by Robert Campion, a Whitby banker, in 1827. It can only be reached by a steepish climb on foot but it is well worth making the effort: from the base of the monument there are stupendous views over the Moors, the Vale of Mowbray and across to the oddly shaped hill called Roseberry Topping. The loftiest of the Cleveland Hills and sometimes called the Matterhorn of Yorkshire, Roseberry's summit towers 1000 feet above Great Ayton.

AROUND GREAT AYTON

GUISBOROUGH

5 miles NE of Great Ayton on the A171

Guisborough is a pleasant market town featuring a broad, cobble-fringed main street with some attractive buildings. A popular market is held here on Tuesdays, Thursdays and Saturdays. The Guisborough Musem

Just to the east of the town, the stark ruins of **Gisborough Priory** (English Heritage) stand on an elevated site overlooked by the Cleveland Hills. Founded by a great landowner in the region, Robert de Brus II, in 1119 the monastery became one of the most powerful in Yorkshire. It was extended in 1200 but almost a century later the whole complex was destroyed by fire. Rebuilding took several generations and was not completed until the late 1300s. A contemporary remarked that the Prior kept 'a most pompous house' and that some 500 households were dependent in some way on the priory. In 1540 the priory's estate was sold to a Thomas Chaloner who cannibalised much of the fabric to grace ornamental gardens at his mansion nearby. That mansion has since disappeared. Of the priory itself, the great arch of the east end is the most striking survival, an outstanding example of Gothic architecture. The priory grounds are a popular venue for picnics.

About 1 mile east of Guisborough, **Tocketts Mill** is a fully restored water-driven corn mill and a Grade II* listed

Tocketts Mill, Guisborough

building. It is one of the most complete mills in the country, with its four floors retaining the original machinery along with an extensive collection of equipment from other mills. Open Sunday afternoons in the summer; Easter Sunday and Monday; and on National Milling Day, the 2nd Sunday in May.

CARLTON IN CLEVELAND

5 miles SE of Great Ayton off the A172

This charming little village, winner of several 'best kept village' awards, is set on either side of Alum Beck which runs through it, flanked by green tree-lined banks. Carlton has a haunted Manor House and a church which was destroyed by fire in 1881 just weeks after its rector had spent years helping to re-build it after an earlier one had been demolished. Another incumbent as rector was Canon John Kyle who fervently maintained the 18th century traditions of the 'squarson' - a parson who was also the village squire. Canon Kyle took the latter of these two roles much the more seriously, riding to hounds, running three farms, boxing with the local lads and also running the village pub, the Fox and Hounds. The Archbishop of York was not pleased that one of his ministers owned a drinking house but the canon pointed out that his proprietorship allowed him to close the pub on Sundays.

INGLEBY GREENHOW

3 miles S of Great Ayton off the B1257

Located on the very edge of the National Park, Ingleby Greenhow enjoys a favoured position, protected from east winds by the great mass of Ingleby Moor. The beckside Church of St Andrew looks small and unimposing from the outside, but inside there is a wealth of rugged Norman arches and pillars, the stonework carved with fanciful figures of grotesque men and animals.

STOKESLEY

3 miles SW of Great Ayton on the A172

This attractive market town lies beneath the northern edge of the moors, its peace only troubled on market day which has taken place here every Friday since its charter was granted in 1223. Nikolaus Pevsner called Stokesley 'one of the most attractive small towns in the county'. The wide cobbled High Street is flanked by rows of elegant Georgian and Regency houses reached by little bridges over the River Leven which flows through the town, and an old water wheel marks the entrance to the town. The River Leven is crossed by the 17th century Pack Horse Bridge which was once the only crossing into the town. Just off the market place stands the 14th century church of St. Peter and St. Paul with woodwork carved by the 'Mouseman of Kilburn'.

The major event in Stokesley's calendar is the Agricultural Show in late September, a gathering that was first held in 1859.

WHITBY

Voted the country's Best Day Out by the *Daily Mail*; voted first of Top 50 Best British Holidays by the *Observer*, and declared the Best Seaside Resort in the UK by *Holiday Which*, Whitby clearly has a lot going for it. Cobbled streets, picturesque waterside houses and a Blue flag sandy beach all contribute to the charm.

The most dramatic approach to one of North Yorkshire's most historic and attractive towns is along the moorland road from Guisborough, the A171. A few miles from the town, the ruins of the great 13th century abbey perched on a huge cliff appear on the horizon. Whitby is famed as one of the earliest and most important centres of Christianity in England; as Captain James Cook's home port, and as the place where, according to Bram Stoker's famous novel,

21 JANE'S KITCHEN

Whitby

A favourite cafe for both vistors and locals alike, together with an adjacent rock shop.

See entry on page 186

Whitby Harbour

outside and very much like a ship inside.' Indeed, the fascinating interior with its clutter of box-pews built in the 1600s and rented by families whose names were put on the sides, iron pillars and long galleries, it was reputedly fashioned by Whitby seamen during the course of the 18th century. The three-decker pulpit is from the same period; the huge ear trumpets for a rector's deaf wife were put in place about 50 years later. Outside, a carved sandstone cross commemorates Brother Caedmon, a member of the Whitby Abbey community whose 7th-century poem, *The Song of Creation*, is the earliest known poem in English.

St Mary's stands atop the cliff: the old town clusters around the harbour mouth far below. Linking them are the famous 199 steps that wind up the hillside: many a churchgoer or visitor has been grateful for the frequent seats thoughtfully provided along the way.

The old port of Whitby developed on the slim shelf of land that runs along the east bank of the River Esk, an intricate muddle of narrow, cobbled streets and shoulder-width alleys. Grape Lane is typical, a cramped little street where ancient houses lean wearily against each other. Young James Cook lived here during his apprenticeship: the handsome house in Grape Lane where he lodged is now the **Captain Cook Memorial Museum**. The rich collection includes period rooms, models, maps and manuscripts, ships' plans, furniture, artefacts from Cook's voyages, and many original drawings, prints and paintings, including one of Cook's notorious contemporary, Captain Bligh of the *Bounty*.

By the early 1800s, old Whitby was full to bursting and a new town began to burgeon on the West bank of the River Esk. The new Whitby, or 'West Cliff', was carefully planned

Count Dracula in the form of a large dog loped ashore from a crewless ship that had drifted into the harbour. The classic 1931 film version of the story, starring Bela Lugosi, was filmed in the original locations at Whitby and there were several reports of holidaymakers being startled by coming across the Count, cloaked and fanged, as he rested between takes. The **Dracula Experience** on Marine Parade gives a lively rendition of the enduring tale with the help of live actors and electronic special effects.

High on the cliff that towers above the old town stand the imposing and romantic ruins of **Whitby Abbey** (English Heritage). In AD 664, many of the most eminent prelates of the Christian Church were summoned here to attend the Synod of Whitby. They were charged with settling once and for all a festering dispute that had riven Christendom for generations: the precise date on which Easter should be celebrated. The complicated formula they devised to solve this problem is still in use today. Just across from the abbey, the Visitor Centre combines the best of modern technology with displays of artefacts in tracing the long history of the site.

A short walk from the abbey is **St Mary's Church**, a unique building 'not unlike a house

22 WHITBY ABBEY

Whitby

The stark and magnificent ruins of Whitby Abbey are much more than a spectacular cliff-top landmark.

See entry on page 187

23 CAPTAIN COOK MEMORIAL MUSEUM

Whitby

In Whitby's Grape lane in a narrow street near the harbour, stands John Walker's house, home to Captain Cook.

See entry on page 187

with the nascent industry of tourism in mind. There was a quayside walk or 'promenade', a bandstand, luxury hotels, and a Royal Crescent of upmarket dwellings reminiscent of Buxton or Cheltenham but with the added advantage of enjoying a sea air universally acknowledged as 'invariably beneficial to the health of the most injured constitution'.

In a dominating position on West Cliff, a bronze statue of Captain Cook gazes out over the harbour he knew so well. Nearby the huge jawbone of a whale, raised as an arch, recalls those other great Whitby seafarers, the whalers. Between 1753 and 1833, Whitby was the capital of the whaling industry, bringing home 2761 whales in 80 years. Much of that success was due to the skills of the great whaling captains William Scoresby and his son, also named William. The elder William was celebrated for his great daring and navigational skills, as well as for the invention of the crow's nest, or masthead lookout. His son was driven by a restless, enquiring mind and occupied himself with various experiments during the long days at sea in the icy Arctic waters. He is most noted for his discoveries of the forms of snow crystals and the invention of the 'Greenland' magnet which made ships' compasses more reliable. The Whitby whaling industry is now, thankfully, long dead, but fortunately the fishing industry is not, as many of Whitby's restaurants bear witness, being famous for their seafood menus.

A popular souvenir of the town is jet stone, a lustrous black stone which enjoyed an enormous vogue in Victorian times. After the death of Prince Albert, jewellery in jet was the only ornament the Queen would allow herself to wear. The Court and the middle classes naturally followed her example and for several decades Whitby prospered greatly from the trade in jet. By 1914, workable deposits of the stone were virtually exhausted and a new generation shunned its gloomy association with death. Recent years have seen a revival of interest in the glossy stone and several shops have extensive displays of jet ornaments and jewellery. The original **Victorian Jet Works**, established in 1867, are open daily and

visitors can see the craftspeople at work as well as purchase jet from a wide range of interesting and contemporary jewellery designs.

On the south-eastern edge of the town the **Whitby Museum and Pannett Art Gallery**, founded in 1823, stands in the attractive setting of Pannett Park. The museum contains a nationally-important collection of Whitby jet jewellery, relics of Captain Cook and the lands he visited, displays on whaling, 60 model ships and many other items from Whitby's past.

The **Whitby Archives Heritage Centre**, which is open all year, holds an exhibition of local photographs and, along with its local history research facilities, has a shop and heritage gallery. Nearby, **The Sutcliffe Gallery** is devoted to the work of the brilliant photographer, Frank Meadow Sutcliffe, who recorded Victorian and Edwardian Whitby in a wealth of beautifully composed, technically immaculate and hugely evocative photographs. There's more Victoriana at the **Museum of Victorian Whitby** which has a re-creation of a 19th-century lane in the town complete with interiors and shop windows along with miniature rooms and settings.

AROUND WHITBY

SANDSEND

2 miles NW of Whitby on the A174

From Runswick Bay, the A174 drops down the notoriously steep Lythe Bank to Sandsend, a pretty village that grew up alongside the

Mulgrave Castle, Lythe

Mulgrave Beck as it runs into the sea at 'sands' end' – the northern tip of the long sandy beach that stretches some two-and-a-half miles from here to Whitby.

The Romans had a cement works nearby, later generations mined the surrounding hills for the elusive jet stone and for alum, and the Victorians built a scenic railway along the coast. The railway track was dismantled in the 1950s but sections of the route now form part of the **Sandsend Trail,** a pleasant and leisurely two-and-a-half hour walk around the village which is made particularly interesting if you follow it with the National Park's booklet describing the route.

LYTHE

4 miles NW of Whitby off the A174

Perched on a hill top, Lythe is a small cluster of houses with a sturdy little church. Just south of the village is **Mulgrave Castle,** hereditary home of the Marquis of Normanby. The castle grounds, which are open to the public, contain the ruins of Foss Castle built shortly after the Norman Conquest. Charles Dickens once spent a holiday at Mulgrave Castle and 'danced on its lawns in ecstasy at its beauty'. It's not known whether the great author witnessed the ancient custom of 'Firing the Stiddy'. This celebrates notable events in the Normanby family and begins with dragging the anvil from the blacksmith's shop, upturning it, and placing a charge of gunpowder on its base. A fearless villager then approaches with a 20 feet long metal bar, its tip red hot, and detonates the powder.

In the 1850s, Mulgrave Castle was leased by an exiled Indian Maharajah, Duleep Singh. He enjoyed going hawking on the moors in full oriental dress and the story is often told of how he had the first road between Sandsend and Whitby constructed because his elephants disliked walking along the beach. Much as one would like to believe this tale, no one has yet proved it to be true.

RUNSWICK BAY

6 miles NW of Whitby, off the A174

A little further down the coast, Runswick Bay is another picturesque fishing village with attractive cottages clinging to the steep sides of the cliff. This perilous position proved disastrous in 1682 when the cliff face collapsed during a violent storm and the whole of Runswick, with the exception of a single cottage, tumbled into the sea. A disaster fund was set up and a new village established.

A rather unexpected sight on the seafront is a thatched cottage, one of the last remaining thatched houses on the Yorkshire coast.

At Runswick, as in most of Yorkshire's remote communities, superstition was once widespread. Even at the beginning of the 20th century, many still believed in witches and almost everyone would avert their gaze or cross the road to avoid someone afflicted with the 'Evil Eye'. In the late 1800s, the Revd Cooper, Vicar of Filey, visited the village and came across a 'perfectly horrible superstition'. Apparently, it was considered unlucky to save a drowning man. The Vicar was told of 'men nearly dragged ashore and then, by the advice of the elders, abandoned to their fate lest ill-fortune should result from saving them'.

STAITHES

9 miles NW of Whitby off the A174

Visitors to this much-photographed fishing port leave their cars at the park in the modern village at the top of the cliff and then walk down the steep road to the old wharf. Take care – one of these narrow, stepped alleys is called Slippery Hill, for reasons that can become painfully clear. The old stone chapels and rather austere houses testify to the days when Staithes was a stronghold of Methodism.

---

24 THE FIRS

Runswick Bay, nr Whitby

A popular family run guest house ideal for visitors wanting to relax and unwind. The homemade food served here is absolutely delicious.

See entry on page 188

The little port is proud of its associations with Captain James Cook. He came here, not as a famous mariner, but as a 17-year-old assistant in Mr William Sanderson's haberdashery shop. James didn't stay long, leaving in 1746 to begin his naval apprenticeship in Whitby with Thomas Scottowe, a friend of Sanderson. Housed in a converted chapel, **The Captain Cook & Staithes Heritage Centre** contains a life-size street scene of 1745 and other displays on Cook's life and local history.

Staithes is still a working port with one of the few fleets in England still catching crabs and lobsters. Moored in the harbour and along the river are the fishermen's distinctive boats. Known as cobles, they have an ancestry that goes back to Viking times. Nearby is a small sandy beach, popular with families (and artists), and a rocky shoreline extending north and south pitted with thousands of rock pools hiding starfish and anemones. The rocks here are also rich in fossils and you may even find ingots of 'fools gold' – actually iron pyrites and virtually worthless.

A little farther up the coast from Staithes rises Boulby Cliff, at 666ft (202m) the highest point on the east coast of England. Near the village of Boulby is the deepest mine in Europe. From depths of between 3600ft and 3900ft thousands of tons of potash are mined every day. This is the only source of potash in the UK. The mining extends some 2 miles under the North Sea.

SALTBURN-BY-THE-SEA

12 miles NW of Whitby on the A174

The charming seaside resort of Saltburn lies at the northern end of the Heritage Coast. It was custom-built in Victorian times and designed for affluent middle-class visitors – so much so that in the early years excursion trains were barred from calling there. Created in the 1860s by the Quaker entrepreneur Henry Pease, Saltburn is set on a cliff, high above a long sandy beach. To transport visitors the 120ft from the elegant little town to the promenade and pier below, an ingenious water-balanced **Tramway** was constructed. It is still in use, the oldest such tramway to have survived in Britain. Saltburn's Victorian heritage is celebrated in mid-August each year with a full programme of events, many of them with the participants clad in appropriate costume. It seems appropriate, too, that such an olde world town should be well-known for its many shops selling antiques and collectables.

Saltburn's genteel image in Victorian times was a far cry from its notoriety in the late 18th century when it was one of the North East's busiest centres for smuggling. The 'King of the Smugglers', John Andrew, had his base here and during a long and profitable career was never apprehended. His story, and that of his partners in villainy, is colourfully recalled at **The Saltburn Smugglers Heritage Centre** next to the Ship Inn of which Andrew was landlord.

From the sea front, a 15-inch gauge miniature railway will take you to the splendid **Italian Gardens** – another Victorian contribution to the town. Here you can take tea on the lawn and explore the **Woodlands Centre** set between the formal pleasure gardens and the wild natural woodlands beyond.

The **Cleveland Way** passes along the coastline here and then takes a steep path up to Huntcliff, once the site of a Roman Signal Station.

---

25 SPRINGHOUSE COTTAGES

Easington

Springhouse is a two-bedroom self-catering cottage near the fishing village of Staithes offering well-equipped modern facilities and fantastic views over the surrounding countryside and out to sea.

See entry on page 188

---

26 WOLD POTTERY

Loftus

This enchanting local pottery displays dynamic collections of both contemporary and traditional designs alongside other local artwork from the North Yorkshire moors and coast.

See entry on page 189

DANBY

12 miles W of Whitby off the A174

Eskdale is the largest, and one of the loveliest, of the dales within the National Park. It is unusual in that it runs east-west, the Esk being the only moorland river that doesn't find its way to the Humber. Instead, the river winds tortuously through the dale to join the sea beneath the picturesque cliffs at Whitby. Along the way, many smaller dales branch off to the north and south – Fryup, Danby, Glaisdale – while even narrower ones can only be explored on foot. The Esk is famed for its salmon fishing, but permits are required. These can be obtained from the local branches of the National Rivers Authority. Walkers will appreciate the Esk Valley Walk, a group of 10 linking walks which traverse the length of the valley.

Close to the head of the Esk Valley, Danby is a busy little village set around a spacious green where Scotch Blackface sheep serve as lawn-mowers. Just outside the village a former shooting lodge set in an idyllic location beside the River Esk houses **The Moors Centre** (free) provides an excellent introduction to the North York Moors National Park. The Centre is set in 13 acres of riverside, meadow, woodland and formal gardens where visitors can either wander on their own or join one of the frequent guided walks. Inside the Lodge various exhibits interpret the natural and local history of the moors. Wild as they look, the moors are actually cultivated land, or perhaps 'managed by fire' is the better term. Each year, gamekeepers burn off patches of the old heather in carefully limited areas called swiddens or swizzens. The new growth that soon appears is a crucial resource for the red grouse which live only in heather moorland, eat little else but heather and find these young green shoots particularly appetising.

The Moors Centre explains all this and more, and there's a bookshop stocked with a wide range of books, maps and guides, and a tea room serving refreshments, including bread and cakes from the Centre's own bakery. A fairly recent addition to the centre's amenities is "Inspired by…", a showcase for local arts and crafts. The centre is open all year round except for January.

For most of the latter half of the 19th century, Danby's vicar was Canon JC Atkinson who married three times, fathered 13 children and authored one of the most fascinating books ever written about rural Yorkshire in Victorian times. His *Forty Years in a Moorland Parish* is still in print and well worth seeking out.

Downstream from The Moors Centre is a superb 14th-century packhorse bridge, one of three to be found in Eskdale. This one is known as **Duck Bridge** but the name has nothing to do with aquatic birds. It was originally called Castle Bridge but re-named after an 18th-century benefactor, George Duck, a wealthy mason who paid for the bridge to be repaired. To the south of Duck Bridge are the remains of Danby Castle, now a private farmhouse and not open to the public. Built in the 14th century, and originally much larger, it was once the home of Catherine Parr, the sixth wife of Henry VIII. In Elizabethan times, the justices met here and the Danby Court Leet and Baron, which administers the common land and rights of way over the 11,000 acres of the Danby Estate, still meets here every year in the throne room. One of the court's responsibilities is issuing licences for the gathering of sphagnum moss, a material once used for stuffing mattresses but now more commonly required for flower arranging.

Duck Bridge

CASTLETON

14 miles W of Whitby off the A171

The main village in Upper Eskdale, Castleton is spread across the hillside above the River Esk. It still has a station on the scenic Esk Valley railway that runs between Whitby and Middlesbrough and a well-used cricket field in a lovely setting on the valley floor. The village's amber-coloured Church of St Michael and St George was built in memory of the men who fell during the First World War; inside there is some fine work by Robert Thompson, the famous 'Mouseman of Kilburn'. The benches, organ screen and panelling at each side of the altar all bear his distinctive 'signature' of a crouching mouse.

LEALHOLM

9 miles W of Whitby off the A171

The *Sunday Times* recently described Lealholm as "one of the prettiest villages in Yorkshire". Its houses cluster around a 250-year-old bridge over the Esk and close by picturesque stepping stones cross the river. The village was one of Canon Atkinson's favourite places – 'Elsewhere , you have to go in search of beautiful views,' he wrote, 'here, they come and offer themselves to be looked at.'

On one of the stone houses in Lealholm, now a tea room and restaurant, a carved inscription reads: 'Loyal Order of Ancient Shepherds' together with the date '1873' in Roman numerals. The Loyal Order ran their lodge on the lines of a men-only London club, but their annual procession through the village and the subsequent festivities were one of the highlights of the autumn.

GLAISDALE

8 miles W of Whitby off the A171

From Lealholm a country lane leads to Glaisdale, another picturesque village set at the foot of a narrow dale beside the River Esk with Arncliffe Woods a short walk away. The ancient packhorse bridge here was built in 1619 by Thomas Ferris, Mayor of Hull. As an impoverished young man he had lived in Glaisdale where he fell in love with Agnes Richardson, the squire's daughter. To see Agnes, he had to wade or swim across the river and he swore that if he prospered in life he would build a bridge here. Fortunately, he joined a ship which captured a Spanish galleon laden with gold. Tom returned to Glaisdale a rich man, married Agnes and later honoured his promise by building what has always been called the **Beggar's Bridge**.

EGTON BRIDGE

7 miles W of Whitby off the A171

This little village set around a bend in the River Esk plays host each year to the famous **Gooseberry Show**. Established in 1800, the show is held on the first Tuesday in August in the village schoolroom. It attracts entrants from all over the world who bring prize specimens in an attempt to beat the current record, established in 2009 and confirmed by the *Guinness Book of Records*, of 2.19oz for a single berry.

St Hedda's Roman Catholic Church is surprisingly large for such a small village. Inside, there are more surprises - a roof painted blue with golden stars and a flamboyant altar made in Munich in the 1860s. Outside, there's another unusual feature, the Mysteries of the Rosary set into

---

27 THE WHEATSHEAF INN

Egton

This charming local inn has a fine reputation with wholesome home cooked food, real ales and cottage accommodation.

See entry on page 189

---

28 HORSESHOE HOTEL

Egton Bridge

An outstanding hotel located at the heart of the North Yorkshire Moors National Park. It offers a varied menu, comfortable accommodation and a selection of real ales.

See entry on page 190

the church walls in coloured pictures. It was at Egton Bridge that the martyr Nicholas Postgate was born in 1596. He was ordained a Roman Catholic priest in France but returned to the moors to minister to those still loyal to the outlawed faith. He travelled disguised as a jobbing gardener and eluded capture for many years. He was finally betrayed for a reward of £20. He was 81 years old when he was hung, drawn and quartered at York. A sad story to be associated with such a delightful village.

GROSMONT

6 miles SW of Whitby off the A169 or A171

Grosmont is the northern terminus of the **North Yorkshire Moors Railway**, the nation's most popular heritage railway, and houses the vintage steam locomotives that ply the 18-mile-long route. It is also on the Esk Valley line with connections to Whitby and Middlesbrough. The station itself has been restored to the British Railways style of 1952 and contains a tea room and two shops with a wide variety of rail-related and other items on sale. In high season as many as eight trains a day in each direction are in service and there are many special events throughout the year. And if you have ever harboured the dream of driving a train, the NYMR offers a range of courses, from one day to a full week, enabling you to realise the fantasy.

GOATHLAND

7 miles SW of Whitby off the A169

The area around Goathland provides some of the wildest scenery in the National Park. Murk Mire Moor, Black Rigg, Howl Moor – the very names conjure up the rigours of these upland tracts where heather reigns supreme. Even those who know the moors well treat its sudden mists and savage storms with respect. The historian of the area, Joseph Ford, recollected hearing as a child of an itinerant trader who travelled the moorland paths selling bottle corks to farmers' wives. During one particularly severe winter it was remarked that he had not paid his usual calls. The following autumn a skeleton was found

Mallyan Spout, Goathland

on Wintergill Moor: the unfortunate victim was only 'identified by the scattered bottle corks lying nearby'. As Ford noted, 'the story was not unusual'.

Goathland today is perhaps best known as 'Aidensfield' – the main location for the television series *Heartbeat*. Mostyn's Garage & Funeral Services (actually the Goathland Garage); The Aidensfield Arms (The Goathland Hotel) and the Aidensfield Stores all attract thousands of visitors each year, as does **Goathland Station** on the North Yorkshire Moors Railway whose vintage steam locomotives have often featured in the series. The station also served as Hogsmeade Station in the film *Harry Potter and the Philosopher's Stone*.

This attractive village 500 feet up on the moors, where old stone houses are scattered randomly around spacious sheep-groomed greens, was popular long before television. Earlier visitors mostly came in order to take the steep downhill path to **Mallyan Spout**, a 70 feet high waterfall locked into a crescent of rocks and trees. They were also interested in Goathland's rugged church and the odd memorial in its graveyard to William Jefferson and his wife. The couple died in 1923 within a few days of each other, at the ages of 80 and 79, and chose to have their final resting place marked by an enormous anchor.

In the award-winning **Goathland Exhibition Centre** you'll find a full explanation of the curious tradition of the Plough Stots Service, performed at Goathland every January. It's an ancient ritual for greeting the new year which originated with the Norsemen who settled here more than a thousand years ago. 'Stots' is the Scandinavian word for the bullocks which were used to drag a plough through the village, followed by dancers brandishing 30-inch swords. This pagan rite is still faithfully observed but with the difference that nowadays Goathland's young men have replaced the 'stots' in the plough harness.

The Centre has copious information about the many walks in the area and can guide you to one of the oldest thoroughfares in the country, Wade's Way. If you believe the legend, it was built by a giant of that name, but it is actually a remarkably well-preserved stretch of Roman road. Another popular walk is the Rail Trail, a 3½ mile route to Grosmont along the disused track of a railway line originally built by George Stephenson.

BECK HOLE

8 miles SW of Whitby off the A169

A mile or so up the dale from Goathland is the pretty little hamlet of Beck Hole. When the North Yorkshire Moors Railway was constructed in the 1830s (designed by no less an engineer than George Stephenson himself), the trains were made up of stage coaches placed on top of simple bogies and pulled by horses. At Beck Hole, however, there was a 1-in-15 incline up to Goathland so the carriages had to be hauled by a complicated system of ropes and water-filled tanks. (Charles Dickens was an early passenger on this route and wrote a hair-raising description of his journey.) The precipitous incline caused many accidents so, in 1865, a 'Deviation Line' was blasted

through solid rock. The gradient is still one of the steepest in the country at 1 in 49, but it opened up this route to steam trains. The original 1 in 15 incline is now a footpath, so modern walkers will understand the effort needed to get themselves to the summit, let alone a fully laden carriage.

Every year, this little village plays host to the **World Quoits Championship**. The game, which appears to have originated in Eskdale, involves throwing a small iron hoop over an iron pin set about 25 feet away. Appropriately enough, one of the houses on the green has a quoit serving as a door knocker.

On the hillside, a mile or so to the west of Beck Hole, is the curiously-named **Randy Mere**, the last place in England where leeches were gathered commercially. An elderly resident of Goathland in 1945 recalled how as a young man he had waded into the lake and emerged in minutes with the slug-like creatures firmly attached to his skin. For those interested in repeating his exploit, the leeches are still there.

LOCKTON

15 miles SW of Whitby off the A169

Lockton is a small, unspoilt village of stone-built houses set around a village green. It is set high above a deep ravine, boasts one of the few duck ponds to have survived in the National Park, and offers some fine walks. About three miles north of the village is the **Hole of Horcum,** a huge natural amphitheatre which, so the story goes, was scooped out of Levisham Moor by the giant Wade. It is now a popular centre for hang gliders.

Hole of Horcom, Lockton

Robin Hood's Bay

ROBIN HOOD'S BAY

5 miles S of Whitby off the A171

Artists never tire of painting this 'Clovelly of the North', a picturesque huddle of red-roofed houses clinging to the steep face of the cliff. Bay Town, as locals call the village, was a thriving fishing port throughout the 18th and 19th centuries. By 1920 however there were only two fishing families left in the Bay, mainly because the harbour was so dilapidated. The industry died out. Today, small boats are once again harvesting the prolific crab grounds that lie along this stretch of the coast.

Because of the natural isolation of the bay, smuggling was quite as important as fishing to the local economy. The houses and inns in the Bay were said to have connecting cellars and cupboards, and it was claimed that 'a bale of silk could pass from the bottom of the village to the top without seeing daylight.' These were the days when press gangs from the Royal Navy were active in the area since recruits with a knowledge of the sea were highly prized. Apparently, these mariners were also highly prized by local women: they smartly despatched the press gangs by means of pans and rolling pins.

Shipwrecks in the Bay were frequent, with many a mighty vessel tossed onto its reefs by North Sea storms. On one memorable occasion in the winter of 1881, a large brig called *The Visitor* was driven onto the rocks. The seas were too rough for the lifeboat at Whitby to be launched there so it was dragged eight miles through the snow and let down the cliffside by ropes. Six men were rescued. The same wild seas threatened the village itself, every storm eroding a little more of the chalk cliff to which it clings. Fortunately, Robin Hood's Bay is now protected by a sturdy sea wall.

Film buffs will want to visit what has been described as "one of the most interesting cinemas in the world". The **Swell Cinema** occupies a former chapel which has been converted to provide a concert hall and cinema incorporating the original 1820's balconied box pews. Patrons are welcome to bring along an extra cushion!

But the most extraordinary building in Robin Hood's Bay is undoubtedly **Fyling Hall Pigsty**. It was built in the 1880s by Squire Barry of Fyling Hall in the classical style although the pillars supporting the portico are of wood rather than marble. Here the Squire's two favourite pigs could enjoy plenty of space and a superb view over the bay. The building is now managed by the Landmark Trust who rent it out to holidaymakers.

Detailed information about the village and the Bay is on display at the **Old Coastguard Station** on The Dock. This National Trust property also houses the National Park Visitor and Education Centre.

About three miles south of Ravenscar, at Staintondale, are three very different animal centres. At the **Staintondale Shire Horse Farm** visitors can enjoy a 'hands-on' experience with these noble creatures, watch a video of the horses working and follow a scenic route around the area. Cart rides are also usually available. There's also a café, souvenir shop, picnic area and a play area with a variety of small farm animals to entertain the children.

At nearby Meeting House Farm, **Pesky Husky** offers the opportunity of meeting and working with some of the world's most charismatic dogs. Expert instruction is provided before setting off on the purpose built circuit where you can become a "musher" for a few hours.

Wellington Lodge Llama Trekking, a variety of treks with llamas is on offer, ranging from a three or four-hour journey to a whole day with a three-course meal included in the price. The llamas have many years of trekking experience and are sure-footed and friendly. They carry heavy loads of food, drink, stools and extra clothing, leaving you free to admire the splendid surroundings. Handlers and specialist guides accompany walkers.

SCARBOROUGH

With its two splendid bays and dramatic cliff-top castle, Scarborough was targeted by the early railway tycoons as the natural candidate for Yorkshire's first seaside resort. The railway arrived in 1846, followed by the construction of luxury hotels, elegant promenades and spacious gardens, all of which confirmed the town's claim to the title 'Queen of Watering Places'. The 'quality', people like the eccentric Earls of Londesborough, established palatial summer residences here, and an excellent train service brought thousands of excursionists from the industrial cities of west Yorkshire.

Even before the advent of the railway, Scarborough had been well-known to a select few. They travelled to what was then a remote little town to sample the spring water discovered by Mrs Tomyzin Farrer in 1626 and popularised in a book published by a certain Dr Wittie who named the site Scarborough Spaw. Anne Brontë came here in the hope that the spa town's invigorating air would improve her health, a hope that was not fulfilled. She died at the age of 29 and her grave lies in St Mary's churchyard at the foot of the castle.

---

29 THE NEWLANDS

Scarborough

Great three star family run hotel halfway between the beach and the town centre perfect for family holidays.

See entry on page 191

---

30 ESPLANADE GARDENS

Scarborough

Beautiful Victorian hotel stylishly renovated for a comfortable stay known for its unrivalled hospitality and delicious breakfasts.

See entry on page 192

---

31 THE EARLSMERE

Scarborough

This magnificent Victorian built property offers luxury accommodation with sea views. It is an ideal place to stay for those who like to be pampered.

See entry on page 193

---

32 FRANCIS TEA ROOMS

Scarborough

Simply oozing character, this delightful tea rooms offers delicious homemade mains, cakes and pastries in an olden day ladies hair salon.

See entry on page 193

---

33 CENTRAL TRAMWAY

Scarborough

The **Central Tramway Company** Scarborough Limited was created and registered in 1880 and still operates in its original corporate form.

See entry on page 194

---

34 THE IVY HOUSE RESTAURANT AND ACCOMMODATION

Scarborough

Formerly an 18th century sea captains house, this stunningly converted beachside home now operates as a successful restaurant with luxury bed and breakfast accommodation above.

See entry on page 195

Scarborough Castle itself can be precisely dated to the decade between 1158 and 1168 - surviving records show that construction costs totalled £650. The castle was built on the site of a Roman fort and signal station and its gaunt remains stand high on Castle Rock Headland, dominating the two sweeping bays. The spectacular ruins often provide a splendid backdrop for staged battles commemorating the invasions of the Danes, Saxons and the later incursions of Napoleon's troops. The surrounding cliffs are also well worth exploring – just follow the final part of the famous Cleveland Way.

As befits such a long-established resort, Scarborough offers a vast variety of entertainment. If you tire of the two sandy beaches, there's **Peasholm Park** to explore with its glorious gardens and regular events, among them the unique sea battle in miniature on the lake. There's also the miniature North Bay Railway which runs for about ¾ miles from the park to the North Bay area of the town. Or you could seek out the intellectual attractions of the **Rotunda Museum,** which re-opened in May 2008 after a comprehensive redevelopment. Described as 'the finest Georgian museum in Britain', this impressive building has now returned to its original role as a Museum of Geology. A sister site to the Rotunda Museum, the **Scarborough Art Gallery** occupies a striking Italianate building in the lovely Crescent Gardens. The gallery houses a permanent collection which has been built up over sixty years through gifts, bequests and purchases to reflect the eclectic mix of the community and the cultural heritage of Scarborough. It also has a popular programme of temporary exhibitions.

The Stephen Joseph Theatre in the Round is well known for staging the premiere performances of comedies written by its resident director, the prolific playwright Sir Alan Ayckbourn. Rather more frivolously, you could explore the futuristic world of holograms at Jimmy Corrigans Amusement Arcade, one of the longest established of the amusement arcades which line the South Bay at Scarborough. And at Scalby Mills, on the northern edge of the town, the **Sea-Life & Marine Sanctuary** offers the chance of close encounters with a huge variety of marine creatures from shrimps to sharks, octopi to eels. A recent addition in 2008 was the Seal Rescue Centre where visitors are invited to sample for themselves what it is like to care for these amazing creatures.

If you happen to be visiting Scarborough on Shrove Tuesday, be prepared for the unusual sight of respectable citizens exercising their ancient right to skip along the highways. This unexpected traffic hazard is now mostly confined to the area around Foreshore Road. Another tradition maintained by local people around this time is the sounding of the Pancake Bell, a custom started by the wives of the town to alert their men folk in the fields and in the harbour that they were about to start cooking the pancakes.

---

35 THE CASTLE TAVERN

Scarborough

This father and daughter team serve a great range of real ales, alongside good value for money themed food nights with live entertainment on weekends.

See entry on page 194

---

36 JEREMY'S

Scarborough

This is one of the premier dining establishments in Scarborough. The modern European cuisine is absolutely superb and popular with customers here.

See entry on page 196

---

37 RENDEZVOUS CAFE

Scarborough

Centrally located, this convenient cafe has charm and style serving tasty homemade dishes and snacks throughout the day.

See entry on page 196

AROUND SCARBOROUGH

CLOUGHTON

4 miles N of Scarborough on the A171

Cloughton village lies less than a mile from the coast and the rocky inlet of Cloughton Wyke. Here, in 1932, a huge whale was cast, or threw itself, ashore. Press photographers and postcard publishers rushed to the scene and paid the smallest local children they could find to pose beside the stranded Leviathan. For a while, Cloughton village was busy with a steady stream of sightseers. Their numbers quickly diminished as the six tons of blubber began to rot. In Cloughton itself, residents came to dread an east wind: it reached them only after washing over the vast hulk lying on the rocks. It's surely the worst thing that has ever happened to this pleasant little village, set around a sharp kink in the A171, where the breezes now – depending on the direction of the wind – either bring a fresh tang of ozone from the sea or a soft perfume of heather from the moors.

RAVENSCAR

10 miles N of Scarborough off the A171

The coastline around Ravenscar is particularly

dramatic and, fortunately, most of it is under the protection of the National Trust which has an Information Centre in Ravenscar. There are some splendid cliff-top walks and outstanding views across Robin Hood's Bay. Ravenscar is the eastern terminus of the 42-mile hike across the moors to Osmotherley known as the **Lyke Wake Walk**.

During the late 19th century there was an unsucceful attempt to turn this scattered village, then known as Peak, into a small town and, although the roads were built, little of the land that was made available to potential buyers was ever developed. Thus, it retains a tranquil air and, along with the small church and a couple of village shops, the only building of any size here is the Raven Hall Hotel. Local legend has it that King George III visited here when it was a private house, while recovering from one of his recurring bouts of mental illness.

FILEY

7 miles SE of Scarborough on the A1039

With its six-mile crescent of safe, sandy beach, Filey was one of the first Yorkshire resorts to benefit from the early 19th-century craze for sea bathing. Filey's popularity continued throughout Victorian times but the little town always prided itself on being

---

38 BRYHERSTONES COUNTRY INN AND LOWFIELD LOG HOMES

Cloughton Newlands, nr Scarborough

A cosy bar serving great food, with nearby self-catering log cabins.

See entry on page 197

---

40 CATH'S DINER

Filey

Found in the Filey's arcade, this family run diner offers up everything from a fried egg sandwich to homemade pies and roast dinners.

See entry on page 199

---

39 THREE JOLLY SAILORS AND PARSONS RESTAURANT

Burniston, Scarborough

Fun family pub and restaurant with a great menu for all tastes.

See entry on page 198

---

41 VICTORIA BAR AND RESTAURANT

Filey

A destination restaurant in a lofty position overlooking the shore, known for its creative fish dishes and warm atmosphere.

See entry on page 200

Cleveland Way, Filey

Just to the north of the town, the rocky promontory known as **Filey Brigg** strikes out into the sea, a massive mile-long breakwater protecting the town from the worst of the North Sea's winter storms. From the Brigg, there are grand views southwards along the six-mile-long bay to the cliffs that rise up to Flamborough Head and Scarborough Castle. Despite the fact that there is no harbour at Filey, it was once quite a busy fishing port and one can still occasionally see a few cobles – direct descendants of the Viking longships that arrived here more than a millennium ago – beached on the slipways.

Filey Brigg is the southern starting point for the oddly-named **Cleveland Way**, odd because only a few miles of the 110-mile footpath actually pass through Cleveland. The path follows the coast as far north as Saltburn-by-the-Sea then turns south to Roseberry Topping and the Cleveland Hills, finally ending up at Helmsley.

rather more select than its brasher neighbour just up the coast, Scarborough. Inevitably, modern times have brought the usual scattering of amusement arcades, fast food outlets and, from 1939 to 1983, a Butlin's Holiday Camp capable of accommodating 10,000 visitors. But Filey has suffered less than most seaside towns and with its many public parks and gardens still retains a winning, rather genteel atmosphere.

Until the Local Government reforms of 1974, the boundary between the East and North Ridings cut right through Filey. The town lay in the East Riding, the parish church and graveyard in the North. This curious arrangement gave rise to some typically pawky Yorkshire humour. If, as a resident of Filey town, you admitted that you were feeling poorly, the response might well be, 'Aye, then tha'll straightly be off t'North Riding' – in other words, the graveyard.

Filey's parish church, the oldest parts of which date back to the 12th century, is appropriately dedicated to St Oswald, patron saint of fishermen, and the Fishermen's Window here commemorates men from the town who died at sea. At the **Filey Folk Museum**, housed in a lovely old building dating back to 1696, you can explore the town's long history, while the **Edwardian Festival**, held every June, re-creates the pleasures of an earlier, more innocent age. In the following month, the town hosts the Filey Regatta. And during the first week of September, the town holds it's annual fishing festival presenting around 70 silver trophies.

SEAMER

3 miles S of Scarborough on the B1261

Seamer lies within an area of waterlogged soil with reeds and alders known as The Carrs. It was at Star Carr in August 2010 that archaeologists discovered what they announced as "the oldest house in Britain". The circular structure has been dated as being made in 8500BC, 500 years earlier than the previous oldest house. The researchers also found a large wooden platform which is believed to be the earliest evidence of carpentry in the country.

CAYTON

3 miles S of Scarborough on the B1261

Cayton is one of only 31 'Thankful Villages' in England. They were so named after the First World War because all of their men came back safely from that horrific conflict. Cayton had all the more reason to be grateful since 43 of its men returned – more than to any other of the Thankful Villages.

An unusual attraction here is the **Stained**

Glass Centre where Valerie Green and her team produce stained glass and leaded lights for churches, hotels, restaurants, public houses and homes throughout the country. Visitors can watch the craftspeople at work, browse in the showroom, examine the exhibition of stained glass or just relax in the tearoom and lovely garden.

Just outside the village is **Playdale Farm Park** which is home to an array of animals, large and small, for visitors to pet or feed. There are also indoor and outdoor play areas, an adventure trail, pedal tractors, indoor and outdoor picnic areas, or you could try the café which serves light lunches and snacks.

HUNMANBY

10 miles S of Scarborough between the A165 and A1039

Here's a question worthy of Trivial Pursuit: 'On which vehicle was the wing mirror first used?' Your answer is almost certainly wrong unless you know about the grave of a 1st century British charioteer uncovered at Hunmanby in 1907. Along with his bones, those of his horses, and fragments of the chariot wheels was a rectangular strip of shiny metal: archaeologists are convinced that this was fixed to the side of the chariot as a mirror so that the driver could see the competitors behind him.

Another curiosity in Hunmanby is the village lock-up with two cells and tiny windows designed for human miscreants, and next to it a circular stone pinfold intended for straying cattle.

HACKNESS

5 miles NW of Scarborough off the A170 or A171

For generations the Forge Valley has attracted sightseers – especially in autumn when the steep wooded banks of the ravine present a dazzling display of colours. There are several splendid walks along this lovely two-mile stretch of the River Derwent, a valley which takes its name from the ancient iron workings of which today not a trace remains. Nothing has survived either of the monastery established at Hackness in AD 681 by the first Abbess of Whitby although

some of its stones were used in the building of St Peter's Church, founded in 1060. Inside the church is a fragment of an Anglo-Saxon cross with inscriptions in English, Latin and runic characters. The grandest building in the village is Hackness Hall (private), a Georgian mansion that is the home of Lord Derwent.

THE VALE OF PICKERING

Not all that long ago, the Vale of Pickering was the Lake of Pickering, an immense stretch of water far larger than any English lake today, about 32 miles long and four to eight miles wide. As the Ice Age retreated, the waters gradually drained away leaving a low-lying plain of good arable soil based on Kimmeridge clay. Much of it remained marshy however and at Star Carr, near Seamer, archaeologists have uncovered "the oldest house in Britain" dating back some 10,500 years. It was part of a Stone Age lake community, where the houses were built on stilts above the water. It is only in comparatively recent times that the Vale has been properly drained, which explains why most of the towns and villages lie around its edge in a rough kind of horseshoe formation.

For much of its length, the Vale is watered by the River Derwent, which was also powerfully affected by the changes that occurred during the Ice Age. Originally it entered the sea near Scarborough but an Ice Age glacier blocked that outlet. The Derwent still flows to within a mile-and-a-half of Scarborough, but then turns abruptly and makes a 90-mile detour through the vale before turning southwards to join the River Ouse near Howden.

The main traffic artery through the vale is the Thirsk to Scarborough road, the A170, which in summer peak periods can become very congested. But you only have to turn off this busy thoroughfare to find yourself in quiet country lanes leading to sleepy market towns and unspoilt villages. To the north rise the intricate folds of the North York Moors: to the south, the Yorkshire Wolds roll gently away towards Beverley, Hull and the River Humber.

PICKERING

This busy little town developed around the important crossroads where the Malton to Whitby, and the Thirsk to Scarborough roads intersect. It's the largest of the four market towns in Ryedale and possibly the oldest, claiming to date from 270 BC when (so it's said) it was founded by a King of the Brigantes called Peredurus. William the Conqueror's attempts to dominate the area are recalled by Pickering's ruined **Castle** (English Heritage), and the many inns and posting houses reflect the town's prosperity during the stage coach era.

The parish church of **St Peter and St Paul** is well worth visiting for its remarkable 15th-century murals. During the glum days of Puritanism, these lively paintings were denounced as idolatrous and plastered over. They stayed forgotten for some 200 years but were rediscovered when the church was being restored in 1851. Unfortunately, the vicar at that time shared the Puritans' sentiments and, despite opposition from his parishioners and even from his bishop, had them smothered again under whitewash. A more liberal successor to the Vicar had the murals restored once again in 1878 and they now give a vivid idea of how cheerful, colourful

and entertaining many English churches were before the unforgivable vandalism of the Puritan years. These superb paintings, sharp, vigorous and well-observed, happily embrace scenes from the Bible, old legends and actual history: a real insight into the medieval mind that had no difficulty in accepting both the story of St George slaying the dragon and the martyrdom of St Thomas à Becket as equally real, and inspiring, events.

Occupying a handsome Regency residence in a lovely riverside setting near the centre of the town, the **Beck Isle Museum** contains a varied collection of bygones relating largely to the rural crafts and living style of Ryedale. Visitors enter through a Printer's Shop of around 1900 with a magnificent Columbian Press of 1854. In the next gallery are models of farm carts, and photographs by the outstanding photographer Sydney Smith who recorded in detail life in Ryedale between the two World Wars. More of his work is seen in the Gallery of Photography along with a collection of cameras and photographic equipment from 1880. Further galleries, all set out as rooms or shops include a dairy, cobblers, village pub, chemist's, costumes, nursery, village store, gents outfitter, Victorian parlour, hardware shop and blacksmith's.

Collectors of antiques can really indulge themselves at the **Pickering Antique Centre** where some 40 dealers display their wares in 3500 square feet of showrooms. The goods on offer include paintings, furniture, china and porcelain, brass and copperware, postcards, books, clocks, silver and plate, old toys and collectables.

If you catch a whiff of sulphurous smoke as you wander around the town, you must be close to the railway station. Pickering is the southern terminus of the **North York Moors Railway** where you can board a steam-drawn train for an 18-mile journey along one of the oldest and most dramatically scenic railways in the country. Thanks to a grant from the Heritage Lottery fund, the Booking and Parcels Office has been restored to how it was in 1937. The station's refreshment room is now a tea room and there's a shop with a wide range of gifts, books and videos.

Just up the road from the station, at the **Pickering Trout Lake,** you can hire a rod and

---

42   PICKERING CASTLE

Pickering

Set in an historic moors-edge market town, this splendid 13th century castle and royal hunting lodge make a fascinating visit for all ages.

See entry on page 199

---

43   POPPIES TRADITIONAL TEAROOMS

Pickering

The smell of home baking oozes from this delightful tea room attracting many locals and visitors to sample the delicious homemade dishes and cakes on offer.

See entry on page 201

tackle and attempt to beat the record for the largest fish ever caught here – it currently stands at a mighty 25lb 4oz (11.45 kg). The owners of the lake are also commercial cider producers pressing apples every autumn. Their Yorkshire Cider is always available during trading hours from the shop.

AROUND PICKERING

NEWTON UPON RAWCLIFFE

4 miles N of Pickering off the A169

A delightful unspoilt village on the southern fringe of the North York Moors National Park, with old stone cottages and farms clustered round the village green and duck pond. A haven of peace in delightful countryside with miles of forest and moor offer wonderful walking and touring. Just to the north of the village is the **North Riding Forest Park.** For a small toll, motorists can drive through the park.

LEVISHAM

7 miles NE of Pickering off the A169

Just to the west of the tiny picturesque village of Levisham, in the scenic valley of Newton Dale, is Levisham Station, one of several stops on the route of the North Yorkshire Moors Railway. This stop is the ideal location for walking with a wide variety of wildlife and flowers within a short distance of the station.

EAST AYTON

13 miles E of Pickering on the A170

Victorian visitors to Scarborough, occasionally

tiring of its urban attractions, welcomed excursions to beauty spots such as the **Forge Valley** near East Ayton. Aeons ago, a sharp-edged glacier excavated the valley; then centuries of natural growth softened its hills, clothed them with over-arching trees and, quite by chance, created one of the loveliest woodland walks in England. For a steady walker, going say four miles an hour, the round trip walk from East Ayton to the old forge from which the valley derives its name – along one side of the river returning on the other, takes about 2.5 hours. A short diversion will lead you to the ruins of **Ayton Castle** at the edge of the road near the junction of the A170 and B1261. Dating from around 1400, this is one of the most southerly of the hundreds of pele towers built in those turbulent times as a protection against invading Scottish marauders. In more peaceful days, many of these towers had a more comfortable mansion added but their defensive origins are still clearly recognisable.

BROMPTON-BY-SAWDON

10 miles E of Pickering on the A170

It was in the medieval church of this small village, on an autumn day in 1802, that William Wordsworth was married to Mary Hutchinson whose family lived at nearby Gallows Hill Farm. 'A perfect woman', he wrote of Mary,

'nobly planned
To warn, to comfort, and command;
And yet a spirit still, and bright
With something of an angelic light'.

Mary's home, now the **Wordsworth Gallery,** hosts an exhibition on the poets Wordsworth and Coleridge, while the medieval barn is now filled with designer

---

gifts, ladies clothes and licensed tea rooms. The gallery is open Tuesday to Saturday all year round.

Wydale Hall (private) was the home of the Squire of Brompton, Sir George Cayley (1773-1857), a pioneer aviator who achieved successful flights with small gliders although it was his coachman who was actually dragooned into being the pilot. Sir George is also credited with inventing the caterpillar tractor.

EBBERSTON

7 miles E of Pickering on the A170

About a mile to the west of Ebberston, in 1718, Mr William Thompson, MP for Scarborough, built for himself what is possibly the smallest stately home in England, Ebberston Hall. From the front, the house appears to be just one storey high, with a pillared doorway approached by a grand flight of stone steps flanked by a moderately sized room on each side. In fact, behind this modest front, there's also an extensive basement – 'deceptively spacious' as the estate agents say. It is now a private house but the exterior can be viewed from the road or churchyard.

THORNTON-LE-DALE

2 miles E of Pickering on the A170

As long ago as 1907, a *Yorkshire Post* poll of its readers acclaimed Thornton-le-Dale as the most beautiful village in Yorkshire. Despite stiff competition for that title, most visitors still find themselves in agreement.

If further proof were needed, just off the A170 near the parish church of All Saints you'll find one of the most photographed houses in Britain. The thatched cottage, set

beside a sparkling beck, has appeared regularly on chocolate boxes, jigsaws and calendars. On the nearby village green there's an ancient cross and a set of wooden stocks and, across the road, are Lady Lumley's Almshouses, 12 dwellings built in 1670 and still serving their original purpose. The North York Moors National Park actually creates a special loop in its boundary to include this picture-postcard village which, somewhat confusingly, is also frequently shown on maps as 'Thornton Dale'.

About 3 miles north of Thornton-le-Dale, the Dalby Visitor Centre is the starting point for the **Dalby Forest Drive** (toll payable), a 9-miile circuit through what was once the royal hunting Forest of Pickering. The Visitor Centre can provide plentiful details of the various amenities available - way marked walks, cycle routes, picnic/barbecue sites, an orienteering course, wildlife observation hide and more. A recent addition to the forest's amenities is **Go Ape!** near the village of Low Dalby. Here visitors can take to the trees and experience an exhilarating course of rope bridges, Tarzan swings and zip slides up to 60 feet above the ground. Pre-booking is essential.

CROPTON

4 miles NW of Pickering off the A170

At this tiny village ales have been brewed from as far back as 1613 even though home-brewing was illegal in the 17th century. Despite a lapse in the intervening decades, brewing returned to the village when, in 1984, the cellars of the village pub were converted to accommodate **Cropton Brewery**, a micro-brewery with a visitors' centre, guided tours and regional dishes served in the pub, The New Inn. In late November each year the inn hosts a Winter Beer Festival when some 80 real ales, traditional ciders and continental beers are on offer in the large marquee.

APPLETON-LE-MOORS

5 miles NW of Pickering off the A170

Located just inside the southern boundary of the Moors National Park, the appealing

46   THE BUCK HOTEL

Thornton-Le-Dale

An outstanding village inn serving real ales and traditional homemade food cooked to order.

See entry on page 202

village of Appleton-le-Moors is noted for its fine church which John Betjeman regarded as "a little gem among moorland churches". Its tower and spire provide a landmark for miles around. It was built in Victorian times to a design by J L Pearson, the architect of Truro Cathedral, and it reflects the same Gothic Renewal style as the Cornish cathedral.

HUTTON-LE-HOLE

10 miles NW of Pickering off the A170

Long regarded as one of Yorkshire's prettiest villages, Hutton-le-Hole has a character all of its own. 'It is all up and down,' wrote Arthur Mee, visiting more than half a century ago, 'with a hurrying stream winding among houses scattered here and there, standing at all angles'. Some sixty years on, little has changed.

Facing the green is the **Ryedale Folk Museum**, an imaginative celebration of 4000 years of life in North Yorkshire. Among the 13 historic buildings is a complete Elizabethan Manor House rescued from nearby Harome and reconstructed here; a medieval crofter's cottage with a thatched, hipped roof, peat fire and garth; and the old village shop and post office fitted out as it would have looked just after Elizabeth II's coronation in 1953. Other exhibits include workshops of

Hutton Beck, Hutton-Le-Hole

traditional crafts such as tinsmiths, coopers and wheelwrights, and an Edwardian photographic studio. The National Park has an Information Centre here and throughout the year there are special events such as a Rare Breeds Day and re-enactments of Civil War battles by the Sealed Knot.

Anyone interested in unusual churches should make the short trip from Hutton-le-Hole to **St Mary's Church, Lastingham**, about three miles to the east. The building of a monastery here in the 7th century was recorded by no less an authority than the Venerable Bede, who visited Lastingham not long after it was completed. That monastery was rebuilt in 1078 with a massively impressive crypt that is still in place – a claustrophobic space with heavy Norman arches rising from squat round pillars. The church above is equally atmospheric, lit only by a small window at one end.

GILLAMOOR

10 miles NW of Pickering off the A170

This pleasant little village is well worth a visit to see its very rare, and very elegant,

---

47 RYEDALE FOLK MUSEUM

Hutton le Hole

Ryedale Folk Museum is a wonderful working museum insight into bygone eras.

See entry on page 204

---

48 THE CROWN

Hutton-Le-Hole

A popular village pub offering the very best in friendly hospitality, wholesome food and real ales.

See entry on page 204

four-faced sundial erected in 1800, and to enjoy the famous **Surprise View**. This is a ravishing panoramic vista of Farndale with the River Dove flowing through the valley far below and white dusty roads climbing the hillside to the heather-covered moors beyond. A bench has conveniently been placed for spectators to enjoy the view.

Also of interest is the nearby village church which was once the church at Bransdale about six miles away. In the late 1700s, Bransdale Church was in good repair but little used; Gillamoor's was dilapidated but the villagers wanted a place of worship. This was achieved by commissioning a single stonemason, James Smith, to remove Bransdale church stone by stone and re-erect it at Gillamoor.

ROSEDALE ABBEY

11 miles NW of Pickering off the A170

To the east of Farndale is another lovely dale, Rosedale, a nine-mile-long steep-sided valley through which runs the River Seven. The largest settlement in the dale is Rosedale Abbey which takes its name from the small nunnery founded here in 1158. Nothing of the old abbey has survived although some of its stones were recycled to build the village houses. A peaceful village now, Rosedale was once crowded with workers employed in iron-ore mines on the moors. It was said that, such was the shortage of lodgings during the 1870s, 'the beds were never cold' as workers from different shifts took turns to sleep in them. The great chimney of the smelting furnace was once a striking landmark on the summit of the moor, but in 1972 it was found to be

unsafe and demolished. Its former presence is still recalled at Chimney Bank where a steep and twisting road, with gradients of 1 in 3, leads up to the moor. High on these moors stands **Ralph Cross**, nine feet tall and one of more than 30 such stone crosses dotted across the moors. It was erected in medieval times as a waymark for travellers and when the North York Moors National Park was established in 1952, the Park authorities adopted Ralph Cross as its emblem.

CHURCH HOUSES

17 miles NW of Pickering off the A170

A few miles north of Hutton-le-Hole, the moorland road comes to Lowna, set beside the River Dove in one of the Moors' most famous beauty spots, **Farndale**. In spring, some six miles of the river banks are smothered in thousands of wild daffodils, a short-stemmed variety whose colours shade from a pale buttercup yellow to a rich orange-gold. According to local tradition, the bulbs were cultivated by monks who used the petals in their medical concoctions. Yorkshire folk often refer to daffodils as Lenten Lilies because of the time of year in which they bloom. The flowers, once mercilessly plundered by visitors, are now protected by law with 2000 acres of Farndale designated as a local nature reserve.

SINNINGTON

4 miles W of Pickering off the A170

At Sinnington the River Seven drops down from the moors and the valley of Rosedale into the more open country of the Vale of Pickering. The stream passes through this tiny village, running alongside a broad green in

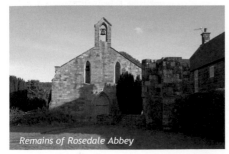

Remains of Rosedale Abbey

49   **THE FEVERSHAM ARMS INN**

Farndale

This is one of the most popular inns in Yorkshire serving a good range of food and real ales.

See entry on page 205

the centre of which stands a graceful old packhorse bridge. At one time this medieval bridge must have served a useful purpose but whatever old watercourse once flowed beneath it has long since disappeared – thus the bridge is known as the 'dry' bridge.

KIRKBYMOORSIDE

7 miles W of Pickering on the A170

Sunset, Kirkbymoorside

Set quietly off the main road, this agreeable market town of fine Georgian houses, narrow twisting lanes, family-owned shops and a cobbled marketplace, straggles up the hillside. After you pass the last house on the hill, you enter the great open spaces of the North York Moors National Park, 553 square miles of outstanding natural beauty which, since they were accorded the status of a National Park in 1952, have been protected from insensitive encroachments. Within the park you don't have to worry about traffic lights – there aren't any. But you may well have to step down firmly on your brakes to avoid sheep crossing the road at their own leisurely and disdainful pace.

Of the several old coaching inns in Kirkbymoorside, the timbered Black Swan is believed to be the most venerable – the intricately carved entrance porch bears the date 1692.

It was in another ancient inn, the King Head's Hotel, that one of the 17th century's most reviled politicians expired. In what is now Buckingham House, but was then part of the adjoining hotel, George Villiers, 2nd Duke of Buckingham died. The duke had been a favourite of Charles II and a member of the notorious 'Cabal' of the king's five most powerful ministers who colluded with him in trying to frustrate the democratic instincts of the elected Parliament. Each letter of the word 'Cabal' represented the initial of one of its five members – Buckingham being the 'B'. The duke had come to Kirkbymoorside to take part in a hunt through the nearby Forest of Pickering. In the heat of the chase he was thrown from his horse and mortally wounded. The duke's retainers carried him to the King's Head Inn where he died later that day. In the parish register for 1687 the passing of a once-mighty politician merited only a laconic, phonetic entry: *Died: April 17th George Viluas: Lord Dooke of Bookingham*.

In a secluded dale about 1½ miles west of the town, tiny **St Gregory's Minster** is a fine example of a Saxon church and is famous for its sun dial which has been dated to around AD 1055.

HELMSLEY

13 miles W of Pickering on the A170

One of North Yorkshire's most popular and attractive towns, with lots of specialty shops, ancient hostelries and a market every Friday, Helmsley lies on the banks of the River Rye on the edge of the North York Moors National Park. The spacious cobbled market square is typical of the area but the Gothic memorial to the 2nd Baron Feversham that stands there

---

50 PENNY BANK CAFÉ

Kirkbymoorside

This is far more than your ordinary café, offering fine cuisine, attentive staff and an additional a la carte menu for the evening.

See entry on page 205

---

51 CASTLEGATE CAFÉ

Helmsley

This traditional tearoom prides itself on offering home baking 'like Grandma used to cook,' with unbeatable hospitality to boot.

See entry on page 206

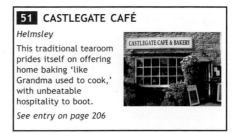

Helmsley

1687. Founded in the early 1100s, seriously knocked about during the Civil War, the castle was in a dilapidated state but its previous owner, the Duke of Buckingham, had continued to live there in some squalor and discomfort. Sir Thomas quickly decided to build a more suitable residence nearby, abandoning the ruins to lovers of the romantic and picturesque.

Winners of Yorkshire in Bloom, 2009, **Helmsley Walled Garden** offers five acres of lovely gardens containing many unusual varieties of flowers, vegetables and herbs. With the castle as its backdrop, it was originally established in the 1700s, but by the late 1900s the garden had become a wilderness. It has now been completely restored and work is currently under way to bring the Victorian glasshouses back into service. Plants, cut and dried flowers, vegetables and herbs are on sale; there's a café, shop and picnic area.

Just to the west of Helmsley rise the indescribably beautiful remains of **Rievaulx Abbey** (English Heritage), standing among wooded hills beside the River Rye – 'the most beautiful monastic site in Europe.' JMW Turner was enchanted by this idyllic landscape; Dorothy Wordsworth, 'spellbound'. Founded in 1131, Rievaulx was the first Cistercian abbey in Yorkshire and, with some 700 people – monks, lay brothers, servants – eventually living within its walls, became one of the largest. Like Kirkham Abbey a few years earlier, Rievaulx was endowed by Walter l'Espec, Lord of Helmsley, still mourning the loss of his only son in a riding accident. The abbey was soon a major landowner in the county, earning a healthy income from farming and at one time owning more than 14,000 sheep. The abbey also had

is not. This astonishingly ornate construction was designed by Sir Giles Gilbert Scott and looks like a smaller version of his famous memorial to Sir Walter Scott in Edinburgh.

The Earls of Feversham lived at **Duncombe Park** whose extensive grounds sweep up to within a few yards of the Market Place. Most of the original mansion, designed by Vanbrugh, was gutted by a disastrous fire in 1879: only the north wing remained habitable and that in its turn was ruined by a second fire in 1895. The Fevershams lavished a fortune on rebuilding the grand old house, largely to the original design, but the financial burden eventually forced them to lease the house and grounds as a preparatory school for girls. Happily, the Fevershams were able to return to their ancestral home in 1985 and the beautifully restored house with its 35 acres of lovely gardens and a further 400 acres of superbly landscaped grounds are now open to the public.

Before they were ennobled, the Fevershams' family name was Duncombe and it was Sir Thomas Duncombe, a wealthy London goldsmith, who established the family seat here when he bought **Helmsley Castle** (English Heritage) and its estate in

---

52 DUNCOMBE PARK
Helmsley

A baroque mansion, built in 1713, with principal rooms restored in late 19th century style and set
amid superb parkland and landscaped gardens.

See entry on page 207

---

53 HELMSLEY WALLED GARDEN
Helmsley

Helmsley Walled Garden is a 5 acre walled garden built in 1758 and set beneath Helmsley Castle.

See entry on page 207

its own fishery at Teesmouth, and iron-ore mines at Bilsdale and near Wakefield.

Looking down on the extensive remains of the Abbey is **Rievaulx Terrace** (National Trust), a breathtaking example of landscape gardening completed in 1758. The cunningly contrived avenues draw your eyes to incomparable views of the abbey itself, to vistas along the Rye Valley and to the rolling contours of the hills beyond. At each end of the terrace is a classical temple, one of which is elaborately furnished and decorated as a dining room.

HAWNBY

16 miles W of Pickering, off the A170

Hawnby was home to the first community of Methodists in Ryedale. This caused a great scandal within the established church. The Methodist rebels were taken before magistrates and charged with disorderly conduct as 'lewd fellows of the baser sort'. That is why, to this day, the village of Hawnby is in two distinct parts: the original village is halfway up the hill, while down at the bottom by the bridge is the settlement the early Methodists built. Within a few years their original houses had been replaced by the ones that stand there now. The village's two chapels also no longer exist – one stands in ruins at Snilesworth on the edge of the moor; the other has been converted into business premises.

The village is close to many hiking trails including the **Cleveland Way** and **Mark Reid's Inn Way**; cycling enthusiasts will enjoy the challenging terrain with trails such as National Cycle Route 65, which passes through the village, and the MTB trails in Boltby Forest. Trout fishing is permitted on Arden Great Lake

for a small fee. Other activities such as hang gliding, clay pigeon shooting, 4x4 off-road driving are available locally.

KIRBY MISPERTON

3 miles SW of Pickering, off the A169

The 375 acres of wooded parkland surrounding Kirby Misperton Hall provide the setting for **Flamingo Land,** a zoo and fun park that is home to more than 1000 birds, animals and reptiles. Red-necked wallabies, meerkats, Bactrian camels, lynx, tigers, rheas, scimitar-horned oryx, bison, sea lions, baboons and guanacos (a South American relative of the camel) are just some of the many exotic creatures in residence. Beyond doubt, the most spectacular sight is that of the flock of pink flamingos gathered around the lake fringed with willow trees. With more than 100 different attractions, including a fun fair with some truly scary rides, an adventure playground and a real working farm, it's no surprise to learn that Flamingo Land is the 4th most visited theme park in the country.

NUNNINGTON

11 miles SW of Pickering off the B1257

Nunnington Hall (National Trust) is a late 17th-century manor house in a beautiful

---

55 SUN INN

Normanby

This is an impressive establishment in the delightful hamlet of Normanby. Produce from Yorkshire is a strong feature on the traditional menu.

See entry on page 208

---

54 INN AT HAWNBY

Hawnby

Simply gorgeous; an award winning inn for food and hospitality many times over.

See entry on page 207

---

56 THE ROYAL OAK COUNTRY INN

Nunnington

This popular inn serves hearty country food in a relaxed and informal public house setting.

See entry on page 208

setting beside the River Rye with a picturesque packhorse bridge within its grounds. Inside, there is a magnificent panelled hall, fine tapestries and china, and the famous Carlisle collection of miniature rooms exquisitely furnished in different period styles to one-eighth life size.

MALTON

Malton has been the historic centre of Ryedale since Roman times. They built a large fort and called it Derventio after the river Derwent beside which it stands. For many years, archaeologists were puzzled by the large scale of the fort, a mystery resolved in 1970 when a building dedication was uncovered which revealed that the fort housed a cavalry regiment, the Ala Picentiana – the extra space was needed to accommodate their horses. Many fine relics from the site, showing the sophisticated lifestyles of the Roman centurions and civilians, can be seen in the **Malton Museum**, along with items from the Iron Age settlement that preceded the Roman garrison.

The River Derwent was vitally important to Malton. The river rises in the moors near Scarborough, then runs inland through the Vale of Pickering bringing an essential element for what was once a major industry in Malton – brewing. In the 19th century, there were nine breweries here, now only the Malton Brewery Company survives. It operates in a converted stable block behind Suddabys Crown Hotel in Wheelgate and welcomes visitors, but telephone them first on 01653 697580.

Charles Dickens stayed in the area with his friend, Charles Smithson, a solicitor, and is believed to have modelled Scrooge's Counting House in *A Christmas Carol* on Smithson's office in Chancery Lane.

Old Malton is located just to the north of the Roman Fort, an interesting and historic area on the edge of open countryside. Nearby villages such as Settrington and their secluded country lanes are home to many famous racehorse stables: if you are up and about early enough you will see the horses out on their daily exercises. In the centre of Old Malton stands a beautiful fragment of **St Mary's Priory**, incorporating a particularly fine Norman doorway. The Priory was built around 1155 by the only monastic order in Christendom to have originated entirely in England – the Gilbertines. The order was founded in 1148 by a Lincolnshire parish priest, St Gilbert of Sempringham.

Parts of the parish church are quite as old as the Priory but one of its most interesting features is relatively modern, the work of the 'Mouseman of Kilburn', Robert Thompson. A gifted woodcarver and furniture maker, Thompson 'signed' all his pieces with a discreetly placed carving of a mouse. There's one on the stout oak door of the church and, inside, the stalls are carved elaborately with all manner of wondrous beasts along with historical and mythical scenes.

---

57 THE BLUE BALL INN

Malton

Formerly a 15th century farmhouse, this charming inn is now well known for its good real ales, warm atmosphere and delectably wholesome English cuisine.

See entry on page 209

---

58 ROYAL OAK

Old Malton

This brilliant hidden gem is famous for its weekly speciality pie night; a real Yorkshire treat!

See entry on page 210

---

59 EDEN CAMP MODERN HISTORY MUSEUM

Malton

Eden Camp will allow you to experience the sights, sounds and even the smells of life on both the Home Front and Front Line during World War Two.

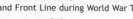

See entry on page 210

A mile or so north of Old Malton is **Eden Camp**, a theme museum dedicated to re-creating the dramatic experiences of ordinary people living through the Second World War. This unique museum is housed in some 30 huts of a genuine prisoner of war camp, built in 1942. Sound, lighting effects, smells, even smoke generators are deployed to make you feel that you are actually there, taking part. Visitors can find out what it was like to live through an air raid, to be a prisoner of war or a sailor in a U-boat under attack. Among the many other exhibits are displays on Fashion in the '40s, Children at War, and even one on Rationing. In 1941, one discovers, the cheese ration was down to 1oz (28 grams) per person a week! More generous portions of food are available in the café, and there's also a bar, gift shop and children's adventure playground.

Gatehouse of Kirkham Priory

Rievaulx). Visitors to Kirkham pass through a noble, exquisitely decorated gatehouse but one of the most memorable sights at the Priory, perhaps because it is so unexpected, is the sumptuous lavatorium in the ruined cloister. Here the monks washed their hands at two bays with lavishly moulded arches supported by slender pillars, each bay adorned with tracery.

AROUND MALTON

KIRKHAM

5 miles SW of Malton off the A64

In a lovely, peaceful setting beside the River Derwent, stand the remains of **Kirkham Priory**. According to legend, the priory was founded in 1125 by Walter l'Espec after his only son was thrown from his horse and killed at this very spot. (A few years later, Walter was to found another great abbey at

CASTLE HOWARD

5 miles SW of Malton off the A64

Lying in the folds of the Howardian Hills about five miles southwest of Malton stands one of the most glorious stately homes in Britain, **Castle Howard**. Well known to TV viewers as the Brideshead of *Brideshead Revisited*, Castle Howard has astonished visitors ever since it was completed in the early 1700s.

Even that world-weary 18th-century socialite Horace Walpole was stirred to enthusiasm: 'Nobody had informed me,' he wrote, 'that at one view I should see a palace, a town, a fortified city, temples on high places ... the noblest lawn in the world fenced by half the horizon and a mausoleum that would tempt one to be buried alive: in short, I have seen gigantic places before, but never a sublime one.'

Winner of York Tourism Bureau's 'Out of Town Attraction of the Year' award, this magnificent 18th-century house has extensive collections and breathtaking

Castle Howard

grounds, featuring temples, lakes and fountains - in all, there are 200 listed building and monuments within the 1000 acre estate. There are various places to stop and enjoy refreshments and also a plant centre and tree nursery. A varied programme of events takes place throughout the year, including the Proms Spectacular and Archaeology Weekends.

Hovingham Hall

Perhaps the most astonishing fact of all concerns the architect of Castle Howard, Sir John Vanbrugh. Vanbrugh had been a soldier and a playwright but until he began this sublime building had never yet overseen the placing of one block of masonry on another.

Castle Howard is open daily between February and November. A land-train is available to transport visitors from the car park to the house, and there is disabled access to many parts.

APPLETON-LE-STREET

4 miles W of Malton off the B1257

Appleton's Grade I listed Saxon church escaped 'improvement' by the Victorians, so it retains much original stonework and has one of the finest Anglo-Saxon towers in the North of England. Inside, effigies date from the 13th and 14th centuries and some interior woodwork dates from 1636. Outside, a statue of the Virgin and Child, defaced at the time of the Reformation, can be seen in a niche above the porch. Set high above the village, All Saints commands magnificent views over the Vale of Pickering.

HOVINGHAM

8 miles W of Malton on the B1257

'Hall, church and village gather round like a happy family', wrote Arthur Mee describing Hovingham some 70 years ago. Today the idyllic scene remains unspoilt, a lovely place boasting no fewer than three village greens. Overlooking one of them is a Victorian school, still in use and boasting an elegant oriel window.

Nearby Hovingham Hall, an imposing Georgian mansion, was built in 1760 for Sir Thomas Worsley, Surveyor General to George III, and almost exactly 200 years later, on June 8th 1961, his descendant Katherine Worsley returned here for a royal reception following her marriage to the Duke of Kent. The Worsley family still live at the Hall so it is only open to visitors for a short time in summer, but you can see its unusual entrance which leads directly off the village green. The huge archway opens, not as you would expect, into a drive leading to the Hall but to a vast riding school and stables through which visitors have to pass. Within the Hall's grounds is the village's cricket pitch, enjoying what is surely the most picturesque setting for the game.

60 HOME FARM HOLIDAY COTTAGES

Slingsby

The perfect countryside escape - two quaint self-catering cottages nestled in a picturesque Yorkshire village.

See entry on page 211

61 THE MALT SHOVEL

Hovingham

A picture postcard pub serving the very best in real ales and good value quality food

See entry on page 212

EAST HESLERTON

7 miles NE of Malton on the A64

This little village is distinguished by one of the many churches gifted by Sir Tatton Sykes of Sledmere House in the mid-1800s. Designed in 13th-century style the church has a fine west portico, a vaulted chancel and an iron screen of very fine workmanship. The north tower has an octagonal belfry and spire, and statues of four Latin Doctors (Ambrose, Augustine, Gregory and Jerome) originally sculpted for Bristol Cathedral.

Old Mill Pond, Wharram Percy

WEST LUTTON

7 miles E of Malton off the A64 or B1253

West Lutton church is yet another of the many repaired or restored by Sir Tatton Sykes in this corner of the East Riding. It stands over-looking the village green and pond, its lych gate reached by a tiny bridge.

62 THE FLEECE INN INCORPORATING THE DROVERS REST

Rillington

Family run pub and restaurant, whose menu adds a twist to the classical pub favourites.

See entry on page 211

63 CROSS KEYS

Thixendale

A popular inn that enjoys a scenic setting, with fine food, well kept ales and attentive hosts.

See entry on page 213

WHARRAM PERCY

7 miles SE of Malton off the B1248

A minor road off the B1248 leads to one of the most haunting sights in the county – the deserted medieval village of **Wharram Percy** (English Heritage). There had been a settlement here for some 5000 years but by the late 1400s the village stood abandoned. For a while the church continued to serve the surrounding hamlets but in time, that too became a ruin. The manor house of the Percy family who gave the village its name, peasant houses dating back to the 13th century, a corn mill, a cemetery complete with exposed skeletons – these sad memorials of a once thriving community stand windswept and desolate. Until fairly recently it was assumed that the villagers had been driven from their homes by the plague but scholars are now certain that the cause was simple economics: the lords of the manor, the Percys, turned their lands from labour-intensive crop cultivation to sheep farming which needed only a handful of shepherds. Unable to find work, the villagers drifted elsewhere.

LOCATION MAP

Accommodation

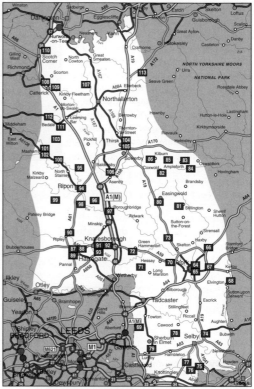

Food & Drink

Food & Drink

YORK & CENTRAL YORKSHIRE

The historic City of York lies in the southern part of the broad Vale of York, a region of rich, agricultural land that stretches some 60 miles northwards from York almost to the River Tees. Although flat itself, there are almost always hills in view: the Hambleton and Cleveland Hills to the east, the Dales and the Pennines to the west. In between lies this fertile corridor of fertile farmland and low-lying meadows, a vast plain bisected by the Great North Road linking London and Edinburgh. Several of Yorkshire's largest rivers - the Swale, the Ure, the Nidd and the Wharfe - debouch into the Vale to join the Ouse.

Apart from York, the main centres of population are the elegant spa town of Harrogate, Knaresborough with its historic castle and spectacular site beside the River Nidd, the cathedral city of Ripon, Northallerton, the county town of North Yorkshire, the brewing centre of Tadcaster

and the smaller settlements of Thirsk, Boroughbridge and Wetherby.

The area boasts one World Heritage Site, the magnificent ruins of Fountains Abbey, near Ripon, and other ecclesiastical sites of note include the uniquely evocative Mount Grace Priory, and the imposing creamy-coloured ruins of Byland Abbey.

Among the stately homes that embellish the region are the Robert Adam-designed Newby Hall, enchanting Ripley Castle where the Ingilby family have lived for 700 years, Sion Hill Hall, 'the last of the great country houses', the baroque masterpiece, Beningbrough Hall, and the noble early 18th century Sutton Park.

And although most of the area is low-lying, if you go to the top of Sutton Bank near Thirsk you can enjoy a panoramic vista of the Vale that James Herriot called "the finest view in England".

Food & Drink

Places of Interest

Places of Interest

YORK

One of the world's great cities, York boasts some 2000 listed buildings, a plethora of outstanding museums, a vibrant cultural life and a huge variety of shops. As an introduction to the city, a walk along the old city walls opens up one of the grandest cityscapes in the country as you walk along the towards York Minster, a sublime expression of medieval faith.

It was the Romans who created the first settlement of any note here, naming their garrison town 'Eboracum'. The Imperial troops arrived here in AD 71 and chose this strategic position astride the Rivers Ouse and Foss as their base for a campaign against the pesky tribe of the Brigantes. From this garrison, the capital of the British Province of the Roman Empire, Hadrian directed the construction of his great wall and a later general, Constantine, was proclaimed Emperor here. The legions finally left the city around AD 410, but the evidence of their three-and-a-half centuries of occupation is manifest all around York in buildings like the **Multangular Tower,** in rich artefacts treasured in the city's museums and even in a pub: at the **Roman Bath Inn** you can see the remains of steam baths used by the garrison residents.

Little is known of York during the Dark Ages but by the 8th century the city had been colonised by the Anglo-Saxons, who named it Eoferwic, and it was already an important Christian and academic centre. The Vikings put an end to that when they invaded in the 9th century and changed the name once again, this time to Jorvik. The story of York during those years of Danish rule is imaginatively told in the many displays at the **Jorvik Viking Centre** in Coppergate, celebrating a 1000-year-old story. This world-famous centre transports visitors back in time to experience the sights, sounds and – perhaps most famously – the smells of 10th-century York. Visitors are shown that, in AD 975, York was a bustling commercial centre where 10,000 people lived and worked. Travelling in state-of-the-art 'time capsules',

visitors are carried past and through two-storey dwellings, enjoying views over back gardens and rooftops, and even glimpsing the Viking Age equivalent of today's Minster. Journeying through representations of real-life Viking Age Britain, you pass through a bustling market thronged with Danes bartering for chickens, corn and other provisions and wares, penetrate dark smoky houses, cross a busy wharf where goods, transported along the rivers Ouse and Foss, are being off-loaded. Both fun and educational, 20 years after it first opened, Jorvik still retains its status as one of the world's iconic attractions, and its many superb features make it an enduring favourite with children and adults alike.

Following the Norman Conquest, the city suffered badly during the Harrowing of the North when William the Conqueror mounted a brutal campaign against his rebellious northern subjects. Vast tracts of Yorkshire and Northumberland were laid waste and some historians reckon that it took more than 100 years for the area to recover from this wholesale devastation.

In later Norman times, however, York entered one of its most glorious periods. It was at this time that **Clifford's Tower** was built, a mightily impressive structure set atop a huge mound. It was built in the shape of a quatrefoil, the only castle in England of this kind. It was originally part of York Castle but was re-named after a man called Clifford was hanged here in 1332.

York Minster, the largest Gothic cathedral in Northern Europe, was begun around 1230 and the work was on such a scale that it would not be completed until two-and-a-half centuries later. Its stained glass windows – there are more than 100 of them – cast a

---

64 JORVIK VIKING CENTRE

York

The world famous **JORVIK** centre in York transports visitors back in time to experience the sights, sounds and - perhaps most famously - the smells of 10th century York

See entry on page 213

York Minster

celestial light over the many treasures within. A guided tour of the Great Tower gives dizzying views across the city; a visit to the crypt reveals some of the relics from the Roman fortress that stood here nearly 2000 years ago.

This superb building has survived three major fires. The first occurred in 1829 and was started by a madman, Jonathan Martin. Believing that God wanted him to destroy the church, he started a fire fuelled by prayer and hymn books. The fire was not discovered until the following morning by which time the east end of the Minster had been severely damaged. A second blaze, in 1840, was caused by a workman leaving a candle burning. As a result of his carelessness, the central part of the nave was destroyed. The

most recent conflagration was in July 1984, shortly after a controversial Bishop of Durham had been installed. Some attributed the fire to God's wrath at the Bishop's appointment; the more prosaic view was that it had been caused by lightning. The subsequent restoration has allowed modern masons and craftsmen to demonstrate that they possess skills just as impressive as those of their medieval forebears.

The network of medieval streets around the Minster is one of the city's major delights. Narrow lanes are criss-crossed by even narrower footpaths – ginnels, snickets or 'snickelways', which have survived as public rights of way despite being built over, above and around. Narrowest of all the snickelways is Pope's Head Alley, more than 100 feet long but only 31 inches wide. The alley became known as Introduction Lane – if you wanted to know someone better, you simply timed your walk along the lane so as to meet the other party half-way. Whip-ma-Whop-ma-Gate, allegedly, is where felons used to be 'whipped and whopped'. Probably the most famous of these ancient streets is **The Shambles**. Its name comes from 'Fleshammels', the street of butchers and slaughter houses. The houses here were deliberately built to keep the street out of direct sunlight, thus protecting the carcasses which were hung outside the houses on hooks. Many of the hooks are still in place.

During these years, York was the second largest city in England and it was then that the town walls and their 'bars', or gates, were built. The trade guilds were also at their most powerful and in Fossgate one of them built the lovely black and white timbered **Merchant Adventurers Hall.** The Merchant Adventurers controlled the lucrative trade in 'all goods bought and sold foreign' and they spared no expense in building the Great Hall where they conducted their affairs beneath a complex timbered roof displaying many colourful banners of York's medieval guilds. To this period, too, belong the **York Mystery Plays**, first performed in 1397 and subsequently every four years.

During Tudor times, York's importance steadily declined but in the 18th century the

---

65 YORK MINSTER

York

York Minster acts as a beacon welcoming all visitors to the City of York. Built over 250 years it is renowned worldwide as an artistic and architectural masterpiece.

See entry on page 214

The Shambles

completely different role as the hub of the railway system in the north. At the heart of this transformation was the charismatic entrepreneur George Hudson, founder of what became the Great Northern Railway. Part visionary, part crook, Hudson's wheeler-dealing eventually led to his disgrace but even then the citizens of York twice elected him as Lord Mayor and he has a street and a pub named after him. It was thanks to Hudson that York's magnificent railway station, with its great curving roof of glass, was built, a tourist attraction in its own right.

Another aspect of railway history is on view at the **York Model Railway**, next door to the station, which has almost one third of a mile of track and up to 28 trains running at any one time.

For real trains, however, a visit to the **National Railway Museum** is a must. The world's largest railway museum, it has 3 enormous halls where you'll find iconic locomotives such as *Mallard,* the world's fastest steam engine, a Japanese Bullet Train, and the Chinese Locomotive, one of the largest steam locomotives ever built in Britain. There's also a wealth of interactive exhibits and daily demonstrations.

A city with such a long and colourful history naturally boasts some fine museums. Set in botanical gardens close to the Minster and beside the River Ouse, the **Yorkshire Museum & Gardens** has an outstanding collection of Roman, Viking and medieval

city re-emerged as a fashionable social centre. Many elegant Georgian houses, of which **Fairfax House** in Castlegate is the most splendid, were built at this time and they add another attractive architectural dimension to the city. Fairfax House was built in the early 1700s and elegantly remodelled by John Carr half a century later. The gracious old house has had an unfortunate history. It passed through a succession of private owners and by 1909 was divided between three building societies and the York City Club. The final indignity came in 1919 when the city council permitted a cinema to be built alongside and its superb first floor rooms to be converted into a dance hall. The York Civic Trust was able to purchase the house in 1981 and has restored this splendid old mansion to its former state of grace. The original furnishings have long since been dispersed but in their place are some marvellous pieces from the Noel Terry collection of fine furniture and clocks which includes many rare and unusual pieces.

The 19th century saw York take on a

Fairfax House - York

artefacts, including the exquisite Middleham Jewel which was discovered close to Middleham Castle. Made of finely engraved gold and adorned with a brilliant sapphire it is one of the most dazzling pieces to have survived from that period.

At the **York Castle Museum** visitors can venture into the prison cell of notorious highwayman Dick Turpin; stroll along Victorian and Edwardian streets complete with fully equipped shops, hostelries and houses; or browse among the more than 100,000 items on display. One of the country's most popular museums of everyday life, its exhibits range from crafts and costumes to automobiles and machine guns, from mod cons and medicines to toys and technology. Recent additions to the museum's amenities include a gift shop and café.

Insights into medieval daily life are provided at **Barley Hall,** a superbly restored late medieval townhouse which in Tudor times was the home of William Snawsell, a goldsmith who became Lord Mayor of York. Visitors can try out the furniture, handle all the pottery, glass and metal wares, and even try on some medieval costumes.

A fairly recent addition to the city's attractions is the **Quilt Museum and Gallery**, opened in June 2008. Housed in a 15th century guildhall, it is Europe's first museum dedicated to quilt making and textile arts and is home to the Quilters' Guild of the British Isles and its world-famous Heritage Quilt Collection.

It's impossible here to list all York's museums, galleries and fine buildings, but you will find a wealth of additional information at the Tourist Information Centre close to one of the historic old gateways to the city, **Bootham Bar.**

AROUND YORK

MURTON

3 miles E of York off the A64

Although a small village, Murton is an important, modern livestock centre and it is also home to the **Yorkshire Museum of Farming**, found at Murton Park. As well as wandering around the fields and pens, visitors can also see reconstructions of a Roman fort, a Danelaw village from the Dark Ages and Celtic Roundhouses along with bumping into Romans, Viking and Saxons. Other attractions at the park include a children's play area, large picnic area, and a café fashioned on a farmhouse kitchen.

ELVINGTON

7 miles SE of York off the B1228

During the Second World War RAF Elvington was the base for British, Canadian and French bomber crews flying missions to occupied Europe. With virtually all its original buildings still intact, the base now provides an authentic setting for the **Yorkshire Air Museum** and is the largest Second World War Bomber Command Station open to the public

---

67 MURTON PARK

Murton

Murton Park. is your gateway to the Yorkshire Museum of Farming, Danelaw Dark Age Village, Brigantium Roman Fort, the Tudor Croft and the Home Front Experience.

See entry on page 216

---

66 MERRICOTE COTTAGES AT VERTIGROW PLANT NURSERY

York

Quality 3-star self-catering accommodation in rural setting just 3 miles from York; adjacent to excellent plant nursery.

See entry on page 215

---

68 THE YORKSHIRE AIR MUSEUM

Elvington

Over the past few years the Yorkshire Air Museum has become one of the most fascinating and dynamic Museums of its type in the country.

See entry on page 214

in the UK. In addition to examining the many exhibits tracing the history of aviation, including a unique Halifax bomber, visitors can visit the control tower, browse among the historic military vehicle collection, watch engineers restoring vintage planes – and enjoy home-cooked food in the NAAFI restaurant. The museum hosts many special events throughout the year and offers conference and corporate event facilities.

TADCASTER

9m SW of York off the A64

The lovely magnesian limestone used in so many fine Yorkshire churches came from the quarries established here in Roman times. Their name for Tadcaster was simply 'Calcaria' – limestone. By 1341 however, brewing had become the town's major industry, using water from the River Wharfe. Three major breweries are still based in Tadcaster: Samuel Smiths, established in 1758 and the oldest in Yorkshire; John Smith's, whose bitter is the best-selling ale in Britain; and Coors Tower Brewery. The distinctive brewery buildings dominate the town's skyline and provide the basis of its prosperity. Guided tours of the breweries are available by prior booking.

Also worth visiting is **The Ark**, the oldest building in Tadcaster dating back to the 1490s. During its long history, The Ark has served as a meeting place, a post office, an inn, a butcher's shop, and a museum. It now houses the Town Council offices and is open to the public in office hours. This appealing half-timbered building takes its name from the two carved heads on the first floor beams. They are thought to represent Noah and his wife, hence the name.

Tadcaster also offers some attractive riverside walks, one of which takes you across the 'Virgin Viaduct' over the River Wharfe. Built in 1849 by the great railway entrepreneur George Hudson, the viaduct was intended to be part of a direct line from Leeds to York. Before the tracks were laid however Hudson was convicted of fraud on a stupendous scale and the route was not completed until 1882.

'Virgin Viaduct', Tadcaster

About four miles southwest of Tadcaster is Hazlewood Castle, now a superb hotel and conference centre. But for more than eight centuries it was the home of the Vavasour family who built it with the lovely white limestone from their quarry at Thevesdale – the same quarry that provided the stone for York Minster and King's College Chapel, Cambridge. Guided tours of the castle with its superb Great Hall and 13th-century Chapel are available by arrangement.

LONG MARSTON

7 miles W of York off the B1224

Lying on the edge of the Vale of York and sheltered by a hill, this peaceful village is an ancient agricultural community. However, in July 1644, its tranquillity was shattered by the

---

69 THE CROOKED BILLET

Saxton, nr Tadcaster

Serving delicious home cooked food packed with locally sourced produce in a lovely community inn.

See entry on page 217

---

70 THE LORD COLLINGWOOD

Upper Poppleton

This popular public house offers the very best in hospitality, food and real ales, and is located in a picture-postcard village.

See entry on page 218

battle of Marston Moor, one of the most important encounters of the Civil War and one which the Royalists lost. The night before the battle, Oliver Cromwell and his chief officers stayed at Long Marston Hall and the bedroom they used is still called The Cromwell Room.

Each year the anniversary of the battle is commemorated by the members of the Sealed Knot and, it is said, that the ghosts of those who fell in battle haunt the site. Certainly, local farmers still occasionally unearth cannonballs used in the battle when they are out ploughing the fields.

NEWTON-ON-OUSE

7 miles NW of York off the A19

About a mile to the south of Newton on Ouse is **Beningbrough Hall** (National Trust), a baroque masterpiece from the early 18th century with seven acres of gardens,

71 THE SPOTTED OX

Tockwith

Cosy and popular public house which has a delicious menu – particularly the Sunday roast!

See entry on page 217

72 THE BAY HORSE INN

Green Hammerton

This family run inn offers a daily changing home cooked menu made with delicious locally sourced produce, with guest accommodation adjacent.

See entry on page 219

73 SIDINGS HOTEL & RESTAURANT

Shipton by Beningbrough

Surrounded by open countryside this hotel and restaurant is an ideal get-away for rail enthusiasts.

See entry on page 220

wilderness play area, pike ponds and scenic walks. There's also a fully-operational Victorian laundry which demonstrates the painstaking drudgery of a 19th-century washing day. A major attraction here is the permanent exhibition of more than 100 portraits on loan from the National Portrait Gallery. Other exhibitions are often held at the Hall – for these there is usually an additional charge. Within the Hall's gardens is a working walled garden whose produce supplies the Walled Garden Restaurant.

SELBY

In 1069 a young monk named Benedict, from Auxerre in France, had a vision. It's not known exactly what the vision was but it inspired him to set sail for York. As his ship was sailing up the Ouse near Selby, three swans flew in formation across its bows. (Three swans, incidentally, still form part of the town's coat of arms.) Interpreting this as a sign of the Holy Trinity, Benedict promptly went ashore and set up a preaching cross under a great oak called the Stirhac. The small religious community he established went from strength to strength, acquiring many grants of land and, in 1100, permission to build a monastery. Over the course of the next 120 years, the great **Selby Abbey** slowly took shape, the massively heavy Norman style of the earlier building gradually modulating into the much more delicate early English style. All of the abbey was built using a lovely cream-coloured stone.

Over the centuries this sublime church has suffered more than most. During the Civil War it was severely damaged by Cromwell's troops who destroyed many of its statues and smashed much of its stained glass. Then in 1690 the central tower collapsed. For years after that the abbey was neglected and by the middle of the 18th century a wall had been built across the chancel so that the nave could be used as a warehouse. That wall was removed during a major restoration during the 19th century but in 1906 there was another calamity when a disastrous fire swept through the building. Visiting this serene and

Selby Abbey

should seek out **St Mary's Church** at Hemingbrough. Built in a pale rose-coloured brick, it has an extraordinarily lofty and elegant spire soaring 190 feet high and, inside, what is believed to be Britain's oldest misericord. Misericords are hinged wooden seats for the choir which could be folded back when they stood to sing. Medieval woodcarvers delighted in adorning the underside of the seat with intricate carvings. The misericord at Hemingbrough dates back to around 1200.

peaceful church today it's difficult to believe that it has endured so many misfortunes and yet remains so beautiful. Throughout all the abbey's misfortunes one particular feature survived intact – the famous Washington Window which depicts the coat of arms of John de Washington, Prior of the Abbey around 1415 and a direct ancestor of George Washington. Prominently displayed in this heraldic device is the stars and stripes motif later adapted for the national flag of the United States. Guided tours of the cathedral are available.

Devotees of railway history will want to pay their respects to Selby's old railway station. Built at the incredibly early date of 1834 it is the oldest surviving station in Britain. From Selby the railway track runs straight as a ruler for 18 miles to Hull – the longest such stretch in Britain.

CARLTON

6 miles S of Selby on the A1041

A mile or so south of Camblesforth, off the A1041, is **Carlton Towers**, a stately home-cum-upmarket hotel that should on no account be missed. This extraordinary building, 'something between the Houses of Parliament and St Pancras Station', was created in the 1870s by two young English eccentrics, Henry, 9th Lord Beaumont, and Edward Welby Pugin, son of the eminent Victorian architect, A.G. Pugin. Together, they transformed a traditional Jacobean house into an exuberant mock medieval fantasy in stone, abounding with turrets, towers, gargoyles and heraldic shields. The richly-decorated High Victorian interior,

AROUND SELBY

HEMINGBROUGH

4 miles E of Selby off the A63

Anyone interested in remarkable churches

---

74 THE NEW INN

Barlby

Bustling village pub known for its fine selection of real ales and popular Sunday roasts, great for all the family with a children's play area in the beer garden.

See entry on page 221

---

75 THE ROYAL OAK INN

Hirst Courtney, nr Selby

Delightful hotel and restaurant, with an adjacent caravan park open in season.

See entry on page 221

---

76 LA ANCHOR BAR & PIZZERIA

Hensall

A surprising treat; the authentic taste of Italy in the middle of picturesque Yorkshire.

See entry on page 222

---

designed in the manner of medieval banqueting halls, contains a minstrels' gallery and a vast Venetian-style drawing room. Both Beaumont and Pugin died in their forties, both bankrupt.

In Carlton village the Comus Inn is the only licensed premises in the country to bear that name. It is believed to have been named after the Greek god of sensual pleasure, Comus, the son of Bacchus.

About 3 miles northeast of Carlton is the village of Drax which, as well as supplying Ian Fleming with a sinister-sounding name for one of the villains in his James Bond thrillers, also provides the National Grid with 7% of all the electricity used in England and Wales. The largest coal-powered power station in Europe, Drax's vast cooling towers dominate the low-lying terrain between the rivers Ouse and Aire. Drax power station has found an unusual way of harnessing its waste heat by channelling some of it to a huge complex of greenhouses covering 20 acres. Part of the heat goes to specially constructed ponds in which young eels are bred for the export market. Guided tours of the power station are available by prior arrangement.

WEST HADDLESEY

5 miles SW of Selby on the A19

At **Yorkshire Garden World** gardeners will find endless inspiration in its six acres of beautiful display and nursery gardens. Organically grown herbs, heathers, ornamental perennials, wild flowers and climbers are all on sale; the gift shop has a huge variety of home made crafts, herbal products, Leeds pottery and garden products; and the many different gardens include a Heather and Conifer Garden, an

Aromatherapy Garden, an Open Air Herb Museum, a Lovers' Garden, and the Hall Owl Maze for children.

SOUTH MILFORD

9 miles W of Selby off the A162

About nine miles west of Selby, near the village of South Milford, is the imposing 14th-century **Steeton Hall Gatehouse**, all that remains of a medieval castle once owned by the Fairfax family. A forebear of the famous Cromwellian general is said to have ridden out from here on his way to carry off one of the nuns at Nun Appleton Priory to make her his bride. He was Sir William Fairfax; she was Isabel Thwaites, a wealthy heiress.

SHERBURN-IN-ELMET

10 miles W of Selby on the A162

This attractive village was once the capital of the Celtic Kingdom of Elmete. Well worth visiting is **All Saints' Church** which stands on a hill to the west and dates from about 1120. Its great glory is the nave with its mighty Norman pillars and arcades. A curiosity here is a 15th-century Janus cross which was discovered in the churchyard during the 1770s. The vicar and churchwarden of the time both claimed it as their own. Unable to resolve their dispute,

---

78 BLACKSMITHS ARMS

Biggin

In a quiet, scenic location this inn holds traditional values serving great real ale and pub food for all.

See entry on page 223

---

77 JUG INN

Chapel Haddesley

Welcoming traditional village inn serving fine cuisine and real ales.

See entry on page 223

---

79 THE SWAN HOTEL

South Milford

Welcoming historic hotel, which lists Dick Turpin's Black Bess and Marilyn Monroe as past guests!

See entry on page 224

they had the cross sawn in half: the two beautifully carved segments are displayed on opposite sides of the south aisle.

RICCALL

4 miles N of Selby on the A19

The ancient village of Riccall was mentioned in the *Domesday Book* and has a church that was built not long after. The south doorway of the church dates back to about 1160 and its fine details have been well-preserved by a porch added in the 15th century. The village's great moment in history came in 1066 when the gigantic King Harold Hardrada of Norway and Earl Tostig sailed this far up the Ouse with some 300 ships. They had come to claim Northumbria from Tostig's half-brother King Harold of England but they were comprehensively defeated at the Battle of Stamford Bridge.

Riccall is popular with walkers: from the village you can either go southwards alongside the River Ouse to Selby, or strike northwards towards Bishopthorpe on the outskirts of York following the track of the dismantled York to Selby railway. This latter path is part of the 150-mile-long Trans Pennine Trail linking Liverpool and Hull.

SKIPWITH

5 miles NE of Selby off the A163

Just to the south of Skipwith, the Yorkshire Wildlife Trust maintains the **Skipwith Common Nature Reserve.** This 500 acres of lowland heath is one of the last such areas remaining in the north of England and is of national importance. The principal interest is the variety of insect and birdlife, but the reserve also contains a number of ancient burial sites.

EASINGWOLD

This agreeable market town lies at the foot of the Howardian Hills, an Area of Outstanding Natural Beauty covering 77 acres of woods, farmland and historic parkland. Easingwold's prosperity dates back to the 18th century when it flourished as a major stage coach post

– at that period the town could offer a choice of some 26 public houses and inns. Until the recent construction of a bypass the old town was clogged with traffic but it is now a pleasure again to wander around the marketplace with its impressive **Market Cross** and, nearby, the outline of the old bull-baiting ring set in the cobbles. Easingwold used to enjoy the distinction of having its own private railway, a two-and-a-half mile stretch of track along which it took all of 10 minutes to reach the main east coast line at Alne. Older residents fondly remember the ancient, tall-chimneyed steam locomotive that plied this route until its deeply regretted closure to passenger traffic in 1948.

A little to the south of Easingwold, on the B1363, is **Sutton Park,** a noble early 18th-century mansion built in 1730 by Thomas Atkinson and containing some fine examples of Sheraton and Chippendale furniture, and much admired decorative plasterwork by the Italian maestro in this craft, Cortese. The ubiquitous 'Capability Brown' designed the lovely gardens and parkland in which you'll find a Georgian ice-house, well-signposted woodland walks and a nature trail. There's also a gift shop and a café.

AROUND EASINGWOLD

STILLINGTON

4 miles E of Easingwold on the B1363

In 1758, one of the great works of English literature almost perished in the fireplace of Stillington Hall. The parson of Coxwold had been invited to dinner and when the meal ended was asked to read from a book he had

just completed. The guests had all wined and dined well and were soon dozing off. Incensed by their inattention the parson threw the pages of his manuscript onto the fire. Fortunately his host, the Squire of Stillington, rescued them from the flames and Laurence Sterne's immortal *Tristram Shandy* was saved for posterity.

HUSTHWAITE

4 miles N of Easingwold off the A19

Old stone houses mingle with mellow Victorian and Edwardian brick and overlooking the village green, where three lanes meet, the Church of St Nicholas still retains its original Norman doorway. Just outside the village, on the road to Coxwold, there's a stunning view across to the Hambleton Hills and the White Horse of Kilburn.

COXWOLD

5 miles N of Easingwold off the A19 or A170

Coxwold enjoys a particularly lovely setting in the narrow valley that runs between the Hambleton and Howardian Hills. At the western end of the village stands the 500-year-old **Shandy Hall,** home of Laurence Sterne, vicar of Coxwold in the 1760s. Sterne was the author of *Tristram Shandy*, that wonderfully bizarre novel which opened a vein of English surreal comedy leading directly to The Goons and the Monty Python team. The architecture of the Hall, Tudor in origin, includes some appropriately eccentric features – strangely-shaped balustrades on the wooden staircases, a Heath Robinson kind of contraption in the bedroom powder-closet by which Sterne could draw up pails of water for his ablutions, and a tiny, eye-shaped

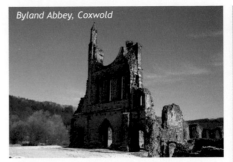
Byland Abbey, Coxwold

window in the huge chimney stack opening from the study to the right of the entrance. A more conventional attraction is the priceless collection of Sterne's books and manuscripts.

The Revd Sterne much preferred the cosmopolitan diversions of London to the rustic pleasures of his Yorkshire parish and rarely officiated at the imposing **Church of St Michael** nearby with its striking octagonal tower, three-decker pulpit and Fauconberg family tombs. A curiosity here is a floor brass in the nave recording the death of Sir John Manston in 1464. A space was left for his wife Elizabeth's name to be added at a later date. The space is still blank. Outside, against the wall of the nave, is Sterne's original tombstone, moved here from London's Bayswater when the churchyard there was deconsecrated in 1969.

Just to the south of Coxwold is **Newburgh Priory,** founded in 1145 as an Augustinian monastery and now a mostly Georgian country house with fine interiors and a beautiful water garden. Since 1538, the Priory has been the home of the Fauconberg family. An old tradition asserts that Oliver Cromwell's body is interred here. Cromwell's daughter, Mary, was married to Lord Fauconberg and when Charles II had her

---

81 **THE WHITE BEAR INN**

Stillington

A well run country pub serving traditional home made food and a selection of five real ales.

See entry on page 226

---

82 **NEWBURGH PRIORY**

Coxwold

Newburgh Priory is a fine stately home in a superb setting with breathtaking views to the Kilburn White Horse in the distance .

See entry on page 225

father's corpse hanged at Tyburn and his head struck off, Lady Fauconberg claimed the decapitated body, brought it to Newburgh and, it is said, buried the remains under the floorboards of an attic room. The supposed tomb has never been opened, the Fauconbergs even resisting a royal appeal from Edward VII when, as Prince of Wales, he was a guest at the Priory. The house is open for guided tours and the extensive grounds are open to the public during the spring and summer months.

From Coxwold, follow the minor road north-eastwards towards Ampleforth. After about two miles, you will see the lovely, cream-coloured ruins of **Byland Abbey** (English Heritage). The Cistercians began building their vast compound in 1177 and it grew to become the largest Cistercian church in Britain. Much of the damage to its fabric was caused by Scottish soldiers after the Battle of Byland in 1322. The English king, Edward II had been staying at the abbey but fled after his defeat, abandoning vital stores and priceless treasures. In a frenzy of looting, the Scots made off with everything the king had left and ransacked the abbey for good measure. The ruined west front of the abbey, although only the lower arc of its great rose window is still in place, gives a vivid impression of how glorious this building once was.

AMPLEFORTH

6 miles N of Easingwold off the A170

Set on the southern slopes of the Hambleton Hills, Ampleforth is perhaps best known for its Roman Catholic public school, Ampleforth College, established by the Benedictine community that came here in 1809, fleeing

from persecution in post-revolutionary France. The monks built an austere-looking abbey in the Romanesque style among whose treasures are an altar stone rescued from Byland Abbey and finely crafted woodwork by the 'Mouseman of Kilburn', Robert Thompson. Visitors are welcome at the abbey and to the grounds, and there's even a tea-room serving home-made scones, cakes and light meals.

KILBURN

6 miles N of Easingwold off the A170

This pleasing small village nestling beneath Sutton Bank was the home of one of the most famous of modern Yorkshire craftsmen, Robert Thompson – the '**Mouseman of Kilburn**'. Robert's father was a carpenter but he apprenticed his son to an engineer. At the age of 20 however, inspired by seeing the medieval wood carvings in Ripon

---

83 WHITE SWAN

Ampleforth

One of the finest pubs in North Yorkshire; a glorious menu which is to be tasted to be believed.

See entry on page 227

---

84 THE FAIRFAX ARMS

Gilling East

Eat, drink and sleep at the highest quality, surrounded by the gorgeous Yorkshire countryside.

See entry on page 228

---

85 WOMBWELL ARMS

Wass

A privately owned free house, which provides the ideal place to stay for lovers of fine ale and delicious food.

See entry on page 229

---

86 MOUSEMAN VISITOR CENTRE

Kilburn

The new Mouseman Visitor Centre will take you on an amazing journey through the life and times of the Mouseman from humble beginnings to furniture legend. Horse in the distance

See entry on page 230

Cathedral, Robert returned to Kilburn and begged his father to train him as a carpenter. An early commission from Ampleforth Abbey to carve a cross settled his destiny: from then until his death in 1955 Robert's beautifully crafted ecclesiastical and domestic furniture was in constant demand. His work can be seen in more than 700 churches, including Westminster Abbey and York Minster. Each piece bears his 'signature' – a tiny carved mouse placed in some inconspicuous corner of the work. According to a family story, Robert adopted this symbol when one of his assistants happened to use the phrase 'as poor as a church mouse'. (Signing one's work wasn't an entirely new tradition: the 17th-century woodcarver Grinling Gibbons' personal stamp was a pod of peas). Robert Thompson's two grandsons have continued his work and their grandfather's former home is now both a memorial to his genius and a showroom for their own creations.

You can see several of the Mouseman's creations in Kilburn village church – there's one perched on the traceried pulpit, another clinging to a desk in the sanctuary, and a third sitting cheekily on the lectern.

From the northern end of the village a winding lane leads to the famous **White Horse**, inspired by the prehistoric White Horse hill-carving at Uffingham in Berkshire. John Hodgson, Kilburn's village schoolmaster, enthused his pupils and villagers into creating this splendid folly in 1857. It is 314 feet long and 228 feet high and visible from as far away as Harrogate and Otley. Unlike its prehistoric predecessor in Berkshire, where the chalk hillside keeps it naturally white, Kilburn's 'White' horse is scraped from grey limestone which needs to be regularly groomed with lime-washing and a liberal spreading of chalk chippings.

HARROGATE

At the heart of this elegant town is the Montpellier Quarter with its abundance of exclusive shops (especially antiques shops), pavement cafés, bars, up-market restaurants and the celebrated Betty's Café tea room. Adjoining this area is the Stray, an area of open parkland some 200 acres (800,000 m2) in size which was created back in 1778 when Harrogate was thriving as the most successful spa town in the north of England. On the Stray, a small pillared and domed building marks the spot where this prosperity was engendered - the site of the Tewitt Well. It was around 1590 that William Slingsby of Bilton Hall near Knaresborough was out walking his dog and discovered a spring bubbling up out of the rock. Tasting the waters, Slingsby found them to be similar to those he had tasted at the fashionable wells of Spaw, in Belgium. Expert opinion was sought and, in 1596, Dr Timothy Bright confirmed the spring to be a chalybeate well and the waters to have medicinal powers – curing a wide variety of illness and ailments from gout to vertigo.

Slingsby's well became known as **Tewit Well**, after the local name for peewits. Other wells were also found in the area, St John's Well in 1631 and the **Old Sulphur Well** which went on to become the most famous of Harrogate's springs. Though this spring had been known locally for years, it was not until

Tewit Well, Harrogate

1656 that the sulphurous, vile-smelling waters, nicknamed 'the Stinking Spaw', began to attract attention. Bathing took place in the evening and, each morning, the patients would drink a glass of the water with their breakfasts. The cupola over the well was erected in 1804.

In order to serve the growing number of people arriving at Harrogate seeking a cure for their ailments, the Queen's Head Hotel was built around 1680. When stagecoaches began to arrive in the 18th century the inn moved with the times and became the first at the spa to serve the needs of the coaches. Many other hotels were built including the Crown Inn, next to the Old Sulphur Well, which became a coaching inn in 1772 and hosted a visit by Lord Byron in 1806. In 1858, Charles Dickens visited the town and described it as 'the queerest place, with the strangest people in it leading the oddest lives of dancing, newspaper reading, and table d'hôte.'

One of the town's most famous hotels, The Majestic, an Edwardian red brick building, survives and was where Edward Elgar stayed while visiting Harrogate. But perhaps the best known Harrogate hotel is The Old Swan. It was here in 1926 that the famous crime writer Agatha Christie took refuge after staging a car accident and disappearing. and sparking off the biggest man-hunt of the time with more than 1000 police and civilians were called in to scour Agatha's local area. It was the first search in England to use aeroplanes.

After 10 days, Bob Tappin, a local banjo player, recognised the author and alerted the police. Colonel Christie was informed and immediately came to collect his wife. Agatha kept her husband waiting before joining him

Pump Room, Harrogate

for dinner, putting her disappearance down to total memory loss caused by the car accident. She had checked in under the name of Theresa Neele - the name of her husband's mistress! It was generally believed that his infidelity and the recent death of her mother had caused her to stage her disappearance. Two years later the couple divorced and Colonel Christie married his mistress. In 1977, the film *Agatha,* starring Dustin Hoffman and Vanessa Redgrave was shot on location at the Old Swan and in the Harrogate area.

The **Royal Pump Room Museum** was built in 1842 to enclose the Old Sulphur Well and this major watering place for spa visitors has been painstakingly restored to illustrate all the aspects of Harrogate's history. Beneath the building the sulphur water still rises to the surface and can be sampled.

There will be few Harrogate residents who have not heard of Betty Lupton, the almost legendary 'Queen of the Wells' who, for over 50 years, dispensed the spa waters, dishing out cupfuls to paying visitors, who were then encouraged to walk off the dubious effects of the medicine by taking a trip around the Bogs Fields, known today as **Valley Gardens**. She conducted her business in the ostentatiously named **Royal Baths Assembly Rooms** which,

---

87 LE JARDIN

Harrogate

In a well loved location overlooking the gardens on Montpellier Parade this bistro is known for its fine food and great hospitality.

See entry on page 230

---

88 ALEXA HOUSE

Harrogate

Comfortable accommodation and outstanding hospitality in an elegant period house a short walk from Harrogate's many attractions.

See entry on page 231

in their heyday, were full of rich visitors sampling the waters. Today, the buildings have been restored to house the **Turkish Baths** where visitors can enjoy a sauna, beauty treatment and massage. The baths are open to the public daily.

Occupying the oldest of the town's surviving spa buildings, originally built in 1806, is the **Mercer Art Gallery**. The Promenade Room has been restored to its former glory and displays a superb collection of fine art along with the Kent Bequest – an archaeological collection that includes finds from both ancient Greece and Egypt.

One of England's most attractive towns and a frequent winner of Britain in Bloom, Harrogate features acres of gardens that offer an array of colour throughout the year, open spaces, and broad tree-lined boulevards. Though its status as a spa town declined following the introduction of the National Health Service, Harrogate is still a fashionable place, a sought after conference location and home of the annual Northern Antiques Fair and the Great Yorkshire Show.

As well as a spa, Harrogate developed into a centre for shopping for the well-to-do and the many old-fashioned shops are typified by Montpellier Parade, a crescent of shops surrounded by trees and flowerbeds. At its heart is an imposing War Memorial designed by Sir Edward Lutyens.

Another attractive aspect of the town is **The Stray**, which is unique to Harrogate and virtually encircles the town centre. The 215 acres of open space are protected by ancient law to ensure that the residents of, and visitors to, the town always have access for sports, events, and walking. The spacious lawns are at their most picturesque during the spring when edged with crocus and

daffodils. Originally part of the Forest of Knaresborough the land was, fortunately, not enclosed under the 1770 Act of Parliament. On The Stray stands the Commemorative Oak Tree, planted in 1902 by Samson Fox to commemorate the ox roasting that took place here as part of the celebrations for Queen Victoria's Jubilee in 1887 and at the end of the Boer War in 1902.

One of Harrogate's major visitor attractions is the **RHS Harlow Carr Botanical Gardens,** just over a mile from the town centre. Established in 1948 by the Northern Horticultural Society and now covering some 58 acres, the gardens feature all manner of plants in a wide variety of landscapes which allows members of the public to see how they perform in the unsympathetic conditions of northern England. The society has also opened a fascinating **Museum of Gardening** and the spring of 2010 saw the opening of a new Learning Centre, designed to be carbon neutral and one of the greenest buildings in the country.

A major summer event is the **Great Yorkshire Show,** a three day event that includes top class show-jumping, displays and demonstrations of various kinds, some 10,000 animals, miles of shopping, a flower show and much, much more.

AROUND HARROGATE

HAMPSTHWAITE

4 miles NW of Harrogate off the A59

This picturesque Nidderdale village lies on an ancient Roman way between Ilkley and Aldborough and traces of Roman tin mining have been found in the area. The village Church of St Thomas has remnants of a Saxon building in the tower and, in the churchyard, is buried Peter Barker. Known as 'Blind Peter', Barker did not let his disability hinder him: he was a skilled cabinet-maker, glazier and musician. The mysterious portrait of the bearded man hanging in the church, painted by the local vicar's daughter, may well be of Blind Peter.

89 MERCER ART GALLERY

Harrogate
The Mercer Art Gallery is home to the district's superb collection of fine art.

See entry on page 231

ALDBOROUGH

4 miles NW of Harrogate off the A59

The ancient Roman town of Isurium Brigantum, or Aldborough, as it is known today, was once the home of the 9th Legion, who wrested it from the Celtic Brigantian tribe. The modern-day focal point of the village is the tall maypole on the village green, around which traditional dances take place each May. At one end of the green is a raised platform which is all that remains of the Old Court House. It bears an inscription recalling that up to 150 years ago the election of members of Parliament was announced here. Below are some well-preserved stocks that are, in fact, only replicas of the originals. The **Aldborough Roman Museum** houses relics of the town's past. This was once a thriving Roman city of vital strategic importance and near the museum are some of the original walls and tessellated pavements of that city.

BURNT YATES

4½ miles NW of Harrogate on the B6165

Located at one of the highest points in Nidderdale, Burnt Yates enjoys some fine views of the surrounding hills and moors. Its tiny village school of 1750 still stands. The original endowment provided for 30 poor boys to be taught the three Rs and for an equivalent number of poor girls to learns the skills of needlework and spinning.

BIRSTWITH

5 miles NW of Harrogate off the B6165

Evidence in the form of a Neolithic axe-head suggests that this one-time estate village in the valley of the River Nidd was a Stone Age settlement in what was to become known as the Forest of Knaresborough. Along with both quarrying and coal-mining, Birstwith also had a cotton mill beside the river – though all that now remains is the weir that was created to ensure a good head of water for the mill-race. One notable visitor to this village was Charlotte Brontë, who stayed with the Greenwood family at Swarcliffe Hall

for about six months in the 1840s, when she was governess to the children. The Hall is now a private boys' school.

RIPLEY

3 miles N of Harrogate off the A61

Twenty-four generations of the Ingilby family have lived at Ripley and in 2010 celebrate 700 years of continuous residence. The family fortune was established when Thomas Ingilby was awarded a knighthood for killing a wild boar in Knaresborough Forest that was charging at King Edward III. The first **Ripley Castle** was built around 1450 but only the sturdy Gatehouse of that building has survived, a worthy portal now to the lovely

Ripley Castle

Tudor and Georgian house beyond. The most striking feature is the Old Tower which has sumptuous old rooms with wood-panelled walls and massive fireplaces. Elsewhere are a priest's hole, only discovered in 1964, richly decorated plaster ceilings, fine paintings, chine, furniture and a magnificent collection of armour and weapons. The castle is set in an outstanding 'Capability Brown' landscape, with lakes, a deer park, and an avenue of tall

90 RIPLEY CASTLE

Ripley

For almost 700 years the Ingilby family has loved their castle and no wonder, given its fabulous treasures, and glorious grounds.

See entry on page 232

beeches over which the attractive towers only just seem to peek. There's also a large Victorian Walled Garden where 150,000 bulbs flower in spring.

During the Civil War the Ingilbys supported the king. Sir William Ingilby and his sister, Jane, both fought on the Royalist side at the disastrous battle of Marston Moor in 1644. After the defeat, they returned to Ripley only do discover that Cromwell himself intended to stay the night there. He received a chilly reception from the Ingilbys; they offered neither food nor a bed. Jane Ingilby, aptly named 'Trooper Jane' due to her fighting skills, was the house's occupant and, having forced the self-styled Lord Protector of England to sleep on a sofa with two pistols pointing at his head, declared the next morning, 'It was well that he behaved in so peaceable a manner; had it been otherwise, he would not have left the house alive.' Cromwell, his pride severely damaged by a woman ordered the immediate execution of his Royalist prisoners and left Trooper Jane regretting staying her hand during the previous night.

In the outer walls of the parish church, built around 1400, are holes said to have been caused by musket balls from Cromwell's firing squad who executed Royalist prisoners here after the battle of Marston Moor. Inside, there is a fine Rood Screen dating from the reign of King Stephen, a mid-14th-century tomb chest, and the stone base of an **Old Weeping Cross** (where one was expected to kneel in the stone grooves and weep for penance) survives in the churchyard.

Ripley, still very much an estate village, is a quiet and pretty place to explore. The unusual architecture is the legacy of Sir William Amcotts Ingilby who in 1827 began to remodel the entire village on one he had seen in Alsace-Lorraine. The original thatched cottages were replaced with those seen today and Sir William even named the Town Hall in French style as the Hotel de Ville.

KNARESBOROUGH

4 miles NE of Harrogate on the A59

This ancient town of pantiled cottages and

Georgian houses is precariously balanced on a hillside by the River Nidd. A stately railway viaduct, 90 feet high and 338 feet long, completed in 1851, spans the gorge. There are many unusual and attractive features in the town, among them a maze of steep stepped narrow streets leading down to the river and numerous alleyways. In addition to boating on the river, there are many enjoyable riverside walks.

The town is dominated by the ruins of **Knaresborough Castle**, built high on a crag overlooking the River Nidd by Serlo de Burgh, who had fought alongside William the Conqueror at Hastings. Throughout the Middle Ages, the castle was a favourite with the court and it was to Knaresborough that the murderers of Thomas à Becket fled in 1170. Queen Philippa, wife of Edward III, also enjoyed staying at Knaresborough and she and her family spent many summers here. However, following the Civil War, during which the town and its castle had remained loyal to the king, Cromwell ordered the castle's destruction.

Also within the castle is the **Old Courthouse Museum** which tells the history of the town and houses a rare Tudor Courtroom. The nearby Bebra Gardens are named after Knaresborough's twin town in Germany and its attractive flower beds are

91 THE GROVES

Knaresborough

A popular establishment offering home made food, bright and contemporary en-suite bedrooms and quality entertainment.

See entry on page 233

92 YE OLDE CHYMIST SHOPPE AND THE LAVENDER ROOMS

Knaresborough

Downstairs, Ye Olde Chymist Shoppe draws in locals and visitors with a sweet tooth while upstairs, the quality, busy and bustling Lavender Rooms seats 38 diners.

See entry on page 232

complemented by luxurious lawns and a paddling pool.

In the Market Square look out for Ye Oldest Chemist's Shop in England which was first recorded in 1720 although the building is probably a hundred years older. The old chemist's drawers, each marked with the scientific name of its contents, are still in place but the pungent potions have been replaced by a wide selection of quality confectionery.

Conyngham Hall, Knaresborough

Knaresborough boasts not only the oldest chemist's shop, but also the oldest tourist attraction in the UK, **Mother Shipton's Cave**, which opened in 1630. It was the birthplace of the famous prophetess and its Petrifying Well has fascinated visitors for generations. The effects that the well's lime-rich water has on objects are truly amazing and an array of paraphernalia, from old boots to bunches of grapes, are on view – seemingly turned to stone. It is little wonder that these were considered magical properties by the superstitious over the centuries or that the well was associated with witchcraft and various other interesting tales.

The foremost tale concerns Mother Shipton, who was said to have been born in a cave next to the well on 6th July 1488 and who has the reputation of being England's most famous fortune-teller. The story says that she was born in the midst of a terrible storm and was soon found to have a strange ability to see the future. As she grew older her prophetic visions became more widely known and feared throughout England. However, the most singular feature about Mother Shipton has to be that she died peacefully in her bed, as opposed to being

burnt at the stake as most witches were at that time.

She had been threatened with burning by, among others, Cardinal Wolsey, when she had warned him on a visit to York that he might see the city again but never enter. True to her prediction Wolsey never did enter York, for he was arrested on a charge of treason at Cawood. Among her many other prophesies she reputedly foretold the invasion and defeat of the Spanish Armada in 1588 and Samuel Pepys recorded that it was Mother Shipton who prophesied the disastrous Great Fire of London in 1666.

While in Knaresborough, it is well worth taking the opportunity to visit the **House in the Rock** hewn out of solid rock by Thomas Hill, an eccentric weaver, between 1770 and 1786. It was Hill's son who renamed the house Fort Montagu and flew a flag and fired a gun salute on special occasions. On the banks of the River Nidd there is also **St Robert's Cave** which is an ancient hermitage. St Robert was the son of a mayor of York who, at the time of his death in 1218, was so beloved that the people of Knaresborough would not allow the monks of Fountains Abbey to bury him. Instead they kept his bones and finally interred him in a place near the altar in the **Chapel of Our Lady of the Crag**. It is guarded by the statue of a larger than life-size figure of a knight in the act of drawing his sword.

In the tradition of this town's reputation for odd characters is 'Blind Jack of Knaresborough'. Jack Metcalfe was born in 1717 and lost his sight at the age of six, but went on to achieve fame as a roadmaker. He was a remarkable person who never allowed

---

93   MOTHER SHIPTON'S CAVE

Knaresborough
Mother Shipton is England's most famous Prophetess. She lived some 500 years ago during the reigns of King Henry VIII and Queen Elizabeth I.

See entry on page 234

his blindness to bar him from any normal activities – he rode, climbed trees, swam, and was often employed to guide travellers through the wild Forest of Knaresborough. He was a talented fiddle player and one of his more roguish exploits was his elopement with Dolly Benson, the daughter of the innkeeper of the Royal Oak in Harrogate, on the night before she was due to marry another man. His most memorable achievement however, was the laying of roads over the surrounding bogs and marshes which he achieved by laying a foundation of bundles of heather, a technique that had never been used before. A **Statue of Blind Jack** in the Market Place, across from Blind Jack's pub has him reclining at his ease on a pavement bench.

Another of Knaresborough's attractive amenities is **Conyngham Hall,** a majestic old house enclosed within a loop of the River Nidd. Once the home of Lord Macintosh, the Halifax toffee magnate, the Hall itself is not open to the public but its landscaped grounds, stretching down to the river, are and provide tennis, putting and other activities.

A mile or so to the south of Knaresborough, **Plumpton Rocks** are popular as an ideal picnic spot. There's an idyllic lake surrounded by dramatic millstone grit rocks and woodland paths that were laid out in the 18th century. It has been declared a garden of special historic interest by English Heritage and is open every weekend, on public holidays, and daily from March to October.

GOLDSBOROUGH

5 miles E of Harrogate off the A59

This rather special village was an estate village from the time of the Norman Conquest until the 1950s when it was sold by the Earl of Harewood to pay enormous death duties. The charming 12th-century **Church of St Mary** has some interesting features including a Norman doorhead and an effigy of a knight. It is also a 'green man church' and the image of the Celtic god of fertility, with his oak-leafed head, is well hidden on one of the many Goldsborough family tombs. In 1859, while the church was being restored, a lead casket was discovered containing Viking jewellery and

coins. In the 1920s, Mary, the daughter of George V and Queen Mary, lived in the village after her marriage and her eldest son, George, was christened in the church.

SPOFFORTH

4½ miles SE of Harrogate on the A661

This ancient village, situated on the tiny River Crimple, is home to the splendid Palladian mansion, **Stockeld Park**, built between 1758 and 1763 by Paine. Containing some excellent furniture and a fine picture collection, the house is surrounded by extensive parkland which offers garden walks. Though privately owned, the house is open by appointment.

Spofforth Castle (English Heritage) is another place of note, an historic building whose sight stirs the imagination, despite its ruined state. The powerful Percy family originally built the castle here in the 16th century to replace the manor house which had been repeatedly laid to waste. The castle itself is now a crumbling ruin after it was destroyed during the Civil War. According to some accounts, the castle was the birthplace of Harry Hotspur.

BECKWITHSHAW

3 miles SW of Harrogate on the B6161

This village, as its name suggests, was once bounded by a stream and woodland though, sadly, most of the trees are now gone. It was once part of the great Forest of Knaresborough and a local legend tells how John O'Gaunt promised John Haverah, a cripple, as much land as he could hop around between sunrise and sunset. By throwing his crutch the last few yards, just as the sun was setting, John Haverah managed to secure himself seven square miles, the remainder of which is today called Haverah Park.

RIPON

Dominating the skyline of this attractive small city is the magnificent **Cathedral of St Peter and St Wilfrid,** the 'Cathedral of the

Dales'. It was founded in 672AD by St Wilfrid who built a church on the high ground between three rivers, the Ure, the Shell and the Laver. It was a remarkable building for its time, built of stone and beautifully adorned with glorious craftsmanship. One relic of that time was discovered in the cathedral grounds in 1976. Known as the Ripon Jewel,it is a small gold roundel inlaid with gemstones and may have been part of a cross or casket. It is currently held in the cathedral treasury. contains the beautiful **Ripon Jewel** found close to the cathedral in 1976. Otherwise, all that remains of St Wilfrid's church is the Crypt, a tiny atmospheric space with, at its northeast corner, a narrow passage known as 'The Needle'. According to the 17th century antiquary, Thomas Fuller, single women whose chastity was suspect were made to squeeze through it. If they were unable to do so, their reputations were irretrievably compromised. "They pricked their credit" Fuller wrote "who could not thread the Needle".

Although it one of the tallest cathedrals in England, Ripon is also the smallest. Begun in the mid-12th century by Archbishop Roger of York, its west front with its twin towers was added in the mid-13th century and is, in Nikolaus Pevsner's opinion, "the finest west front in England". The east choir was completed in 1286, and there was further rebuilding in the early 1600s. Its status was still that of a collegiate church and it was not until the creation of the Diocese of Ripon in 1836 that it was upgraded to a cathedral.

Throughout the Middle Ages, Ripon prospered: its market charter had been granted by King Alfred in the 9th century and, at one time, Ripon produced more woollen cloth than Halifax and Leeds. The

collapse of the woollen industry saw a rise in spur manufacture in the 16th century and their fame was such that Ripon spurs were referred to in the old proverb: 'As true steel as a Ripon rowel.'

Fortunately, for today's visitor, the Industrial Revolution, and all its associated implications, by-passed Ripon and it was not until the early 20th century that the town flourished, though briefly, as a spa. However, many ancient customs and festivals have survived down the centuries. Perhaps the most famous is the sounding of the 'Wakeman's Horn' each night at 9pm in the marketplace. Dating back to the 9th century, the Wakeman was originally appointed to patrol the town after the nightly curfew had been blown and, in many ways, this was the first form of security patrol. The Wakeman was selected each year from the town's 12 aldermen and those choosing not to take office were fined heavily. Today, this old custom is revived in the Mayor-making Ceremony when the elected mayor shows great reluctance to take office and hides from his colleagues.

The heart of the city is the Market Place where the most distinctive feature is a lofty obelisk which was erected in 1702 to replace the market cross. Restored in 1781, at its summit are a horn and a rowel spur, symbolizing Ripon's crafts and customs. Situated at the edge of the square are the picturesque, half-timbered 14th-century **Wakeman's House** and the attractive Georgian **Town Hall**.

The Spa Baths building, opened in 1905 by the Princess of Battenberg, is a reminder of Ripon's attempt to become a fashionable spa resort. With no spring of its own, the town had to pipe in sulphur mineral water from Aldfield near Fountains Abbey. However, the scheme failed, though the building, which now houses the city's swimming pool, is a fine example of art nouveau architecture. The **Ripon Spa Gardens** with its 18-hole putting course, flat green bowling, nine hole crazy golf, tennis courts, bandstand and café, is still a pleasant place for a stroll.

Near the cathedral is Ripon's old **Courthouse** that was built in 1830 on the site

---

94 **THE WATER RAT**

Ripon

In an idyllic location on the banks of the river in the city of Ripon; this inn is known for fine dining and excellent hospitality.

See entry on page 234

Ripon Workhouse

of an earlier (17th-century) Common Hall, used for the Quarter Sessions and the Court Military. Adjacent to this fine Georgian courthouse is a Tudor building that was part of the Archbishop of York's summer palace.

Also not far from the cathedral is the House of Correction, built in 1686 which served as the local prison between 1816 and 1878 and then became the police station until the late 1950s. This austere building is now home to the **Prison and Police Museum**, established in 1984, which depicts the history of the local police force as well as giving visitors a real insight into the life of a prisoner in Victorian times. Almost as unfortunate as those prisoners were the inmates of **Ripon Workhouse**, the city's most recent museum. The restored vagrants' wards of 1877 provide a chilling insight into the treatment of paupers in Yorkshire workhouses and the displays include a 'Victorian Hard Times Gallery'.

Horse racing at Ripon dates back to 1713 and the present course opened in 1900. Meetings are held between April and August and the course is widely regarded as one of the most beautiful in the country.

AROUND RIPON

WATH

4 miles N of Ripon off the A1

Although closed for major repairs throughout

2010, the stately home of **Norton Conyers,** just to the south of Wath, is expected to re-open for the 2011 season. Dating back to the mid-1300s, with Tudor, Stuart and Georgian additions,, has been owned by the Graham family since 1624 - with just one break. In 1865, the 7th baronet's extravagance forced him to sell the house. Fortunately, his son's marriage to an heiress enabled him to buy it back 17 years later.

Undoubtedly, the house's main claim to fame is the visit made by Charlotte Brontë in 1839. During her stay here the novelist heard the story of Mad Mary, supposedly a Lady Graham. Apparently Lady Graham had been locked up in an attic room, now tantalisingly inaccessible to the public. Charlotte eventually based the character of Mrs Rochester in her novel *Jane Eyre* on this unfortunate woman. Visitors to the hall will also see the famous painting of Sir Bellingham Graham on his bay horse, as Master of the Quorn hunt. It is rumoured that ownership of the painting was once decided on the throwing of a pair of dice. Other family pictures, furniture and costumes are on display and there's a lovely 18th-century walled garden within the grounds which will remain open through 2010.

SKELTON

3 miles SE of Ripon off the B6265

This charming little village has some surviving cottages, dating from 1540, which are built from small handmade bricks with pantiled roofs. A ferry used to cross the River Ure, at this point, to Bishop Monkton and, in 1869, it was the scene of a notorious hunting accident. Members of the York and Ainsty

---

95 NORTON CONYERS HALL AND GARDENS

Norton Conyers, nr Ripon

The house is set in a fine park. The large 18th century walled garden has herbaceous borders flanked by yew hedges, and an Orangery with an attractive little pool in front of it.

See entry on page 235

Hunt boarded the ferry in order to follow a fox that had swum across the river. Half way across the horses panicked, capsizing the boat, and the boatman, along with five hunt members, were drowned. Just outside the village is **Newby Hall,** one of the area's finest stately homes. It was built in the 18th century and designed by Robert Adam. Much of the house is open to the public including the splendid Billiard Room with its fine portrait of Frederick Grantham Vyner. An ancestor of the family that has lived here since the mid-1800s, Frederick was murdered by Greek bandits after having been kidnapped. The house is perhaps most famous for its superb tapestries and there is also a fine collection of Chippendale furniture.

Another major attraction here is the 25 acres of award-winning gardens. It was the present owner's father who transformed a 9-hole golf course into these delightful grounds which also contain a Woodland Discovery Walk, a miniature railway, plenty of attractions for children, a plant stall, shop and restaurant.

BOROUGHBRIDGE

7 miles SE of Ripon on the B6265

In the last two years Boroughbridge Marina, on the River Ure, has also gone from strength to strength, its berths full and with a healthy waiting list to boot.

The bridge over the River Ure, from which this attractive and historic town takes its name, was built in 1562 and formed part of an important road link between Edinburgh and London. Busy throughout the coaching days with traffic passing from the West Riding of Yorkshire to the North, Boroughbridge is now bypassed by the A1(M) and has returned to its former unassuming role of a small wayside town. It boasts a goodly number of Georgian houses and inns.

In Hall Square, the former open-fronted Butter Market has been developed into a small museum of locally made or locally used artefacts. The exhibits range from an early 19th century bread oven to railway memorabilia and dairy equipment from local farms.

On the western outskirts of the town, beside Roecliffe Lane, rise the **Devil's Arrows**, three massive Bronze Age monoliths which form Yorkshire's most famous ancient monument. Thought to date from around 2000BC, the tallest is 22 feet high, higher than anything at Stonehenge. The monoliths stand in a line running north-south and are fashioned from millstone grit which has been seriously fluted by weathering. A local legend attributes the great stones to the Devil suggesting that they were, actually, crossbow bolts that he fired towards nearby Aldborough which, at the time, was a Christian settlement.

STUDLEY ROGER

2 miles SW of Ripon off the B6265

The only World Heritage Site in Yorkshire, **Fountains Abbey** (National Trust) is the most

---

96 NEWBY HALL & GARDENS

Skelton, nr Ripon

Newby Hall and Gardens, near Ripon in North Yorkshire, is one of England's renowned Adam Houses, and home to spectacular treasures and antiques as well as 25 acres of stunning landscaped gardens.

See entry on page 235

---

97 THE BLACK BULL INN

Boroughbridge

This is a historic inn full of character and traditional features with a modern twist. It offers great accommodation, traditional favourites and real ales.

See entry on page 236

---

98 THORPE LODGE B&B

Littlethorpe, nr Ripon

A listed Georgian building with large bedrooms and a superb garden.

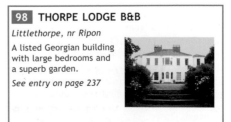

See entry on page 237

sublime of all the ecclesiastical ruins in Yorkshire. The remains are also the most complete of any Cistercian abbey in Britain. Founded in 1132, the first buildings housed just 12 monks of the order. The abbey reached its peak in the 15th century with the grandiose designs of Abbot Marmaduke Huby, whose beautiful tower still stands as a reminder of just how rich and powerful Fountains became. In fact, the abbey was run on such businesslike lines that, at its

Fountains Abbey

height, as well as owning extensive lands throughout Yorkshire, it had an income of about £1000 a year, then a very substantial sum indeed.

Studley Royal Water Gardens in

which still stands in the abbey's grounds and part of which is open to the public.

The magnificent **Studley Royal Gardens**, also National Trust, were created in the early 18th century before they were merged with nearby Fountains Abbey in 1768. Started by John Aislabie, Chancellor of the Exchequer and founder of the South Sea Company that spectacularly went bust in 1720, the landscaping took some 14 years. It then took a further 10 years to complete the construction of the buildings and follies found within the gardens. With a network of paths and the River Skell flowing through the grounds, these superb gardens. Provide a magical experience.

NORTH STAINLEY

4½ miles NW of Ripon on the A6108

Just to the south of the village, the **Lightwater Valley Theme Park** is set in 175 acres of scenic grounds. The Park boasts 'Ultimate' – the biggest roller-coaster in the world (authenticated by the *Guinness Book of Records*), the Rat Ride,

The Dissolution hit the abbey as it did all the powerful religious houses. The abbot was hanged, the monks scattered, and its treasures taken off or destroyed. The stonework, however, was left largely intact, possibly due to its remote location. In 1579, Sir Stephen Proctor pulled down some of its outbuildings, in order to construct **Fountains Hall**, a magnificent Elizabethan mansion

99 THE GRANTLEY ARMS

Grantley, nr Ripon

This hidden gem is definitely a must if you are visiting the area. It is well known for its stunning location, quality food, ale and hospitality.

See entry on page 238

Falls of Terror, and the Viper to name just a few and there are also plenty of more appropriate activities for younger children. Also within the grounds is a Bird of Prey Centre, and Lightwater Village which offers a wide variety of retail and factory shops, a garden centre, restaurant and coffee shop.

KIRKBY MALZEARD

6 miles NW of Ripon off the A6108

Dating back to the 11th century, the **Church of St Andrew** is noted for its associations with witchcraft. Apparently, the north-eastern corner of the churchyard was favoured by practitioners of the black arts for conducting their strange rituals and charms. Black magic aside, the church has been pealing its bells for more than 400 years and records show that in 1591 one of the bells was recast – the process taking place inside the church building.

This traditional Yorkshire village is also one of the few places in the country that can boast its own Sword Dance. Certainly a pagan ritual, thought to date back to prehistoric times, the performance of the dance is supposed to make the grass grow tall and to wake the earth from her winter's sleep.

Many of the farms around the village are dairy farms and at Kirby Malzeard Dairy they still produce the traditionally made Coverdale cheese. Very much a local speciality, it is one of the few remaining Dales' cheeses still made though, at one time, each dale had its own particular variety.

WEST TANFIELD

6 miles NW of Ripon on the A6108

This attractive village on the banks of the River Ure is home to a remarkable Tudor

---

100	**THE BULL INN**

West Tanfield

A former coaching inn with comfortable accommodation and a menu offering a fine selection of appetising dishes.

See entry on page 239

---

gatehouse known as the **Marmion Tower**. Overlooking the river and with a beautiful oriel window, the tower is open to the public. For many years, West Tanfield was associated with the powerful Marmion family and the 14th-century Church of St Nicholas contains many effigies commemorating the family.

Though the purpose of the **Thornborough Circles**, which lie just outside the village, remains a mystery, these late Neolithic or early Bronze Age oval earthworks are very impressive, especially from the air.

GREWELTHORPE

6½ miles NW of Ripon off the A6108

Just outside the village, at 850ft above sea level, is the **Himalayan Garden & Sculpture Park** which has a fine display of the rarer and more unusual varieties of Species and Hybrid Rhododendrons as well as Azaleas, Magnolias, Cornus and other Himalayan plants. The plants are for sale, as are the sculptures of which there are 150 pieces. Opening times are restricted but visits can be made by appointment.

North of the village are the beautiful **Hackfall Woods** through which the River Ure flows. During the 19th century the Victorians developed the woodland, creating waterfalls and transforming the 18th-century follies that had been built here into splendid vantage points. Following a period of neglect which began with the sale of the woodland in the 1930s, the Hackfall Woods are now in the care of the Woodland Trust and the area is being gradually restored to its 19th-century condition.

WELL

8 miles NW of Ripon off the B6267

This pretty village takes its name from St Michael's Well which was already being venerated long before the Romans came here and one of them built a spacious villa near the well. Part of the tessellated pavement of that villa is now on display in the parish church, which is itself a venerable building with foundations that date back to Norman times. The church's greatest treasure is a font cover dating from 1325, one of the oldest in the country. It was a gift to the church from Ralph Neville, Lord of Middleham, who also founded the line of almshouses near the church which were rebuilt by his descendants in 1758.

MASHAM

9 miles NW of Ripon on the A6108

Set beside the River Ure, Masham (pronounced *Massam*) is a very picturesque place with a huge marketplace at its heart. The ancient Church of St Mary stands in one corner, a school founded in 1760 in another, while at the centre is the market cross surrounded by trees and flowers. The size of the marketplace reflects Masham's historical importance as a market town and its position, between the sheep-covered hills and the corn growing lowlands, certainly helped to support its flourishing trade. The sheep fairs held in the town in the 18th and 19th centuries were among the largest in the country and in September the **Masham Sheep Fair** revives those heady days, giving visitors the chance of seeing many rare breeds of sheep and goats as well as witnessing events such as dog agility and sheep racing.

The town is famed for its beer, boasting two celebrated breweries – Theakston's and Black Sheep. **Theakston's Brewery**, noted for its Old Peculier brew, was founded in 1827 by two brothers, Thomas and Robert. Adjoining the brewery today is a modern visitor centre which illustrates the process of brewing and the art of cooperage. Those taking the tour (which must be pre-booked) should be aware that there are two flights of steep steps along the route and the tour is not suitable for children under 10. Interestingly, the name of the famous brew derives from the fact that Masham in medieval times had its own Peculier Court (meaning special rather than odd) – an ecclesiastical body with wide-ranging powers.

The **Black Sheep Brewery** is also well worth a visit. It is owned by another Theakston, Paul, who is the 5th generation of this famous brewing family. The vessels, plants and methods employed here are from a bygone age and currently produce seven different ales, including a Monty Python Holy Grail ale which was specially commissioned to celebrate the 30th anniversary of the cult comedy series. The brewery also offers a guided tour and visitors get the chance to sample the traditionally made ales. In addition to the working brewery, the old Maltings building is home to a 'sheepy' shop and a popular bistro.

ILTON

9½ miles NW of Ripon off the A6108

This village is close to one of the area's most interesting and unusual features – the **Druid's Temple**. Though the name suggests that this was an ancient meeting place for pagan worshippers, the charming folly was built in the 1820s by William Danby of the nearby Swinton Estate. Resembling a miniature Stonehenge, the folly was inspired by a similar temple Danby saw on his travels in Europe and his building project was intended to provide work for local unemployed people. It is considered one of the best Druidic follies in the country. From Ilton village it can be reached by following part of the long-distance footpath known as the Ripon Rowel Walk.

---

101 **FANCY THAT TEA ROOM**

Masham

It is the smell of home cooking that attracts people to this delightful establishment in the historic town of Masham.

See entry on page 240

---

102 **THEAKSTON BREWERY & VISITOR CENTRE**

Masham

A guided tour will take you through the brewing process at the famous Theakston Brewery.

See entry on page 240

SNAPE

9½ miles NW of Ripon off the B6268

This quiet and unspoilt village, where the original timber-framed cottages stand side by side with their more modern neighbours, is still dominated by its castle as it has been for centuries. Reached via an avenue of lime trees, **Snape Castle** has a famous, if somewhat complicated, royal connection as it was the home of Lord Latimer of Snape (a member of the Neville family), the first husband of Catherine Parr, Henry VIII's last wife. The Nevilles owned the castle for more than 700 years and its beautiful chapel, still used by the villagers, saw the marriages of many Latimers and Nevilles.

Set in over 1000 acres of parkland, **Thorp Perrow Arboretum** is unique to Britain, if not Europe, in that it was the creation of one man, Colonel Sir Leonard Ropner (1895-1977). Sir Leonard travelled all over the world collecting rare and unusual species for Thorp Perrow and today the hundreds of trees he enthusiastically collected are in their prime. The arboretum was initially Sir Leonard's private hobby but after his death his son, Sir John Ropner, decided to open the 85-acre garden to the public and the arboretum is now one of the area's prime attractions. A treasure trove of specimen trees, woodland walks, nature trail, tree trails, a large lake, picnic area and children's play area, the arboretum also embraces the Milbank Pinetum, planted by Lady Augusta Milbank in the mid-19th century, and the medieval Spring Wood dating back to the 16th century. Thorp Perrow provides interest all year round but perhaps the most popular time is the spring when you can witness one of the finest and most extensive plantings of daffodils in

Snape Castle

the north of England, among them some old and unusual varieties. In addition to the fascinating collection of trees, visitors will also find an information centre, a tea room and a plant sales area.

An additional attraction at Thorp Perrow is the **Bird of Prey & Mammal Centre** a bird-of-prey, captive-breeding and conservation centre which has been created within a large, formerly derelict walled garden. There are more than 75 birds from all continents of the world and regular flying demonstrations three times a day, weather permitting. The recently opened Mammal Centre shelters a variety of animals with red squirrels, meerkats and wallabies amongst the most popular with visitors.

---

103 **THORP PERROW ARBORETUM, WOODLAND GARDEN AND FALCONRY CENTRE**

Snape

Thorp Perrow Arboretum is one of the finest private collections of trees and shrubs in the country.

See entry on page 241

THIRSK

This pleasing market town has become famous as the home of veterinary surgeon Alf Wight, better known as James Herriot, author of *All Creatures Great and Small*, who died in 1995. In his immensely popular books, Thirsk is clearly recognisable as 'Darrowby'. A £1.4m tribute to the celebrated vet. **The**

World of James Herriot, is housed in his original surgery in Kirkgate and offers visitors a trip back in time to the 1940s, exploring the life and times of the world's most famous country vet. There's also the opportunity to take part in a TV production, and a Visible Farm exhibit where you can explore farm animals inside and out!

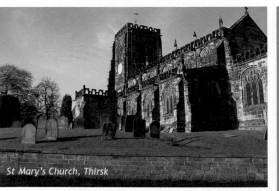
St Mary's Church, Thirsk

Just across the road from the surgery is the birthplace of another famous son of Thirsk. The building is now the town's Museum and a plaque outside records that Thomas Lord was born here in 1755: 30 years later he was to create the famous cricket ground in Marylebone that took his name. A more recent celebrity whose home was in Thirsk was Bill Foggitt (died Sep 2004, aged 91), renowned for his weather forecasts based on precise observations of nature.

This pleasant small town of mellow brick houses has a sprawling Market Place and the magnificent 15th-century **St Mary's Church** which is generally regarded as the finest parish church in North Yorkshire. It was here that the real life 'James Herriot' married his wife, Helen. Cod Beck, a tributary of the River Swale, wanders through the town, providing some delightful – and well-signposted riverside walks.

Thirsk appeared in the *Domesday Book* not long after William the Conqueror had granted the Manor of Thirsk to one of his barons, Robert de Mowbray. The Mowbrays became a powerful family in the area, a fact reflected in the naming of the area to the north and west of Thirsk as the Vale of Mowbray. In the early 1100s the family received permission to hold a market at Thirsk but then blotted their copybook by rebelling against Henry II in 1173. The rebellion failed and their castle at Thirsk was burnt to the ground. Not a trace of it remains. The market however is still thriving, held twice-weekly on Mondays and Saturdays. An old market by-law used to stipulate that no butcher be allowed to kill a bull for sale in the market until the beast had been baited by the town dogs. That by-law was abandoned in the early 1800s and the bull-ring to which the animal was tethered has also disappeared.

Thirsk's **Ritz Cinema,** first opened in 1912 as The Picture House, is unusual in that it is run entirely by volunteers. The original

---

104 THE BLACK LION BAR AND BISTRO

Thirsk

Beautiful refurbishment and exquisite cuisine awaits in this stylish bar and bistro with specialty game menu all year round.

See entry on page 242

---

105 THE WORLD OF JAMES HERRIOTT

Thirsk

The original and cosy home of James Herriot providing a fascinating insight into his life.

See entry on page 241

---

106 THE ANGEL INN

Topcliffe, nr Thirsk

This attractive inn offers fabulous pub grub, real ales, en suite guest accommodation and a beautiful function room in the heart of Thirsk.

See entry on page 243

balcony seating arrangements have been retained but the screen and equipment are all very up-to-date.

On the edge of Thirsk, housed in a mid-Victorian maltings, **Treske** specialises in producing bespoke furniture and designer upholstery fabrics. Among Treske's most notable commissions are some 400 chairs for the OBE chapel in St Paul's Cathedral, bedroom furniture for the College of St George's, Windsor Castle, and period replica furniture for the monks' cells at Mount Grace Priory. The showrooms are open daily and group tours of the workshop are available by arrangement.

On the outskirts of the town is **Thirsk Racecourse,** known to devotees of the turf as the 'Country Racecourse'. There are around 12 race meetings each year.

AROUND THIRSK

BOLTBY

5 miles NE of Thirsk, off the A170

Boltby is an engaging village tucked away at the foot of the Hambleton Hills, close to where the oddly-named Gurt of Beck tumbles down the hillside and, depending on how much rain has fallen on the moors, passes either under or over a little humpback bridge. On the plain below is Nevison House, reputed to be the home of the 17th-century highwayman, William Nevison, 'Swift Nick' as Charles II dubbed him. Some historians claim that it was Swift Nick, not Dick Turpin, who made the legendary ride on Black Bess from London to York to establish an alibi.

SUTTON-UNDER-WHITESTONECLIFF

3 miles E of Thirsk on the A170

Boasting the longest place-name in England, Sutton is more famous for the precipitous cliff that towers above it, **Sutton Bank**. For one of the grandest landscape views in England, go to the top of Sutton Bank and look across the vast expanse of the Vale of York to the Pennine hills far away to the west. The real-life James Herriot called it the 'finest view in England'. He knew this area well since his large veterinary practice covered the farms from here right over to the Dales. A continuation of the Cleveland Hills, the Hambleton Hills themselves lead into the Howardian Hills: together they form the mighty southwest flank of the North York Moors.

There's a National Park Information Centre at the summit of Sutton Bank and a well-marked Nature Trail leads steeply down to, and around, **Lake Gormire**, an Ice Age lake trapped here by a landslip. Gormire is one of Yorkshire's only two natural lakes, the other being Semerwater in Wensleydale. Gormire is set in a large basin with no river running from it: any overflow disappears down a 'swallow hole' and emerges beneath White Mare Cliffs.

Sutton Bank used to be a graveyard for caravans because of its steep (1 in 3) climb and sharp bends. On one July Saturday in 1977, some 30 vehicles broke down on the ascent and five breakdown vehicles spent all day retrieving them. Caravans are now banned from this route. Sutton Bank may be tough on cars but its sheer-sided cliffs create powerful thermals making this a favoured spot for gliders and bright-winged hang-gliders.

Lake Gormire, Sutton-under-Whitestonecliff

SOWERBY

1 mile S of Thirsk on the B1448

Georgian houses stand beside a majestic avenue of lime trees, an old packhorse bridge crosses Cod Beck, footpaths lead across fields and the quiet stream provides a peaceful refuge. All-in-all, an attractive village.

KIRBY WISKE

4 miles NW of Thirsk off the A167

Sion Hill Hall, about four miles northwest of Thirsk, is celebrated as the 'last of the great country houses'. Its light, airy and well-proportioned rooms, all facing south, are typical of the work of the celebrated Yorkshire architect, Walter Brierley - the 'Lutyens of the North'. He completed the building in 1913 for Percy Stancliffe and his wife Ethel, the wealthy daughter of a whisky distiller. The rooms haven't altered one bit since they were built, but the furniture and furnishings certainly have. In 1962, the Hall was bought by Herbert Mawer, a compulsive but highly discerning collector of antiques. During the 20 years he lived at Sion Hill, Herbert continued to add to what was already probably the best collection of Georgian, Victorian and Edwardian artefacts in the north of England. Furniture, paintings, porcelain, clocks (all working), and ephemera, crowd the 20 richly furnished rooms and make Sion Hill a delight to visit. A recent addition to the many sumptuous displays is a charming exhibition of dolls from the early 1900s. Visits are by prior arrangement only and the guided tour takes about one hour. Refreshments, served in the original kitchen, are included.

NORTHALLERTON

The county town of North Yorkshire, Northallerton boasts a grand medieval church, a 15th-century almshouse and, of more recent provenance, a majestic County Hall built in 1906 and designed by the famous Yorkshire architect Walter Brierley. The oldest private house in Northallerton is Porch House which bears a carved inscription with the date 1584. Charles I stayed here as a guest in 1640 and returned seven years later as a prisoner.

The town's broad High Street is almost half a mile long and is typical of the county's market towns. (Wednesday and Saturday are the market days here.) In stage coach days Northallerton was an important stop on the Great North Road and several old coaching inns still stand along the High Street. The most ancient is The Old Fleece, a favoured drinking haunt of Charles Dickens during his several visits to the town. It's a truly Dickensian place with great oak beams and a charming olde-worlde atmosphere. The Old Fleece recalls the great days of the stage coach which came to an abrupt end with the arrival of the railway in 1840. One day in 1847, a coach called the *Wellington* made the whole of the 290-mile journey from Newcastle to London, via Northallerton, completely empty. The era of this romantic - if uncomfortable and extremely expensive - mode of transport was over.

Northallerton has many old buildings of interest, including an ancient Grammar School whose history goes back to at least 1322. The school was rebuilt in 1776 at the northern end of the High Street - a building that is now a solicitors' office. By the end of the 19th century the school had 'no great reputation' and by 1902 only 13 pupils were registered. Things went from bad to worse the next year when the headmaster was convicted of being drunk and disorderly. Fortunately, the school, now **Northallerton College** and in new buildings, has recovered its reputation for academic excellence.

Two miles north of the town of Northallerton, a stone obelisk beside the A167 commemorates the **Battle of the Standard,** fought here in 1138. It was one of the countless conflicts fought between the English and the Scots, and also one of the bloodiest with more than 12,000 of the Scots, led by King David, perishing under a rain of English arrows. The battle took its name from the unusual standard raised by the English: the mast of a ship mounted on a wagon and, crowning its top, a pyx containing the consecrated Host.

Danby Wiske Village Green

AROUND NORTHALLERTON

DANBY WISKE

4 miles NW of Northallerton off the A167 or B6271

This pleasant little village takes its name from the Danby family, once great landowners with huge properties across North Yorkshire, and the little River Wiske. It has a moated former rectory and a village green overlooked by a traditional hostelry, The White Swan.

CATTERICK VILLAGE

9 miles NW of Northallerton off the A1

This is an ancient settlement with an attractive village green and a nearby race-course which, every Sunday, hosts the largest street market in England. Ever since the time of the Romans, when the settlement was known as *Cataractonium*, Catterick has been

associated with the armed forces. Located on the Roman highway between London and Hadrian's Wall, the garrison was also close to the place where Paulinus, Bishop of York baptised 10,000 Christians in the River Swale. Today, the army garrison (the largest in Europe) is some three miles to the west. RAF Leeming lies just south of the village.

Catterick's connections with Lord Nelson are not immediately obvious but it was Alexander Scott, vicar of Catterick in 1816 who was at the admiral's side when he died at Trafalgar. Also, Nelson's sister-in-law, Lady Tyrconnell lived at nearby **Kiplin Hall,** a beautiful Jacobean country house famed for its wonderful interior plasterwork and medieval fishponds. The hall also contains many mementoes of Nelson and Lady Hamilton. On display in the Blue Room is a folding library chair from Nelson's cabin on *HMS Victory*. The hall also has a strong American connection since it was built by the 1st Lord Baltimore who was instrumental in founding the state of Maryland whose capital city bears his name.

---

108 THE BRIDGE HOUSE HOTEL

Catterick Bridge

This grand 15th century hotel commands a stunning location on the banks of the River Swale with a reputation for high standards in all areas.

See entry on page 245

---

107 THE WHITE SWAN INN

Danby Wiske

A 17th century traditional inn, popular with walkers. Offers real ales and ensuite accommodation.

See entry on page 244

---

109 THE LAKESIDE COUNTRY CAFE

Ellerton upon Swale, nr Catterick

Gorgeous hidden gem offering delicious home-made food, and a range of clothing and gifts from independent retailers.

See entry on page 246

MOULTON

11 miles NW of Northallerton off the A1

This small village is home to two fine 17th-century manor houses that were built by members of the Smithson family. The Manor House, in the village centre, was originally built in the late-16th century and was improved greatly in the mid-17th century. Just to the south stands **Moulton Hall**, built by George Smithson following his marriage to Eleanor Fairfax in 1654. Similar in size to the original Smithson family home and somewhat resembling it, this elegant manor house with its beautiful carved staircase is now in the hands of the National Trust. Visits are by arrangemnt with the tenant, Viscount Eccles

MIDDLETON TYAS

12 miles NW of Northallerton off the A1

Situated in a sheltered position yet close to the Great North Road, the position of the village church, away from the village centre and at the end of a long avenue of trees seems strange. However, when the Church of St Michael was built it served not only Middleton Tyas but also Moulton and Kneeton (the latter no longer in existence), between which Middleton lay.

ALDBROUGH

14 miles NW of Northallerton off the B6275

To the west of the village lies the enormous complex of earthworks known as **Stanwick Camp**. The series of banks and ditches were excavated in the 1950s and their discovery also revealed that the constructions had been carried out in the 1st century. The site, open to the public, is now owned by English Heritage.

110 KING WILLIAM IV INN

Barton

A traditionally styled community inn known for its delicious Yorkshire food and unusual entertainment.

See entry on page 247

PIERCEBRIDGE

17 miles NW of Northallerton on the A67

This picturesque village in upper Teesdale was once an important Roman fort – part of a chain of forts linking the northern headquarters at York with Hadrian's Wall. (Another fort in the chain can be found to the south, at Catterick.) The Romans are thought to have originally chosen Piercebridge as a suitable river crossing back in 70AD, when Cerialis attacked the British camp at Stanwick. The extensive remains of the fort can be dated from coin evidence to around 270AD. The site is always open, though the finds from the excavations are housed in the Bowes Museum at Barnard Castle.

BEDALE

7½ miles SW of Northallerton on the A684

Bedale's broad and curving main street leads to the beautiful parish **Church of St Gregory** at the northern end. Recorded in the *Domesday Book* and incorporating architectural styles from the 12th to the 14th centuries, the building has a fine fortified tower and a striking medieval wall-painting of a left-handed St George. Just inside the churchyard is an old building dating from the mid-1600s which served as a school in the

111 THE PANTRY

Bedale

This tea room is extremely popular with lovers of home cooking. It has a fine reputation for its friendly hospitality and homemade food.

See entry on page 248

112 THE BAY HORSE INN

Crakehall

Attractive village inn known for its fine brand of hospitality, delicious pies and real ales.

See entry on page 248

18th century.

Across the road from the church is **Bedale Hall,** a Grade I listed Palladian-style mansion with a superb ballroom. The Hall houses the town library and local museum. The north front of the building is a particularly fine example of the Georgian architecture which gives Bedale its special character. Within the grounds of the Hall is an 18th century Ice House, an underground chamber where ice was stored in winter for use during the summer months. Another building of interest, at the other end of the town, is the 18th-century **Leech House** beside the beck, so called because it was once used by the local chemist to store his leeches.

Leech House, Bedale

This pleasant little market town with its many fine Georgian buildings and old coaching inns developed around the point where the Saxon track from Ripon joined the route from Northallerton to Wensleydale. Traders met here and in 1251 Henry III granted a charter for a weekly market every Tuesday which still flourishes today. The market cross still stands at the top of Emgate, a narrow street leading from the river to the marketplace.

CRAKEHALL

8½ miles SW of Northallerton on the A684

Crakehall has a huge village green with a small church, a 16th century pub and an enormous former country seat of the Duke of Leeds, Crakehall Hall (private), overlooking it. Part of the 5-acre green serves as the village's cricket pitch and is in regular use during the summer.

Sometime around 1090AD the *Domesday Book* commissioners arrived in Crakehall and noted details of a mill on the beck that runs through this picturesque village. More than 900 years later there's still a mill on the very same spot. The present Crakehall Water Mill building dates from the 1600s; its mighty machinery from the 18th and 19th centuries. The Mill was still working until 2003 but at

the time of writing it is not open to the public on a regular basis.

OSMOTHERLEY

5 miles NE of Northallerton off the A19

Long-distance walkers will be familiar with this attractive moorland village since it is the western starting point for the **Lyke Wake Walk** which winds for more than 40 miles over the moors to Ravenscar on the coast. At the centre of the village is a heavily carved cross and, next to it, a low stone table which was probably once a market stall and also served John Wesley as a pulpit.

About a mile northeast of the village, **Mount Grace Priory** (English Heritage & National Trust) is quite unique among Yorkshire's ecclesiastical treasures. The 14th-century building set in tranquil surroundings was bought in 1904 by Sir Lothian Bell who decided to rebuild one of the well-preserved cells, a violation of the building's 'integrity' that would provoke

113 MOUNT GRACE PRIORY

Saddlebridge

In this unusual monastery, the best-preserved priory of the Carthusian order in Britain, you can see how hermit-monks lived 600 years ago.

See entry on page 248

Mount Grace Priory, Osmotherley

14th-century monastic house. The Carthusians were an upper-class order whose members dedicated themselves to solitude – even their meals were served through an angled hatch so they would not see the servant who brought them. Most visitors find themselves fascinated by Mount Grace's sanitary arrangements which were ingeniously designed to take full advantage of a nearby spring and the sloping site on which the Priory is built. Along with discovering what life was like for a monk in this almost hermit-like order, visitors can also wander around the remains of the Great Cloister and outer court, and see the new monks' herb garden designed specifically to aid contemplation and spiritual renewal. Mount Grace Priory is open all year though times are limited in the winter months.

howls of outrage from purists if it were proposed today. When English Heritage inherited the Carthusian Priory, however, it decided to go still further by reconstructing other outbuildings and filling them with replica furniture and artefacts to create a vivid impression of what life was like in a

LOCATION MAP

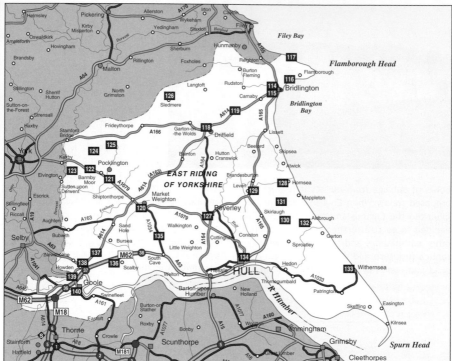

EAST YORKSHIRE

The south-eastern corner of Yorkshire tends to be overlooked by many visitors. If only they knew what they were missing. Beverley is one of the most beguiling of Yorkshire towns and its Minster one of the greatest glories of Gothic architecture. The whole town has the indefinable dignity you might expect from a community that was a capital of the East Riding in former days when Hull, just six miles to the south, was still a rather scruffy little port.

To the east and south of Beverley lies the old Land of Holderness, its character quite different from anywhere else in Yorkshire. A wide plain, it stretches to the coast where for aeons the land has been fighting an incessant, and losing, battle against the onslaught of North Sea billows. The whole length of the Holderness coast is being eroded at an average rate of three inches a year, but in some locations up to three feet or more gets gnawed away. At its southernmost tip, Spurn Point curls around the mouth of the Humber estuary, a cruelly exposed tip of land whose contours get re-arranged after every winter storm. The coastal towns and villages have a bleached and scoured look to them, perhaps a little forbidding at first. It doesn't take long however for visitors to succumb to the appeal of this region of wide vistas, secluded villages and lonely shores.

Further north, the Wolds are a great crescent of chalk hills that sweep round from the coast near Flamborough Head to the outskirts of Hull. There were settlers here some 10,000 years ago – but never very many. In the early 1700s, Daniel Defoe described the area as 'very thin of towns and people' and also noted the 'great number of sheep'. Little has changed: the Wolds remain an unspoilt tract of scattered farmsteads and somnolent villages with one of the lowest population densities in the country. Artists remark on the striking quality of the light and air, and on the long views that open up, across undulating hills to the great towers of the Minster at York. The Wolds never rise above 800 feet but the open landscape makes them particularly vulnerable to winter snowstorms: children have been marooned in their schools, the dipping and twisting country roads, even in recent years, have been blocked for weeks at a time.

The area boasts some magnificent coastal scenery, notably at Flamborough Head and at Bempton Cliffs with their countless colonies of birds. Inland are some magnificent stately homes, including medieval Wressle Castle, the Elizabethan gems of Burton Agnes and Burton Constable halls, the noble Georgian pile of Sledmere House and the Victorian extravaganza of Carlton Towers.

BRIDLINGTON

This bustling seaside resort with its manifold visitor amusements and attractions has been understandably popular since early Victorian times. The attractions include a vast, 10-mile stretch of sandy beach, a busy harbour where fishing boats land their catches on the quayside, and a wealth of amusements. Bayside Pleasure Park caters for all ages; Gasworx Skatepark is a huge state-of-the-art park for skateboarding, rollerblading and BMX biking.

Then there's **Beside the Seaside**, an all-weather venue where visitors can take a promenade through Bridlington's heyday as a resort, sampling the sights, sounds and characters of a seaside town. Film shows and period amusements such as antique coin-in-the-slot games and a Punch & Judy Show, displays reconstructing a 1950s boarding house as well as the town's maritime history – the museum provides a satisfying experience for both the nostalgic and those with a general curiosity about the town's past. The museum is owned and run by a body called the Lords Feoffees, a charitable trust established in 1636.

Penny arcades were once an indispensable feature of seaside resorts. At the **Old Penny Memories Museum** you can see 'What the Butler Saw', have your fortune told, test your strength on the Minigrip, discover your matrimonial prospects, pit your skills against a pinball machine, and enjoy a host of other entertainments on the extensive collection of antique slot machines – and all for just one old penny each. There's also a sixties café with lots of colourful memorabilia of the period.

At the **Bridlington Harbour Museum** the main exhibit is the traditional sailing coble *Three Brothers* which was built in 1912 and is moored in the harbour. The museum displays photographs, a diorama of fishing techniques and a video presentation. There's also an art gallery where paintings by local artists can be purchased.

Lovers of the Art Deco style should find a reason to visit to the Royal Hall at **The Spa Bridlington**. The ballroom and theatre are exquisitely adorned in the short-lived 1930s fashionable vogue. The Spa has recently had a multi-million-pound redevelopment and was re-launched as the East Coast's premier entertainment venue in the spring of 2008. It hosts concerts by top bands, quality drama, dancing, exhibitions, music and more. Outside The Spa, the Spa Gardens are currently undergoing a £6.7m upgrade.

Bridlington's multifarious attractions distract most visitors from the Old Town which lies half a mile inland from the beach. Narrow, medieval streets are lined with unspoilt buildings many of which are now tea rooms, speciality and antiques shops. Also within the Old Town is **Bridlington Priory** which was one of the wealthiest in England until it was ruthlessly pillaged during the Reformation. Externally it is somewhat unprepossessing, but step inside and the majestic 13th-century nave is unforgettably impressive.

A corner of the Priory churchyard recalls one of the most tragic days in the town's history. During a fearsome gale in January 1871, a whole fleet of ships foundered along the coast. Bridlington's lifeboat was launched but within minutes it was "smashed to matchwood"; most of its crew perished. Twenty bodies were washed ashore and later

---

114 THE GEORGIAN ROOMS

Bridlington

Browse through the antiques centre, or relax in the tea rooms and garden with some award winning treats.

See entry on page 249

---

115 BURLINGTON'S RESTAURANT

Bridlington

A great husband and wife team run this well loved restaurant famed for its delicious English cuisine with continental twists.

See entry on page 249

buried in the churchyard here; it was estimated that 20 times as many souls found a watery grave. This awesome tragedy is still recalled each year with a solemn service of remembrance and the lifeboat is drawn through the town.

Sewerby Hall, Bridlington

Another dangerous event, though fortunately not fatal, occurred during Queen Henrietta Maria's visit to Bridlington in February 1643. She landed here on a Dutch ship laden with arms and aid for her beleaguered husband, Charles I. Parliamentary naval vessels were in hot pursuit and having failed to capture their quarry, bombarded the town. Their cannon balls actually hit the Queen's lodging. Henrietta was forced to take cover in a ditch where, as she reported in a letter to her husband, 'the balls sang merrily over our heads, and a sergeant was killed not 20 paces from me.' At this point Her Majesty deemed it prudent to retreat to the safety of Boynton Hall, three miles inland and well beyond the range of the Parliamentary cannons.

These stirring events, and many others in the long history of Bridlington and its people, are vividly brought to life with the help of evocative old paintings, photographs and artefacts in the **Bayle Museum**. Quite apart from its fascinating exhibits the museum is well worth visiting for its setting inside the old gatehouse to the Priory, much of it built in the late 12th century. The museum is owned and run by a charitable trust called the Lords Feoffees, who also run Beside the Seaside in the New Town.

On the north-eastern outskirts of Bridlington is **Sewerby Hall**, a monumental mansion built on the cusp of the Queen Anne

and early Georgian years, between 1714 and 1720. Set in 50 acres of garden and parkland (where there's also a small zoo), the house was purchased by Bridlington Borough Council in 1934 and opened to the public two years later by Amy Johnson, the dashing, Yorkshire-born pilot who had captured the public imagination by her daring solo flights to South Africa and Australia. The Museum of East Yorkshire here houses some fascinating memorabilia of Amy's pioneering feats along with displays of motor vehicles, archaeological finds and some remarkable paintings among which is perhaps the most famous portrait, painted by Van Dyck, of Queen Henrietta Maria, wife of Charles I. Queen Henrietta loved this romantic image of herself as a young, carefree woman, but during the dark days of the Civil War she felt compelled to sell it to raise funds for the doomed Royalist cause which ended with her husband's execution. After passing through several hands, this haunting portrait of a queen touched by tragedy found its last resting place at Sewerby Hall.

Other amenities at Sewerby Hall include a pitch and putt course, putting green, children's play area, tearooms, craft units and a souvenir and gift shop.

Close by is **Bondville Miniature Village**, one of the finest model villages in the country. The display includes more than 1000 hand-made and painted characters, over 200 individually crafted buildings, and carefully created scenes of everyday life, all set in a beautifully landscaped one acre site. The Village is naturally popular with children who

---

116 SEWERBY HALL AND GARDENS

Sewerby

Sewerby Hall is situated 2 miles northeast of the seaside resort of Bridlington, on the East Yorkshire coast.

See entry on page 250

are fascinated by features such as the steam train crossing the tiny river and passing the harbour with its fishing boats and cruisers.

AROUND BRIDLINGTON

FLAMBOROUGH

4 miles NE of Bridlington on the B1255.

At **Flamborough Head,** sea and land are locked in an unremitting battle. At the North Landing, huge, foam-spumed waves roll in between gigantic cliffs, slowly but remorselessly washing away the shoreline. Paradoxically, the outcome of this elemental conflict is to produce one of the most picturesque locations on the Yorkshire coast, much visited and much photographed.

Flamborough has a long and lively maritime history, not least for being the site of one of the most stubborn naval battles in British history. It was fought in the waters off Flamborough Head between an American squadron led by John Paul Jones and two British ships of war. Spectators on the coast were transfixed by this intense battle that eventually led to the defeat of the British, when British Captain Pearson surrendered his sword to John Paul Jones. Shortly afterwards, Jones's ship began to sink and he was lucky to escape with his life.

Victorian travel writers, in their time, also came to appreciate and honour Flamborough, not just for its dramatic setting but also for its people. They were so clannish and believed in such strange superstitions. No boat would ever set sail on a Sunday; wool could not be wound in lamplight; anyone who mentioned a hare or pig while baiting the fishing lines was inviting doom. No fisherman would leave harbour unless he was wearing a navy-blue jersey, knitted by his wife in a cable, diamond mesh peculiar to the village and still worn today. Every year the villagers would slash their way through Flamborough in a sword-dancing frenzy introduced here in the 8th century by the Vikings. Eventually, local fishermen grew weary of this primitive role so although the sword dance still takes place it is now performed by boys from the primary school, wearing white trousers, red caps and the traditional navy-blue jerseys.

Flamborough's parish church contains two particularly interesting monuments. One is the **Tomb of Sir Marmaduke Constable** which shows him with his chest cut open to reveal his heart being devoured by a toad. The knight's death in 1518 had been caused, the story goes, by his swallowing the toad which had been drowsing in Sir Marmaduke's lunchtime pint of ale. The creature then devoured his heart. The other notable monument is a statue of St Oswald, patron saint of fishermen. This fishing connection is renewed every year, on the second Sunday in October, by a service dedicated to the **Harvest of the Sea,** when the area's seafarers gather together in a church decorated with crab pots and fishing nets.

Flamborough Head's first, and England's oldest surviving **lighthouse,** is the octagonal chalk tower on the landward side of the present lighthouse. Built in 1674, its beacon was a basket of burning coal. The lighthouse that is still in use was built in 1806. Originally signalling four white flashes, developments over the years have included a fog horn in 1859 and, in more recent years, a signal of radio bleeps. Until it was automated in 1995, it was the last manned lighthouse on the east coast. Visitors can take a 20-minute tour, climb the 119 winding steps and gaze out from the lantern room.

Flamborough Head

Boat trips around the lighthouses are also available during the season.

The South Landing area of Flamborough Head is designated as a Local Nature Reserve and an attractive feature here is the **Sculpture Trail**. There are currently 16 sculptures made from various materials and the subjects include two donkeys hand-crafted with cement, a Totem Pole intricately carved with objects associated with the sea, and various living willow sculptures. Each of the sculptures was inspired by tales told by local people drawing on the area's local history.

Just to the north of Flamborough is **Danes Dyke,** a huge rampart 4 miles long designed to cut off the headland from hostile invaders. The Danes had nothing to do with it, the dyke was in place long before they arrived. Sometime during the Bronze or Stone Age, early Britons constructed this extraordinary defensive ditch. A mile and a quarter of its southern length is open to the public as a Nature Trail.

BEMPTON

3 miles N of Bridlington on the B1229

Bempton Cliffs, 650 feet high at their loftiest point, mark the most northerly tip of the great belt of chalk that runs diagonally across England from the Isle of Wight to Flamborough Head. The sheer cliffs at Bempton provide an ideal nesting place for huge colonies of fulmars, guillemots, puffins and Britain's largest seabird, the gannet, with a wingspan six feet wide. In Victorian times, a popular holiday sport was to shoot the birds from boats. Above them, crowds gathered to watch gangs of 'climmers' make a hair-raising descent by rope down the cliffs

Bempton Cliffs

to gather the birds' eggs. Most were sold for food, but many went to egg collectors. The climmers also massacred kittiwakes in their thousands: kittiwake feathers were highly prized as accessories for hats and for stuffing mattresses. The first Bird Protection Act of 1869 was specifically designed to protect the kittiwakes at Bempton. A ban on collecting eggs here didn't come into force until 1954. Bempton Cliffs are now an RSPB bird sanctuary, a refuge during the April to August breeding season for more than 200,000 seabirds making this the largest colony in England. The RSPB provides safe viewpoints allowing close-up watching and there's also a visitor centre, shop and refreshments.

BARMSTON

5 miles S of Bridlington off the A165

The road leading from Barmston village to the sands is just over half a mile long: in Viking times it stretched twice as far. The whole of this coast is being eroded at an average rate of three inches every year, and as much as three feet a year in the most vulnerable locations. Fortunately, that still leaves plenty of time to visit Barmston's village pub before it tumbles into the sea!

CARNABY

2 miles SW of Bridlington on the A614

A short drive from Bridlington along the A614 will bring you to **John Bull - World of Rock** which has become a premier tourist attraction in this part of East Yorkshire and really is a great day out. Whether you are

---

117 **RSPB'S BEMPTON CLIFFS NATURE RESERVE**

Bempton Cliffs

Part of England's largest seabird colony, visitors can watch the birds here, among which are puffins and gannets.

See entry on page 250

young or old, you will be fascinated as you discover the history and delights of rock making. The older generation will particularly revel in the smell of the old-fashioned way of making toffee and the interesting bygone displays. Animation and taped conversation accompany you as you explore the establishment which is described as a total sensory experience. You can even try your hand at making a personalised stick of rock. Next door is John Bull's Candy Kingdom, a well-equipped indoor adventure play area.

Burton Agnes Hall

Also in Carnaby, set in 3½ acres of natural woodland, is the **Park Rose Owl & Bird of Prey Centre**, home to a variety of eagle owls, hawks, buzzards, vultures and owls. There are daily flying displays, weather permitting, and the centre runs courses on falconry.

BURTON AGNES

5 miles SW of Bridlington on the A166

The overwhelming attraction in this unspoilt village is the sublime Elizabethan mansion, Burton Agnes Hall, but visitors should not ignore **Burton Agnes Manor House** (English Heritage), a rare example of a Norman house: a building of great historical importance but burdened with a grimly functional architecture, almost 800 years old, that chills one's soul. As Lloyd Grossman might say, 'How could anyone live in a house like this?'

Burton Agnes Hall is much more appealing. An outstanding Elizabethan house, built between 1598 and 1610 and little altered, Burton Agnes is particularly famous for its splendid Jacobean gatehouse, wondrously decorated ceilings and overmantels carved in oak, plaster and alabaster. It also has a valuable collection of paintings and furniture from between the 17th and 19th centuries – including a portrait of Oliver Cromwell 'warts and all' – and a large collection of Impressionist paintings. The gardens are extensive with more than 2000 plants, a maze and giant board games in the Coloured Gardens. Other visitor facilities include an ice cream parlour, a dried-flower and herb shop, a children's animal corner, and an artists' studio. A very popular addition is the plant sales where numerous uncommon varieties can be obtained. The Impressionist Café, open throughout the Hall's season, seats 64 inside and, in good weather, 56 outside. Licensed and offering only the very best in home cooking, the café serves some particularly delicious scones.

FOSTON ON THE WOLDS

7 miles SW of Bridlington off the B1249 or A165

If you can't tell a Gloucester Old Spot from a Saddleback, or a Belted Galloway from a Belgian Blue, then take a trip to **Cruckley Animal Farm** where all will become clear. This working farm supports many different varieties of cattle, sheep, pigs, poultry and horses. Some of the animals are endangered – Greyfaced Dartmoor and Whitefaced Woodland Sheep, for example, and the farm also safeguards all seven breeds of rare British pigs.

The farm has been approved by the Rare Breeds Survival Trust since 1994 and is the only farm in East Yorkshire to achieve this accolade. Enormously popular with children, the 60-acre farm is home to more than 50 varieties of farm animals. There are daily milking demonstrations, seasonal events such as sheep-clipping and harvesting, and a children's paddock with hand-reared small animals where the undoubted star is Cecil the Vietnamese pot-bellied pig.

RUDSTON

4 miles W of Bridlington on the B1253

'Fold upon fold of encircling hills, piled rich and golden' – such was the author Winifred Holtby's fond memory of the Wolds landscape around Rudston where she was born in 1898. The village is dominated by the prehistoric **Rudston Monolith**. This colossal block of stone, a daunting symbol of some misty pagan belief, stands challengingly close to Rudston's Christian parish church. Twenty-five feet (7.6m) high, it is the tallest standing stone in Britain. Winifred Holtby left the village and became a leading figure in London literary circles, editor of the influential magazine *Time and Tide*, but in her own books it was those 'rich and golden hills' that still enthralled her. In her most successful novel, *South Riding*, the fictional Riding is unmistakably recognisable as the Wolds among whose gently rolling acres she had spent her childhood.

Rudston Monolith

GREAT DRIFFIELD

Located on the edge of the Wolds, Great Driffield is a busy little market town at the heart of an important corn growing area. A cattle market is held here every Thursday; a general market on both Thursday and Saturday. All Saints Parish Church, dating back to the 12th century, has one of the highest towers in the county and some lovely stained glass windows portraying local nobility.

The town hosts a variety of events throughout the year. These nclude The Yorkshire Trucking Spectacular held in May, The Yorkshire Motoring Festival and the Driffield Agricultural Show which has been held in July each year since 1854. It attracts some25,000 visitors and is reckoned to be the largest one day agricultural show in England. Also in July is the Festival Week which culminates in a colourful parade through the streets of decorated floats. Then in August the Annual Traction Rally features a cavalcade of machines driving through the Town Centre along with vintage vans and lorries.

Great Driffield was once the capital of the Saxon Kingdom of Dear, a vast domain extending over the whole of Northumbria and Yorkshire. It was a King of Dear who, for administrative convenience, divided the southern part of his realm into three parts, 'thriddings', a word which gradually evolved into the famous 'Ridings' of Yorkshire.

AROUND GREAT DRIFFIELD

HARPHAM

4½ miles NE of Great Driffield off the A614

To the south of this village, where a manor

---

118 INSPIRATION CAFÉ BAR

Driffield

A delightful café run by a friendly family offering tasty homecooked treats.

See entry on page 251

---

119 ST QUINTIN ARMS

Harpham

This is a picturesque and child friendly village pub. Food, real ales and accommodation are all available.

See entry on page 251

house once stood, stands **Drummers Well** which gained its interesting name during the 14th century. Then, the Lord of the Manor, in the midst of holding an archery day, accidentally pushed his drummer boy into the well, where he subsequently drowned. The boy's mother, who was also the local wise woman, on hearing the news proclaimed that from then on the sound of drumming from the well would precede the death of any member of the lord's family.

KIRKBURN

3 miles SW of Great Driffield on the A614

The architectural guru Nikolaus Pevsner considered **St Mary's Church** in Kirkburn to be one of the two best Norman parish churches in the East Riding. Dating from 1119, the church has an unusual tower staircase, a richly carved and decorated Victorian screen, and a spectacular early Norman font covered with carved symbolic figures.

MILLINGTON

12 miles SW of Great Driffield off the B1246

A popular and pleasant walk leads from this tiny hamlet of old cottages and farmhouses to **Millington Woods.** This ancient ash woodland is a nature reserve teeming with all kinds of wildlife.

NUNBURNHOLME

13 miles SW of Great Driffield off the A1079

This small village close to the Yorkshire Wolds Way was named after the Benedictine nuns who first settled here. The village has a 1000-year-old Saxon cross elaborately carved with arches, animals and representations of the Madonna. It was also here that the famous ornithologist the Reverend Francis Orpen Morris was born. Heavily influenced by the 18th -century naturalist Gilbert White, Morris penned the multi-volumed *History of British Birds.*

SOUTH DALTON

13 miles SW of Great Driffield off the B1248

The most prominent church in East Yorkshire,

St Mary's Church, has a soaring spire more than 200 feet high, an unmistakable landmark that has been described as 'an arrow in the breast of the Wold'. Built in 1861 for Lord Beaumont Hotham, the church was designed by the famous Victorian architect JL Pearson and is regarded as one of his best works.

GOODMANHAM

14 miles SW of Great Driffield off the A1079

Goodmanham is always mentioned in accounts of early Christianity in northern England. During Saxon times, according to the Venerable Bede, there was a pagan temple at Goodmanham. In 627AD its priest, Coifu, was converted to the Christian faith and with his own hands destroyed the heathen shrine. Coifu's conversion so impressed Edwin, King of Northumbria, that he also was baptised and made Christianity the official religion of his kingdom. Other versions of the story attribute King Edwin's conversion to a different cause. They say he was hopelessly enamoured of the beautiful Princess Aethelburh, daughter of the King of Kent. Aethelburh, however, was a Christian and she refused to marry Edwin until he had adopted her faith.

MARKET WEIGHTON

16 miles SW of Great Driffield on the A614/A1069

Recorded in the *Domesday Book* as 'Wicstun', Market Weighton is a busy little town where mellow 18th-century houses cluster around an early Norman church and a Green with a duck pond. Buried somewhere in the churchyard is William Bradley who was born at Market Weighton in 1787 and grew up to become the

tallest man in England. He stood 7 feet 8 inches high and weighed 27 stones. William made a fortune by travelling the country and placing himself on display. He was even received at Court by George III who, taking a fancy to the giant, gave him a huge gold watch to wear across his chest.

POCKLINGTON

14 miles SW of Great Driffield off the A1079

Set amidst rich agricultural land with the Wolds rising to the east, Pocklington is a lively market town with an unusual layout of twisting alleys running off the marketplace. Its splendid church, mostly 15th century but with fragments of an earlier Norman building, certainly justifies its title as the Cathedral of the Wolds (although strictly speaking Pocklington is just outside the Wolds). William Wilberforce went to the old grammar school here and, a more dubious claim to fame, the last burning of a witch in England took place in Pocklington in 1630.

Founded in Anglo-Saxon times by 'Pocela's people', by the time the *Domesday Book* was compiled Pocklington was recorded as one of the only two boroughs in the East Riding. A market followed in the 13th century, but it was the building in 1815 of a canal linking the town to the River Ouse, and the later

arrival of the railway, that set the seal on the town's prosperity.

The people of Pocklington have good reason to be grateful to Major P. M. Stewart who, on his death in 1962, bequeathed **Stewart's Burnby Hall and Gardens** to the town. The eight acres of gardens are world-famous for the rare collection of water-lilies planted in the two large lakes. There are some 80 varieties and in the main flowering season from July to early September they present a dazzling spectacle. The Major and his wife had travelled extensively before settling down at Burnby and there's a small museum in the Hall displaying his collection of sporting trophies. On summer Sunday afternoons, the gardens are the venue for concerts given by some of Yorkshire's most popular bands.

A mile outside the town is **Kilnwick Percy Hall**, a magnificent Georgian mansion of 1784 built for the Lord of the Manor of Pocklington. It now houses the Madhyamaka Centre, the largest Buddhist settlement in the western world. Visitors can stay in converted stables at the Hall, either to take part in one of the residential courses or to use as a base for exploring the area. There's a modest charge for full board; smoking and drinking alcohol are not allowed.

A few miles to the south of Pocklington is **Londesborough Park,** a 400-acre estate which was once owned by the legendary railway entrepreneur, George Hudson. He had the York to Market Weighton railway diverted here so that he could build himself a comfortable private station. The railway has now disappeared but part of its route is included in the popular long-distance footpath, the Wolds Way, which passes through the park.

---

121 THE YORKWAY MOTEL

Pocklington

Superb accommodation, fine food and a warm welcome awaits you at this popular motel adjacent to the A1079.

See entry on page 252

---

122 THE STEER INN

Wilberfoss

This is an ideal place to stay for visitors to Yorkshire, with 15 comfortable en-suite bedrooms for guests.

See entry on page 253

---

123 THE HALF MOON INN

Newton upon Derwent

Picture postcard establishment in delightful village, renowned for its quality food and real ales.

See entry on page 253

BISHOP WILTON

14 miles W of Great Driffield off the A166

A small and unspoilt village between Stamford Bridge to the west and Pocklington to the south, Bishop Wilton was a country retreat for the bishops of York in Saxon times. The Saxons – whose bishops gave the village its name – began the lovely village church, which has a fine Norman chancel arch and doorway. The remarkable black-and-white marble flooring is copied from the Vatican.

STAMFORD BRIDGE

16 miles W of Great Driffield off the A166

Everyone knows that 1066 was the year of the Battle of Hastings but, just a few days before that battle, King Harold had clashed at Stamford Bridge with his half-brother Tostig and Hardrada, King of Norway who between them had mustered some 60,000 men. On a rise near the corn mill is a stone commemorating the event with an inscription in English and Danish. Up until 1878, a Sunday in September was designated 'Spear Day Feast' in commemoration of the battle. On this day, boat-shaped pies were made bearing the impression of a spear, in memory of the Saxon soldier in his boat who slew the single Norseman defending the wooden bridge

over the River Derwent. Harold's troops were triumphant but immediately after this victory they marched southwards to Hastings and a much more famous defeat.

SLEDMERE

7 miles NW of Great Driffield on the B1252/B1253

Sledmere House is a noble Georgian mansion built by the Sykes family in the 1750s when this area was still a wilderness infested with packs of marauding wolves. Inside, there is fine furniture by Chippendale and Sheraton, and decorated plasterwork by Joseph Rose. The copy of a naked, and well-endowed, Apollo Belvedere in the landing alcove must have caused many a maidenly blush in Victorian times, and the Turkish Room – inspired by the Sultan's salon in Istanbul's Valideh Mosque – is a dazzling example of oriental opulence. Outside, the gardens and the 220 acres of parkland were landscaped by Capability Brown.

The Sykes family set a shining example to other landowners in the Wolds by agricultural improvements that transformed a 'blank and barren tract of land' into one of the most productive and best cultivated districts in the county. They founded the famous Sledmere Stud, and the second Sir Tatton Sykes spent nearly two million pounds on building and restoring churches in the area. Sledmere House itself was ravaged by fire in 1911. Sir Tatton was enjoying his favourite lunchtime dessert of rice pudding when a servant rushed in with news of the fire and urged him to leave the house. 'First, I must finish my pudding, finish my pudding,' he declared, and did so. An armchair was set up for him on the lawn and Sir Tatton, then 85 years old,

---

124 **THE CARPENTERS ARMS**

Fangfoss

Real ale lovers will love it at The Carpenters Arms, which serves three real ales and excellent pub cuisine.

See entry on page 254

---

125 **THE FLEECE INN**

Bishop Wilton

Fine old traditional hostelry offering excellent home-cooked food, real ales and en suite rooms.

See entry on page 254

---

126 **SLEDMERE HOUSE**

Sledmere

There has been a **manor house** at Sledmere since medieval times. The present house was built in 1751 by Sir Christopher Sykes 2nd Baronet.

See entry on page 255

Sledmere House

'followed the progress of the conflagration' as the household staff laboured to rescue the house's many treasures. After the fire, Sledmere was quickly restored and the Sykes family is still in residence. The house is open to the public and music lovers should make sure they visit between 2 and 4pm on Wednesday or Sunday when the enormous pipe organ is being played.

Across the road from Sledmere House are two remarkable, elaborately detailed, monuments. The **Eleanor Cross** – modelled on those set up by Edward I in memory of his Queen, was erected by Sir Tatton Sykes in 1900; the **Wagoners Memorial** designed by Sir Mark Sykes, commemorates the 1000-strong company of men he raised from the Wolds during the First World War. Their knowledge of horses was invaluable in their role as members of the Army Service Corps. The finely-carved monument is like a 'storyboard', its panels depicting the Wagoners' varied duties during the war. In the main house itself, a recently re-designed exhibit tells the story of the Wagoners Special Reserve through old photographs, memorabilia and some of the medals they were awarded.

WEST LUTTON

10 miles NW of Great Driffield off the A64 or B1253

West Lutton church is yet another of the many repaired or restored by Sir Tatton Sykes in this corner of the East Riding. It stands

overlooking the village green and pond, its lych gate reached by a tiny bridge.

BEVERLEY

In medieval times, Beverley was one of England's most prosperous towns and it remains one of the most gracious with a wealth of Georgian half-timbered town houses. Its greatest glory is the **Minster** whose twin towers, built in glowing magnesian limestone, soar above this, the oldest town in East Yorkshire. More than two centuries in the making, from around 1220 to 1450, the Minster provides a textbook demonstration of the evolving architectural styles of those years. Among its many treasures are superb, fine wood carvings from the Ripon school, and a 1000 year old *fridstol*, or sanctuary seat. Carved from a single block of stone, the fridstol is a relic from the earlier Saxon church on this site. Under Saxon law, the fridstol provided refuge for any offender who managed to reach it. The canons would then try to resolve the dispute between the fugitive and his pursuer. If after 30 days no solution had been found, the seeker of sanctuary was given safe escort to the county boundary or the nearest port. The custom survived right up until Henry VIII's closure of the monasteries.

Unlike the plain-cut fridstol, the canopy of the 14th-century Percy Shrine is prodigal in its ornamentation – 'the finest piece of work of the finest craftsmen of the finest period in British building.' The behaviour of some visitors to this glorious Shrine was not, it

127 THE POPPY SEED

Beverley

Outstanding delicatessen and coffee shop serving quality home-cooked food prepared to the highest standards.

See entry on page 255

113

seems, always as reverent as it might have been. When Celia Fiennes toured the Minster in 1697 she recorded that the tomb of 'Great Percy, Earle of Northumberland was a little fallen in and a hole so bigg as many put their hands in and touch'd the body which was much of it entire.' Great Percy's remains are now decently concealed once again.

As well as the incomparable stone carvings on the shrine, the Minster also has a wealth of wonderful carvings in wood. Seek out those representing Stomach Ache, Toothache, Sciatica and Lumbago – four afflictions probably almost as fearsome to medieval people as the Four Riders of the Apocalypse.

Close by is the **North Bar,** the only one of the town's five medieval gatehouses to have survived. Unlike many towns in the Middle Ages, Beverley did not have an encircling wall. Instead, the town fathers had a deep ditch excavated around it so that all goods had to pass through one of the gates and pay a toll. North Bar was built in 1409 and, with headroom of little more than 10 feet, is something of a traffic hazard, albeit a very attractive one. Next door is Bar House, in which Charles I and his sons stayed in the 1630s. Another visitor to the town, famous for very different reasons, was the highwayman Dick Turpin who, in 1739, was brought before a magistrates' hearing conducted at one of the town's inns. That inn has long since gone and its site is now occupied by the Beverley Arms.

St Mary's Church, just across the road

from the Beverley Arms, tends to be overshadowed by the glories of Beverley Minster. But this is another superb medieval building, richly endowed with fine carvings, many brightly coloured, and striking sculptures. A series of ceiling panels depicts all the Kings of England from Sigebert (623-37AD) to Henry VI. Originally, four legendary kings were also included, but one of them was replaced in recent times by a portrait of George VI. Lewis Carroll visited St Mary's when he stayed with friends in the town and was very taken with a stone carving of a rabbit – the inspiration, it is believed, for the March Hare in *Alice in Wonderland*. Certainly the carving bears an uncanny resemblance to Tenniel's famous drawing of the Mad Hatter.

The wide market square in the heart of the town hosts a Saturday market every week with as many as 140 different stalls. The square is graced by an elegant **Market Cross,** a circular pillared building rather like a small Greek temple. It bears the arms of Queen Anne in whose reign it was built at the expense of the town's two Members of Parliament. At that time of course parliamentary elections were flagrantly corrupt but at Beverley the tradition continued longer than in most places – in 1868 the author Anthony Trollope stood as a candidate here but was defeated in what was acknowledged as a breathtakingly fraudulent election.

The Guildhall nearby was built in 1762 and is still used as a courtroom. The impressive interior has an ornate plasterwork ceiling on which there is an imposing Royal Coat of Arms and also the familiar figure of Justice holding a pair of scales. Unusually, she is not wearing a blindfold. When an 18th-century town clerk was asked the reason for this departure from tradition, he replied, 'In Beverley, Justice is not blind.'

The **Beverley Art Gallery** contains an impressive collection of local works including those by Frederick Elwell RA.

In early 2010, the town began installing its **Medieval Guilds & Crafts Town Trail** which focusses on the medieval guilds that were the

Inside the Guildhall, Beverley

foundations of Beverley's wealth with a series of public artworks. The installations depict the role played by millers, musicians, bakers, blacksmiths, bricklayers, armourers and other less well-known craftsmen.

When the project is completed, there will be 39 works of art in all.

Just outside the town on Westwood Common, is **Beverley Racecourse,** one of Britain's oldest flat racing courses where racing was first recorded in the 1690s.

From Beverley, serious walkers might care to follow some or all of the 15-mile **Hudson Way,** a level route that follows the track of the old railway from Beverley to Market Weighton. The route wanders through the Wolds, sometimes deep in a cutting, sometimes high on an embankment, past an old windmill at Etton and through eerily abandoned stations.

Skidby Mill

East Riding Rural Life where the farming year is chronicled using historic implements and fascinating photographs. The displays feature the Thompson family, who owned Skidby Mill for more than a century, and other local characters.

AROUND BEVERLEY

SKIDBY

4 miles S of Beverley off the A164

In the 1800s more than 200 windmills were scattered across the Wolds. Today, **Skidby Mill** is the only one still grinding grain and producing its own wholemeal flour. Built in 1821, it has three pairs of millstones powered by four 12-metre sails, each weighing more than 1.25 tonnes.

The mill is run, weather permitting, by the miller and mill volunteers between Wednesdays and Sundays, and produces various grades of wholemeal flour from East Riding-grown 'Hereward' variety grain, which is available for purchase in the mill shop, along with a wide range of souvenir and other items, and books. The Mill's courtyard contains various exhibits including a blacksmith's forge, and a café. At the side of the mill is a sheltered garden picnic area, Wildlife Garden and pond.

At the same location is the **Museum of**

HOLDERNESS

Lordings, there is in Yorkshire, as I guess
A marshy country called Holdernesse.

With these words Chaucer begins the Summoner's story in the *Canterbury Tales*. It's not surprising that this area was then largely marshland since most of the land lies at less than 10 metres above sea level. The name Holderness comes from Viking times: a 'hold' was a man of high rank in the Danelaw, 'ness' has stayed in the language with its meaning of promontory. The precise boundaries of the Land of Holderness are clear enough to the east where it runs to the coast, and to the south where Holderness ends with Yorkshire itself at Spurn Point. They are less well-defined to the north and west where they run somewhere close to the great crescent of the Wolds. For the purposes of this book, we have taken as the northern limit of Holderness the village of Skipsea, where, as you'll discover, some early Norman Lords of Holderness showed a remarkable lack of loyalty to their King.

Hornsea Mere

HORNSEA

This small coastal town with its Blue Flag beach can boast not only one of the most popular visitor attractions in Humberside, **Freeport Hornsea**, a quaint timber village with some 40 retail outlets, but also Yorkshire's largest freshwater lake, **Hornsea Mere**. The mere, an RSPB nature reserve, is two miles long and one mile wide and provides a refuge for more than 170 species of birds and a peaceful setting for many varieties of rare flowers. Human visitors are well provided for, too, with facilities for fishing, boating and sailing.

Hornsea also has an award-winning mile-long promenade, well-tended public gardens and a church built with cobbles gathered from the shore.

The excellent **Hornsea Museum**, established in 1978, is a folk museum that has won numerous national awards over the years as well as being featured several times on television. The museum occupies a Grade

II listed building, a former farmhouse where successive generations of the Burn family lived for 300 years up until 1952. Their way of life, the personalities and characters who influenced the development of the town or found fame in other ways, are explored in meticulously restored rooms brimming with furniture, decorations, utensils and tools of the Victorian period. The kitchen, parlour and bedroom have fascinating displays of authentic contemporary artefacts, and the museum complex also includes a laundry, workshop, blacksmith's shop and a barn stocked with vintage agricultural implements.

In Swallow Cottage next door, children can undergo the Victorian school experience under the tutelage of 'Miss Grim' – writing on slates, having good deportment instilled and, above all, observing the maxim 'Silence is Golden.' The cottage also houses a comprehensive and varied display of early Hornsea pottery, various temporary exhibitions, and, in summer, a refreshment room for visitors. Remarkably, this outstanding museum is staffed mainly by volunteers.

For a satisfying shop-till-you-drop experience, **Hornsea Freeport** – the 'Independent State of Low Prices' – is hard to beat. There are discounts of up to 50 per cent or more on everything from designer wear, children's wear and sportswear to chinaware, kitchenware and glassware. There are themed leisure attractions and bright, fun-filled play areas to keep the children amused. One of these, **Butterfly World,** is home to more than 200 species of colourful butterflies.

Just to the north of the town, **Honeysuckle Farm** promises a great day out for all the family. There are shire horses giving cart rides, other farm animals, indoor and outdoor play areas, woodland walks, picnic areas and a souvenir shop. There's also a tea room and an ice cream parlour selling ice creams made with milk from the farm's own Jersey cows.

A mile or so west of Hornsea stands **Wassand Hall**, a handsome Regency house in

---

128 **HORNSEA FOLK MUSEUM**

Hornsea

Established in 1978, the excellent **Hornsea Folk Museum** occupies a Grade II listed former farmhouse where successive generations of the Burn family lived for 300 years up until 1952.

See entry on page 256

Wassand Hall, Hornsea

wonderfully tranquil surroundings overlooking Hornsea Mere which is actually part of the Estate. Owned by the same family since 1520, the Hall has a fine collection of 18th and 19th century paintings, including portraits of past owners of Wassand Hall and their relations. There are also collections of English and European silver, furniture and porcelain. The grounds include some lovely walled gardens and a woodland walk. The hall and grounds are only open on selected days during the summer.

AROUND HORNSEA

ATWICK

2 miles NW of Hornsea on the B1242

Atwick is a picturesque village on the coast, just two miles north of Hornsea. It has been a regular winner of local – and, in 1997, county – awards in the Britain in Bloom competition.

Like Hornsea, Atwick once had its own mere. Some years ago, excavations in its dried-up bed revealed fossilised remains of a huge Irish elk and the tusk of an ancient elephant, clear proof of the tropical climate East Yorkshire enjoyed in those far-off days.

SKIPSEA

5 miles NW of Hornsea on the B1242

When William the Conqueror granted Drogo de Bevrere the Lordship of Holderness, Drogo decided to raise his **Castle** on an island in the shallow lake known as Skipsea Mere. Built mostly of timber, the castle had not long been completed when Drogo made the foolish mistake of murdering his wife. In the normal course of events, a Norman lord could murder whomever he wished, but Drogo's action was foolish because his wife was a kinswoman of the Conqueror himself. Drogo was banished and his lands granted to a succession of other royal relatives, most of whom also came to a sticky end after becoming involved in rebellions and treasonable acts. The castle was finally abandoned in the mid-13th century and all that remains now is the great motte, or mound, on which it was built and the earth ramparts surrounding it.

WEST NEWTON

5 miles S of Hornsea off the B1238

To the south of the village of West Newton is **Burton Constable Hall,** named after Sir John Constable who, in 1570, built a stately mansion here which incorporated parts of an even older house, dating back to the reign of King Stephen in the 1100s. The Hall was again remodelled, on Jacobean lines, in the 18th century and contains some fine work by

---

129 HARE & HOUNDS

Leven

The place to go for a home-cooked hearty meal, real ale and friendly hospitality.

See entry on page 256

---

130 BURTON CONSTABLE HALL

Burton Constable

Burton Constable is a large Elizabethan mansion set in a 300 acre park with nearly 30 rooms open to the public.

See entry on page 257

Chippendale, Adam and James Wyatt. In the famous Long Gallery with its 15th- century Flemish stained glass, hangs a remarkable collection of paintings, among them Holbein's portraits of Sir Thomas Cranmer and Sir Thomas More, and Zucchero's Mary, Queen of Scots. Dragons abound in the dazzling Chinese Room, an exercise in oriental exotica that long pre-dates the Prince Regent's similar extravaganza at the Brighton Pavilion. Thomas Chippendale himself designed the fantastical Dragon Chair, fit for a Ming Emperor. Outside, there are extensive parklands designed by Capability Brown, and apparently inspired by the gardens at Versailles. Perhaps it was this connection that motivated the Constable family to suggest loaning the Hall to Louis XVIII of France during his years of exile after the Revolution. (Louis politely declined the offer, preferring to settle rather closer to London, at Hartwell in Buckinghamshire.) Also in the grounds of the Hall are collections of agricultural machinery, horse-drawn carriages and 18th-century scientific apparatus.

The descendants of the Constable family still bear the title 'Lords of Holderness' and along with it the rights to any flotsam and jetsam washed ashore on the Holderness peninsula. Many years ago, when the late Brigadier Chichester Constable was

congratulated on enjoying such a privilege, he retorted, 'I also have to pay for burying, or otherwise disposing of, any whale grounded on the Holderness shore – and it costs me about £20 a time!' The huge bones of one such whale are still on show in the grounds of the Hall.

WITHERNSEA

The next place of interest down the Holderness coast is Withernsea. Long, golden sandy beaches stretch for miles both north and south, albeit a mile further inland than they were in the days of William the Conqueror. Over the years, 22 towns and villages have been lost to the encroaching sea.

Withernsea hosts an outdoor market every Thursday, Saturday, Sunday and Bank Holidays, has a promenade nearly a mile long, and a beautifully landscaped open space, Valley Gardens, that has recently been refurbished and hosts free outdoor concerts in the season.

The old **Lighthouse** is a striking feature of the town and those energetic enough to climb the 144 steps of the 127-ft tower are rewarded by some marvellous views from the lamp room. The lighthouse was decommissioned in 1976 and now houses two small museums. One is dedicated to the history of the Royal National Lifeboat Institution; the other to the actress Kay Kendall. Her grandfather helped build the lighthouse in 1892 and was the last coxswain of the deep sea lifeboat. Kay was born in Withernsea and later achieved great success in the London theatre as a sophisticated comedienne but she is probably best remembered for the rousing trumpet solo she

---

131 WRYGARTH INN

Great Hatfield

Known for its great facilities and chilled out atmosphere, this inn serves delicious homemade food with conference facilities and crazy golf available.

See entry on page 258

**132 GEORGE &
DRAGON**

Aldbrough,

Gorgeous 16th century Inn, with a delicious home-made menu.

See entry on page 259

**133 THE
LIGHTHOUSE**

Withernsea
The Museum is run by
Withernsea Lighthouse
uniquely towers 127 feet above the town.

See entry on page 260

Spurn Point, Withernsea

PATRINGTON

*4 miles SW of Withernsea
on the A1033*

Shortly after it was built, **St Patrick's Church** at Patrington was dubbed 'Queen of Holderness', and Queen it remains. "It sails like a galleon of stone over the wide, flat expanse of Holderness" wrote John Betjeman. This sublime church took more than 100 years to build, from around 1310 to 1420, and it is one of the most glorious examples of the eye-pleasing style known as English Decorated. Its spire soars almost 180 feet into the sky making it the most distinctive feature in the level plains of Holderness. St Patrick's has the presence and proportions of a cathedral although only enjoying the status of a parish church. A parish church, nevertheless, which experts consider among the finest dozen churches in Britain for architectural beauty. Patrington's parish council go further: a notice displayed inside St Patrick's states unequivocally, 'This is England's finest village Church.' Clustering around it, picturesque Dutch-style cottages complete an entrancing picture and just to the east of the village the Dutch theme continues in a fine old windmill.

delivered in the Ealing Studios hit film *Genevieve*. The museum shows video excerpts from some of her most popular films.

South of Withernsea stretches a desolate spit of flat windswept dunes. This is **Spurn Point** which leads to Spurn Head, the narrow hook of ever-shifting sands that curls around the mouth of the Humber estuary. This bleak but curiously invigorating tag end of Yorkshire is nevertheless heavily populated – by hundreds of species of rare and solitary wild fowl, by playful seals, and also by the small contingent of lifeboatmen who operate the only permanently manned lifeboat station in Britain. Please note that this is a National Nature Reserve and a toll is payable beyond the village of Kilnsea. Access to Spurn Head itself is only on foot.

AROUND WITHERNSEA

HOLMPTON

3 miles S of Withernsea off the A1033

RAF Holmpton was built between 1951 and 1952 and started its operational life in 1953 as an Early Warning Radar Station. It was equipped with a massive Nuclear Bunker almost 100ft below ground and covering nearly 35,000 sq.ft. This **Underground Bunker** is now open to the public with fully guided tours lasting about an hour and a half. The tours visit all the working and living areas as well as the Weapons of Mass Destruction Gallery, all brought to life with films, shows and demonstrations.

HALSHAM

4 miles W of Withernsea off the B1362

Halsham was once the seat of the Constable family, Lords of Holderness, before they moved to their new mansion at Burton Constable. On the edge of Halsham village, they left behind their imposing, domed mausoleum built in the late 1700s to house ancestors going back to the 12th century. The mausoleum is not open to the public but is clearly visible from the B1362 Hull to Withernsea road.

HEDON

10 miles W of Withernsea off the A1033

Founded around AD 1130 by William le Gros, Lord of Holderness, Hedon quickly became a port and market town of great importance. Its market still takes place every Wednesday in the square with its row of Georgian shops and early 19th-century dwellings. Nearby, in St Augustine's Gate, is the handsome Town Hall, built in 1692. From time to time, the town's Civic Silver Collection is on display here. It includes the oldest civic mace in the country, dating back to 1415. The volunteer-run **Hedon Museum** (free) has displays of maps, photographs and artefacts relating to the history of Hedon and Holderness; these are changed regularly. Limited opening times.

PAULL

12 miles W of Withernsea off the A1033

Fort Paull's role as a frontier landing and watch point goes back to at least Viking times. Henry VIII built a fortress here in the mid-1500s; a second fort was added at the time of the Napoleonic wars. Charles I based himself at Fort Paull for some time during the Civil War; Winston Churchill visited its anti-aircraft installations during the Second World War.

Today, the spacious 10-acre site on the bank of the Humber Estuary offers a wide variety of attractions for all the family. In addition to the historical displays, including rare period and contemporary artillery, there are classic military vehicles, an array of waxwork creations, a parade ground where re-enactments take place, an assault course for youngsters, a Bird of Prey Centre, museum, gift shop, bar and restaurant. The fort also has the world's only Blackburn Beverley aircraft.

HULL

Although unmistakably part of Yorkshire, Hull also has the freewheeling, open-minded character of a cosmopolitan port. The port area extends for seven miles along the Humber with 10 miles of quays servicing a constant flow of commercial traffic arriving from, or departing for, every quarter of the globe. Every day, a succession of vehicle ferries link the city to the European gateways of Zeebrugge and Rotterdam.

Hull's history as an important port goes back to 1293 when Edward I, travelling north on his way to fight the Scots, stopped off here and immediately recognised the potential of the muddy junction where the River Hull flows into the Humber. The king bought the land from the monks of Meaux Abbey (at the usual royal discount) and the settlement thenceforth was known as 'Kinges town upon Hull'.

The port grew steadily through the centuries and at one time had the largest fishing fleet of any port in the country with more than 300 trawlers on its register. The port's rather primitive facilities were greatly improved by the construction of a state-of-the-art dock in 1778. Now superseded, that dock has been converted into the handsome **Queen's Gardens**, one of the many attractive open spaces created by this flower-conscious city which also loves lining its streets with trees, setting up fountains here and there, and planting flower beds in any available space.

Waymarked walks such as the **Maritime Heritage Trail** and the **Seven Seas Fish Trail,** with 41 species depicted make the most of the city's dramatic waterfront. The tourist information centre also publishes a leaflet detailing the Hull Ale Trail, a guide to almost 30 of the city's hostelries. Remarkably, despite the battering Hull received in World War II, many splendid Victorian pubs have survived with their opulent furnishings and decoration intact.

A visit to Hull is an exhilarating experience at any time of the year but especially so in early October. Back in the late 1200s the city was granted a charter to hold an autumn fair. This began as a fairly modest cattle and sheep mart but over the centuries it burgeoned into the largest gathering of its kind in Europe. **Hull Fair** is now a two week extravaganza occupying a 16-acre site and offering every imaginable variety of entertainment. That takes care of October, but Hull also hosts an Easter Festival, an International Festival (some 300 events from mid-June to late July), a Jazz on the Waterfront celebration (August), an

Queen's Gardens

fine collection of scrimshaw. A more unusual museum is the **Spurn Lightship.** Once stationed on active duty 4.5 miles east of Spurn Point, the 200-ton, 33-metre long craft is now moored in Hull's vibrant Marina. Visitors can explore the 75-year-old vessel with the help of its knowledgeable crew. Another aspect of the city's maritime heritage can be investigated in the **Arctic Corsair,** the city's last sidewinder trawler. Former trawlermen recount the hazardous conditions endured by deep sea trawler men in the 1960s.

International Sea Shanty Festival (September) and a Literature Festival in November.

Throughout the rest of the year, Hull's tourism office modestly suggests you explore its 'Marvellous Museums – Fabulous and Free' – a quite remarkable collection of eight historic houses, art galleries and museums, all with free entry. Perhaps the most evocative is the **Wilberforce House Museum** in the old High Street. William Wilberforce was born here in 1759 and, later, it was from here that he and his father lavished thousands of pounds in bribes to get William elected as Hull's Member of Parliament. Nothing unusual about that kind of corruption at the time, but William then redeemed himself by his resolute opposition to slavery. His campaign took more than 30 years and William was already on his deathbed before a reluctant Parliament finally outlawed the despicable trade. Re-opened in 2007 after a £1.6m refit, the museum presents a shaming history of the slave trade along with a more uplifting story of Wilberforce's efforts to eliminate it for ever.

Other stars of the 'Magnificent Eight' are **The Ferens Art Gallery** which houses a sumptuous collection of paintings and sculpture that ranges from European Old Masters (including some Canalettos and works by Franz Hals) to challenging contemporary art and sculptures by Henry Moore and Barbara Hepworth. Occupying the monumental former Dock Offices, the **Hull Maritime Museum** celebrates seven centuries of Hull's maritime heritage and includes a

The city's noisiest museum is the **Streetlife Transport Museum** which traces 200 years of transport history. Visitors are transported back to the days of horse-drawn carriages, steam trains, trams and penny-farthing cycles. There are curiosities such as the 'Velocipede', the Automobile à Vapeur (an early steam-driven car), and Lady Chesterfield's ornamental sleigh, caparisoned with a swan, rearing unicorn and a panoply of bells to herald her approach.

One of Hull's largest and most impressive buildings is the Victorian **Guildhall** which houses a wonderful collection of paintings, sculptures, antiques, silver, Civic Insignia and the unique Hull Tapestry which took 12 years to complete. **The Hands on History Museum** is housed in the former Grammar School with a genuine Tudor schoolroom dating back to 1583. Upstairs, there's a fascinating collection of Ancient Egyptian tomb furniture and the mummy of an Ancient Egyptian priest. And then there's the **Hull & East Riding Museum of Archaeology** where you

---

134 **THE DEEP**

Hull

This award-winning Yorkshire family attraction is home to 40 sharks and over 3,500 fish.

See entry on page 260

can stroll through an Iron Age Village, visit a Roman bath-house, encounter mysterious Bronze Age warriors and inspect dinosaur bones. There are more relics of these ever-fascinating creatures at **Dinostar - The Dinosaur Experience.** The exhibition of fossils and dinosaurs includes a full size T-Rex skull and Triceratops leg bones you can touch. Dinostar is only open on Sundays and school holidays.

At **The Deep,** the world's only submarium, visitors can have a close encounter with the ocean's greatest predator. There are some 40 sharks here and more than 3500 fish. Visitors can walk through the deepest viewing tunnel in Europe, some 10 metres deep, as sharks circle above them. In the Slime! exhibit you can discover animals that ooze, stick and slide to survive. A recent addition to the displays is the ultimate shark film in 4D, a 20-minute spectacular with theatrical effects.

Hull offers a huge choice of shops but the most spectacular shopping venue is Prince's Quay, a £300 million development that stands on 500 huge stilts. It has 4 "decks", some 75 different shops, and a 10-screen fully digital cinema complex.

AROUND HULL

HESSLE

5 miles W of Hull off the A63

At Hessle the River Humber narrows and it was here that the Romans maintained a ferry, the *Transitus Maximus*, a vital link in the route between Lincoln and York. The ferry remained in operation for almost 2000 years until it was replaced in 1981 by the **Humber Bridge** whose mighty pylons soar more than 500 feet above the village.

It is undoubtedly one of the most impressive bridges on earth, and also one of the least used – someone described it as

the least likely place in Britain to find a traffic jam. With an overall length of 2428 yards (2220m), it is one of the world's longest single-span bridges. For more than a third of a mile only four concrete pillars, two at each end, are saving you from a watery death. From these huge pylons gossamer cables of thin-wired steel support a gently curving roadway. Both sets of pylons rise vertically, but because of the curvature of the earth they actually lean away from each other by several inches. The bridge is particularly striking at night when the vast structure is floodlit.

The great bridge dwarfs Cliff Mill, built in 1810 to mill the local chalk. It remained wind-driven until 1925 when a gas engine was installed. Although it is no longer working, the mill provides a scenic feature within the **Humber Bridge Country Park.** This well laid out park gives visitors a true back-to-nature tour a short distance from one of modern man's greatest feats of engineering. The former chalk quarry has been attractively landscaped, providing a nature trail, extensive walks through woodlands and meadows, picnic and play areas, and picturesque water features. Another attractive feature of the park is the **Phoenix Sculpture Trail** which connects ten unique sculptural seats, each made from a different material - locally sourced wood, stone, earth and steel. A leaflet available from the tourist information centre will help

Humber Bridge, Hessle

you find Iris overlooking the pond, the Leaf Spirit in the woods or Odonata in the amphitheatre.

NORTH FERRIBY

9 miles W of Hull off the A63

It was here, in 1946, that some late Bronze Age boats dating from 890BC to about 590BC were found on the shore. Made from planks held together with strips of yew, they indicate that travel on the River Humber began much earlier than had been previously thought. A model of the boats can be seen in Hull's Transport and Archaeology Museum.

WELTON

10 miles W of Hull off the A63

A little further south is the pretty village of Welton where a stream flows past the green, under bridges and into a tree-encircled duck pond. It has a church dating from Norman times which boasts a striking 13th-century doorway and Pre-Raphaelite windows made by William Morris' company of craftsmen. In the graveyard stands a memorial to Jeremiah Found, a resilient local reputed to have outlived eight wives.

The notorious highwayman Dick Turpin was not a local but his villainous, if romantic, career came to an end at Welton village when he was apprehended inside the Green Dragon Inn. Local legend has it that this establishment gave him hospitality before he was taken off to the magistrates at Beverley who committed him to the Assizes at York where he was found guilty and hanged in 1739.

BRANTINGHAM

11 miles W of Hull off the A63

The village of Brantingham, just off the A63, is worth a short diversion to see its remarkable **War Memorial,** once described as 'lovingly awful'. Conceived on a monumental scale, the memorial was built using masonry recycled from Hull's old Guildhall when that was being reconstructed in 1914. Various stone urns placed around the village came from the same source.

SOUTH CAVE

14 miles W of Hull off the A63

The village of South Cave is, officially, a town with its very own Town Hall in the marketplace. The name is said to be a corruption of South Cove since the southern part of the parish is set around a backwater of the Humber. The village is separated into two distinct areas by the grounds of the Cave Castle Golf Hotel. This building dates back to Elizabethan times and was once the home of George Washington's great grandfather.

HOWDEN

18 miles W of Hull on the A63

Despite the fact that its chancel collapsed in 1696 and has not been used for worship ever since, **Howden Minster** is still one of the largest parish churches in East Yorkshire and

---

135 THE TIGER INN

North Newbald

Family-run pub in delightful village, offering excellent home-cooked food and real ales.

See entry on page 261

---

136 WARDS HOTEL

Gilberdyke

Outstanding traditional inn serving good old-fashioned English food and real ales.

See entry on page 262

---

137 THE ROYAL OAK

Portington

Traditional village in serving delicious homemade food and hand pulled real ale throughout the year.

See entry on page 263

Howden Minster

most exquisite small buildings in England.

When the medieval Prince-Bishops of Durham held sway over most of northern England, they built a palace at Howden which they used as a pied-à-terre during their semi-royal progresses and as a summer residence. The Hall of that 14th-century palace still stands, although much altered now.

Howden town is a pleasing jumble of narrow, flagged and setted streets with a picturesque stone and brick Market Hall in the marketplace. The celebrated aircraft designer Barnes Wallis knew Howden well: he lived here while working on the R100 airship which was built at Hedon airfield nearby. It made its maiden flight in 1929 and successfully crossed the Atlantic. At the nearby Breighton Aerodrome, a World War II bomber base, is the **Real Aeroplane Museum** which boasts a fine collection of vintage military and civilian aircraft. Probably the most interesting aircraft is the Aeronca 100, first registered in March 1937 and known as 'Jeeves' because of its registration: G-AEVS. Other exhibits illustrate the history of flight through the work of Yorkshire aviation pioneers.

About four miles northwest of Howden are the striking remains of **Wressle Castle**, built in 1380 for Sir Henry Percy and the only surviving example in East Yorkshire of a medieval fortified house. At the end of the Civil War, three of the castle's sides were pulled down and much of the rest was destroyed by fire in 1796. But two massive towers with walls six feet thick, the hall and kitchens remain. The castle is not open to the public but there are excellent views from the village road and from a footpath that

also one of its most impressive, cathedral-like in size. From the top of its soaring tower, 135 feet high, there are wonderful views of the surrounding countryside – but it's not for the faint-hearted. The ruined chapter house, lavishly decorated with a wealth of carved mouldings, has been described as one of the

---

138 JAY JAY'S

Howden

Chic cafe bar serving tapas and fresh stone baked pizzas, also a brilliant venue for live music

See entry on page 264

---

139 THE FERRYBOAT INN

Howden

Sail the night away in this unique inn, their Angler's breakfast is a real weekend treat.

See entry on page 265

Wressle Castle

runs alongside the River Derwent. A fine old windmill nearby provides an extra visual bonus.

GOOLE

20 miles W of Hull on the A614

Goole's name comes from the Old English word for a ditch, appropriately since the town stands on reclaimed marshland. It is one of the most important ports on the east coast, handling more than 3 million tonnes of cargo a year, despite the fact that it is some 45 miles

Goole Docks

from the sea. The town stands at the hub of a waterways network that includes the River Ouse, the River Don (known here as the Dutch River), the River Aire and the Aire & Calder Navigation. The **Yorkshire Waterways Museum** (free), located on the dockside, tells the story of Goole's development as a canal terminus and also as a port connecting to the

North Sea. The museum displays model ships and many photographs dating from 1905 to the present day. Visitors can explore an original Humber Keel, *Sobriety*, and watch crafts people at work. There are also boat trips around Goole Docks at weekends.

More of the town's history is in evidence at **Goole Museum & Art Gallery** (free) which displays ship models, marine paintings and a changing programme of exhibitions. Other attractions in the town include its refurbished Victorian Market Hall, open all year Wednesday to Saturday, and a well-equipped Leisure Centre which provides a wide range of facilities for all ages.

In recent years, Goole has redeveloped its town centre and the main shopping street, Boothferry Road, is now pedestrianised.

---

140 THE YORKSHIRE WATERWAYS MUSEUM

Goole
The Yorkshire Waterways Museum offers an extensive collection which tells the story of the Port of Goole

See entry on page 265

LOCATION MAP

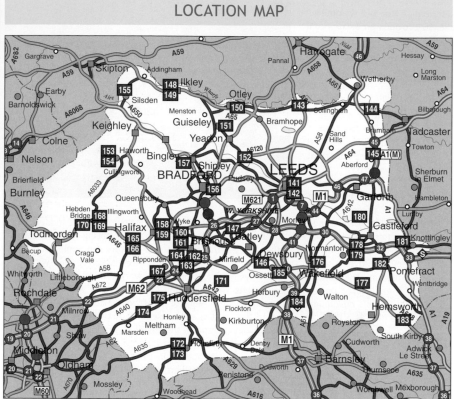

WEST YORKSHIRE

With a rich industrial and cultural heritage, a host of magnificent stately homes, a clutch of world-class museums and galleries, and superb Pennine scenery that ranges from the awesome to the enchanting - clearly, West Yorkshire has a lot to offer. The industrial heritage is celebrated at the National Coal Mining Museum at Overton, at the World Heritage Site of Saltaire near Bradford, and in the marvellous array of monumental civic buildings that are such a feature of West Yorkshire towns. The old perception of West Yorkshire as a place of smoking mill chimneys and bleak Wuthering Heights-style moors is surprisingly durable even though most of the chimneys have gone and many of the mills have been converted into upmarket apartments.

The county's stately homes range in time from the captivating Elizabethan charm of Oakwell Hall, through the graceful Queen Anne pile of Bramham Park, to the opulent Georgian mansions of Harewood House, Nostell Priory and Temple Newsam House, concluding with the elegant Edwardian country seat of Lotherton Hall.

Culturally, the county has produced two major sculptors, Henry Moore and Barbara Hepworth, who are celebrated at venues such as the Yorkshire Sculpture Park at West Bretton and in galleries throughout the region. David Hockney was born in Bradford and one of the largest collections of his work can be seen at nearby Saltaire. Bradford has also been declared a World City of Film by UNESCO because of its hugely popular National Media Museum. Popular culture of another kind is in evidence at Holmfirth where much of BBC-TV's longest running situation comedy, *Last of the Summer Wine*, was filmed.

But the place that most cultural pilgrims to West Yorkshire seek out is The Parsonage at Howarth. The Brontë family moved here in 1820 and, surrounded by the wild Pennine landscape, the three sisters, Charlotte, Anne and Emily, were inspired to write some of the most famous novels in the English language. Now a museum dedicated to the tragic sisters, this fine Georgian house is a starting point for a 40-mile footpath that takes in many of the places that feature in the Brontë novels.

Food & Drink

Places of Interest

LEEDS

In recent years, the city of Leeds has seen something of a renaissance. Its waterfront, neglected and derelict for so long, is now buzzing with new developments. Abandoned warehouses have been imaginatively transformed into fashionable bars, restaurants and tourist attractions, all less than 15 minutes walk from the shopping centre. Debenhams has opened a flagship store in the heart of the city and other high profile stores are also flocking to the city. Perhaps the most talked about store is Harvey Nichols whose Knightsbridge emporium enjoyed a heightened reputation in the 1990s thanks to the BBC series *Absolutely Fabulous*. In parallel with these developments the Aire and Calder Navigation, which commenced construction in 1704, is being transformed to enable leisure traffic to use the waterway as well as freight.

The city is also a major European cultural centre with its own opera and ballet companies, Northern Ballet Theatre and Opera North, while the West Yorkshire Playhouse, regarded as the 'National Theatre of the North', provides a showcase for classic British and European drama as well as work by new Yorkshire writers. The Leeds International Film Festival, held every October since 1986, has hosted major world premieres for films such as *Brassed Off*.

The Victoria Quarter is firmly established as the 'Knightsbridge of the North'. The stylish shopping development specialises in top international names: Prada, Hugo Boss, Paul Smith, and Vivienne Westwood to name but a few.

Leeds boasts some outstanding galleries and museums. Located right next to the monumental Town Hall, the **Leeds City Art Gallery** showcases an exceptional collection of Victorian and French Post-Impressionist paintings, along with major works by Courbet, Lowry, Sickert, Stanley Spencer and Bridget Riley. Linked to the gallery is the **Henry Moore Institute**, the first centre in Europe devoted to the display and study of sculpture of all periods. There's also a Craft and Design shop selling cards, jewellery and pottery; and an art library.

The **Thackray Medical Museum**, one of the largest museums of its kind in Europe, possesses more than 25,000 extraordinary objects in its collection. They range from a surgical chain saw and Prince Albert's Medical Chest through to a 17th-century correction frame. Visitors can listen in to the thoughts and feelings of a surgeon, his assistants and Hannah Dyson, an 11-year-old girl whose leg has been crushed in a factory accident, as they prepare for the amputation of Hannah's leg. Or you might prefer to walk through a giant gut in Bodyworks and find out exactly why your tummy rumbles.

The **Royal Armouries Museum** occupies a multi-million pound purpose-built building and traces the development of arms and armour from the 5th century BC to modern times with more than 8500 artefacts on show, among them Henry VIII's tournament armour. The museum utilises interactive computer displays, videos, films, music and poetry to tell the story of arms and armour in battle, self-defence, sport and fashion. Outside, the Tiltyard features jousting and hunting tournaments daily from April to September, while a bustling Menagerie Court includes displays of falcons, hunting dogs and horses. Visitors can also see a gunmaker, armourer and wardrobe mistress at work.

Located in the magnificent Leeds Institute building on Millennium Square, **Leeds City Museum** promises an exciting and fun day out for visitors of all ages. Here you can come face-to-face with the 'Leeds Tiger' (a stuffed Bengal tiger), step into 'Ancient Worlds', see the final resting place of the Leeds Mummy, and even dig for fossils in the 'Life on Earth' gallery.

141 HENRY MOORE INSTITUTE

Leeds

The Henry Moore Institute in Leeds is a unique resource devoted exclusively to sculpture, with a programme comprising exhibitions, collections and research.

See entry on page 266

Kirkstall Abbey, Leeds

A few miles north of Leeds city centre, in Roundhay Park, is one of the UK's most popular garden tourist attractions and home to the largest collection of tropical plants outside Kew Gardens – **Tropical World**. Visitors can follow the 'Tropical Trail' into an Amazon rain forest where waterfalls tumble into jungle pools and birds of every hue fly through the trees. There's also a 'Desert World' and a 'Nocturnal House' where fruit bats, monkeys, bush babies and rock cavies reside – animals that can normally only be seen during twilight hours.

Leeds in the 1880s is the theme of **Abbey House Museum** where visitors can experience the signs and sounds of everyday life in Victorian Leeds, learn about a city steeped in history and walk through the carefully reconstructed streets of a once small market town. Just across the road from the museum **Kirkstall Abbey** is one of the most complete ruins in this part of Yorkshire and is set in glorious parkland along the banks of the River Aire. Building started in 1152 by the Cistercians and was completed within a generation, so Kirkstall is regarded by many as representing Cistercian architecture at its most representative. It was executed with typical early Cistercian austerity as can be seen in the simplicity of the outer domestic buildings. The bell tower, a 16th century addition, was in contravention of the rule of the Order that there were to be no stone bell towers as they were considered an unnecessary vanity.

Armley Mills, once the world's largest woollen mill, is now the award-winning **Leeds Industrial Museum.** It contains exhibits dating from the 18th and 19th centuries showing the history of textiles, clothing, engines and locomotive manufacture in the area. The museum also illustrates the history of cinema projections, including the first moving pictures taken in Leeds, as well as 1920s silent movies. During the regular 'working weekends' several exhibits are operated including water wheels and a steam engine.

Two miles south of the city centre, at Moor Road Railway Station, is the **Middleton Railway** which claims to be the world's oldest working railway, established by an act of parliament in 1758. Visitors can ride on the train the way miners would have travelled to work, examine the "Leeds built" locomotive collection in the Engine House, and visit the cafe and shop. There's more industrial heritage at **Thwaite Mills** where you will find a fully restored, working 19th century watermill in an lovely riverside setting. This is one of the last remaining examples of a water-powered mill in Britain

To the southwest of the city is **Temple Newsam House**, often referred to as the 'Hampton Court of the North'. Set in 1000 acres of parkland landscaped by 'Capability' Brown (entry to which is free), this Tudor-Jacobean gem boasts extensive collections of decorative arts displayed in their original room settings. Among them is one of the largest collections of Chippendale furniture in the country. Within the Temple Newsam

---

142 **THWAITE MILLS WATERMILL**

Leeds

One of the last remaining examples of a water-powered mill in Britain, **Thwaite Mills** is situated in beautiful riverside surroundings just two miles from Leeds city centre.

See entry on page 266

House estate is the country's largest approved Rare Breeds Centre – **Home Farm**. Visitors to this working farm will see pigs, goats, horses and poultry alongside interesting displays of vintage farm machinery and past farming methods.

AROUND LEEDS

HAREWOOD

8 miles N of Leeds on the A61

One of the grandest stately homes in the country, **Harewood House** was built at a time when many of the most illustrious names in the history of English architecture, interior decoration, furniture making and landscape gardening were at the peak of their powers.

For the creation of Harewood in the mid-1700s, Edwin Lascelles was able to employ the dazzling talents of Robert Adam, John Carr, Thomas Chippendale and 'Capability' Brown. Edwin's son, Edward, was one of the first to patronise a young artist named JMW Turner and many of Turner's paintings are still here along with hundreds by other distinguished painters collected by later generations of the family.

Many of the finest of them are displayed in a superb gallery that extends along the whole west end of the house. Among the masterpieces on show are works by Bellini, Titian, Veronese, El Greco and Tintoretto, while family portraits by Reynolds, Hoppner and Gainsborough look down from the silk-covered walls of the opulent drawing rooms. Along with superb gardens, charming walks, a bird garden which is home to some 120 exotic species, an adventure playground,

Harewood House

boat trips on the lake, and an extensive events and exhibitions programme, Harewood House is indisputably one of Yorkshire's must-see attractions.

WETHERBY

19 miles NE of Leeds off the A1

Situated on the Great North Road, at a point midway between Edinburgh and London, Wetherby was renowned for its coaching inns, of which the two most famous were The Angel and The Swan & Talbot. It is rumoured that serving positions at these inns were considered so lucrative that employees had to pay for the privilege of employment in them!

The town has remained unspoilt and has a quaint appearance with a central marketplace that was first granted to the Knights Templar. Many of the houses in the town are Georgian, Regency, or early Victorian. Apart from its shops, galleries, old pubs, and cafés, there is also a popular racecourse nearby. Another feature is the renowned 18th-century bridge with a long weir which once provided power for Wetherby's corn mill and possibly dates from medieval times. The bridge once carried traffic along the Great North Road; the A1 now by-passes the town.

About five miles south of Wetherby, **Bramham Park** is noted for its magnificent gardens, 66 acres of them, and its pleasure grounds which cover a further 100 acres. They are the only example of a formal, early 18th-century landscape in Britain. Temples, ornamental ponds, cascades, a two-mile long avenue of beech trees and one of the best

143 HAREWOOD HOUSE

Harewood

Designed in 1759 by John Carr, Harewood House is the home of the Queen's cousin, the Earl of Harewood.

See entry on page 267

wildflower gardens in the country are just some of the attractions. In early June, the park hosts the Bramham Horse Trials. The house itself, an attractive Queen Anne building, is open to groups of six or more by appointment only.

BOSTON SPA

9 miles NE of Leeds off the A1

Set beside the broad-flowing River Wharfe, this attractive little town enjoyed many years of prosperity after a Mr John Shires discovered a mineral spring here in 1744. The spa activities have long since ceased. There's a pleasant riverside walk which can be continued along the track of a dismantled railway as far as Tadcaster in one direction, Wetherby in the other. The town's impressive 19th-century church is notable for its stately tower and the 36 stone angels supporting the nave and aisles.

BRAMHAM

8 miles NE of Leeds off the A1

Bramham Park is one of Yorkshire's most exquisite country houses and is special for a number of reasons. The house itself dates from the Queen Anne era. It was built between 1698 and 1710, for Robert Benson, Lord Bingley, Lord Mayor of York and Kord Chamberlain to Queen Anne. The house is superbly proportioned in an elegant and restrained classical style. The final effect is more French than English and indeed the gardens were modelled on Louis XIV's Versailles, with ornamental canals and ponds, beech groves, statues, long avenues and an arboretum with an legant furniture and paintings by major artists such as Kneller and

Bramham Park, Wetherby

Sir Joshua Reynolds. Despite its grandeur, this is still a family home, the residence of Nick and Rachel Lane Fox and their five children.

ABERFORD

13 miles E of Leeds on the B1217

To the southeast of this village stands an elegant Edwardian mansion, **Lotherton Hall and Gardens**, providing a fascinating insight into life in those serene days before the First World War. It was once the home of the Gascoigne family who were local land and coal mine owners. They were also enthusiastic travellers and collectors with a discriminating taste that is evident in the family paintings, furnishings and works of art on display. The house, gardens and estate were given to the citizens of Leeds in 1968 by Sir Alvary and Lady Gascoigne, together with a handsome endowment fund. This has allowed the council to add to the collections which now include superb 19th- and 20th-century decorative art as well as costume and Oriental art. Other attractions include the Edwardian formal gardens, a walled garden with some quirky spiral topiary, a bird garden with more than 200 species of rare

---

144 THE CROWN HOTEL

Boston Spa

Intimate hotel with a superb restaurant, in an ideal location for exploring the region.

See entry on page 267

---

145 THE ARABIAN HORSE

Aberford

Lovely welcoming pub, with a tempting menu and a roaring 18th Century open fireplace in winter.

See entry on page 268

and endangered birds, a 12th-century Chapel of Ease, red deer park and café.

BATLEY

6 miles S of Leeds on the A653

This typical industrial town is home to the **Bagshaw Museum** (free), housed inside a strangely Gothic residence in Wilton Park. The museum was founded by the Bagshaw family and many of the collections here were gathered by them on their travels, including items brought back from Alaska by Violet Bagshaw in her 100th year! There are all manner of exhibits, ranging from ancient Egypt to Asia and the Americas, displayed in the exotic interior of this Victorian house. Perhaps the most popular exhibits are found in the 'Gods, Divine Creatures and Mythical Beasts' gallery, showcasing beautiful decorative arts from India, China, Africa and Japan. In the museum park there are nature trails and also the **Butterfly Conservation Centre** (free) which houses a rich assortment of butterflies, many of which are close to extinction in the wild.

Elsewhere in the town there is the **Batley Art Gallery** which plays host to a changing programme of exhibitions that, in particular, feature local artists. In the historic Alexandra Mill there is the **Yorkshire Motor Museum** (free). The collection of around 40 classic and vintage cars on display here ranges from a Benz Motor Wagon of 1885 to the latest Ferrari F40. The museum also boasts the only surviving Bramham – chassis number 128.

BIRSTALL

6 miles SW of Leeds on the A653

This town is home to **Oakwell Hall**, an Elizabethan manor house that dates from 1583 and is one of England's most charming historic houses. Now set out as a 17th-century home, the panelled rooms contain a fine collection of oak furniture, reproduction soft furnishings and items of domestic life. The gardens are stocked with period plants, including culinary and medicinal herbs, while the grounds are now Oakwell Hall Country Park. Charlotte Brontë visited the Hall in the

19th century and it appears as 'Fieldhead' in her novel *Shirley*.

DEWSBURY

8 miles SW of Leeds on the A653

Dewsbury is an extremely old town which once had considerable influence. It has one of the region's oldest town centres with an imposing Town Hall designed by Henry Ashton and George Fox. It also has a number of other notable public and commercial buildings, a substantial shopping area (with some 443,500 square feet of retail floor space) and a famous open market, the largest in Yorkshire.

According to legend, **Dewsbury Minster** is situated at the very spot where, in AD 627, St Paulinus baptised converts to Christianity in the River Calder. The main body of the church dates from the 12th century but the tower was erected in 1767 to a design by the eminent York architect, John Carr. The interior has some interesting features, among them fragments of an Anglo-Saxon cross and coffin lids. The Minster is perhaps best known for its custom of tolling the 'Devil's Knell' on Christmas Eve to ward off evil spirits with a

Dewsbury Minster

bell known as Black Tom. There are Brontë connections here. Patrick Brontë was curate of Dewsbury between 1809-11, and Charlotte taught at Wealds House School nearby. The school was run by a Miss Wooler who later gave her away when she was married.

Re-opened in August 2010 after extensive restoration and refurbishment, the **Dewsbury Museum** (free) in Crow Nest Park is dedicated to childhood and takes visitors on a fascinating journey right back to the first decades of the 20th century, as seen through the eyes of a child.

GOMERSAL

8 miles SW of Leeds on the A643

This ancient village, which featured in the *Domesday Book*, is home to another house that featured in Charlotte Brontë's famous novel, *Shirley*. The **Red House Museum and Brontë Gallery**, which dates back to 1660, was the home of woollen cloth merchants the Taylor family. Charlotte often came here to see her close friend Mary Taylor in the 1830s. The house features as 'Briarmains' in the novel. Today the house is just as the two young Victorian ladies would have remembered it, and it faithfully portrays middle-class domestic life of the time. There is an elegant parlour and a stone-floored

kitchen while, outside in the restored barn, the Secret's Out Gallery explores the author's connections with the Spen Valley. The museum shop sells period toys and gifts and the garden has been re-created from 19th century maps of the site.

ILKLEY

Surrounded by fine unspoiled scenery, with Ilkley Moor and the famous Cow and Calf rocks positioned just above the town, Ilkley is a very attractive spa town. The Victorian bath house still exists, and the recently refurbished Ilkley Pool and Lido, one of the country's last remaining outdoor public swimming pools, continues the spa theme.

Originally an Iron Age settlement, Ilkley was eventually occupied by the Romans who built a camp here to protect their crossing of the River Wharfe. They named their town *Olicana*, so giving rise to the present name with the addition of the familiar *ley* (Anglo-Saxon for 'pasture'). Behind the medieval church is a grassy mound where a little fort was built and in the town's museum are altars carved in gritstone, dedicated to the Roman gods.

The spring at **White Wells** (free) brought more visitors to the town in the 18th century. A small bath house was built where genteel and elderly patients were encouraged to take a dip in the healing waters of the heather spa. Two baths were built here, one of which can still be used. Early Victorian times saw the development of the Hydros – hydropathic treatment hotels – providing hot and cold

---

146 THE LEGGERS

Dewsbury

Originally a hay loft, this beautifully converted inn overlooks the canal basin offering plenty of real ales and home cooked food.

See entry on page 268

---

147 RED HOUSE

Gomersal

This delightful house now looks very much as it would have done in Charlotte Bronte's time when she used it as a model for the Briarmains of her novel *Shirley*.

See entry on page 269

White Wells, Ilkley

treatments based on the idea of Dr Preissnitz of Austria who in 1843 became the director of Britain's first Hydro at nearby Ben Rhydding.

The coming of the railways from Leeds and Bradford in the 1860s and '70s, during a period of growth in the Yorkshire woollen industry, saw the town take on a new role as a fashionable commuter town. Wool manufacturers and their better-paid employees came, not only to enjoy the superb amenities, but to build handsome villas. If Bradford and Leeds were where people made their brass, so it was said at the time, then it was usually at Ilkley that it was spent. Even today, Ilkley sports some remarkable and opulent Victorian architecture.

Ilkley's patrons and well-to-do citizens gave the town a splendid Town Hall, Library, Winter Gardens and King's Hall and a sense of elegance is still present along The Grove. It is still a delight to have morning coffee in the famous Betty's coffee house and discerning shoppers will find a wealth of choice, some in a perfectly preserved Victorian arcade complete with potted palms and balconies. Charles Darwin stayed in the town during the publication of "The Origin of Species", a visit which is commemorated by the town's Darwin Gardens and the Millennium Maze.

Between the remains of the Roman fort and the River Wharfe lie the **Riverside Gardens**, a favourite place for a stroll that might lead over a 17th-century packhorse bridge across the river. On the side of this bridge, beside the stone steps, the flood levels of the river have been marked, along with the dates. On the opposite side of the river is The Lido, one of the few surviving outdoor swimming pools in Yorkshire. Its idyllic surroundings and extensive terraces make it a popular place in summer. Next to the Lido is an indoor pool open all year round. From the Lido a footpath leads up to Middleton Woods, in May a sea of bluebells.

Housed in a building that dates from the 15th, 16th and 17th centuries, complete with mullioned windows, carved beams and an interesting wall privy, **Manor House** (free) tells the history of Ilkley from its prehistoric roots through to its development as a Victorian spa town. Upstairs is an art gallery hosting a programme of temporary exhibitions throughout the year.

A very different kind of museum, the **Ilkley Toy Museum** displays one of the finest private collections of toys in the north of England with its oldest exhibit dating back to 350BC. Amongst the many exhibits are dolls, dolls houses, teddies, tin plate toys, lead figures and games. The museum shop stocks a selection of unusual and traditional toys, games and jigsaw puzzles for sale, together with a range of Ilkley Toy Museum gifts and souvenirs.

Regular events in the town include the Ilkley Literature Festival, a 17-day long event in early October, and the Ilkley Music Festival. The town is also home to the Airedale Symphony Orchestra and is the starting point for the Dales Way long distance footpath, an 80-mile trail which passes through Wharfedale en route to Bowness on Windermere in the Lake District.

One of the most famous West Yorkshire attractions has to be **Ilkley Moor**, immortalised in the well-known song, "On Ilkla Moor Baht'at" (On Ilkley Moor without a Hat). The song is widely regarded as Yorkshire's county "anthem" and gives its name to the local area known as "Baht'at" Country. Few places in the north can equal

---

148 EMPORIO ITALIA

Ilkley

The Italian owner and his chefs bring an authentic taste of Italy to Ilkley in relaxed surroundings reminiscent of a *ristorante* in the south of Italy.

See entry on page 269

---

149 MANOR HOUSE MUSEUM

Ilkley

The Manor House is a very old house dating back to the Middle Ages with later alterations and additions.

See entry on page 270

Ilkley Moor or, more correctly, Rombalds Moor. The moorland, much of it still covered in heather, is also an area of national importance for its archaeology. There is a series of mysteriously marked cup and ring stones dating from the Bronze Age. Almost in the centre of the moor is an ancient stone circle, no doubt a site of some religious importance. Only the keen walker is likely to find these, located high up on the moor, but there is a fine example of a cup and ring stone in the lower part of St Margaret's churchyard in Queen's Road.

Cow and Calf Rocks, Ben Rhydding

AROUND ILKLEY

BEN RHYDDING

1 mile E of Ilkley off the A65

'A few weeks spent at Ben Rhydding seem to effect a complete change in the system', wrote one Victorian visitor to the spa. 'I have seen delicate women, scarcely able to walk feebly round the garden on their first arrival, become strong enough to walk to the Hunting-tower, a lovely point in the heart of the moor at some distance from the house.'

The original Ben Rhydding Hydropathic Hotel, opened in 1844 by a consortium of Leeds businessmen, was built in the Scottish baronial style so popular at the time. By 1908, interest in hydropathy had declined and the exuberant building became the Ben Rhydding Golf Hotel. Later it was turned into flats but finally demolished in 1955.

Athough the name suggests some Scottish connection – and the surrounding scenery certainly has a Caledonian grandeur – 'Ben Rhydding' is actually derived from nearby Bean Rhydding, or bean clearing.

Looking at a map of the area around Ilkley, many people's attention is drawn to the curiously named **Cow and Calf Rocks** which form a striking moor-edge landmark above Ben Rhydding. The Cow is a great gritstone outcrop concealing an old quarry, popular with climbers, while the free-standing Calf is a giant boulder.

BURLEY IN WHARFEDALE

3 miles SE of Ilkley on the A65

Mentioned in the Anglo-Saxon Chronicle in 972AD as Burhleg and in the *Domesday Book* as Burghelai, Burley remained a small riverside settlement until the 1790s when the Industrial Revolution reached the village. Many of the terraces of stone-built cottages, designed for the mill workers, have survived and are now regarded as highly desirable residences. Burley's population has doubled since the 1920s but the Main Street is still lined with Yorkshire stone cottages and houses, and the surrounding hills frame every view.

OTLEY

6 miles SE of Ilkley on the A660

Although it now forms part of the Leeds Metropolitan District, Otley has retained its distinctive character, still boasting a busy cobbled marketplace and many little alleyways and courtyards. Each May the Wharfedale Agricultural Show, founded in 1799 and the oldest show of its kind in

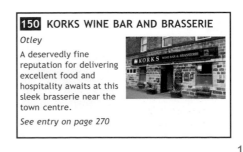

150 KORKS WINE BAR AND BRASSERIE

Otley

A deservedly fine reputation for delivering excellent food and hospitality awaits at this sleek brasserie near the town centre.

See entry on page 270

England, is held in a nearby field.

Even older is Prince Henry's Grammar School, founded in 1602 by James I and named after his eldest son. In front of the building in Manor Square is a statue of Thomas Chippendale, the great furniture maker who was born in Otley in 1718. In 1754 Chippendale published *The Gentleman and Cabinet-Maker's Director* which was immensely influential in both Britain and the USA. His own workshop produced a comparatively small number of pieces but he gave his name to a style that dominated a generation and is still highly prized.

In addition to the statue on the front of the Grammar School, Otley's most famous son is commemorated by a plaque on the wall of Browns Gallery which records that Thomas Chippendale was born in 1718 in a cottage that stood on this spot.

Otley's parish church dates from Saxon times although the main body was constructed in the 11th century. An unusual memorial close by is a stone model of Bramhope Railway Tunnel with its impressive crenellated entrance portals. It was built in the 1830s on the Leeds-Thirsk railway line and more than 30 labourers died during its construction – a tragic loss of life which the model commemorates.

An attractive feature of the town is **The Chevin Forest Park,** a forested ridge above the town which can be reached by a delightful walk that starts in the town. There is also a pleasant walk along the River Wharfe.

GUISELEY

7 miles SE of Ilkley on the A65

Guiseley boasts the most famous fish and chip shop in the world, Harry Ramsden's.

Harry's career as the world's most successful fish frier began in Bradford where he was the first to offer a sit-down fish and chips meal. He moved to Guiseley in 1928 and the original white-painted wooden hut, 10 feet by 6 feet, in which he started business is still on the site today. The present building holds its place in the *Guinness Book of Records* as the world's busiest fish and chip restaurant, serving nearly one million customers each year and still using Harry's secret recipe for the batter. The franchise has steadily expanded over the years and there are now 35 fish and chip shops bearing his name across the country.

HAWORTH

The story of the Brontë family at Haworth Parsonage captures the imagination almost as powerfully as the stirring, passionate novels that were written there. The family moved here in the winter of 1820 - the Revd Patrick Brontë and his wife Maria, and five young daughters. Despite its exposed position on the slopes of Penistone Hill, Haworth seems to have been a singularly unhealthy location. An official report on the village some years later noted that the average age at death was just over 25 years - about the same as in

152 EAT! IN HORSFORTH

Horsforth

Just off the main Leeds ring road, a popular eatery serving breakfasts, snacks, salads and hot dishes from early morning to lunchtime.

See entry on page 270

151 THE DROP INN

Guiseley

With a new lease of life, this popular village inn offers delicious pub grub, famous carveries and great Yorkshire brews.

See entry on page 271

153 COBBLES AND CLAY - THE ART CAFE

Haworth

Novel organic and fair trade cafe with pottery painting workshops for customers to paint their own pieces and take away.

See entry on page 272

the most squalid areas of London. This fearsome mortality did not spare the Brontës. Barely eighteen months after the move to Haworth, Mrs Brontë was dead; four years later the two eldest daughters, Maria (11) and Elizabeth (10) died within a few weeks of each other.

Though all the remaining children did receive an education, it was in a somewhat haphazard way and they spent much of their time with each other isolated at the parsonage. After various attempts at working, generally as teachers, the girls, and their brother Branwell, all returned to the parsonage in the mid-1840s and this is when their writing began in earnest.

Taking their inspiration from the surrounding bleak and lonely Haworth Moor and from the stories they made up as children, the three sisters, Anne, Charlotte, and Emily, under male *noms de plume*, all became published authors. Branwell, though by all accounts a scholar, sought refuge in opium and in visit to the local inn. Then the tuberculosis that had attacked the family earlier returned and, one by one, Patrick s children succumbed to the terrible disease. The Revd Brontë'lingered on until 1861 and then he too joined his gifted but ill-fated children in the family vault of Haworth church.

Their handsome Georgian house, built in 1777, is the focus of most Brontë pilgrimages. It is now owned by the Brontë Society and known as the **Brontë Parsonage Museum**. The Society has restored the interior to resemble as closely as possible the house in which the sisters lived with their father and brother. There are exhibitions and displays of contemporary material, personal belongings, letters, and portraits, as well as

Remains of Top Withins

a priceless collection of manuscripts, first editions, and memorabilia in the newer extension. Perhaps the most atmospheric room in this deeply evocative house is the Dining Room. Over against one wall is the sofa on which Emily expired in 1848; nearby is the rocking chair used by Anne. In the centre stands the square table around which the sisters would pace, arm in arm, reading their work out loud, debating and criticising each other's work.

Once a bleak moorland town in a dramatic setting that fired the romantic imaginations of the Brontë sisters, Haworth has been transformed into a lively, attractive place, with wonderful tea houses, street theatre, and antique and craft shops, very different to how it must have been in the Brontë's days. It was then a thriving industrial town, squalid amidst the smoke from its chimneys, filled with the noise of the clattering looms which were rarely still. It is worth exploring the ginnels and back roads off the steeply rising high street, to get a feeling of what the place was like when the Brontës lived here.

Many visitors are drawn to the area by the story of the family and the **Brontë Way**, a 40-mile linear footpath with a series of four guided walks, links the places that provided inspiration to the sisters. The most exhilarating and popular excursion is that to **Top Withins**, a favourite place of Emily's and the inspiration for the 'Wuthering Heights' of the novel. The route also takes into account a great variety of scenery, from wild moorlands to pastoral countryside.

Brontë enthusiasts can also sit in the Black Bull, where Branwell sent himself to an

---

154 BRONTË PARSONAGE MUSEUM

Haworth
Set between the unique village of Haworth and the wild moorland beyond, this homely Georgian house still retains the atmosphere of the Brontës time.

See entry on page 272

early grave on a mixture of strong Yorkshire ale, opium, and despair. The Post Office, from where the sisters sent their manuscripts to London publishers, is still as it was, as is the Sunday School at which they all taught. Sadly, the church which they all attended no longer exists, although Charlotte, Emily, and Branwell (Anne is buried in Scarborough) all lie in a vault in the new church which dates from 1879.

The countryside around Haworth inspires the modern visitor as much as it did the Brontës. This is excellent walking country and it is worth taking a trip through the **Penistone Hill Country Park**, following the rough track by old moorland farms to the Brontë Falls and stone footbridge. For the energetic, the path eventually leads to the deserted ruins of Top Withins Farm, said to have been the inspiration for the setting of *Wuthering Heights*.

As well as attracting devotees of the Brontë legend, Haworth is also popular with steam railway fans. The town is the headquarters of the **Keighley & Worth Valley Railway,** a thriving volunteer-run enterprise which serves 6 stations, most of them still gas-lit, in the course of its 4¼ mile route. The railway owns a large and varied collection of steam and heritage diesel locomotives and everything combines to re-create the atmosphere of the days of steam. There are daily services during July and August, and intermittent services throughout the rest of the year. Many scenes for the classic film *The Railway Children* (1970) were filmed on the railway, mostly on the stretch between Keighley and Oxenhope. Oakworth

Station in the film is indeed the actual Oakworth station, and the house of stationmaster Perks, played by Bernard Cribbins, is just over the level crossing.

AROUND HAWORTH

OAKWORTH

1 mile N of Haworth on the B6143

Those visiting Oakworth may find its Edwardian station, on the Keighley and Worth Valley Railway line somewhat familiar. In fact, not only did it feature in the classic film *The Railway Children*, but also in episodes of the TV series *Sherlock Holmes*.

KEIGHLEY

3 miles N of Haworth on the A650

The centre of Keighley is dominated by impressive Victorian civic buildings and a beautifully set out covered shopping precinct where the statue of legendary local giant, Rombald, stands. The parish church, also in the centre, is famous as the site where the Revd Patrick Brontë often officiated at marriages. The graveyard contains 15th-century headstones, as well as a crude cross made from four carved heads which is believed to be Saxon in origin.

Close to the town centre is Cliffe Castle which, despite its name, is actually a grand late-19th century mansion complete with a tower, battlements and parkland. It was built for local mill owners, the Butterfields, but now houses the **Keighley Museum** which concentrates of the fascinating local topography and geology of Airedale as well

Keighley and Worth Valley Railway

155 DALESBANK HOLIDAY PARK

Silsden, nr Keighley

For a real taste of the Yorkshire countryside, visit this beautiful country park with bed and breakfast accommodation, caravan and camping facilities and a traditional bar and restaurant.

See entry on page 273

as the history of the town. Also on display is the hand loom, complete with unfinished cloth, used by Timmy Feather, the last hand loom weaver in England. Part of the building is still furnished and decorated in the lavish style of the 1880s.

Lying at the junction of the Rivers Worth and Aire, this bustling textile and engineering town still retains a strangely nostalgic air of the Victorian Industrial Revolution. It's especially evident in the labyrinth of ginnels and terraces which lie amid the many elaborately decorated mills. There are delightful carvings and on one early mill chimney are three heads, one wearing a top hat; in contrast is the classical French-styled Dalton Mills in Dalton Lane with its ornate viewing gallery.

Keighley is the northern terminus of the **Keighley and Worth Valley Railway** which runs to Haworth and Oxenhope. This restored steam railway line passes through some attractive small villages and some notable stations complete with vintage advertising signs, gas lighting and coal fires in the waiting rooms. At Ingrow Station, the **Museum of Rail Travel** contains some fascinating items connected with Victorian travel, among them three small locomotives, coaches in various liveries, the clock from Manchester's Mayfield Station, and an interesting collection of posters and other memorabilia from the golden age of steam.

Celebrating another form of transport, the **Keighley Bus Museum** has a collection of more than 50 buses, coaches, trolleybuses and ancillary vehicles, mainly with West Yorkshire connections and dating from 1924 to 1982.

Above the town, by way of escaping the industrial past, one might enjoy a walk in Park Woods, taking the cobbled path to Thwaites Brow which affords magnificent views of the town below.

The **Worth Way** is an interesting five mile walk from the heart of industrial Keighley to the eastern edge of the Worth Valley at Oxenhope. This landscape has changed little since the time when Mrs Gaskell wrote about the area while visiting Charlotte Brontë in 1856.

East Riddlesden Hall

RIDDLESDEN
4 miles NE of Haworth off the A629

Parts of **East Riddlesden Hall** (National Trust) date back to Saxon times. The main building, however, was constructed in the 1630s by James Murgatroyd, a wealthy Halifax clothier and merchant. A charming example of a 17th-century manor house, the gabled hall is built of dark stone with mullioned windows, and it retains its original central hall, superb period fireplaces, oak panelling, and plaster ceilings. The house is furnished in Jacobean style, which is complemented by carved likenesses of Charles Stuart and Henrietta Maria. Within the extensive grounds is one of the largest and most impressive timber framed barns in the North of England which now houses a collection of farm wagons and agricultural equipment.

OXENHOPE
2 miles S of Haworth on the A6033

This village contains more than 70 listed buildings, including a Donkey Bridge, two milestones, a mounting block, a cowshed, and a pigsty. The early farmhouses had narrow mullioned windows which gave maximum light for weaving and some had a door at first-storey level so that the pieces could be taken out. The first mill here was built in 1792 and, during the 19th century, there were up to 20 mills producing worsted.

Many scenes for *The Railway Children* were set here in 1970 using local views and local people. The village station is the terminus of the **Keighley and Worth Valley Railway.** The station hosts steam engine events and has an exhibition of engines, including one used in the filming of *The Railway Children.*

Oxenhope has become well-known locally for its annual **Straw Race.** Participants (in fancy dress) have to carry a bale of straw with them as they drink a pint of beer in each of the 5 village pubs and carry the bale up a hill. Two local bands add to the jolly atmosphere and over the years the event has raised some £300,000 for local charities.

STANBURY

2 miles W of Haworth off the B6143

Close to the village stands **Ponden Mill** which was, in the heyday of Yorkshire's textile industry, one of the largest working mills in the country. At the height of production, cloth from Ponden Mill was exported around the world. Though the vast majority of the mills have now closed and the Yorkshire textile industry is virtually a thing of the past, Ponden Mill is still open, this time as a retail centre selling all manner of textiles from home furnishings and linens to country clothing. To round off your visit, have a look in the clog shop where traditional methods of manufacture are still on show. There's also a licensed tearoom/restaurant on site.

BRADFORD

Recently designated by UNESCO as the world's first City of Film, Bradford's most popular attraction is undoubtedly the re-named **National Media Museum** which houses the 5-storey high IMAX, one of the largest cinema screens in the world. If you suffer from vertigo you'll need to close your eyes as the huge, wrap-around screen shows such heart-stopping scenes as roller-coaster rides and Alpine mountaineering. There's plenty to keep you occupied here for hours – virtual reality exhibits, the Kodak Gallery which leads you on a journey through the history of popular photography, an extensive TV display which ranges from the world's first TV

pictures to the very latest, and much, much more. A recent addition is a vast new space presenting world-class exhibitions on photography, film, TV and new media.

A short walk from the museum brings you to Bradford's latest two cultural offerings, the **Impressions Gallery** and **Bradford 1 Gallery** which have changing programmes of photography and art exhibitions respectively.

Of related interest is Britain's only **Museum of Colour.** 'The World of Colour' gallery looks at the concept of colour, how it is perceived and its importance. Visitors can see how the world looks to other animals, mix coloured lights and experience strange colour illusions. In the 'Colour and Textiles' gallery you can discover the fascinating story of dyeing and textile printing from Ancient Egypt to the present day. Computerised technology allows you to take charge of a dye-making factory and decorate a room.

Occupying a spectacularly exuberant Victorian pile in Lister Park, the collections at the **Cartwright Hall Art Gallery** (free) reflect the diverse cultural mix that helps to make Bradford the vibrant and unique city it has become in the 21st century. From Victorian paintings and sumptuous Indian silks to works by David Hockney, this gallery is as interesting and far-reaching as the city itself.

Also in Lister Park is the most striking building in this city of impressive buildings, **Lister's Mill.** Its huge ornate chimney dominates the city's northern skyline and it's claimed that it is wide enough at the top to drive a horse and cart around. The mill fell silent some years ago though its exterior has

Lister's Mill, Bradford

been cleaned up and it is currently being converted into up-market apartments.

The **Bradford Industrial Museum** (free) celebrates the city's industrial heritage. It is housed in a huge worsted spinning mill complex built in 1875 and re-creates life in Bradford in late Victorian times. Open all year, the museum also offers horse-bus and tram rides, a shire horse centre, a reconstructed mill owner's house and the working men's back to back cottages. The complex also includes a café, shop and picnic area.

Bolling Hall Museum (free) is a primarily 17th century mansion house containing period furnished rooms as well as temporary exhibitions. The furnishings come from the collections of Bradford Museums, Galleries and Heritage. Amongst the fine furniture on display is a superb bed made for Harewood House by Thomas Chippendale.

Unique in the UK, the **Peace Museum** (free) covers the history of non-violence movements and conflict resolution.

A rather quirkier sign of the city's former riches is **Undercliffe Cemetery**. Here the wool barons were buried, each in a more opulent Gothic mausoleum than the last. It is easy to spend an hour here admiring the Victorian funereal art on show with the cityscape laid out before you.

The **Cathedral Church of St Peter** and its small precinct provides an oasis of calm in this busy city. The present church is some 500 years old but the first evidence of worship on the site is provided by the remains of a Saxon preaching cross. Today the cathedral contains many items of interest, including beautiful stained glass windows, some of which were designed by William Morris, carvings and statuary, including a memorial sculpture by

John Flaxman who considered it one of his best memorial tablets.

No visit to Bradford would be complete without attending a show at the magnificent **Alhambra Theatre**, an Edwardian extravaganza that has been meticulously restored and is now a popular venue for major touring companies and blockbuster West End shows. The city's other major entertainment venue is St George's Concert Hall.

AROUND BRADFORD

SHIPLEY

4 miles N of Bradford on the A6037

Although Shipley town is mainly industrial, **Shipley Glen** is a very popular area for tourists. Within the grounds is a narrow gauge, cable hauled tramway, built in 1895, that carries passengers a quarter of a mile up the side of a steep hill, passing en route through Walker Wood, famous for its bluebells.

In Shipley itself, the **Saltaire Brewery** is a state of the art micro-brewery. It features

Shipley Glen

---

156 BOLLING HALL MUSEUM

Bradford

Bolling Hall offers visitors a fascinating journey through the lives and times of the Bradford families for whom it provided a home over five hundred years.

See entry on page 274

---

157 SHIPLEY GLEN CABLE TRAMWAY

Shipley, nr Bardford

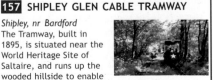

The Tramway, built in 1895, is situated near the World Heritage Site of Saltaire, and runs up the wooded hillside to enable visitors to reach the delights of Shipley Glen.

See entry on page 274

a Visitor Centre with a mezzanine bar and an exhibition about the science of brewing.

The Bracken Hall Countryside Centre has displays and exhibitions relating to the local landscape, archaeology, history, geology and natural history of the local area.

ESHOLT

7 miles N of Bradford off the A6038

This pleasant village was for many years the setting for the TV soap *Emmerdale* until the congestion caused by the filming led the producers to build a replica of the village within the grounds of Harewood House near Leeds. Just outside the village is the award-winning **St Leonard's Farm Park** where there are lots of different animals to feed and pet, play and picnic areas, nature trails, a gift shop and café.

Salt's Mill, Saltaire

THORNTON

4 miles W of Bradford on the B6145

Thornton is an essential stopping place on the Brontë trail for it was here that the three sisters were born, at No. 74 Market Street, now open to the public as the **Brontë Birthplace**. Their father was the vicar of Thornton and one of the treasures of his parish church is a font, inscribed with the date 1687, in which Charlotte, Emily and Anne were all baptised. Charlotte was only four years old, her two sisters still toddlers, when the family moved a few miles northwest to Haworth where their father had been appointed rector.

SALTAIRE

4 miles NW of Bradford off the A657

A UNESCO World Heritage Site, **Saltaire** takes its name from the benevolent industrialist Sir Titus Salt (1803-1876) who founded it, and the River Aire which runs through this model village. Salt was determined to provide his workers with everything essential for a decent standard of living. Built between 1851 and 1876, the facilities in the village were

designed to cater for all their needs – health, leisure and education. High quality housing was provided and almshouses were available rent-free for the elderly and infirm. They also received a pension, some 40 years before the first state pensions were introduced in the UK. But there were no public houses in Saltaire.

The spiritual needs of the work force were attended to by the elegant Congregational church which has been described as the most beautiful Free Church in the north of England.

A statue of Titus Salt stands in nearby Robert's Park (where swearing and gambling were banned) above the figures of a llama and an alpaca whose wool he imported for spinning in his mills.

Titus Salt's ban on the sale of alcohol in Saltaire has finally been overturned. The Victoria Boat House on the banks of the River Aire was built in 1871 but has recently been converted into a stylish bar and restaurant.

Occupying part of what used to be the Saltaire Club and Institute, built in 1871, is the **Museum of Reed Organs and Harmoniums** which has a collection of around 100 instruments, including harmonicas and an American organ, which are demonstrated from time to time, and some of which are available for visitors to try. Original catalogues, posters, trade cards and glass plate negatives create a lively impression of the industry in its heyday.

Saltaire isn't completely locked in the past. The former Salt's Mill has been converted into a shopping mall and also houses the **1853 David Hockney Gallery** which displays one of the largest collections in the world of paintings by the internationally acclaimed artist who was born in Bradford in 1937.

Another building of interest is the **Saltaire United Reformed Church,** a unique Italianate construction built by Sir Titus in 1853 and where he was buried in the Mausoleum in 1876. Rather unusually, Sunday visitors can also take refreshment in the café here.

If you visit Saltaire in September you can enjoy the **Saltaire Festival,** a 10-day long celebration that includes exhibitions, live music, markets, a beer festival and comedy nights. Sir Titus Salt built his factories beside the Leeds and Liverpool Canal and railway to facilitate the distribution of his products. Today, the canal has 1.5 hour circular boat trips.

HALIFAX

Halifax has been dubbed "the most complete Victorian town in Britain". Amongst its numerous impressive examples of municipal architecture from that period is one glorious building from the previous century, **Piece Hall.** It was originally built as a Cloth Hall housing some 300 merchants selling 'pieces' of woven woollen cloth. Today the Hall contains forty bespoke shops ranging from designer glassware to traditional and old-fashioned sweets. It has a large quadrangle where regular markets are held on Fridays and Saturdays, surrounded by colonnades and balconies behind which are some 40 specialist shops. On Thursdays a flea market is held here and there's a lively and varied programme of events for all the family throughout the season. There's also an art gallery with a varied programme of contemporary exhibitions and workshops, a visitor centre, museum, cafes and bars.

The **Town Hall** is another notable building, designed by Sir Charles Barry, architect of the Houses of Parliament, and there's an attractive Borough Market, constructed in cast iron and glass with an ornate central clock.

Halifax also boasts the largest parish church in England. Of almost cathedral sized proportions, the **Church of St John** dates from the 12th and 13th centuries although most of the present building is from the 1400s. It has a lovely wooden ceiling, constructed in 1635, and visitors should look out for 'Old Tristram', a life-sized wooden effigy of a beggar, reputedly based on a local character. It was designed to serve as the church poor box – and still does.

There are many hidden places in old Halifax to explore. From Shear's Inn, an old weavers' inn near the town centre, one can walk up the cobbled Boy's Lane, very little changed from Victorian times, or trace out the ancient *Magna Via*, a medieval path to the summit of Beacon Hill. In Gibbet Street stands a grisly reminder of the past – a replica of the Halifax guillotine, the original blade being kept in the Piece Hall Museum. Halifax appears to have been unique in using the guillotine to execute condemned criminals. It is reported that if the offender was to be executed for stealing an animal, the end of a rope was fastened to the pin holding the blade in place and tied to the animal, which was then driven off, causing the pin to pull out and the blade to drop. The use of the guillotine was first recorded in 1286; the last two offenders to die by this method perished in 1650.

Situated next to Halifax railway station, **Eureka!** is Britain's first and only interactive museum designed especially for children between three and 12 years old. With more than 400 larger than life exhibits and exciting activities available, Eureka! opens up a fascinating world of hands-on exploration. A team of 'Enablers' helps children make the most of their visit; there are regular temporary exhibitions, and the complex includes a café and gift shop.

Now a vibrant complex of businesses, galleries, theatre, design and book shops, **Dean Clough** is housed in a magnificent Victorian carpet mill that stretches for two-thirds of a mile. Built between 1840 and 1870 by the Crossley family, this mill was once home to one of the world's leading carpet factories. It ceased production in

1982. The complex also includes artists studios and workshops, a café/bar and a licensed restaurant.

Shibden Hall and Park, about a mile out of town, is somewhere very special that should not be missed. The Old Hall lies in a valley on the outskirts of the town and is surrounded by 90 acres of parkland. The oldest part of this distinctive timber framed house dates from 1420 and has been carefully furnished to reflect the various periods of its history. The 17th-century aisled barn behind the Hall houses a fine collection of horse-drawn vehicles and the original buildings have been transformed into a 19th-century village centre with a pub, estate worker's cottage, saddler's, blacksmith's, wheelwright's and potter's workshop. The grounds of the Hall are now a public park with a boating lake, pitch and putt, children's playground, miniature railway, café and visitor centre.

On the northern outskirts of the town is the **Bankfield Museum**, the home between 1837 and 1886 of Edward Akroyd, the largest wool manufacturer in Britain. He lavished money and attention on the building, transforming it from a modest town house into a magnificent Italianate mansion with elaborate ceilings, staircases and plasterwork. After his death, his sumptuous

Shibden Hall, Halifax

home became a museum and now houses an internationally important collection of textiles and costumes from around the world. Contemporary crafts are also featured and the museum hosts an interesting programme of temporary exhibitions, workshops, seminars, master classes and gallery demonstrations. Here, too, is a Toy Gallery, the Duke of Wellington's Regimental Museum and the Marble Gallery that sells contemporary crafts. Surrounding his house, Akroyd built a model village called Akroydon that, with its terraced houses, allotments, park and church was the first 'urban' village.

AROUND HALIFAX

BRIGHOUSE

4 miles SE of Halifax on the A643/A644

Brighouse lies in the so called "golden triangle" commuter belt between Halifax, Ripponden and Brighouse with convenient access to the M62. Currently, there is an extensive programme of renovation of Brighouse mills which are being converted

---

158 SHIBDEN HALL

Halifax

For over 300 years this was the Lister's family home, but Shibden Hall itself is even older, built in 1420. Generations have lived and worked here and today the hall reflects this continual development.

See entry on page 274

---

159 BANKFIELD MUSEUM

Halifax

Set in a Victorian mill owner's house, there is an important collection of textiles, various objects from around the world plus a programme of exhibitions and activities.

See entry on page 275

---

160 BLAKELEY'S FISH AND CHIP RESTAURANT

Brighouse

A superb family run restaurant serving a wide range of fish dishes popular with locals and visitors.

See entry on page 276

into loft style apartments.

The **Smith Art Gallery** is named after its founder, William Smith, Mayor of Brighouse in 1893. He was passionate about art and amassed a large collection of works that reflect the tastes of the late Victorian period, pieces like Atkinson Grimshaw's Mossy Glen and Marcus Stone's Silent Pleading. One of the two galleries displays his collection as a permanent exhibition; the other has a programme of temporary exhibitions, including work by local artists, as well as touring exhibitions by national and internationally renowned artists.

SOWERBY BRIDGE

2 miles SW of Halifax on the A58

Sowerby Bridge has a flower-bedecked canal wharf, a reputation as a gourmet destination, many specialist shops, an award-winning sculpture trail and, in the spirit of the times, a solar-powered market.

The town has a rather odd connection with the Brontës. For a while, Branwell Brontë worked as a booking clerk at the railway station here. He was dismissed in March 1842 when discrepancies were found in his accounts. Branwell also worked in the same role at nearby Luddenden Foot where he was a member of the library at the White Swan inn. (At that time, several hostelries provided this amenity for their patrons.) A condition of membership of the library stipulated 'sobriety and decorous conduct' on pain of a fine of 2d (0.8p) for each offence. This requirement must have caused Branwell some difficulty as he was a scandalously heavy drinker.

An important crossing of both the Rivers Ryburn and Calder in medieval times, and possibly as far back as the Roman occupation,

---

161 THE OLD SHIP INN

Brighouse

This award winning pub is a haven for real ale lovers and serves excellent pub food.

See entry on page 275

---

162 THE CLOUGH HOUSE INN

Rastrick, nr Brighouse

This inn dates back to the early 1800s and serves fresh local produce and a selection of real ales.

See entry on page 277

---

163 THE DUKE OF YORK

Stainland

A truly remarkable pub offering wholesome home cooked food, a well stocked bar and a great atmosphere in which to relax with friends.

See entry on page 278

---

164 BRANCH ROAD INN

Upper Greetland

An immensely popular inn with a friendly host, offering homecooked food made from local ingredients.

See entry on page 278

---

165 THE WORKS

Sowerby Bridge

Originally an old workshop, The Works offers a great place to meet with friends, dine with a partner and enjoy a wide selection of refreshments, including 9 real ales.

See entry on page 279

---

166 THE ALMA INN AND FRESCO ITALIAN RESTAURANT

Sowerby Bridge

This is one of Yorkshire's finest inns. It offers superb home-cooked food in its Italian restaurant and offers luxurious accommodation.

See entry on page 280

Sowerby Bridge first had water-powered mills as early as the 14th century. The mills, first used for grinding corn, moved into textile production and by the 1850s were all steam-driven. Greenups Mill, built in 1792, was the first integrated woollen mill in Yorkshire with all the textile processes brought under one roof. Sowerby Bridge also boasted one of the first turnpike roads in Britain, constructed in 1735. Just a short time later the Calder and Hebble Navigation, surveyed by John Smeaton, the designer of the Eddystone Lighthouse, was opened in 1770, followed by the Rochdale Canal in 1804. A reminder of the busy days of the canal is **Tuel Lane Lock and Tunnel** which joined the two man-made waterways. It re-opened in 1996 and it is a grand sight to watch the narrowboats negotiating what is the deepest lock in the country.

RIPPONDEN

6 miles SW of Halifax on the A58

Ripponden lies in the valley of the Ryburn, a tributary of the Calder. An ancient packhorse bridge crosses the river and, right beside it is the Old Bridge Inn, one of the oldest inns in Yorkshire. It was already in existence in 1313 and its interior, with its sloping floors and different levels, has been compared to a funfair crazy house. Back in the 1980s a group of customers founded the Pork Pie Appreciation Society which now holds an annual **Pork Pie Festival** at the inn where butchers from around the country display their offerings.

MYTHOLMROYD

5 miles W of Halifax on the A646

Prior to the 1600s, the valley bottom in what is now Mytholmroyd was marshy and of little

167 EL GATO NEGRO TAPAS

Ripponden

This stylish and funky tapas restaurant serves a wide range of mouth-watering dishes cooked by reputable chef Simon Shaw.

See entry on page 281

use as foundations for a village, though some of the outlying farms in the area date from the late 14th century. However, with the need to build more mills close to a supply of water, the land was improved and Mytholmroyd joined the age of the Industrial Revolution.

Each spring the town is host to the **World Dock Pudding Championships**. Dock Pudding is unique to this corner of the county and is made from the weed *Polygonum Bistorta* or sweet dock (which should not be confused with the larger docks that are commonly used for easing nettle stings). In spring the plant grows profusely and local people pick it by the bagful. The docks are then mixed with young nettles and other essential ingredients and cooked to produce a green and slimy delicacy the appearance of which is found by many to be rather off-putting. It is usually served with bacon and/or an egg after having been fried in bacon fat and is believed to cure acne and cleanse the blood.

Mytholmroyd is also home to **Walkley Clogs,** one of the last UK producers to make and sell the genuine article. The owners claim that clogs keep your feet cool in summer and warm in winter, and welcome visitors to watch them being made.

TODMORDEN

12 miles W of Halifax on the A646

This is another typical mill town that grew with the expansion of the textile industry. Before the 19th century, Todmorden had been a spartan place with many of the villagers eking out frugal lives by hand loom weaving. Following the building of the first mill here, Todmorden began to grow and the highly ornate and flamboyant public buildings were, in the main, built by the mill owners. Though many towns which owe their existence to industry also bear the scars, Todmorden has retained all its charm and character and is an excellent place to visit for those interested in architecture. It boasts a magnificent **Town Hall** designed by John Gibson and opened in 1875. One of the finest municipal buildings of its size in the country, the grand old building stands half in Yorkshire and half in

Lancashire. So the ornate carving in the pediment represents the farming and iron trades of Yorkshire in the right panel; the cotton trade of Lancashire in the left.

Few towns can boast of having been the birthplace of two Nobel Prize-winners but Todmorden can: John Cockcroft who won the prize for Physics in 1951 and Geoffrey Wilkinson who the prize for Chemistry in 1973.

HEBDEN BRIDGE

6 miles NW of Halifax on the A646

Rochdale Canal, Hebden Bridge

Hebden Bridge has been described as the "jewel in the crown" of Calderdale. This former mill town is characterised by the stepped formation of its houses which are stacked one above the other up the steep sides of the Calder valley. Today, the heart of the town, St George's Square, is packed with arts and crafts shops, vegetarian and specialist organic cafes, and restaurants, pubs serving fine Yorkshire real ale, delicatessens, arts and crafts shops and designer or specialised clothing shops. Here you'll also find the octagonal Methodist chapel which is believed to be the oldest in the world still in use. And, adjacent to the white Lion Inn is the 18th century **Hebden Bridge Mill** which has been lovingly restored and is now home to various stylish shops, restaurants and craft workshops.

The **Rochdale Canal**, which slices through the town, was completed in 1798. It was constructed to link the Calder and Hebble Navigation with the Bridgewater and Ashton canals from Lancashire. Used by commercial traffic since 1939, the canal has been repaired and sections of it, including that between Hebden Bridge and Todmorden, are now open to traffic. Motor boat cruises are available from the marina and horse-drawn trips can be enjoyed along the canal.

To the northwest of Hebden Bridge, at Colden, is the **Land Farm Sculpture Garden and Gallery**, a delightful woodland garden created over some 30 years from a barren Pennine hillside that faces north and is 1000ft above sea level.

From Hebden Bridge a riverside walk leads to **Hardcastle Crags** (National Trust, free), 400 acres of unspoilt woodlands encompassing deep rocky ravines, tumbling streams, oak, beech and pine woods and some of the best examples of upland meadows in the country. At the heart of the site is **Gibson Mill**, a 19th century former cotton mill. It went out of business in the early 1900s. It has recently been redeveloped by the Trust as an example of sustainable tourism. So the mill has no mains electricity, gas, water or sewers - the only outside service is the telephone. There are many hands-on family-orientated exhibits allowing visitors to learn more about the industrial

---

168 **WATERGATE LICENSED TEA ROOM & TEA GARDEN**

Hebden Bridge

This is one of West Yorkshire's finest tea rooms and has a fantastic courtyard overlooking the river.

See entry on page 282

---

169 **WHITE LION HOTEL**

Hebden Bridge

This traditional coaching inn is set in an attractive riverside location. It serves fresh home cooked food and real cask ales.

See entry on page 282

and social heritage of the mill and the natural surroundings of Hardcastle Crags.

HEPTONSTALL

7 miles NW of Halifax off the A646

This picturesque hilltop village, one of the main tourist centres in Calderdale, overlooks Hebden Bridge and Hardcastle Crags. Within this beautiful wooded valley there are several attractive walks along purpose built footpaths.

Occupying what used to be the village grammar school, **Heptonstall Museum** has a range of displays reflecting life in the area over the last four centuries. Two of the school's long black oak desks have survived, complete with graffiti, as well as the Headmaster's desk and a fine collection of Victorian school books. The story of the Cragg Vale Coiners is told, a tale of a small band of local men who produced counterfeit coins and committed murder to escape capture. Also on display are photographs from the Alice Longstaff Collection which gives unique insights into local life between the 1960s and 1990s.

Heptonstall is one of only three places in Britain where two churches occupy the same churchyard. In this case, the original church, which dates from 1256, was struck by lightning in the 1830s and a new church was built next to the ruin. Within one of the three churchyards is the grave of David Hartley, the leader of the Cragg Vale Coiners, who was hung in 1770 in York. In another is buried Sylvia Plath, the American wife of the former Poet Laureate Ted Hughes.

Every year, on Good Friday, the **Paceggers Play** takes place in Weavers Square. It's an ancient method of story-telling with actors

---

170 WHITE LION

Heptonstall

This impressive stone-built inn sells real ale, quality fresh food and has several guest rooms available all year round.

See entry on page 283

---

dressed in elaborate costumes recounting the legend of St George.

HUDDERSFIELD

With its steep, often cobbled streets, millstone grit cottages and imposing Victorian public buildings and houses, Huddersfield has a very distinctive character all of its own. Friedrich Engels described it as "the most handsome manufacturing town in the north of England". The town flourished in Victorian times and its most impressive buildings date from that era. The stately railway station, regarded as having the finest façade of any station building in England, was designed by James Pritchett of York and built between 1846-50, to be followed by the Town Hall (!881) which has a sumptuously decorated interior and one of the best concert halls in the north.

The **Tolson Memorial Museum** (free) has displays that range from the tools of the earliest settlers in the area to modern day collections contributed by local people. One of the most popular exhibits is the collection of vintage vehicles and motoring memorabilia in the 'Going Places' collection. The collection includes Britain's rarest car - the three-wheeled LSD - which was manufactured in Huddersfield between 1919 and 1924. Other displays trace the story of the Industrial Revolution, so important to the growth of the town, and the political protests it engendered.

Huddersfield Art Gallery holds the Kirklees Collection of British Art covering the last 150 years, with a lively programme of exhibitions that feature contemporary works from regional, national and international artists. The permanent exhibition features works by internationally renowned artists such as Francis Bacon, LS Lowry, Walter Sickert, Frank Auerbach and Henry Moore.

Amongst the many legacies of the Victorians are two splendid public parks. Spread across the valley side, Beaumont Park is a 21-acre expanse with some stunning Pennine views; Greenhead Park attracts around half a million visitors each

Huddersfield Canal

home to a marina. In 1794, work began on the **Huddersfield Narrow Canal**, linking the town with Ashton-under-Lyne. Its centrepiece, the Standedge Tunnel, took 17 years to complete and is the longest, highest and deepest canal tunnel in the country. The **Standedge Experience** at Marsden houses an exciting and interactive exhibition telling the story of the canal and the tunnel. Trips in a glass-topped boat take visitors through the 3.25 mile long tunnel in a 30-minute journey. The surrounding countryside offers a wide range of activities including walking, cycling and fishing, and this area of outstanding natural beauty is also a haven for wildlife.

year and its many amenities include bowling greens, tennis courts, ornamental gardens, steam hauled miniature railway and a colossal war memorial.

Huddersfield is proud of the fact that the sport of Rugby League was created in 1895 at the George Hotel in Huddersfield. Today, the George is still a hotel but it also houses a permanent exhibition celebrating the game. The **Gillette Rugby League Heritage Centre** displays a collection of rare memorabilia, ancient caps and jerseys, valuable medals and trophies, old programmes and pictures. Plasma screens and floor-to-ceiling graphics record the game's history in a vivid and user-friendly format. The Centre is open at weekends only

The town's two canals have been vitally important to Huddersfield's development. They helped to link Huddersfield not only with the national canal network but also with other industrial towns. Completed in 1780 and paid for by the Ramsden family, the **Huddersfield Broad Canal** was constructed to link the town with the Calder and Hebble Navigation. The canal's Aspley Basin is today

Huddersfield's earliest roots can be found on the 1000-ft high Castle Hill which has been occupied as a defence since the Stone Age. Simple tools, flints, bone needles, combs and pottery dating back to 2000BC have been unearthed here. The much later ramparts of an Iron Age fort, built here around 600BC can still be seen. In 1147 the Normans repaired the earthworks and built a motte and bailey castle which was apparently used as a base for hunting. The hill was also used as a beacon when England was threatened by the Spanish Armada, and again during the Napoleonic wars. The lofty Jubilee Tower, built in 1897 to celebrate Queen Victoria's Diamond Jubilee, is the most recent structure on the summit and was funded by public subscription. Inside the tower there's a museum which traces the hill's 4000 years of history.

AROUND HUDDERSFIELD

DENBY DALE

8 miles SE of Huddersfield on the A635/A636

The pleasant village of Denby Dale is, of course, famous for its production of gigantic meat pies. The first of these Desperate Dan-sized dishes was baked in 1788 to celebrate George III's return to sanity; later ones

---

171 THE BLACKSMITHS ARMS

Kirkheaton

Commanding stunning views over the surrounding countryside this rural inn offers delicious Yorkshire food and local brews in a great atmosphere.

See entry on page 284

marked the victory of Waterloo and Queen Victoria's Jubilee. The 1928 monster meal was organised to raise funds for the Huddersfield Royal Infirmary but the festivities were almost cancelled when the organisers discovered that a large part of the pie had gone bad. Four barrowloads of stinking meat were secretly spirited away.

Perhaps because of that mishap, no more great pies were attempted until 1964 when it was decided to commemorate the four royal births of that year. On this occasion two walls of Mr Hector Buckley's barn, in which the pie had been baked, had to be demolished to get it out. The most recent pie was made in 2000 as part of the town's Millennium celebrations. It weighed a hearty 12 tonnes and contained 100kg of John Smith's Best Bitter.

Rising high above the village is the TV mast at Emley, 330 metres high and the tallest self-supporting structure in Britain. Another striking landmark nearby is the long railway viaduct of the Penistone Line that spans the Dearne valley at Denby Dale.

CLAYTON WEST

8 miles SE of Huddersfield on the A636

A popular attraction at Clayton West is the **Kirklees Light Railway**, a 15" gauge steam railway which runs along the old Lancashire & Yorkshire Clayton West branch line. The track passes through gently rolling farmland for about four miles with a quarter-mile long tunnel adding to the thrill. The large station/ visitor centre at Clayton West provides passengers with comfortable, spacious surroundings to await their train or take advantage of the light refreshment café and the souvenir shop. The railway operates daily during the season and every weekend throughout the year.

ARMITAGE BRIDGE

2½ miles S of Huddersfield on the A616

This village is home to the **North Light Gallery** which is housed in a converted 18th century textile mill. The gallery concentrates on hosting major exhibitions of the very best in 20th-century and

contemporary art while, throughout the year, the North Light Studio holds classes and a programme of weekend workshops.

HONLEY

3 miles S of Huddersfield off the A616

The centre of this delightful little Pennine village has been designated as a site of historic interest. There are charming terraces of weavers' cottages, many interesting alleyways, and the old village stocks still stand in the churchyard of St Mary's. The Coach and Horses Inn has strong connections with the Luddite movement of the early 1800s. It was here, in 1812, that two Luddites, Benjamin Walker and Thomas Smith, spent the night drinking after murdering a mill owner at nearby Marsden. They were later arrested, convicted and executed at York. Not far from the inn is another interesting feature – an old well dated 1796 whose date stone warns passers-by they will be fined 10 shillings (50p) for 'defouling' the water.

The village is well-known because of its Honley Show in June, one of the most prestigious, best attended and well respected rural shows in the country. Now in its 78th year, the show provides a remarkable range of activities, agricultural events, stands and displays.

FARNLEY TYAS

4 miles S of Huddersfield off the A626 or A629

Set on a 900ft-high hillo, Farnley Tyas is another attractive Pennine village with scattered stone farmhouses and barns, and 18th- and 19th-century workers' cottages grouped around the crossroads. It is mentioned in the *Domesday Book* as 'Fereleia': the Tyas part of its name comes from the Le Teyeis family which owned much of the land hereabouts from the 13th century.

MELTHAM

5 miles S of Huddersfield on the B6107/B6108

A typical Pennine mill town, Meltham is mostly Victorian but with a handsome Georgian parish church dating from 1786 which is challenged in size by the spacious Baptist Chapel, rebuilt in 1864. Only two mills have survived but the Meltham Mills Band, founded in 1846, is still thriving and has won many competitions throughout the country, including the British Open Championship which it won three years in a row.

Meltham used to have an assembly plant for building tractors. The **David Brown Tractor Museum** showcases memorabilia and archives from the history of that once well-known company. The displays includes one of the first tractors built here in 1943 and also the last tractor built here. Limited opening times.

HOLMFIRTH

6 miles S of Huddersfield on the A6024/A635

BBC-TV's longest running situation comedy, *Last of the Summer Wine*, ran for 37 years and transmitted its last series in the summer of 2010. Compo and his companions have made this little Pennine town familiar to viewers around the world. Visitors can enjoy an authentic bacon buttie in the Wrinkled Stocking Tea Room, gaze at Nora Batty's cottage and sit in the famous pub. And there are plans underway to create a Last of the Summer Wine Museum using original sets and props.

---

172 **LAST OF THE SUMMER WINE EXHIBITION**

Holmfirth

Back in the early 1970s, the sleepy Pennine town of Holmfirth was turned head over heels by the introduction of three rascally men.

See entry on page 284

---

173 **ROTCHER COFFEE BAR**

Holmfirth

A popular licensed coffee bar that also serves a good choice of home baking, snacks and hot dishes.

See entry on page 285

The rest of the town offers a network of side lanes, courts and ginnels (alleyways) while the terraces of weavers' cottages are typical of a town famous for its production of wool textiles. In recent years, the influx of *Last of the Summer Wine* tourists has generated the growth of a number of speciality shops and galleries, including the Ashley Jackson Gallery featuring the distinctive watercolour paintings of brooding moorland by the popular artist.

Holmfirth has a lovely Georgian church, built in 1777-8 in neo-classical style to the designs of Joseph Jagger. The gable faces the street and the tower is constructed at the eastern end against a steep hillside.

During the first half of the 20th century a comprehensive range of traditional saucy seaside postcards was produced by Bamforths of Holmfirth. The company also printed hymn sheets and, rather surprisingly, made many early silent movies. Bamforths also owned a cinema in the town which has recently been restored as **Picturedrome,** complete with a bar. The re-instated building now hosts a wide range of film events and other entertainment, and also displays a selection of the vintage postcards.

Holmfirth hosts several festivals throughout the year; there's the annual Folk Festival in May; the Holmfirth Arts Festival in June and the Holmfirth Music Festival in October.

As with so many moorland villages, there is a lot of surrounding water and in its time Holmfirth has suffered three major floods. The worse occurred in 1852 when the nearby Bilberry Reservoir burst its banks, destroying mills, cottages and farms, and killing 81 people. A pillar near the church records the height the waters reached.

HOLMBRIDGE

7 miles S of Huddersfield on the A6024

This charming village stands at the head of a steep-sided valley and enjoys picture postcard views of the Pennines and the Holme valley. There are cottages here dating from the 1700s and the area is known for its unusual style of architecture, four-decker

Marsden Moor Estate

some stunning views. Public footpaths criss-cross this land which, as well as providing grazing for sheep, is home to numerous moorland birds including golden plover, grouse, curlew, snipe and twite. Meanwhile, the moorland's deep peat provides a habitat for acid-loving plants and for animals that can survive in this bleak and exposed environment.

GOLCAR

3 miles W of Huddersfield
off the A62 or A640

About a mile south of the oddly-named Scapegoat Hill the **Colne Valley Museum** is housed in three 19th century weavers' cottages near the parish church. Visitors can see a loom chamber with working hand looms and a Spinning Jenny; a weavers' living room of 1850 and a gas-lit clogger's shop of 1910. On two weekends a year, a craft weekend is held when many different skills are demonstrated. Light refreshments are available and there's also a museum shop. Run entirely by its members, the museum has featured many times on TV and is open weekends and Bank Holidays throughout the year but party visits can be arranged at other times.

cottages dug into the hillside. The lower cottage is approached from the front, the upper cottage is reached by a steep flight of stone steps leading round the back.

HEPWORTH

7 miles S of Huddersfield on the A616

What is one to make of a village that lies on the River Jordan, has a house that has always been known as Solomon's Temple (although no one knows why), and a parcel of land called Paradise, the only place it is said where fruit trees will grow? There are some other curious names here, including Meal Hill, where the Romans brought their hand-mill stones to grind corn, and **Barracks Fold** where, during the plague, the healthy barricaded themselves against the infected. There are still some triangular patches of land in the village that are believed to contain the common graves of the plague victims.

MARSDEN

7 miles SW of Huddersfield on the A62

Situated at the head of the Colne Valley, this village is an historic Trans-Pennine crossing point with the Standedge rail, canal tunnels and a packhorse route that leads out of the valley.

Situated above the village is the **Marsden Moor Estate** (National Trust), a tract of nearly 6000 acres of Pennine moorland that is full of industrial architecture and provides

---

174 **PENNY'S PANTRY**

Slaithwaite

Excellent home cooking in a popular daytime eating place right by a bridge on the Huddersfield Narrow Canal.

See entry on page 285

---

175 **ROSE & CROWN**

Golcar

A remarkable pub with friendly hosts, offering a well stocked bar, hearty Sunday roasts and a warm welcome to all.

See entry on page 285

WAKEFIELD

One of the oldest towns in Yorkshire, Wakefield stands on a hill guarding an important crossing of the River Calder. Its defensive position has always been important and it was the Battle of Wakefield in 1460, when the Duke of York was defeated, that gave rise to the mocking song *The Grand Old Duke of York*.

Many students of the Robin Hood legends claim that the famous outlaw had his origins in Wakefield. As evidence they cite the Court Rolls in which one Robin Hode is noted as living here in the 14th century with his wife Matilda. Also medieval in origin are the **Wakefield Mystery Plays** which explore Old and New Testament stories in vivid language.

Wakefield Cathedral

There are four main streets in the city, Westgate, Northgate, Warrengate and Kirkgate, which still preserve the medieval city plan. One of the most striking surviving buildings of that time is the tiny Chantry Chapel on Chantry Bridge which dates from the mid-1300s and is the best of only four such examples of bridge chapels in England. It is believed to have been built by Edward IV to commemorate the brutal murder of his brother Edmund. Grandest of all though is **Wakefield Cathedral** which was begun in Norman times, rebuilt in 1329 and refashioned in 1470 when its magnificent 247-ft high spire – the highest in Yorkshire – was added. The eastern extension was added in 1905 and was considered necessary after the church became a Cathedral in 1888. Other interesting buildings in the town include the stately Town Hall, the huge County Hall, the recently restored Victorian Theatre Royal and many fine Georgian and Regency terraces and squares.

Wakefield's cultural attractions include **Wakefield Art Gallery**, housed in an attractive former Victorian vicarage just a short stroll from the town centre. Collections include many early works by locally born sculptors Henry Moore and Barbara Hepworth along with important work by many other major British modern artists. Currently, work is well underway for the construction of a £26m art gallery and creative centre, The Hepworth Wakefield, which is scheduled to open in May 2011. It will showcase the present gallery's treasures as well as the Gott Collection of more than 1200 images of Yorkshire.

Wakefield Museum, located in an 1820s building next to the Town Hall, was originally a music saloon and then a Mechanics' Institute. It now houses collections illustrating the history and archaeology of Wakefield and its people from prehistoric times to the present day. There is also a permanent display of exotic birds and animals garnered by the noted 19th-century traveller, naturalist and eccentric Charles Waterton, who lived at nearby Walton Hall where he created the world's first nature reserve. Also of interest is the **Stephen G Beaumont Museum** (free) which houses an unusual exhibition of medical memorabilia and exhibits telling the story of the West Riding Pauper Lunatic Asylum that was founded in 1818 and only closed in 1995. The exhibition

---

176 **THE HORSE AND GROOM WAKEFIELD**

Wakefield

The rural location of Heath Common just outside Wakefield City is the home of the Horse and Groom popular for its real ales, real cider, humble pub food, pub traditions and real welcome.

See entry on page 286

Sandal Castle, Wakefield

includes restraining equipment, a padded cell, photographs dating from 1862 plus medical and surgical equipment and documents. The museum, which has a scale model of the early 19t-century building, is only open on Wednesdays.

Just south of the city centre stands **Sandal Castle**, a 12th-century motte-and-bailey fortress that was later replaced by a stone structure. It overlooks the site of the Battle of Wakefield in 1460. Such was this castle's importance that Richard III was planning to make Sandal his permanent northern stronghold when he was killed at Bosworth Field. Today all that remains are ruins as the castle was destroyed by Cromwell's troops after a siege in 1645. From the castle there are magnificent views across the Calder Valley. Discoveries made during recent excavations of the site can be found in Wakefield's Interpretive Centre.

To the north of the city centre, **Clarke Hall** is a late-17th century brick-built gentleman farmer's residence with contemporary and replica furnishings and now used as a living history museum. Because of its size the Hall is reserved for use by school

groups during term time. The gardens have also been restored in 17th century style and there's a modern visitor centre with exhibits and displays relating to the history of the Hall and its owners.

About 5 miles southeast of Wakefield, **Nostell Priory** is one of the most popular tourist venues in this area. The word 'priory' is misleading since it evokes the picture of an ecclesiastical structure. But Nostell is in fact a large Palladian building erected on the site of an old Augustinian priory. It was in 1733 that the owner, Sir Rowland Winn, commissioned James Paine to build a grand mansion here. Paine was only 19 at the time and this was his first major project. Thirty years later, only half the state rooms were constructed and Sir Rowland's son, also named Rowland, engaged an up and coming young designer to complete the decoration. The young man's name was Robert Adam and between 1766 and 1776 his dazzling designs produced an incomparable sequence of interiors.

There was a third man of genius involved in the story of Nostell Priory – the cabinet maker Thomas Chippendale. What is believed to be his 'apprentice piece', made around 1735, is on display here – an extraordinary doll's house six feet high and replete with the most elaborate detail, every minuscule door, window or desk drawer functioning perfectly. Today, Nostell Priory can boast the most comprehensive collection in the world of Chippendale's work.

Another interesting piece of furniture is John Harrison's Clock. John was the son of Nostell Estate's carpenter and went on to solve the Longitude problem. The movement of the clock on display here is made entirely of wood.

177 NOSTELL PRIORY

Nostell, nr Wakefield

Nostell Priory takes its name from the 12th century Augustinian Priory dedicated to Saint Oswald.

See entry on page 286

AROUND WAKEFIELD

CASTLEFORD

9 miles NE of Wakefield on the A656

It was here at Castleford that the Romans crossed the River Aire and then built a fort to protect this important crossing. Sadly little remains of the settlement that the Romans called 'Legioleum', although archaeological finds from that period can be seen in the town's excellent Castleford Museum Room at the town library. Here, not only are these remains exhibited but there are also displays on the lives of ordinary people in Victorian Castleford.

The home of Allison's flour, which is still stone-ground on the banks of the river, Castleford was also, in 1898, the birthplace of the internationally-renowned sculptor Henry Moore. One of the most influential artists of the 20th century, the town has honoured its famous son with Moore Square, a fine area of York stone paving with a series of large stone archways that stands close to the place where the family's home once stood – the house itself was demolished in the 1970s.

Shopaholics will no doubt make a bee-line for the Junction 32 Outlet Village (formerly Freeport) which is Europe's largest shopping village and offers a wide selection of shops, including many designer names. Next door to Junction 32 is the recently opened Xscape development, housing one of the largest indoor real snow ski slopes in Europe. The complex, incorporates an ice climbing wall, multiplex cinema, bowling alley, shops and restaurants all under one roof.

NORMANTON

4 miles E of Wakefield off the A655

A former mining town, Normanton has a spacious park, a moat round a hill where the Romans built a camp, and a large, mostly 15th-century church with a fine 500-year-old font. The stained glass windows here are something of an oddity since none of them originally belonged to the church. They were part of a collection amassed by a 19th-century resident of the town who was himself a glass painter and bequeathed the unrelated pieces to the church. The most striking is a 15th-century *Pietà* in the east window which has been identified as Flemish in origin.

PONTEFRACT

8 miles E of Wakefield off the M62/A1

Shakespeare alluded to the town in his plays

---

178 BRIDGE INN

Whitwood

Well established inn with lovely accommodation, and delicious food being cooked up in the bar and restaurant.

See entry on page 287

---

179 THE RISING SUN AND PALM COURT

Whitwood

Two excellent adjacent restaurants managed by the same able woman, offering a more traditional English dining experience alongside a taste of the Mediterranean.

See entry on page 288

---

180 THE BOAT PUB AND RESTAURANT

Allerton Bywater

This pub is well worth seeking out. Good food, real ales and warm hospitality are the main priorities here.

See entry on page 289

---

181 THE GOLDEN LION HOTEL

Ferrybridge

A warm welcome is assured to all at this hotel standing in a glorious spot alongside the River Aire.

See entry on page 289

---

182 PONTEFRACT CASTLE

Pontefract

In the Middle Ages, **Pontefract Castle** was one of the most important fortresses in the country.

See entry on page 290

as 'Pomfret' – a place of influence and power, often visited by kings and their retinues. The great shattered towers of **Pontefract Castle** stand on a crag to the east of the town. Built by Albert de Lacy in the 11th century, it was one of the most formidable fortresses in Norman England. In medieval times it passed to the House of Lancaster and became a Royal Castle. Richard II was imprisoned here and murdered in its dungeons on the orders of Henry Bolingbroke who then assumed the crown as Henry IV.

The castle was a major Royalist stronghold during the Civil War, after which it was destroyed by Cromwell's troops. Today it remains as a gaunt ruin with only sections of the inner bailey and the lower part of the keep surviving intact. There is an underground chamber, part of the dungeons where prisoners carved their names so that they might not be utterly forgotten. The unfortunate Richard II may have been incarcerated in this very chamber.

Many of the streets of Pontefract evoke memories of its medieval past with names such as Micklegate, Beast Fair, Shoe Market, Salter Row and Ropergate. Modern development has masked much of old Pontefract but there are still many old Georgian buildings and winding streets.

The town's most famous products, of course, are Pontefract Cakes. Liquorice root has been grown here since monastic times and there's even a small planting of liquorice in the local park. The town celebrates this unique heritage with the five day **Pontefract Liquorice Fayre** in mid-August which includes two days of jousting, archery and battle re-enactments at Pontefract Castle.

WINTERSETT

6 miles SE of Wakefield off the A638

Found on the historic estate of Walton Hall, once the home of the famous 19th-century naturalist Charles Waterton, is the **Heronry and Waterton Countryside Discovery Centre**, which provides information and exhibitions about the surrounding country park, which includes two reservoirs and woodland that was once part of the ancient Don Forest. The centre is open Tuesday to Friday and Sundays all year round.

ACKWORTH

8 miles SE of Wakefield off the A628

Reputedly the largest village in Europe, Ackworth is home to the famous **Ackworth School,** founded by the Quakers in 1779 as a boarding school for Quaker boys and girls in 1779. Today it has 580 boys and girls of many different faiths.

Outside the village a Plague Stone can still be seen beside the road, where villagers would leave money in exchange for food that was brought here when Ackworth was cut off during an outbreak of the Plague.

RYHILL

8 miles SE of Wakefield on the B6428

The village of Ryhill is mentioned in the *Domesday Book* as part of land granted to Robert de Lacy by William the Conqueror. Known as Rihella, in 1124 Robert de Lacy transferred lands including Ryhill to Nostell Priory, where it remained in the control of the Nostell canons until the Dissolution of the Monasteries in 1654. A prosperous London merchant, Sir Rowland Winn, bought the Nostell estate and Ryhill village; the estate has remained in the hands of the Winn family ever since. Ryhill attracts many visitors for its three beautiful reservoirs - popular for fishing, sailing and bird-watching - for its Heronry Centre and for some famous nature walks.

WEST BRETTON

5 miles S of Wakefield on the A637

One of the leading attractions of the area is found conveniently close to junction 38 of

183 THE ARMS AT UPTON

Upton

Family orientated inn serving great fresh pub grub, real ales with live entertainment and lovely beer garden.

See entry on page 291

Yorkshire Sculpture Park

The boathouse, built in the 1820s, has been restored as a visitors' centre while the rest of the 240-acre park offers ample opportunity for walking and viewing wildlife at close quarters. Just to the northwest lies Woolley Edge, from where there are wonderful views out across Emley Moor and, on a clear day, all the way to Barnsley.

OVERTON

5 miles SW of Wakefield off the A642

A visit to the **National Coal Mining Museum** for England at Caphouse Colliery in Overton includes a guided tour 450 feet underground during which each visitor is provided with a hat, belt and battery, so that the true atmosphere of working life underground is captured. There are also indoor exhibitions and videos, outdoor machine displays, a working steam winder, train rides and, for children, an adventure playground and some friendly pit ponies.

the M1. The **Yorkshire Sculpture Park** draws in some 200,000 visitors a year and since you only pay a small charge for parking it represents amazing value for money. Changing exhibitions of sculpture are set in the beautiful 18th-century parkland of Bretton Hall, 200 acres of historic landscape providing a wonderful setting for some of the best sculpture to be seen in Britain today by artists from around the world.

Alongside the programme of indoor and outdoor exhibitions, more permanent features include the YSP collection of works in many different styles (from 19th-century bronzes by Rodin to contemporary sculptures), and a display of monumental bronzes by Henry Moore sited within the adjacent 100-acre Bretton Country Park.

WOOLLEY

6 miles S of Wakefield off the A61

Despite being surrounded by industrial towns, Woolley has managed to retain its rural air and its old hall, now a course and conference centre, standing on land that was originally enclosed as a hunting park during the reign of Henry VII. Just to the northeast lies **Newmillerdam Country Park and Boathouse** which was, in the 19th century, part of the Chevet Estate and a playground for the local Pilkington family.

184 THE GARDENERS ARMS

Crigglestone

After much renovation and installation of fantastic facilities, this inn now holds an enviable reputation serving delicious home cooked food and real ales.

See entry on page 290

185 THE BREWERS PRIDE & MILLERS BAR AND RESTAURANT

Osset

A truly independent freehouse offering exceptional food and well kept ales, with an additional a la carte restaurant, ideal for those special occasions.

See entry on page 292

SOUTH YORKSHIRE

South Yorkshire is dominated by the four urban centres of Sheffield, Barnsley, Rotherham and Doncaster. Sheffield's prosperity was founded on steel and, in particular, cutlery, but today it has become a cultural hotspot with a wealth of museums, theatres, concert halls and galleries. There are few ancient buildings but, as "England's greenest city" it has the great advantage of being on the edge of the spectacular Peak District National Park. To the north of Sheffield is Barnsley, whose prosperity came from the rich seams of coal that surround it. To the east lies Rotherham, where iron ore has been mined and smelted since the 12th century. While its wealth is certainly based upon metal, Rotherham is proud of the fact that 70% of its area is rural, giving the town a green and leafy appearance.

Further east again is the charming riverside town of Doncaster, which was established by the Romans and today has the air of a pleasant market town. Doncaster was once one of the country's most important centres of steam locomotive manufacture and it is famous for having built the *Mallard* which still holds the record for the top speed attained by a steam train. Today, though, Doncaster is best known as the home of the St Leger, Britain's oldest classic horse race.

Elsewhere in the county visitors can discover the delights of Roche Abbey, a 12th-century Cistercian house, Conisbrough Castle, which boasts the oldest stone keep in England, and the faded Victorian grandeur of Brodsworth Hall.

LOCATION MAP

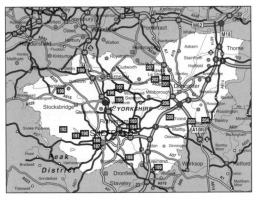

SHEFFIELD

England's fourth-largest city is still busy with its steel, cutlery, engineering and tool-making industries but in recent years Sheffield has re-invented itself. It is now a vibrant, international, multi-cultural city and a world-class centre for sport, headquarters of the government-backed UK Sports Institute and with an impressive array of international venues. There are facilities for ice-skating, dry skiing and two indoor climbing centres. It has also recently overtaken Leeds as the fastest-growing city in Yorkshire, thanks to a forward-looking programme of new housing and public spaces that continue to draw students in their thousands, many of whom choose to stay on in Sheffield after they've finished their studies.

Among the city's many museums is the **Kelham Island Museum** which is located in one of the city's oldest industrial areas and stands on a man-made island that was created more than 900 years ago. Inside the museum buildings visitors can witness the sights and sounds of industrial Sheffield through working machinery, activity areas and event days. A new mezzanine floor displays the museum's transport collection. This includes the famous Sheffield Simplex car, built in 1920, the Sharron Laycock car, Richardson Light car, Ner-a-car motorcycle and a Rolls Royce jet engine. The museum was badly damaged by the floods of 2007 and forced to close but has now re-opened.

Sheffield's industrial heritage is also celebrated at the **Weston Park Museum** which recently completed a £17m refurbishment. The animated new displays are specially designed to delight even the youngest visitors and range from Egyptian Mummies, to a traditional butcher's shop, from Snowy the polar bear to living ants and bees. The city's collections of beautiful, varied and unusual treasures are brought to life by fascinating histories, incredible facts and hands-on interactives.

Sheffield has several outstanding galleries devoted to the visual arts. The **Millenium Gallery** has helped to establish the city as a cultural force in the north of England. A remarkable building of white columns and striking glass arches, it holds four unique galleries that showcase not only Sheffield's impressive metalware collection but also provide space to show the city's wonderful collection of paintings, drawings and natural history exhibits. One gallery hosts visiting installations from the Victoria & Albert museum and other distinguished collections from throughout the country.

Nearby, the **Graves Gallery** has recently been refurbished and repainted, giving prominence to works by legendary artists such as Turner and Cézanne. New displays take visitors on a lavish journey through the collections, spanning the 16th to the 21st century and including works by famous names such as Edward Coley Burne-Jones and Bridget Riley, and local heroes such as George Fullard and Derrick Greaves.

Then there's the **Ruskin Gallery** with its eclectic collection of minerals, paintings, drawings, and ornithological prints. Also on display are medieval manuscripts, books and architectural plaster casts from Ruskin's own collection.

Another gallery of interest, the **Site Gallery** is devoted to international contemporary art. One of the largest contemporary visual art and media centres in the country, the gallery also offers darkroom

Sheffield Cathedral

and digital imaging facilities, as well as photographic and digital courses in the recently created education suite.

Sheffield's most picturesque museum is undoubtedly the **Bishop's House Museum** which dates from around 1500 and is the earliest timber-framed house still standing in the city. Many original features have survived and the bed chamber and great parlour are furnished in the style of the home of a prosperous 17th century yeoman. There are also displays on Sheffield in Tudor and Stuart times, and changing exhibitions on local history themes.

Tucked away in a former church hall on Ecclesall Road is one of Sheffield's best-kept secrets, the **Traditional Heritage Museum.** It is made up of fully reconstructed shops, workshops and offices from 1850-1950, and provides many insights into what Sheffield was like in years gone by.

At **Abbeydale Industrial Hamlet** the time frame is the 1700s. This unique complex of industrial works on the banks of the River Sheaf boasts the world's only surviving intact crucible steel furnace. There's also a tilt forge with massive tilt hammers, four dam-driven water wheels, a gleaming steam engine and some workers' cottages.

One of the UK's most interesting and comprehensive collections of nineteenth and twentieth century glass can be seen at the University of Sheffield's **Turner Museum of Glass** . From drinking glasses to contemporary installations the museum celebrates the skill and artistry of glassmakers. Pieces by all the major European and American glassmakers are on display and the collection is unrivalled in its display of work from the 1920s to the 1950s.

Sheffield is noted for its huge variety of shops. **Meadowhall** is one of Europe's largest shopping centres with more than 270 stores. High street names, designer boutiques and speciality craft stores provide a formidable retail experience. The complex also contains many places to eat, an 11-screen cinema, crèche and an award-winning programme of events.

And if you want to just relax, the city's most peaceful spot has to be the 19 acres of **Sheffield Botanical Gardens,** first opened in 1836. There are actually 15 distinct gardens featuring some 5,500 species from all over the world and including the National Collections of Weigela and Diervilla.

Also offering a tranquil refuge are the boat cruises along the Sheffield & Tinsley Canal which follows the Don Valley. Boats leave from the quay area which has a continental café bar with an outside patio and a craft shop.

---

186 BISHOPS' HOUSE

Sheffield

Bishops' House is the best preserved timber-framed house in Sheffield.

See entry on page 293

---

187 SHEFFIELD BOTANICAL GARDENS

Sheffield

This 19-acre site is a green haven within our busy city and has recently undergone a major restoration programme.

See entry on page 293

AROUND SHEFFIELD

NORTH ANSTON

10 miles E of Sheffield on the B6060

This village, separated from its neighbour South Anston by the main road, is home to the **Tropical Butterfly House, Wildlife and Falconry Centre** where you can, if you wish, hold a tarantula or fondle a snake. Children can cuddle a bunny or bottle feed a calf. There are also spectacular falconry displays and entertaining parrot shows. The centre, open all year, includes a well-stocked butterfly house, an Animal Nursery, Farmyard Corner, nocturnal reptile room, nature trail, children's play area and a gift shop.

RENISHAW

9 miles SE of Sheffield on the A616

This sizeable village gives its name to **Renishaw Hall**, home of Sir Reresby and Lady Sitwell which is located about a mile or so to the northwest. The beautiful formal Italian gardens and 300 acres of wooded park are open to visitors, along with an Orangery housing the National Collection of Yuccas, a nature trail, a Sitwell family museum, an art gallery, a display of Fiori de Henriques antique sculptures in the Georgian stables, and a café. The Hall itself is open to group and connoisseur tours by special arrangement only.

Renishaw Hall

WALES

9 miles SE of Sheffield on the B6059

A mile or so to the west of Wales, the **Rother Valley Country Park** provides excellent facilities for water sports including sailing, windsurfing, canoeing and jet skiing, as well as a cable water ski tow. Visitors can hire equipment or use their own, and training courses from beginner to instructor level are available in various water sports. Other attractions include a lakeside golf course, a Craft Centre with craftspeople at work, cycle

hire, gift shop, cafeteria – and Playdales, a 'mega play area' for children under 14.

CROSSPOOL

4 miles W of Sheffield on the A57

Intriguingly, it was a fit of pique that led to the building of **The Bell Hagg Inn** in Crosspool. Back in the 1830s a certain Dr Hodgson offered the vicar of Stannington (a village across the River Rivel from Crosspool) a large donation for the church funds. But Hodgson was well known as a gambler and frequenter of pubs so the vicar declined the generous offer. Incensed by this rebuff,

---

188 THE ROYAL OAK

Beighton

The traditional homemade food here is absolutely delicious. The pub is building up a fantastic reputation in the area.

See entry on page 294

---

189 THE BEEHIVE

Harthill

This quality public house is well renowned for its excellent food, friendly atmosphere and well kept ales.

See entry on page 294

---

190 THE ROYAL HOTEL

Dungworth

Welcoming family run public house on the edge of the Peak District offering quality cuisine, family room and en suite rooms.

See entry on page 295

---

191 PLOUGH INN

Low Bradfield

A popular pub, serving home cooked food in a picturesque and scenic location at the heart of the Peak District National Park.

See entry on page 296

Strines Reservoir

Hodgson bought the land directly opposite the church and built the pub there, a monument to drinking that no one attending Divine Service at Stannington church could possibly overlook. It clings to the cliffside, a defiant piece of architecture obviously intended to make a statement.

ROTHERHAM

The town's most striking building is undoubtedly the **Church of All Saints**. With its soaring tower, pinnacled buttresses and battlements, and imposing porch, it is one of the finest examples of perpendicular architecture in Yorkshire. It dates mainly from the 15th century although there is evidence of an earlier Saxon church on the site.

A church here was listed in the *Domesday Book* and in 1161 the monks of Rufford Abbey were granted the right to prospect for and to smelt iron, and to plant an orchard, and from that day industry has existed side by side with agriculture.

About half the land area of the Borough of Rotherham is actually rural but it was heavy industry that put the town on the map. From the mid-1700s, the Walker Company of Rotherham was famous for cannons, their products serving to lethal effect at the Battle of Trafalgar and in the American War of Independence. They also built bridges, among them Southwark Bridge in London and the bridge at Sunderland. Another famous bridge builder was born here in 1901: Sir Donald Coleman Bailey invented the Bailey Bridge which proved to be of great military value, especially during the Second World War.

The town also had lighter industries. Rockingham Pottery, produced here in the late 18th and early 19th century, is now highly prized by collectors. There's a fine collection at the **Clifton Park Museum,** a stately building whose interior has changed little since it was built in 1783 for the Rotherham ironmaster, Joshua Walker. The most breathtaking piece is the spectacular Rhinoceros Vase which stands almost four feet high and was the first ever one-piece porcelain vase cast. In addition, the museum houses a collection of other Yorkshire pottery, English glass, silver and British oil paintings and watercolours. The grounds around Clifton House form the largest urban park in the Borough which has 10 urban parks altogether, along with three country parks, seven golf courses, 10 swimming pools and a leisure centre.

192 THE STRINES INN

Sheffield

With stunning views over the Strines reservoir this historic and charming inn offers four poster accommodation, with a stunning bar and restaurant.

See entry on page 297

193 CAFE OASIS

Rotherham

This newly opened cafe offers an impressive variety of snacks, lunches and breakfasts as eat in or takeaway.

See entry on page 295

Another museum of interest is the **York and Lancaster Regimental Museum** in the Central Library. The regiment had strong ties with South Yorkshire, its recruits drawn mainly from Barnsley, Sheffield and Rotherham. The displays include historic uniforms, campaign relics and more than 1000 medals, among them nine Victoria Cross groups. There are also sections on local militia, rifle volunteers and territorials.

Rotherham's latest attraction, opened in 2007, is the **South Yorkshire Transport Museum** at Aldwarke which features an interesting collection of vintage buses and commercial vehicles. Various displays and other transport-related artefacts help recall the story of transport in the region. Opening times are limited.

Wentworth Woodhouse, Rotherham

Dramatically set within the former Templeborough steelworks, **Magna** was the UK's first science adventure park. This imaginative exploration of the power of the four natural elements – earth, air, fire and water – offers visitors the opportunity of experiencing the full power of lightning, firing a water cannon, manoeuvring a real JCB digger, getting close to a tornado and blowing up a virtual rock face. In the Living Robots Show predator robots pursue each other in an epic struggle to survive and breed. In the Power Pavilion, after donning overalls and cap for your 'shift', you can shed a few pounds by creating electricity on a giant treadmill, test your strength in a self-lifting chair, attack a target with a giant catapult and discover how much you would weigh on the planets Mars or Jupiter. The site also has a restaurant, cafeteria, picnic areas and shops.

About 6 miles northwest of the town, the palatial 18th-century mansion **Wentworth Woodhouse** boasts the longest frontage in England, some 600 feet long. The house is not open to the public but is clearly visible from its park. Also visible are a number of follies and monuments dating from the 1700s. The most curious of these is the Needle's Eye which consists of a tower with a stone urn on top and is pierced by a carriageway. Legend says it was built in response to a wager by the

Marquis of Rockingham, owner of Wentworth Woodhouse, that he could drive through the eye of a needle. One structure which *is* open (on Sunday afternoons during the season), is the Wentworth Mausoleum which was built in 1788 in memory of the 2nd Marquis.

Also open to the public are the adjacent **Wentworth Woodhouse Gardens** comprising some 16 acres of walled and landscaped areas. Features include a replanted maze, a bear pit, ornamental and Japanese gardens, 'hot walls', and a wealth of stone and water features. The site also contains the National Plant Collections of rhododendrons, camellias and magnolias, an adventure playground, craft units and a coffee shop.

A little further afield, near the village of Maltby, are the dramatic ruins of **Roche Abbey** (English Heritage). The abbey dates from the 12th century and takes its name from the rocky limestone of the riverside site. The majestic remains of this great abbey stand in a landscape fashioned by 'Capability' Brown in the 1770s as part of the grounds of Sandbeck Park, home of the Earls of Scarborough.

---

194 **SOUTH YORKSHIRE TRANSPORT MUSEUM**

Aldwarke

The new Museum - now called the **South Yorkshire Transport Museum** - is situated just off the A6123 on Waddington Way at Aldwarke.

See entry on page 298

BARNSLEY

The county town of South Yorkshire, Barnsley stands on the River Dearne and derived its Victorian prosperity from the rich seams of coal hereabouts. It has an appropriately imposing Town Hall although the building is comparatively recent, completed in 1933. Opposite the town hall, the **Cooper Gallery** is a lively centre for the arts which hosts a varied programme of exhibitions throughout the year as well as housing a fine permanent collection.

The town's most impressive museum is actually located a few miles to the west, in the village of Cawthorne. **Cannon Hall** is a magnificent 18th-century country house set in formal gardens and historic parkland. It offers unique collections of pottery, furniture, glassware and paintings, along with the 'Charge Gallery' which documents the story of the 13th/18th Royal Hussars. There's a tea room open at weekends and a gift shop.

About a mile to the south of Barnsley is the **Worsbrough Mill Museum and Country Park**. The Grade II listed mill dates from around 1625. A steam mill was added in the 19th century and both have been restored to full working order to form the centrepiece of an industrial museum. Wholemeal flour, ground at the mills, can be bought here. The mill is set within a beautiful 200-acre country park, whose reservoir attracts a great variety of birds including heron.

AROUND BARNSLEY

ELSECAR

5 miles S of Barnsley on the B6097

Situated in the pretty conservation village of Elsecar, just off the M1 (J36), the **Elsecar Heritage Centre** is located within the former ironworks and colliery workshops of the Earl Fitzwilliam. Restored historical buildings now house an antiques centre, individual craft workshops, tea rooms and exhibitions of Elsecar's past. The steam

railway here is the focus for many events such as Thomas and Friends and Elsecar Wartime weekend. There are also walks alongside the Dearne and Dove Canal.

WORTLEY

8 miles SW of Barnsley on the A629

The ancestral home of the Wortley family, **Wortley Hall,** was built in the late 1500s on the site of an older residence; over the centuries it has been much altered and even left to decay. Restoration work was carried out in the late 18th and early 19th centuries, and it was also around this time that the landscaping and ornamental planning of the grounds and gardens took place. The 26 acres of gardens are laid out in the Italianate style.

In the village itself are the school and schoolhouse built in 1874 by the Wortley family and only closed in 1993, while the

---

195 ELSECAR HERITAGE CENTRE

Elsecar

The Elsecar Heritage Centre nestles within the beautiful South Yorkshire countryside and dates from the early 1800's

See entry on page 298

---

196 ELEPHANT & CASTLE BAR & RESTAURANT

Hemingfield, nr Barnsley

This family orientated business is a great place to eat out for young and old with special deals almost every day of the week.

See entry on page 299

---

197 OLD MOOR WETLANDS CENTRE RSPB

Wombwell

There are five hides out on the Old Moor Wetlands Centre RSPB reserve and one overlooking the bird-feeding garden.

See entry on page 299

---

oldest house in Wortley, Tividale Cottage, was practically rebuilt and modernised in 1983. In the early 1700s this was the home of headmaster William Nevison, and the cottage is thought to have been the birthplace of his son, the highwayman John Nevison.

PENISTONE

9 miles SW of Barnsley off the A628

Perched 700 feet above sea level, Penistone forms a gateway to the Peak District National Park which extends for some 30 miles to the south of the town. Penistone's oldest building is the 15th-century tower of its parish church which overlooks a graveyard in which ancestors of the poet William Wordsworth are buried. Later centuries added an elegant Dissenters' Chapel (in the 1600s) and a graceful Cloth Hall in the 1700s.

THURLSTONE

9 miles SW of Barnsley off the A628

Thurlstone developed when the first settlers realised that the nearby moors provided extensive grazing for sheep and the lime-free waters of the River Don were ideal for the washing of wool. Today the village still has some fine examples of the weavers' cottages which sprang up during the early 19th century, the best of which can be seen on Tenter Hill. Here the finished cloth would have been dried and stretched on 'tenters' – large wooden frames placed outside on the street which gave the road its name.

The village's most famous son was Nicholas Saunderson, born in 1682, who was blinded by smallpox at the age of two. He taught himself to read by passing his fingers over the tombstones in Penistone churchyard – 150 years before the introduction of Braille.

---

198 THE HUNTSMAN

Thurlstone

A proper old-fashioned pub; real ales, hearty local food and a great atmosphere.

See entry on page 300

Nicholas went on to attend grammar school and rose to become Professor of Mathematics at Cambridge University.

DUNFORD BRIDGE

15 miles SW of Barnsley off the A628

The hamlet of Dunford Bridge is only shown on very large scale maps but if you are travelling westwards from Barnsley on the A628, after 13 miles or so you will see a sign for Stanhope Inn off to the right. It's well worth seeking out this grand old hostelry, originally built in the 1800s as a shooting lodge for the Cannon Hall Estate. It stands beside the entrance to the Woodhead railway tunnel which runs beneath the moors for more than three miles. When the tunnel opened in 1852 it was twice as long as any other in the world. In the snug of the Stanhope Arms there's an interesting display of memorabilia regarding the tunnel and the camp built for the Tunnel Tigers - the men who built it.

SILKSTONE

4 miles W of Barnsley off the A628

The travel writer Arthur Mee dubbed Silkstone's parish church 'The Minster of the Moors' and it is indeed a striking building. Parts of the church date back to Norman times but most of it was built during the golden age of English ecclesiastical architecture, the 15th century. Outside, there are graceful flying buttresses and wonderfully weird gargoyles. Inside, the ancient oak roofs sprout floral bosses on moulded beams, and old box-pews and lovely medieval screens all add to the charm.

The old stocks just outside **The Ring o' Bells** are another sign of the antiquity of this former mining village.

CAWTHORNE

4 miles W of Barnsley on the A365

This pretty village noted for its lavish 'Britain in Bloom' displays offers three other attractions. **Cannon Hall Museum, Park & Gardens** is centred around a 17th century

Cannon Hall, Cawthorne

house containing some fine furniture, paintings, glassware and pottery placed in period rooms and galleries.

The charming **Victoria Jubilee Museum** occupies a reconstructed part cruck-frame building and features local and natural history, costumes and a fascinating array of eccentric Victoriana.

During the season the **Maize Maze at Cawthorne** promises lots of family fun. In addition to the maze, there are tractor rides, go-karts, organised games, play areas - and home-made ice cream.

DONCASTER

The Romans named their riverside settlement beside the River Don *Danum*, and a well-preserved stretch of the road they built here

---

199 CANNON HALL MUSEUM

Cawthorne

Set in 70 acres of historic parkland and gardens, Cannon Hall Museum provides an idyllic and tranquil setting for a day out.

See entry on page 300

---

can be seen just west of Adwick le Street. The town stood on the Great North Road and a reminder of the stagecoach days is the fine old coaching inn, the Salutation. Doncaster boasts other impressive Georgian and Regency buildings, notably the imposing Mansion House built in 1748 and designed by James Paine. Dominating the skyline is **The Minster of St George** which was rebuilt in 1858 by Sir George Gilbert Scott. It is an outstanding example of Gothic revival architecture with its lofty tower, 170 feet high, crowned with pinnacles. The lively Frenchgate Shopping Centre is enhanced by a stately Corn Exchange building of 1875, and a market which takes place every Tuesday, Friday and Saturday.

Doncaster was once one of the most important centres for the production of steam engines. Thousands were built here, including both the *Flying Scotsman* and *Mallard*. *Mallard* still holds the record for the fastest steam train in the world, achieving a top speed of 126mph in July 1938. For a further insight into the history of the town and surrounding area, there is **Doncaster Museum & Art Gallery** which contains several exciting and informative exhibitions on the various aspects of natural history, local history and archaeology. Although the present buildings only opened in 1964, the museum celebrates its centennial in 2010. The art gallery's best-known painting is *Giants Refreshed* by legendary railway artist, Terence Cuneo. It depicts two mighty LNER locomotives being refitted and refurbished at Doncaster Works. Housed in the same building is the **Regimental Museum of the King's Own Yorkshire Light Infantry**, which reflects the history of this famous local regiment and has one of the largest collections of military medals in the UK.

There is no-one connected with the racing fraternity who has not heard of the St Leger, one of the oldest classic races, which has been held at Doncaster since 1776. **Doncaster Racecourse** provides a magnet for all horse-racing enthusiasts and there are a total of 26 meetings each year. Back in 1909, the racecourse played host to the very first Aviation Meeting when pioneer aviators from

Doncaster Racecourse

around the world landed their flimsy craft here. Modern aviation buffs will enjoy Aeroventure, the South Yorkshire Aviation Museum which is housed in the original hangars and other buildings of RAF Doncaster. Exhibits include a replica of the Bleriot XI, other full size aircraft and helicopters.

Overlooking the town, Cusworth Hall is home to the **Museum of South Yorkshire**

---

200 **CUSWORTH HALL (MUSEUM OF SOUTH YORKSHIRE LIFE)**

Doncaster

Cusworth Hall is an imposing 18th century country house set in extensive landscaped parklands. It houses the Museum of South Yorkshire Life.

See entry on page 301

---

201 **CUSWORTH HALL TEA ROOM**

Cusworth

This charming tea room offers delicious homemade cuisine throughout the day with decadent chocolate workshops and evening buffets available.

See entry on page 301

---

202 **MARR LODGE**

Marr

Traditional home-cooked food is the order of the day at this fine establishment, which stands in its own grounds.

See entry on page 302

Life. The Hall is a splendid Georgian mansion built in the 1740s and set in a landscaped park. The interior features varied displays on the social history, industry, agriculture and transport in the area.

AROUND DONCASTER

NORTON

8 miles N of Doncaster off the A19

This sizeable village is located close to the borders with North and West Yorkshire and was once busy with farming, mining and quarrying. Nowadays it's a peaceful place, a tranquil base for commuters to Doncaster and Pontefract. Its most impressive building is the ancient parish church of **St Mary Magdalene** whose splendid 14th century west tower is considered by many to be the finest in Yorkshire. Once there was also a priory here, standing beside the River Went, but now only a fragment of wall remains. However, the old water mill has survived.

STAINFORTH

7 miles NE of Doncaster off the A18 or A614

Stainforth was once an important trading centre and inland port on the River Don. It also stands on the banks of the Stainforth & Keadby Canal which still has a well-preserved dry dock and a 19th-century blacksmith's shop. This area of low, marshy ground was drained by Dutch engineers in the 1600s to produce rich, peaty farmland. The place has retained the air of a quiet backwater, a little-explored area of narrow lands and pretty hamlets, the fields drained by slow-flowing dykes and canals. The rich peat resources are commercially exploited in part but also provide a congenial home for a great deal of natural wildlife.

FISHLAKE

10 miles NE of Doncaster off the A614

Set along the banks of the River Don, which is known here as the Dutch River, Fishlake is effectively an island since it is surrounded by rivers and canals and can only be entered by crossing a bridge. It's a charming village with a striking medieval church famous for its elaborately carved Norman doorway, an ancient windmill and a welcoming traditional inn.

SANDTOFT

13 miles NE of Doncaster off the A18

Sandtoft's **Trolleybus Museum** contains the world's largest collection of preserved trolleybuses and other vehicles of the same era. Visitors can see the buses in action, ride on them, and browse among the many related artefacts on show. Opening times are restricted.

BRANTON

4½ miles E of Doncaster off the B1396

Surrounded by agricultural land, Brockholes Farm has been a working farm since 1759 and one where the traditional farming skills have been passed down from one generation to the next. Known today as the **Yorkshire Wildlife Centre,** it is a combination of working farm, zoo and riding school. It is home to a fascinating collection of animals from small ferrets to rare breeds of farm animals. The pride of place in the farm is given to a herd of pedigree Limousin cattle, powerfully impressive beasts. But there is also a wide range of exotic animals including llamas, wallabies, monkeys and zebra. A "Woodland Walk" reveals red and fallow deer. Promised for 2010 is a new attraction, a pride of 13 lions rescued from a Romanian zoo.

FINNINGLEY

7 miles SE of Doncaster on the A614

A unique feature of this pleasant village close to the Nottinghamshire border is its five village greens, the main one having a duck pond complete with weeping willows. Finningley is a living village with a well-used Village Hall, originally a barn which later served as the village school. Finningley has a beautiful Norman church with a rectors' list dating back to 1293 and a post office which has been in the same family for five

generations. The year 2004 saw the opening of the international **Robin Hood Aiport** outside the village, which utilised the runways from the old RAF base, built just before World War II and later the home base of the famous Vulcan bombers. The airport has led to increased development and investment in the area while not disturbing Finningley's traditional appeal.

BAWTRY

9 miles SE of Doncaster on the A614

This pleasant little market town stands close to the Nottinghamshire border and in medieval times it was customary for the Sheriff of South Yorkshire to welcome visiting kings and queens here. In the mid-1500s the then Sheriff, Sir Robert Bowes, accompanied by 200 gentlemen dressed in velvet, together with 4000 yeomen on horseback, greeted Henry VIII and – in the name of Yorkshire – presented him with a purse containing the huge sum of £900 in gold. Close to the county border, the first house is known simply as "No. 1, Yorkshire".

Today's Bawtry is an upmarket and exciting town with very good shopping in select boutiques, and an impressive selection of excellent and stylish restaurants. A happy mix of stunning buildings, small

---

203 SCARBOROUGH ARMS

Tickhill

This handsome ivy clad inn is known for its large range of cask marque ales and excellent brand of hospitality.

See entry on page 302

---

204 THE SHIP

Bawtry

This handsome village inn is run by a charismatic couple with a fine reputation for delivering delicious food and award winning ales.

See entry on page 304

boutiques, antique shops and sophisticated restaurants, Bawtry remains the quintessential English town. Many of the buildings are grand three-storey Georgian affairs that help the town maintain a tranquil and restrained appearance. Once a coaching stage post along the old Great North Road, it continues its proud tradition of offering great food and drink to visitors with a range of elegant eateries. The opening of the Robin Hood Airport nearby has led to increased investment in the area and Bawtry is set to see more changes and improvements in goods and services on offer while maintaining its traditional attractions.

THORPE SALVIN

14 miles S of Doncaster off the A57

This attractive village is home to the now-ruined Thorpe Salvin Hall, which dates from 1570 and is thought to have been the inspiration for Torquilstone in Sir Walter Scott's *Ivanhoe*.

CADEBY

4 miles SW of Doncaster off the A630

Listed in the *Domesday Book* as 'Catebi', this pleasant little village is surrounded on all sides by prime agricultural land. For centuries Cadeby had no church of its own; parishioners had to travel some two miles to the parish church in Sprotbrough. Then in 1856 the owners of the huge Sprotbrough estate, the Copley family, paid for a church to be built in Cadeby. It was designed by Sir George Gilbert Scott, the architect of St Pancras Station in London, and resembles a medieval estate barn with its steeply pitched roofs and lofty south porch. A century and a

Conisbrough Castle

half later, Cadeby is again without a church since Sir George's attractive church has been declared redundant.

CONISBROUGH

5 miles SW of Doncaster on the A630

The town is best known for the 11th-century **Conisbrough Castle** (English Heritage) which features prominently in one of the most dramatic scenes in Sir Walter Scott's novel *Ivanhoe*. The most impressive medieval building in South Yorkshire, Conisbrough Castle boasts the oldest circular keep in England. Rising some 90 feet and more than 50 feet wide, the keep stands on a man-made hill raised in Saxon times. Six huge buttresses some 6 feet thick support walls that in places are 15 feet deep. Visitors can walk through the remains of several rooms, including the first floor chamber where the huge open fireplaces give one a fascinating insight into the lifestyle of Norman times. The castle also offers a visual presentation, a visitor centre and a tea room.

Close by is the parish **Church of St Peter's** which is the oldest building in South Yorkshire, dating back to around 675AD. Much of the original Saxon structure remains and

---

205 THE GARDEN ROOM

Braithwell

Excellent daytime dining in converted farm buildings in a village easily reached from Doncaster, Rotherham and the M18 (J1). Eat inside or out on the garden patio.

See entry on page 305

---

206 CONISBROUGH CASTLE & VISITOR CENTRE

Conisbrough

Conisbrough Castle has been standing guard over the Dearne valley for nearly 850 years and is now open for families to enjoy all year round.

See entry on page 306

the church is also notable for a stone tomb chest with a fine carving of St George slaying the dragon which is believed to be one of the oldest such carvings in England.

SWINTON

8 ½ miles SW of Doncaster on the A6022

This is the town that is home to the world-famous Rockingham porcelain; the story of the amazing small country pottery which grew to become the king's porcelain manufacturer before falling into bankruptcy is told in a special gallery at Clifton Park Museum, Rotherham. However, here in Swinton itself visitors can still see the secluded Swinton Pottery site where, in beautiful surroundings, the Waterloo Kiln (built in 1815) and the Pottery Ponds are the only surviving landmarks of the renowned Rockingham Porcelain works.

BRODSWORTH

6 miles NW of Doncaster on the B6422

Just outside the village, **Brodsworth Hall** (English Heritage) is a remarkable example of a Victorian mansion that has survived with many of its original furnishings and decorations intact. When Charles and Georgiana Thellusson, their six children and 15 servants moved into the new hall in 1863 the house must have seemed the last word in both grandeur and utility. A gasworks in the grounds supplied the lighting and no

Brodsworth Hall

fewer than eight water closets were distributed around the house, although rather surprisingly only two bathrooms were installed.

More immediately impressive to visitors were the opulent furnishings, paintings, statuary and decoration. The sumptuous reception rooms have now a rather faded grandeur and English Heritage has deliberately left it so, preserving the patina of time throughout the house to produce an interior that is both fascinating and evocative. A vanished way of life is also brought to life in the huge kitchen and the cluttered servants wing. The Hall stands in 15 acres of beautifully restored Victorian gardens, complete with a summer house in the form of a classical temple, a target range where the family practised its archery, and a pets cemetery where the family dogs - and a prized parrot with the unimaginative name of Polly - were buried between 1894 and 1988. There is also a fascinating exhibition illustrating the family's obsession - yachting.

Also in Brodsworth is the **Markham Grange Steam Museum** which, rather unexpectedly, is sited inside a garden centre. The museum contains six large stationary steam engines, nearly all of which are more than 100 years old. The engines can be seen working on Wednesdays, Sundays and Bank Holidays.

---

207 BRODSWORTH HALL AND GARDENS

Brodsworth

One of England's most complete Victorian country houses, **Brodsworth Hall** was opened to the public in 1995 following a major programme of restoration and conservation.

See entry on page 306

Accommodation, Food & Drink and Places to Visit

The establishments featured in this section includes hotels, inns, guest houses, bed & breakfasts, restaurants, cafés, tea and coffee shops, tourist attractions and places to visit. Each establishment has an entry number which can be used to identify its location at the beginning of the relevant county chapter.

In addition full details of all these establishments and many others can be found on the Travel Publishing website - www.findsomewhere.co.uk. This website has a comprehensive database covering the whole of the United Kingdom.

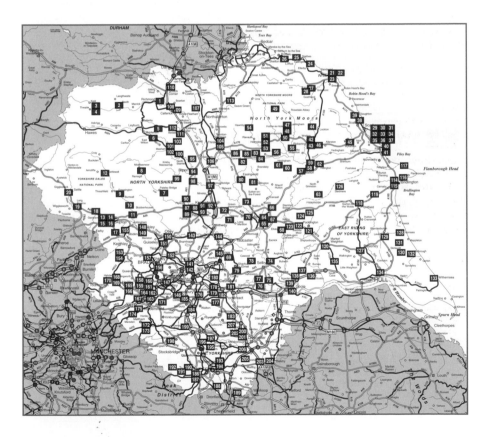

1 SIP COFFEE

18 King Street, Richmond,
North Yorkshire DL10 4HP
Tel: 01748 822877

Located in the heart of historic Richmond, **Sip Coffee** was created in 2006 by and has quickly become very popular with both locals and visitors. As you might expect from the name, there's an excellent choice of coffees but the menu also offers a wide variety of teas and other hot and cold drinks. The freshly baked paninis with a wide choice of fillings are both tasty and good value for money and like most of the food and drinks on offer can be eaten in or taken away.

Sip Coffee has been owned by Andy Gaines for the past two years and he has developed it greatly as a popular and successful business. Since he took over the coffee shop has benefited from a new interior and exterior and many locals and visitors who discover it return. Inside, 18 diners can be seated with a further two outside and children are always welcomed. Sip Coffee is open Monday to Saturday from 9am to 4pm, and between 10am and 3pm on Sundays. If you are after somewhere to enjoy a morning/afternoon coffee or something for lunch Sip Coffee is definitely worth a look.

2 SWALEDALE FOLK MUSEUM

The Green, Reeth, North Yorkshire DL11 6QT
Tel: 01748 884118
website: www.swaledalemuseum.org

The **Swaledale Folk Museum** was opened in 1974, and is based in the old Methodist School, which took its first pupils in 1836. It is a fascinating repository of over 1,000 objects connected with living and working in the Dale. If you want to learn about lead miniing this is the place for you, where lead and its associated rocks, minerals and fossils were yielded up by the hard labour of the miners. You can see the tools they used, trace their progress through the landscape via nineteenth century maps, and imagine what it must have been like to work underground with only candlelight for a guide.

Sheep farming been the mainstay of Swaledale agriculture since Tudor Times. As a thriving community the Dale was also home to many skilled trades and crafts; tinsmithing, joinery and stonemasonry, all represented in the Museum. While work was hard outside, it was no less easy inside. There are displays of domestic equipment from washing tubs and dollies to early electric irons.

Keeping the house clean, and the family fed was a labour intensive job, but did not preclude time for entertainment. The strange iron spring with a spike is for playing knurr & spell. There are nineteenth century quoits, and a whole section on the local brass and silver bands. There are many old photographs, which show Reeth as it was in the early twentieth century, and faces that are still familiar.

3 SWALEDALE WOOLLENS

Strawbeck, Muker in Swaledale, Richmond,
North Yorkshire DL11 6QG
Tel: 01748 886251
e-mail: mail@swaledalewoollens.co.uk
website: www.swaledalewoollens.co.uk

Swaledale Woollens was founded in Muker in Swaledale more than 30 years ago by villagers reviving the old cottage industry of knitting. Here in one of the most beautiful areas of Northern England the tradition of hand knitting in local wool goes back more than 400 years to the days of Queen Elizabeth I. It was Elizabeth who set a new fashion by wearing hand knitted stockings and, with demand increasing, every family in the Dale - men, women and children - became involved in knitting woollen stockings. By the end of the 19th century however, changes in fashions together with the arrival of knitting machines ended most of the Dales hand knitting trade.

Swaledale Woollens is now owned and run by Kathleen Hird who carries on using local Swaledale and Wensleydale wool for the knitwear. There are more than 30 people knitting from their homes and producing a unique range of quality woollen knitwear. The wool provided for the knitters is mainly from Swaledale sheep, but use is also made of the different shades and textures provided by the nearby Wensleydale breed and Welsh hill sheep. The Swaledale, Wensleydale and Welsh wools are spun at the only remaining traditional worsted Woollen Mill in Bradford. Then it is dyed in to soft country colours and delivered to Muker. Real horn buttons are used on many of the garments. Kathleen takes it to her team of conscientious knitters then collects it when the ladies and gentlemen have knitted or crocheted it into garments.

The shop stocks a wide range of high quality knitwear, including sweaters, cardigans, hats, gloves, rugs, hangings, shawls, scarves, slippers and socks. It also stocks sheepskin slippers, gloves and rugs. What better choice could there be for a quality and unique, hand-crafted gift for yourself, friends and family? And you can also place your order online from the comfort of home!

Swaledale Woollens is open from 10am to 5pm every day except Christmas Day and Boxing Day. The shop closes at 4pm during November, December, January and February.

4 MUKER VILLAGE STORE AND TEASHOP

The Village Store, Muker, Richmond, North Yorkshire DL11 6QG
Tel: 01748 886409
e-mail: mukerteashop@btinternet.com
website: www.mukervillage.co.uk

Nestled within the heart of Swaledale in the village of Muker guests will find this charming store and teashop. **Muker Village Store and Teashop** is run by a lovely local couple; Nick and Alison. They have been opening both the store and teashop for the past four years, bringing convenience and hospitality to locals and visitors to the area.

The shop portion of the business offers its customers a full stock of everyday household items that you might find at any local shop, but they also display a whole host of locally made produce from cheese, to chutneys, jams and farm eggs. The shop opens daily from 9am-5pm Monday to Friday and from 9:30am-5pm on Sundays.

The teashop adjacent opens every day from 11am-5pm apart from Tuesdays when it is closed. Both Nick and Alison share the cooking with Nick's speciality savoury dishes and Alison taking care of the home baking and cakes. Popular dishes here include Cream Teas, homemade scones, fruit cake and good old Yorkshire rarebit.

One guest bedroom is available all year round in twin or double format. Found just above the teashop with a generous breakfast tariff and four star rating it is a wonderful place to stay and soak up quiet village life.

5 THE QUEENS HEAD

Finghall, North Yorkshire DL8 5ND
Tel: 01677 450259
e-mail: enquiries@queensfinghall.co.uk
website: www.queensfinghall.co.uk

With a fascinating heritage, **The Queens Head** stands in the heart of the quiet village of Finghall. Dating back to the 1700's, this beautiful old inn oozes character from her very core with well preserved gnarled oak beams, real stone fires and wooden floors bearing testament to her age. The inn enjoys picturesque surroundings with glorious views across the countryside from the patio balcony, and a more mysterious view into the 'Wild Woods,' rumoured to be the place where author Kenneth Grahame took his inspiration for his classic tale 'Wind in the Willows.'

The inn's owner Ian Vipond only took over the inn 18 months ago, but believes the inn embodies all the qualities that make a public house special. Using a quote by Dr Samuel Johnson as his guiding light, Ian believes he serves his community well – 'There is nothing which has yet been contrived by man, by which so much happiness is produced, as by a good tavern or inn.' Ian has over thirty years of experience in the trade and has put it to good use, sympathetically refurbishing the inn to an impressive four star status.

The inn now houses two luxurious double rooms and one well equipped family room, each with en suite facilities. These make the perfect base from which to explore rural North Yorkshire with the inn excellent facilities to hand and the market towns of Leybrun, Badale and Richmond just a short drive away.

The inn opens every session and all day on weekends, offering a fine choice of real ales, lagers, wines and spirits. Food is available between 12-2pm and 6-9pm each day and is exceedingly popular; necessitating booking to avoid disappointment on weekends. The food is prepared by notable head Chef Andrew Megson who has devised a range of menus to showcase the delicious produce he sources locally. An assortment of mains, pub classics, vegetarian options and grills are available with both an 'Early Bird' and Sunday lunch menu operating also. Typical mains include medallions of beef fillet with haggis, grilled sea bream, slow roasted belly pork, roasted duck and pan fried venison along with wild mushroom risotto and Cassoulet. Andrew's skills can also be turned to cater for a range of functions able to be booked at the inn, please call for details.

6 JERVAULX ABBEY

Jervaulx, Ripon,
North Yorkshire HG4 4PH
Tel: 01677 460266 / 01677 460391
e-mail: ba123@btopenworld.com
website: www.jervaulxabbey.com

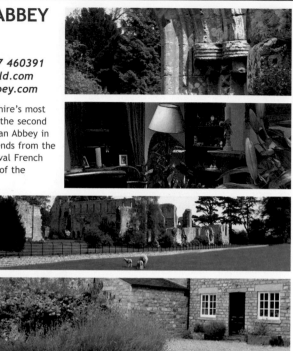

Jervaulx Abbey is one of Yorkshire's most popular destinations, reputably the second largest privately owned Cisterican Abbey in the UK. The name Jervaulx extends from the River Ure or Jer, and the medieval French word for valley; 'Vaulx,' a relic of the French monks who built the abbey shortly after the Norman Conquest which saw them arrive in this pretty area of the country. Once one of the most prosperous and wealthiest religious houses in Yorkshire, the abbey was known for its sheep rearing, and horse breeding; owning half of Wendsleydale. The monks were also known for the invent of a soft blue cheese similar to the Roquefort cheese of the monks' native region in France, now known globally as the Wendsleydale cheese.

The abbey is now in ruins after the dissolution of the monasteries in the 16th century under the rule of Henry VIII, but is frequented by many visitors who are invited to take their time exploring the weather beaten stones and glorious surrounding countryside with the help of various written guides.

The abbey was bought by Major Burdon and his wife in 1971. Following his death in 1980, it is now owned and run by his younger son Ian and his wife Carol and their daughter Anna. They work hard to conserve the abbey for both their visitors and history's sake. The family also own the Tea Room across the road from the abbey which provides a peaceful place to enjoy a light snack in between perusing various aspects of the abbey.

The tea room stocks a delicious selection of home baked food including lunches, vegetarian dishes, all day snacks and a range of freshly baked cakes and scones. There is a plant centre adjacent stocking a beautiful array of herbaceous perennials, shrubs and garden pots.

The family also provide five star accommodation in the form of bed and breakfast, available all year round in their stunningly renovated country house, which also lies on the Jervaulx estate. Guests can choose from four beautifully appointed rooms, three of which have full en suite facilities and the fourth a private bathroom with a jacuzzi bath. Rooms are elegantly decorated, affording guests the tranquillity and comfort to continue their enjoyable visit to the abbey and the area further. A small caravan site is also found on the estate, perfect for families and couples touring the North.

Ian and Carol also welcome requests from those wanting to hold an event at the abbey and have recently held various evenings from wedding blessings and ceremonies to plays and charity events, please call for details.

7 THE BIRCH TREE INN

Wilsill, Harrogate, North Yorkshire HG3 5EA
Tel: 01423 711131
website: www.thebirchtree.net

The **Birch Tree** is a fine old country inn standing in an Area of Outstanding Natural Beauty just west of Wilsill and a short drive from Pateley Bridge. Licensees Ken and Lynn, who recently bought the pub in July 2010, are continuing a tradition of hospitality serving traditional beers and are now a genuine freehouse. Ken brings a wealth of talent and experience on the culinary side, and Lynn does an equally excellent job front of house. It's a favourite place for locals to meet for a chat over a glass of wine or two and regular ales are: Timothy Taylor Landlord, Black Sheep and Tetley's, with an occasional guest ale adding to the choice. Food is served lunchtimes from Wednesday and evening meals are served from Tuesday night. Sunday you will find mouth-watering traditional roasts on offer as well as the full menu. Ken's menus provide plenty of choice for all tastes and appetites, with classics like steak and ale pie, ham, egg and chips, steaks, curries, gammon, lasagne and liver and bacon among the favourites. Jumbo haddock, salmon and scampi feature among the fish choices, and there are always several vegetarian options. Thursday is steak night, and fish & chips are a crowd pleaser on Friday nights. For guests taking a break the inn has three attractively decorated and furnished en suite bedrooms.

8 HOW STEAN GORGE

Lofthouse, Pateley Bridge,
North Yorkshire HG3 5SF
Tel: 01423 755666
e-mail: info@howstean.co.uk
website: www.howstean.co.uk

Visitors heading for **How Stean Gorge** had better prepare for adventure with more activities and opportunities for exploration than any other place in North Yorkshire. Located in the heart of Nidderdale, this stunning limestone gorge is almost 1 kilometre in length and up to 20 metres deep. Narrow paths and footbridges are cut through the spectacular steep-sided ravine with views over the unusually shaped rocks below; carved out by the torrent of waters that rush over them. Guests can simply stroll around the gorge taking in the thrill of nature or book themselves onto an adventure day for friends and families.

Options include braving the 'Iron Way,' a network of metal beams and cables set into the rock, abseiling down the gorge face itself, exploring caves, wading through the water and sitting under waterfalls and truly testing your nerve. Stag do's, hen do's and corporate events can all be given an adrenaline injection through visiting the gorge for one of these days. Guests can also extend their stay by camping on site with your own tent or spending a night in the six-man tipi. A great restaurant and tearoom is also on site selling a delicious selection of homemade cakes, lunches, teas and ice creams – just what you need after an icy plunge into the gorge.

9 OLD SCHOOL TEA ROOM

Main Street, Hebden, Skipton,
North Yorkshire BD23 5DX
Tel: 01756 753778
e-mail: magseagle@yahoo.com
website: www.theoldschooltearoom.co.uk

Located in an idyllic setting, and only a 5 minute drive from Grassington is the popular Old School Tea Room. Housed within the old Hebden school, the charming premises dates back to 1875 and was transformed into the much loved tea room in February 2008.

Maggie came across the Old School Tea Room when she got lost during a walk from Grassington and ended up in Hebden Village. Falling for the special atmosphere of the building and the wonderful location, she decided to take up the challenge to run this establishment for future walkers.

The food here is second to none, and with dishes such as beef casserole, steak and ale pie and vegetable cannelloni, visitors will be spoilt for choice. As well as hearty meals, light snacks are also available including sandwiches, paninis, platters and salads. For those looking for something sweet, the delicious cream teas, with freshly made scones, whipped cream and preserves go down a treat! The selection of homemade cakes is also extremely tempting. The tea room is open 10am – 5pm throughout the week except Tuesdays (open everyday throughout July and August).

10 HOWGILL LODGE

Barden, Skipton, North Yorkshire BD23 6DJ
Tel: 01756 720655 e-mail: enq@howgill-lodge.co.uk
website: www.howgill-lodge.co.uk

Howgill Lodge is located in seven acres of magnificent countryside in the heart of the Yorkshire Dales National park. Comprising bed and breakfast accommodation within a glorious 17th century barn conversion, self catering caravans and a tent and touring site; Howgill is the ideal spot for all kinds of holidaymakers looking to enjoy some of Yorkshire's finest views. The site has been family owned since 1970 with Fiona and Tony and their children Robert and William being the most recent editions to take over. Rural walks and local attractions couple with the sites award winning facilities to make for a hassle free holiday all year round.

Garden Centres and Nurseries

www.findsomewhere.co.uk
For people who want to explore the United Kingdom

11 BOLTON ABBEY

Bolton Abbey Estate Office, Bolton Abbey, Skipton, North Yorkshire BD23 6EX
Tel: 01756 718009
website: www.boltonabbey.com

Bolton Abbey near Skipton is the Yorkshire Estate of the Duke and Duchess of Devonshire. Situated in Wharfedale, in the Yorkshire Dales National Park this historic estate is a magnet for visitors drawn to its breathtaking landscapes and excellent facilities.

Visitors have flocked to Bolton Abbey for over one hundred years. On an August Bank Holiday in the 1890's the railway brought 40,000 people to Bolton Abbey; nearly as many people as now visit York in a week. After the First World War visitors arrived by train in their "Sunday Best" with the children carrying buckets, spades and fishing nets. Some fathers never got much further than the Devonshire Arms' Refreshment Room, but many removed their boots and rolled up their trousers to paddle with their children by the sandy river bank. Little has changed over the years; visitors still come to see the landscape that inspired artists like Turner and Landseer, and poets such as Wordsworth.

As the name suggests Bolton Abbey was originally a large monastic Estate, based around the 12th century priory. Legend has it that the Priory was established in 1120 by Cecily de Romille as an expression of her grief following the drowning of her son in the nearby Strid. Today, the ruins of the Priory set in an incomparable position overlooking the river Wharfe will evoke the past glories of the Estate whilst the restored and thriving parish church shows that the Estate is still very much a living community.

12 BLUE BELL INN

Middle Lane, Kettlewell, Skipton,
North Yorkshire BD23 5QX
Tel: 01756 760230
website: www.bluebellkettlewell.co.uk

The delightful Blue Bell Inn can be found at the heart of the Yorkshire Dales National Park at Kettlewell. It is located close to the River Wharfe and has six en-suite letting rooms that are available all year round. Three of these are located on the ground floor and special breaks are available (ring for details). New licensees have recently taken over the running of the Blue Bell Inn and offer a warm welcome to customers, be they new or old.

Four real ales are served and three of these are brewed locally at the Copper Dragon Brewery in Skipton – the other is a regular rotating guest ale. Delicious food is served every lunch time and evening and in the summer months food times are extended to midday to 5pm and 6pm to 9pm. Meals can be chosen from the printed menu and additional choices are available from the daily specials board. Such is the popularity of dining here it is advisable to book for larger parties. Children are welcomed and the good hospitality matches the quality facilities and cooking. Open all day every day the Blue Bell Inn is an ideal place to stop off for a relaxing refreshment, bite to eat or place to stay. Dogs are welcome.

13 HEMMINGWAYS TEA ROOMS

10-11a Craven Court, Skipton,
North Yorkshire BD23 1DG
Tel: 01756 798035

Hemmingways Tea Rooms is undoubtedly one of Yorkshire's best eating establishments. It can be found in Craven Court, which is an undercover courtyard off Skipton's main street. The tea rooms have been privately owned and run since 2003 and are surrounded by varying independent businesses.

Hemingways is extremely popular with locals but also attracts plenty of visitors through its doors to indulge in the delicacies on offer. Local produce is used as much as possible and this adds to the quality of the dishes served. Home cooking is a strong focus of this dog friendly establishment. Hot dishes, snacks, drinks and desserts can all be enjoyed here. Homemade soups, muffins and omelettes are available and there is plenty of choice when it comes to filled sandwiches, toasties and salads. For those with a larger appetite there is a good range of hot dishes including traditional favourites such as meat lasagne and traditional fried fillet of haddock. There are other options such as salmon and broccoli pancakes as well as many vegetarian choices. Children are well catered for and younger diners can choose a meal from the special kids menu. Daily specials are listed on the blackboard.

Hemmingways Tea Rooms certainly give customers a little taste of Yorkshire – with an occasional continental twist. Everyone is welcome here, whether it be for a cup of tea or a lunch time meal. There is seating for around 80 customers inside and around 50 more can be seated on the balconies.

Gifts are also sold at the tea rooms. The establishment is open Monday to Saturday between 9.30am and 5pm and from midday on Sunday until 4pm.

All in all, Hemmingways is one of Yorkshire's finest tea rooms and a visit is highly recommended. All major credit cards accepted. Disabled access is not a problem.

14 THE CRAVEN MUSEUM

Town Hall, High Street, Skipton,
North Yorkshire BD23 1AH
Tel: 01756 706407 Fax: 01756 706412
e-mail: museum@cravendc.gov.uk
website: www.cravendc.gov.uk

Crammed full of fascinating exhibits, the **Craven Museum** is a great place to explore the history of Skipton and the Craven Dales. The museum displays collections of local history, archaeology, natural history, art and geology in a small but very popular museum situated in the Town Hall at the top of Skipton's busy market place. Temporary exhibitions vary from community projects to items on loan from other museums. Admission is free and the museum is open all year round.

16 SKIPTON CASTLE

Skipton, Yorkshire BD23 1AQ
Tel: 01756 792442
e-mail: info@skiptoncastle.co.uk
website: www.skiptoncastle.co.uk

Guardian of the gateway to the Yorkshire Dales for over 900 years, this unique fortress is one of the most complete and well-preserved medieval castles in England. Standing on a 40-metre high crag, fully-roofed Skipton Castle was founded around 1090 by Robert de Romille, one of William the Conqueror's Barons, as a fortress in the dangerous northern reaches of the kingdom.

Owned by King Edward I and Edward II, from 1310 it became the stronghold of the Clifford Lords withstanding successive raids by marauding Scots. During the Civil War it was the last Royalist bastion in the North, yielding only after a three-year siege in 1645. 'Slighted' under the orders of Cromwell, the castle was skilfully restored by the redoubtable Lady Anne Clifford and today visitors can climb from the depths of the Dungeon to the top of the Watch Tower, and explore the Banqueting Hall, the Kitchens, the Bedchamber and even the Privy!

Every period has left its mark, from the Norman entrance and the Medieval towers, to the beautiful Tudor courtyard with the great yew tree planted by Lady Anne in 1659. In the castle grounds visitors can see the Tudor wing built as a royal wedding present for Lady Eleanor Brandon, niece of Henry VIII, the beautiful Shell Room decorated in the 1620s with shells and Jamaican coral and the ancient medieval chapel of St. John the Evangelist. The Chapel Terrace, with its delightful picnic area, has fine views over the woods and Skipton's lively market town.

www.findsomewhere.co.uk
For people who want to explore the United Kingdom

Places to Visit

15 SPENCER'S CAFE & BISTRO

6 Victoria Square, Skipton, North Yorkshire BD23 1JF
Tel: 01756 795482
e-mail: spencerscafebistroskipton@googlemail.com

Hidden away in Victoria Square, Skipton, you will find a magnet for lovers of fine cuisine. **Spencer's Cafe and Bistro** is located just yards from the main street in the bustling market town of Skipton. Owner Adam Wilcock opened the cafe 3 ½ years ago and as a professional chef himself the food is superb. Wherever possible local produce is used and a lot of it is ordered in fresh daily. The dishes available are of the highest quality and the printed menu has plenty for customers to choose from.

There is a good range of filled sandwiches, ciabattas, paninis and wraps. Toasties, jacket potatoes and salads are all available. For those customers who have a bigger appetite there are choices including sausage and mash (three seasoned pork sausages served on a bed of mashed potato, smothered in a rich homemade onion gravy), giant Yorkshire pudding (a giant oven cooked pudding filled with two pork sausages, potatoes and seasoned vegetables smothered with homemade onion gravy), four egg omelette (served with salad and a variety of fillings), lasagne (a rich meat lasagne served with salad garnish), and lamb casserole (a rich casserole served with mash or jacket potatoes).

The menu changes every six months and additional choices like lamb shank are available from the daily specials board. The homemade scones served at Spencer's Cafe Bistro are definitely worth a try and so are the waffles on offer. The waffles are dusted and served with maple syrup.

Background music and the friendly and helpful waitress service all add to the ambience of the establishment. There is room for 42 customers inside spread across the ground and first floor. The courtyard provides extra space for diners on a warmer day. If you do find yourself in the town of Skipton the cafe is definitely worth a look. It is an ideal place to relax after a hard day's work or shopping trip. Spencer's Cafe and Bistro is open seven days a week between 9am and 5pm. Disabled access is not a problem.

17 THE SLATERS ARMS

Crag Lane, Bradley, nr Skipton,
North Yorkshire BD20 9DE
Tel: 01535 632179
e-mail: philipcook951@btinternet.com
website: www.theslatersarms.co.uk

The Slaters Arms has been a public house for over 150 years and is steeped in history and tradition. It opened in 1858 and retains many of its original features such as beautiful oak beamed ceilings and a huge open fireplace which still houses a roaring fire in the colder weather. The decor of the inn befits its history well, as the walls are adorned with a hundreds of mugs, plates and brass plaques from years gone by. The feel of yesteryear continues in the furniture which is comfortable whilst retaining a rustic feel.

The inn's owners Phil and Rosemary have been running the inn since 2001 and have just as much character as their beautiful inn. They are proud of the inn's heritage and preserve it by offering their customers the fine food, drink and service for which they have gained their notable reputation. The inn's fine canal side location affords it stunning views across the waters and the Aire Valley, particularly in the beer garden which functions as a true sun trap throughout the year.

Open every session and all day on Sundays, Phil and Rosemary always offer guests a choice of four real ales. The local's favourite is Taylor's Golden Best; however other ales from local breweries are forever rotating to sample. A fine selection of wine and spirits are also stocked behind the charming bar, where a friendly chat is always waiting.

The food served at Slaters is a real crowd pleaser, drawing regulars back day on day. Phil and Rosemary's Chef Tim works hard to ensure that there is something for everyone on his menu, which samples a range of traditional pub dishes and some more creative versions. Owing to popularity, it's recommended that guests book on weekends. Tim's speciality is Lamb Henry, marinated in mint and honey before being slow roasted with a rich jus. Other dishes include Cajun chicken salad, bolognaise lasagne, spinach and ricotta cannelloni and the delicious pork loin served with apple sauce and black pudding. The fish dishes here particularly popular with dishes like griddled Scottish salmon served with a lemon pickle, or the chefs own beer battered haddock fillet. Regardless of what you choose, all the ingredients used in your dish are sourced from within Yorkshire, offering a true Yorkshire taste to all the meals. There is no food on Mondays, but guests can come and enjoy a meal here from Tuesday to Saturday from 12-2pm and 6-9pm, and on Sundays from 12-7:30pm. All major credit cards accepted apart from American Express and Diners.

18 THE OLD SWAN INN

High Street, Gargrave, Skipton, North Yorkshire BD23 3RB
Tel: 01756 749232
e-mail: theoldswangargrave@googlemail.com
website: www.theoldswaninn.co.uk

The Swan Inn stands adjacent to the A65 in the heart of the village of Gargrave, just a short drive from Skipton on the way to Settle. It has had many previous occupations, including a coaching inn in the 17th century when it was believed to be built, and latterly a post office, morgue and blacksmiths. Today it operates as a successful inn, being perfectly located for guests wanting a comfortable base whilst touring the Yorkshire Dales and moors, with the Lake District also within driving distance.

Kate and Daniel took over the Swan in April 2009 and have quickly built up a steady clientele of locals and visitors to the area. Locals say that they have put the inn back on the map, giving the village a sense of community once again.

They offer up a wide range of food and drinks, noted for quality as well as quantity. There are three real ales available at all times; with Black Sheep, Tetleys and Hobgoblin making regular appearances. A good wine list also accompanies these, with plenty of other spirits, lagers and soft drinks available. Food is available Monday to Friday 12-3pm and 6-9pm, and from Saturday 12-9pm and Sundays 12-8pm. Kate and Daniel employ a professional chef who has designed the menus here himself. Customers are guaranteed that each dish is prepared fresh each day from only the very best in local produce. Guests can choose from the main menu which samples a variety of meat, grills, fish and vegetarian dishes, or select something from the regularly changing specials menu; often showcasing the area's best seasonal dishes. Popular mains include goat's cheese and chive stuffed chicken breast with a creamy mustard sauce, Black Sheep steak and ale pie, homemade creamy fish pie and the succulent 8oz sirloin steak. Other favourites include moules mariniere, homemade beef lasagne and a creamy mushroom stroganoff with rice timbale. Guests can also choose from the light bites menu which offers up a good range of sandwiches, hot baguettes and salads. Bar snacks are also available throughout the day from classic beef burgers with fries, to nachos laden with guacamole salsa and sour cream to your liking. Children are welcome to dine, and can choose from their own small menu or take half portions from the main menu at a reduced price. On Sundays however, a traditional roast is served with a choice of three meats, perfect for pleasing the whole family.

Kate and Daniel also provide fantastic guest accommodation all year round with two double rooms, one twin room, one single room and one family room available. The tariff includes a hearty breakfast – ideal for waking you up after a night spent at the inn's Saturday disco at the end of every month. Cash only please.

19 THE BOARS HEAD HOTEL

9 Main Street, Long Preston, Skipton, North Yorkshire BD23 4ND
Tel: 01729 840217
e-mail: boarsheadhotel@hotmail.co.uk
website: www.hotelyorkshiredales.co.uk

Nestled between the picturesque villages of Settle and Skipton in the equally appealing village of Long Preston, is **The Boars Head Hotel**. This magnificent building stands on the main street, once a former coaching inn and post house dating back to the 16th century in parts. Although it has recently been refurbished under its new owners, the inn retains all of its old character with well preserved oak beamed ceilings and a beautiful open fireplace.

Karina and Paul moved into the inn in the summer of 2010 along with Paul's parents Brenda and Derek. Together the family make up a very friendly and able team. Although it's the family's first venture into the hospitality trade, they are seeing many repeat visitors; a testament to how well they are doing.

They open all day everyday, serving a good variety of real ales from both local and national breweries. Dogs are welcome in the bar and beer garden, which makes a lovely retreat during the summer; commanding glorious views across the National Park.

Food is also available everyday between 12-9pm when both a main menu and a specials board operate. The family aim to stay true to their roots and serve up a host of delicious Yorkshire food, and their traditional menu reflects this, although some more adventurous dishes are usually found too. Described as great 'pub grub' – some favourite dishes include Cumberland sausages in a large Yorkshire pudding with mash and peas, homemade steak pie, scampi and chips and an all day breakfast. The grill also offers a tempting array with succulent steaks, slow roasted lamb Henry and butterfly Cajun chicken. Vegetarians are also very well catered for with a separate menu including dishes like spinach and feta goujons, Feuillete Epinard and vegetable satay. Local produce is used where possible, and all dishes are cooked fresh to order.

Karina and Paul also offer their guests a choice of five contemporary en suite rooms. Perfect for touring the surrounding area, a mixture of room sizes are available to suit families, singles and couples. The room tariff includes a generously portioned breakfast, sure to set you up for a hike across the dales. The hotel accepts credit cards.

20 GIGGLESWICK TEA ROOMS & VILLAGE SHOP

3 Church Street, Giggleswick, nr Settle, North Yorkshire BD24 0BE
Tel: 01729 822592
e-mail: vinewoods@yahoo.co.uk

Situated in the heart of the village of Giggleswick you can find the delightful Giggleswick Tea Rooms and Village Shop. What this place lacks in size it makes up for in hospitality and delicious food. Sharon Woodvine took over here in December 2009 and has built up a thriving business in a fairly short period of time. The premises house the village shop, selling many essentials and contains a fine old fashioned sweet shop.

The quaint tea rooms, which has a slate floor, seats eight inside with room for 13 more in the pretty rear courtyard, which is home to an attractive water feature. When it is too cold outside there is a fantastic old range, which keeps diners warm and cosy in winter months. All dishes available are listed daily on the blackboard and are cooked fresh to order. There is plenty of choice from fresh fish dishes to filled paninis and sandwiches. Breakfasts are particular popular at Giggleswick Tear Rooms and the traditional sweet shop is a favourite among the local students. Giggleswick Tea Rooms and Village Shop is open seven days a week in summer and six days in winter. Disabled access is not a problem.

21 JANE'S KITCHEN

18 Sandgate, Whitby, North Yorkshire YO22 4DB
Tel: 01947 602861

Standing in the heart of the popular historic town of Whitby, **Jane's Kitchen** can be found close to the harbour and Whitby Bridge. It is becoming extremely well known in the area and it is a favourite with many locals and visitors. Jane and Bill Wilson have owned the cafe for the past year and have owned the Rock Shop next door for more than 30 years.

Jane does the majority of the cooking here and all dishes are homemade and cooked to order. There is a fantastic selection of dishes to choose from including breakfasts, homemade chilli, curry and a fine range of delicious homemade cakes and scones. Carrot cake is Jane's speciality and if you taste it you will understand why so many people come here to sample it. As a main dish scampi and chips is one of the favourites and if you still have room left it will be hard to resist one of the many tempting homemade desserts which include bread & butter pudding and sticky toffee pudding. Jane's Kitchen seats 32 inside, four outside and is open until 5pm every day (except from Mondays in December and on Christmas day).

22 WHITBY ABBEY

Whitby, North Yorkshire YO22 4JT
Tel: 01947 603568
website: www.english-heritage.org.uk

The stark and magnificent ruins of **Whitby Abbey** are much more than a spectacular cliff-top landmark. Since prehistory, successive generations have been drawn to this dramatic headland as a site of settlement, religious devotion and even literary inspiration.

23 CAPTAIN COOK MEMORIAL MUSEUM

Grape Lane, Whitby, Yorkshire YO22 4BE
Tel: 01947 601900
website: www.whitby-uk.com

In Whitby's Grape lane in a narrow street near the harbour, stands John Walker's house, home to Captain Cook. Cook lodged in the attic of this house from 1746 to 1749 while serving as an apprentice to ship owner John Walker. Visitors can see displays and models relating to Cook's life and voyages and can also see where Cook slept.

At the very top of the house, in the ship-timbered attic, the young James Cook pursued his winter studies by candlelight; huddled by the chimney breast for warmth, he must often have looked across the river to the shipyards where, later, the ships he would use on his famous voyages – Endeavour, Resolution, Adventure and Discovery would be built.

James Cook's explorations started at the house in Grape Lane, Whitby, from where his skills, courage and adventurous spirit took him to sail, as he himself said, "...not only as far as man has gone before, but as far as it is possible for man to go."

24 THE FIRS

26 Hinderwell Lane, Runswick Bay, nr Whitby,
North Yorkshire TS13 5HR
Tel: 01947 840433   Fax: 01947 841616
e-mail: mandy.shackleton@talk21.com
website: www.the-firs.co.uk

Situated at the top of the bank in Runswick Bay on the
North Yorkshire Coast just a short walk from the picturesque
seafront, The Firs is a quality four star family run guesthouse
which has 12 en-suite rooms. All of the rooms are spacious,
comfortable and individually decorated, six are on the
ground floor of which four have been purpose built for
mobility access with wet rooms and grab rails.

Having been in the same family ownership since 1985,
The Firs is extremely popular with repeat visitors who come
here to relax and unwind. There is a lovely homely
atmosphere here and the extensive breakfast menu and
daily changing choice of evening meals are absolutely
delicious. All meals are cooked to order and menus for evening meals are devised using seasonal
fresh local produce. Fresh local fish is a speciality.

All dietary requirements can be easily catered for (please ring for details).

The Firs is not licensed, guests and diners are more than welcome to Bring their Own which will
be chilled (if needed) opened and served for you.

25 SPRINGHOUSE COTTAGES

3 Springhouse Cottages, Easington,
Saltburn-by-the-Sea, Cleveland TS13 4UE
Tel: 01287 640226 / 07956344132
e-mail: holiday@springhousecottages.co.uk
website: www.springhousecottages.co.uk

Springhouse is a two-bedroom self-catering cottage near the fishing
village of Staithes. Owners Amanda and Adrian Pearson's property
offers well-equipped modern facilities and fantastic views over the
surrounding countryside and out to sea. The cottage was converted by
the owners with love and skill from an old blacksmith's barn. The
work took ten months and was completed in May 2009. The whole of
the property is at least 200 years old and when they started the work
it had not been lived in for 35 years.

The ground floor comprises a kitchen-diner, cloakroom and a living
room with leather settees, a log-burning stove and underfloor
heating. One the first floor are two bedrooms - a double (which has a
large walk in wardrobe and a 26" LCD TV and DVD player) and a twin,
both with en suite facilities. This lovely pantile-roofed cottage has
two sets of patio doors, into the kitchen-diner and living room, and
outside is a terrace with garden furniture that commands terrific
views. Springhouse is an ideal base for relaxing or walking the dog, while sporting facilities
available nearby include golf, fishing, sailing and riding. Staithes, on the Cleveland Way, is two
miles away, and also within easy reach are Runswick Bay, Whitby, Guisborough, Pickering and
Kirkby Moorside.

26 WOLD POTTERY

79 High Street, Loftus,
Saltburn-by-the-Sea, Cleveland TS13 4HG
Tel: 01287 640100
e-mail: woldpottery@yahoo.co.uk
website: www.woldpottery.co.uk

For more than 50 years Wold Pottery has been
producing pieces to delight buyers and owners at
home and overseas. Jill Christie has long been
passionate about pottery, working in the finest
traditions of the studio pottery movement. In 1973
she was apprenticed to Aidan Dixon, who founded
the Pottery in its original location near Beverley. At Aidan's wheel she learnt throwing and
decorating techniques and took over the business in 1985. To meet the growing needs of
commissioning for customers the Pottery moved into a 19th century butchers shop on the main
street of Loftus. In 2008 the premises were extended to house the Gallery, fulfilling Jill's dream of
having the workshop and the gallery under one roof.

Jill produces earthenware of a lightness and clarity that is never equalled by stoneware. The
output includes a wide range of domestic and decorative pieces; some are embossed with real
leaves, others feature lattice work, and the classic Wolds colours of sea green, browns and blues
are often to be seen. The Gallery houses a collection of original works by Jill and other people in
a variety of media, including oils, watercolours, ceramics, sculpture, silks, soaps and candles -
gifts at all prices for all occasions, and almost everything made in and around the Moors and
Coast.

27 THE WHEATSHEAF INN

Egton, Whitby, North Yorkshire YO12 1TZ
Tel: 01947 895271
e-mail: info@wheatsheafegton.com
website: www.wheatsheafegton.com

The Wheatsheaf Inn is found snugly tucked away in the village of
Egton with the outstanding beauty of the National Park and the
Yorkshire moors on its doorstep. The inn has been owned and run
by Nigel and Elaine for the past ten years, whose hands on
approach in running the inn has served them well; forging a
sturdy reputation for charm and class. The inn itself dates back
to the early 17th century, and retains a true period feel. Live
fires, traditional furniture and earthy tones allow for an intimate
dining experience in what is very much a local pub.

Elaine is the chef here, offering her guests a delicious set of
dishes between 12-2pm Tuesday to Sunday and 6-8:30pm Tuesday
to Saturday. Her dishes include hearty lamb shanks, chicken and smoked bacon puff pastry pie,
sirloin steak, and steak and mulled wine pie. Vegetarians can sample dishes like white nut and
artichoke heart roast or sundried tomato and mozzarella ravioli in basil sauce, whilst children
have their own menu. Elaine also offers guests a decadent dessert menu, although her mini trio of
desserts option is ever popular. Adjacent to the inn is a beautifully converted cottage for self
catering or B&B, with two double rooms and a family suite available. It has its own rear courtyard
complete with table tennis and a games room converted from an old pigsty. For a taste of
traditional country living with all the mod cons, stay here.

28 HORSESHOE HOTEL

Egton Bridge, Whitby, North Yorkshire YO21 1XE
Tel: 01947 895245
e-mail: paul@thehorseshoehotel.co.uk
website: www.thehorseshoehotel.co.uk

The outstanding **Horseshoe Hotel** is a former country house which dates back to the 18th century. It can be found at Egton Bridge in the heart of the North Yorkshire Moors National Park. This charming country inn is run by Paul and Alison Underwood, their daughter Holly and grandson Theodore. It is set in beautiful grounds on the River Esk and offers a friendly and relaxed atmosphere, varied menu, and comfortable accommodation.

The Underwood family took over here three years ago and the place is becoming a real magnet for keen walkers and tourists. There are six guest double rooms available here with three of them offering en-suite facilities. Each is individually furnished, decorated to a high standard and available all year round. The tariff includes a breakfast that will last you all day. Ring for details.

The extensive menu has a strong focus on fresh local produce and diners can enjoy the food inside or out in the superb beer garden on warmer days. Although a chef is employed in peak season Alison always oversees the kitchen making sure the food, listed on a daily blackboard, is spot on. Starters include soup of the day prepared with fresh ingredients and served with rustic bread, homemade chicken liver pate: served with toast and salad garnish, and warm chicken & bacon salad with balsamic dressing.

All of the main courses are reasonably priced and there are plenty of traditional options such as fish pie poached white, smoked fish and prawns, topped with creamy mashed potato and cheddar cheese; sirloin steak cooked to your liking and served with a traditional garnish; and home baked ham, egg & chips.

For those with a lighter lunch time appetite there is a good range of jacket potatoes, sandwiches and hot baguettes.

The bar here is well stocked and there is a comprehensive wine list as well as traditional, hand-pulled beers. There are five real ales to enjoy with Black Sheep and John Smiths the regulars, and an annual beer festival is held in July or August.

Walkers and motorists alike will find Egton Bridge an ideal centre from which to explore this delightful area. The child-friendly hotel is within very easy reach of the seaside resorts of Whitby, Sandsend, Staithes, Robin Hood's Bay and Runswick Bay. A Roman road and fort, the North Yorkshire Moors Railway, Goathland (Heartbeat Country) and Castle Howard are all nearby.

29 THE NEWLANDS

80 Columbus Ravine, Scarborough, North Yorkshire YO12 7QU
Tel: 01723 367261
e-mail: newlandshotel@btconnect.com
website: www.thenewlandshotel.co.uk

The traditional seaside resort of Scarborough is home to two long sandy bays with a variety of attractions to entertain any visitor with indoor pools, a Sea Life Centre, adventure golf courses, cricket grounds, boating lakes and the famous Spa Grand Hall; regularly showing various theatre and concert performances. With so much to do, it's ideal for a family holiday but also has the beautiful North Yorkshire moorland to explore by foot or steam railway nearby.

The Newlands is a popular three star family run hotel in the North Bay area of Scarborough, just ten minutes from the town centre and the same distance from the golden sands of the beach. Pauline Sutton and her daughter Debbie and her partner Stuart offer the warmest of welcomes to their hotel; a distinctive red brick Victorian building, handsomely decorated throughout. The family are in their fourth season at Newlands, and see many repeat visitors year by year; tribute to their wonderful hospitality.

There are seven rooms in total to choose from; with two large family rooms, four double rooms and one single room. All the rooms apart from the single have full en suite facilities; whereas the single has its own separate shower room. Rooms afford comfort and space, with the use of the hotels TV lounge also available for guests looking for a quiet night in. Evening meals at the hotel are available on request between 6:30-7:30pm, with a different selection of traditional dishes home cooked fresh to order each night. If guests prefer to dine out, the family are more than happy to recommend the best restaurants and bars in the area with many within easy walking distance. Pauline is the cook, and is known throughout Scarborough for her breakfasts which are as tasty as they are generous. She offers a hearty full English breakfast each morning from 8-9:30am with a range of continental and lighter options also available; whatever you choose, she guarantees it will fill you up for the whole day. Meals are enjoyed in the hotels spacious dining room, with tables laid individually for each party morning and night. Its sunny colours and bustling atmosphere make for a charming start to the day.

Parking is to the front of the property on the roadside; however parking permits are available from the hotel free of charge. Cash and cheque only please.

30 ESPLANADE GARDENS

24 Esplanade Gardens, South Cliff, Scarborough, North Yorkshire YO11 2AP
Tel: 01723 360728
e-mail: dekquy@aol.com
website: www.esplanadegardensscarborough.co.uk

Scarborough offers much for both families and couples looking for a holiday in Yorkshire, with plenty of attractions within the town itself, and much more further afield. Scarborough sports two glorious beaches and a bustling town centre with a host of cafes, restaurants, theatres, sporting facilities and spas. The well known towns of Whitby, York and Ryedale are just a short drive away, making Scarborough a convenient base for exploring.

Esplanade Gardens is the perfect hotel for that base, just 200 yards from the cliff lift, and a fifteen minute walk to the town centre and harbour. The Hotel takes its name from the famed Italian Gardens and is overlooked by the picturesque Olivers Mount. The Italian Gardens are perfect for a quiet afternoon stroll. The hotel itself is a charming Victorian building dating back to 1874, full of attractive period features coupled with modern styling and comforts.

Its hosts, Jenny and Derek have been running the hotel for over four years now and have built up an impressive reputation for hospitality as evidenced in their visitor's book.

There are ten en suite rooms to choose from in a range of sizes from family rooms to doubles and twins. Each room is tastefully decorated with contemporary colours and sumptuous fabrics; affording a luxurious and modern feel to any stay here. Children are more than welcome to stay with families, with extra cots and additional bedding available on request. Each day is started with a hearty breakfast between 8-9am served in the striking dining area, with a beautiful feature wall and matching dining chairs. Guests can choose from a 'proper fry up' or a range of lighter options to suit any appetite or dietary requirement

including vegetarian. The homely lounge bar adjacent also offers a range of tasty snacks and treats throughout the day from toasted sandwiches to burgers and salads. The bar is also fully licensed so guests are free to spend an evening relaxing with a good ale and good company if they prefer.

Jenny and Derek open all year round, but are closed for the Christmas period and in January apart from New Years Eve. Parking permits for the area are provided free of charge allowing for easy parking on arrival and throughout your stay. All major credit cards accepted.

31 THE EARLSMERE

5 Belvedere Road, South Cliff, Scarborough YO11 2UU
Tel: 01723 361340
e-mail: info@theearlsmere.co.uk
website: www.theearlsmere.co.uk

Lavish and elegant accomodation is what you wil find at The Earlsmere-a magnificent Victorian built property,which also has some views down to the sea. The interior is superb in every department and has many eye-catching and original features, including stained glass windows.

Owners Lynne and Peter Marsh have been here for eight years and have many returning visitors. The Earlsmere is the perfect place to stay for those who like to be pampered. There are five luxury en-suite rooms that have been completed to an extremely high standard. Each has been tastefully decorated and thoughtfully equipped and there is wireless internet access available to every room. Some of the rooms have slight sea views and all of them are located upstairs. Flexible breakfast times, and free internet access to all rooms.

This splendid hotel enjoys a peaceful location and is situated just a two minute walk from the seafront and a ten minute walk to the town centre. The Earlsmere can be found in the historical South Cliff area of Scarborough overlooking the playing fields of a Private School. No parking problems, as The Earlsmere is located outside the restricted area.

32 FRANCIS TEA ROOMS

7 South Street, South Cliff, Scarborough,
North Yorkshire YO11 2BP
Tel: 01723 350550
website: www.francistearooms.co.uk

As you enter **Francis Tea Rooms** the delightful aroma of good old fashioned home baking embraces you, followed swiftly by a warm welcome from the team within. Owner Wendy has been running Francis for three years with the help of her hardworking team; Barbara, Joy, Helen, Roz, Jane and Jules.

Known locally for its unrivalled home cooking, Francis offers its guests a handsome selection of homemade breakfasts, lunches, snacks, cakes and pastries each day fresh from the oven. Open from 9:30am-4pm Tuesday to Saturday and from 9:30am-3:30pm on Sundays, it's popular with those who enjoy all the things that make a tea room special; as Francis uses hand-embroidered tablecloths and proper delicate china crockery – making for a charming afternoon tea.

The tea rooms themselves are not without character either, as they once functioned as an old Scarborough hair salon with individual styling rooms for the shy ladies who would not be seen in public with un-styled hair. Wendy has kept many of the original features, and pleasingly all the solid wooden mirrors are still intact; simply oozing charm.

Booking is recommended from Thursday-Sunday, cash and cheque only please.

33 CENTRAL TRAMWAY

Marine Parade, Scarborough, Yorkshire YO11 2ER
Tel: 01723 501754
website: www.funimag.com

The **Central Tramway Company** Scarborough Limited was created and registered in 1880 and still operates in its original corporate form. The lift, designed for steam operation and first opened to the public in August 1881, is located in the real center of the South Bay, linking the city to the shore just beside the Grand Hotel.

Below the track and about 60 feet from the top station the steam operated winch gear was housed. The driver of the lift had no view of the cars and relied on an indicator with other visual aids such as string tied on to the haulage rope, and chalk marks on the winch drums to indicate the arrival of the cars at the top and bottom stations. In 1910 steam was abandoned and the gear converted to electric drive. In 1932 the cars were replaced and the motor placed under the top station. Control was from a driving position at the top of the station with full view of the cars. For emergency use each car is fitted with a screw on and wedge safety brake which operates on a safety rail down the center of each track and the rail also carries the rollers for the support of the cables.

35 THE CASTLE TAVERN

49 Castle Road, Scarborough, North Yorkshire YO11 1BG
Tel: 01723 365626 e-mail: jamesricescarborough@yahoo.co.uk

Just a short walk from the centre of Scarborough, is The Castle Tavern. The "Tavern" sees a steady clientele who enjoy a laid back atmosphere and great amenities. The family run pub, managed by Jimmy Rice and daughter Trudy, is open all day every day, serving great value food, real ales, largers and bitters. There is a different theme every night, Monday - Curry Night: 2 curries & bottle of wine £10. Wednesday - Steak Night: 2 steaks & bottle of wine £15. Thursday - Meal Deal Night: Meal & drink only £5 (*selected meals & drinks only*). Saturday: Karaoke and Disco with the occasional live band. Sunday Day: Traditional Sunday lunch only £4.95, served with "giant" Yorkshire pudding. Children's meal's available. Sporting fans can also catch up on all the big sports. Free Wi-Fi available.

34 THE IVY HOUSE RESTAURANT AND ACCOMMODATION

49 Sandside, Scarborough, North Yorkshire YO11 1PG
Tel: 01723 361675
e-mail: enquiries@theivyhousescarborough.com
website: www.theivyhousescarborough.com

The Ivy House Restaurant and Accommodation is situated on an unrivalled location right on the harbour and beach in Scarborough. This affords the Ivy House glorious views year round allowing guests to watch this popular seaside town change with the seasons.

Current owners, Alison and George Tuby took over in June 2009 and have since given the building a complete refurbishment. Once a former 18th century sea captains house, it is now the talk of the town operating as a successful restaurant with luxury bed and breakfast accommodation above.

Alison and George's daughters Sammy-Jo and Jade helped their parents with the style and decor decisions and their passion for interior design is evident throughout. Combining 21st century chic with 18th century furniture gives both the restaurant and the bedrooms a wickedly luxurious and elegant feel. There are six stunning suites to choose from; all of which take their names from Pirates of the Caribbean – perhaps the Tuby family were channelling the spirit of the sea captain when they made their decisions... Room features include king size beds, family mezzanine rooms, plasma TVs, sea views, living fires and personal touches like slippers and spa gowns that make your stay special.

The restaurant opens from 9am-10pm in season seating up to seventy-five people indoors and thirty-six more on the harbour front patio. Not surprisingly the specialty here is the seafood, the majority of which is caught fresh each morning. The rest of the menu however is also popular with a great selection of creative and wholesome dishes. Popular main dishes include 100% beef short crust pastry pie, Cumberland sausage whirl with mash and rich gravy, and the hot seafood platter which includes scampi tails, queen scallops, premium white fish and goujons. Lighter bites are also available with plenty of sandwiches, paninis, toasties, jackets and salads on offer. The dessert menu here also demands deserved attention; with a mouth-watering array of homemade cakes, scones and treats fresh from the oven each day. Favourites include the warm apple pie, waffles and the treacle sponge. Equally difficult to resist is the Tuby's special Yorkshire cream tea.

Whether dining or staying for longer, guests can rest assured there is plenty to see and do in the area whilst uncovering some of Scarborough's history. Families and children also have the option of visiting the Tuby's funfair; conveniently just across the road at Lunar Park.

36 JEREMY'S

33 Victoria Park Avenue, Scarborough,
North Yorkshire YO12 7TR
Tel: 01723 363871
e-mail: info@jeremysrestaurant.me.uk
website: www.jeremysrestaurant.me.uk

Since it opened in November 2009 **Jeremy's** has become one of the premier dining establishments in Scarborough. Nearby hoteliers and B&B owners have tried it and now regularly recommend it to their many guests.

Owners Jeremy and Anne Hollingsworth totally refurbished the premise before opening it last year. Jeremy has been a professional chef since 1984 and has worked as head chef in many restaurants that have been awarded Michelin Stars and Rosettes. With that in mind it comes as no surprise how well executed each of his delicious dishes are. The modern European cuisine is extremely popular with customers here. Starters include red onion tatin with kidderton ash goat's cheese & basil pesto; and among the favourite mains is Anna's organic slow-roast belly pork with mash, carrot & swede puree & bobbi beans. Be sure to leave room for one of the many tempting desserts or puddings.

Around 46 diners can be seated inside and there is room for a further 14 guests on the front patio. Food orders are taken Wednesday – Saturday between 5.30pm and 9.30pm and between 12 noon and 3pm for Sunday lunch.

37 RENDEZVOUS CAFE

1-5 Northway, Scarborough, North Yorkshire YO11 1JH
Tel: 01723 372970

Rendezvous Cafe is located centrally in Scarborough nearby the main train station. Its convenient location and personable staff make it a popular haunt with both locals and visitors alike who enjoy the great selection of food and drink.

The cafe has been in the Dack family for over twenty years, with Nigel taking the helm for the past three. Open every day apart from Christmas Day between 8:30am-6pm Monday to Saturday and from 9am-5pm on Sundays, the cafe sees many repeat visitors. Working on a first come first served basis, guests can choose from a variety of special and set menus – or just choose whatever takes their fancy from the display counter. Dishes range from tasty homemade scones and cakes to hearty breakfasts and homemade pies. On Sundays guests can enjoy a traditional roast dinner with all the trimmings. A good range of teas, coffees and hot drinks are on offer alongside a range of soft drinks and juices. Children are welcome at all times. Cash only please.

38 BRYHERSTONES COUNTRY INN AND LOWFIELD LOG HOMES

Cloughton Newlands, nr Scarborough,
North Yorkshire YO13 0AR
Tel: 01723 870744
e-mail: bryherstones@btinternet.com
website: www.bryherstones.info

The lovely **Bryherstones Country Inn** sits between Cloughton and Staintondale in North Yorkshire, within the North Yorkshire National Park, and close to the coast. It offers something for everyone, and is brimming with charm and character; there is always a friendly welcome waiting inside. Owners Paul and Sally have restored Bryherstones to its former glory (it was owned very successfully by Paul's family from 1983-95), and are proud of their fine home-cooked menu and excellent hospitality. The menu is freshly cooked and locally-sourced, and there is a great variety from the printed menu and the daily changed specials board. There is a very popular Traditional Sunday Dinner on Sunday

afternoons, which is always advisable to book in advance. The large garden at the rear of the Inn provides a large play area for children - the perfect location on those summer days.

One and a half miles away, within the grounds of the property, are two new Scandinavian log houses, available all year around on a self-catering basis. There is no better way to experience the National Park than in these natural wooden cabins, with outstanding facilities. One sleeps a group of six and the other a group of four.

39 THREE JOLLY SAILORS AND PARSONS RESTAURANT

2 High Street, Burniston, Scarborough, North Yorkshire YO13 0HJ
Tel: 01723 871259
e-mail: threejollysailor@aol.com

This fine public house and restaurant has been put on the map for great food, real ales and hospitality by Gavin and Lucy, since they took over in December 2009. **The Three Jolly Sailors and Parsons Restaurant** has flourished through word-of-mouth, as the recommendations have flooded in, and is popular with the locals and visitors holidaying by the sea.

Naturally, it is the food which is the star of the show here, and everyone in the family will love this menu which is full of fresh tasty dishes, and is kind to your wallet as well! For starters there is a delicious variety of single dishes, such as bite-sized fishcakes of traditional haddock served with lemon mayonnaise, and creamy garlic mushrooms with a melted cheese topping, served with half a ciabatta roll, as well as sharing platters, which are perfect for a big group. The salad menu is extensive, and brilliant for warmer weather when you want something lighter to eat; favourites include bang bang chicken, with crunchy slaw, a peanut & chilli satay dressing and crispy noodles, and mature cheddar and green apple tossed with mixed leaves & drizzled with honey mustard dressing.

The main menu consists of traditional dishes, like steak & Copper Dragon ale pie and The Jolly's special chicken kiev, as well as a selection of fish dishes and burgers, which can be made to exactly your tastes. All of the meat from the Three Jolly Sailors' grill is sourced by nearby Halders of Staintondale – you can't get fresher. The specials include Surf & Turf, a 8oz rump steak with Whitby scampi, and grilled lemon chicken breast with a lemon and herb butter and jacket potato. The desert menu has its own heavenly chocolate section; who could resist a warm chocolate brownie or white chocolate & mascarpone cheesecake to finish off a lovely meal? Children will be spoilt for choice by "The Captains" children's menu.

Food is served Sunday-Thursday 12noon-8pm, and Friday-Saturday 12noon-9pm (the Sunday lunch carvery is served between 12noon and 4pm, and then the restaurant will be closed until 5pm to clean up.). It is always advisable to book to avoid disappointment, particularly Friday to Sunday. On Friday there is a fun pub quiz from 8pm, and on Saturdays there is entertainment from 9pm.

40 CATH'S DINER

Station Avenue, Filey,
North Yorkshire YO14 9AQ
Tel: 01723 514664

Open every day from 7:30am apart from Christmas
Day, Cath's diner serves a handsome selection of
freshly made hot and cold sandwiches, main meals,
snacks and drinks. Located just a stone's throw from
the railway station at Filey inside an arcade, this
family run place sees many visitors despite its
hidden location. Cath has worked in the cafe for
five years, but became a business partner with
Craig just last year. Her friendly demeanour and
dedication to her business makes her a truly warm
and welcoming host.

Cath cooks up everything from a fried egg
sandwich to homemade steak and ale pie
throughout the day, although she tells us her most
popular dishes are the breakfasts and Sunday
lunches. A full roast is offered each Sunday, when
booking is recommended owing to popularity.
Children and pensioners can take advantage of her
money saving deals, making it a common haunt for
all ages. Cash only please.

42 PICKERING CASTLE

Castlegate, Pickering, Yorkshire YO18 7AX
Tel: 01751 474989
website: www.english-heritage.org.uk

Set in an historic moors-edge market town, this
splendid 13th century castle and royal hunting lodge
make a fascinating visit for all ages. Explore the walls
and towers overlooking deep moats. Take the steps up
the man-made mound to the shell-keep, for wonderful
views of the North York Moors.

www.findsomewhere.co.uk
For people who want to explore the United Kingdom

Places to Stay

41 VICTORIA COURT BAR AND RESTAURANT

The Crescent, Filey, North Yorkshire YO14 9JF
Tel: 01723 513237

The popular seaside town of Filey in North Yorkshire is home to **Victoria Court Bar and Restaurant**, found in a lofty location overlooking the gardens and the shore. It holds an unbeaten reputation for outstanding dining for both lunch and dinner. Its owners Richard and Jill Bell have been running Victoria for over 28 years and have turned it into quite the destination restaurant. Both locals and guests from further afield flock to dine here with its beautiful decor and even more stunning food.

Open all year round, but closed on Tuesdays, guests can visit Victoria Court throughout the day, with food available between 12-2pm and 6-9pm. The restaurant and bar area seats up to 35 guests with seating for another 35 in a private function room. The bar area, elegant and full of atmosphere, is always fully stocked and staffed by charming and helpful aides. Diners can choose from a range of drinks or wines.

Richard has been a professional chef for a phenomenal 47 years, leaving his knowledge about food and flavour second to none. Over the years he has carefully cultivated a selection of menus to suit every appetite, palette and budget.

Owing to its seaside location, Richard's menus are unsurprisingly laden with countless sumptuous seafood dishes, however all dishes are cooked fresh to order using the very best in local Yorkshire produce. The a la carte menu which operates in the evenings offers up starters such as homemade chicken liver pate, Norwegian prawn cocktails, hot chicken chunky salad topped with Granny Bell's own recipe dressing, and plaice filled with fresh salmon mayonnaise in a light batter. The main courses also feature much plaice, with breaded, deep fried, grilled and goujons varieties. Haddock and scampi also feature on the menu along with a vegetarian nut roast, several varieties of chicken, pork and specialty pies. Guests can also opt for something from the grill, with plenty of handsome cuts of Yorkshire meat on offer. Desserts include local ice cream, sherry trifle, apple or banana fritters and meringue glace.

For those desiring a lighter lunch, there are also plenty of options, including homemade soup, supreme Scottish scampi with a salad garnish, and the popular 'mushroom moments' which features lightly battered mushrooms filled with pate and served with hot stilton sauce. A simple, but delicious selection of omelettes, sandwiches and hot baguettes are also available. Children are welcome to dine from the main menu with half portions. All major credit cards accepted apart from American Express and Diners. Closed during the first two weeks of February. For annual holidays.

43 POPPIES TRADITIONAL TEAROOMS

37 Burgate, Pickering, North Yorkshire   YO18 7AU
Tel: 01751 477741
e-mail: poppiesteas@gmx.co.uk

Situated just yards from the centre of well known Pickering, in Burgate, stand **Poppies Traditional Tearooms**. New owners Louis and Tracy took over here in June 2010 and with a wealth of experience in the catering and cooking industries they are taking to their new venture like ducks to water.

The interior of the establishment has undergone major refurbishment and now has an elegant and stylish feel to it. Work is also being completed on the exterior, giving the tearooms a more fresh and inviting feel. A warm welcome will always greet you here as will the lovely aroma of home baking. It is a smell that takes many customers back to their youth and attracts locals and visitors to come and sample the delicacies on offer. There is room to seat 22 diners in the cosy establishment.

Tracy is in charge of things in the kitchen and with nine years experience cooking professionally she has everything under control, cooking delicious homemade food to order. Her husband Louis, who has plenty of experience in the catering industry is in charge of the front of house, greeting people in a warm and friendly manner.

Although the menu is yet to be finalised you can guarantee that most of the dishes will be homemade with additional daily specials. Customers can enjoy a selection of quiches, homemade desserts and plenty of home-baked cakes, which are displayed elegantly in a glass cabinet. Among the most popular specials are chicken and bacon pasta bake, salmon and broccoli quiche and chocolate and strawberry trifle.

The tearooms are child friendly and for youngsters wanting something to eat half portions are offered at half the price.

Poppies Traditional Tearooms are open six days a week from 10am Friday to Wednesday and are closed on Thursday.

Disabled access is not a problem although there are no disabled toilet facilities. Only cash and cheque are accepted here.

44 SWAN COTTAGE

Newton upon Rawcliffe, Pickering, North Yorkshire YO18 8QA
Tel: 01751 472502

The delightful **Swan Cottage** can be found in the picturesque village of Newton upon Rawcliffe. The B&B overlooks the village green and the village pond and is an ideal setting for wildlife enthusiasts. Newton upon Rawcliffe is a beautiful place in the North Yorkshire Moors National Park and the guest house is a perfect base for visitors and walkers wanting to explore the area. Owners Christine and Austin Harrison offer three en-suite guest rooms, which like the rest of the cottage, are full of style and character. Dating back to the early 19th century the cottage is next door to the village pub, where excellent food and real ales are available.

46 THE BUCK HOTEL

Chestnut Avenue, Thornton-le-Dale, Pickering,
North Yorkshire YO18 7RW
Tel: 01751 474212
e-mail: paul.tiffany@btopenworld.com

The Buck Hotel is an outstanding inn in the lovely village of Thornton-Le-Dale. It can be found on the A170, a short drive east from Pickering. Paul and Joanne Tiffany have been the leaseholders here since December 2009. The Buck Hotel is open every session in the week and all day on Sundays. There are two real ales on offer – Tetleys and Old Speckled Hen. It is hoped that more real ales will be available shortly. The menu is fairly traditional and all of the dishes are homemade and cooked to order. Food is available each day (apart from Mondays – except Bank Holidays) between 12pm – 2.30pm and 5.30pm – 8pm.

There is accommodation all year round. The three en-suite rooms are all located upstairs, but other than that disabled access is not a problem. The tariff includes a hearty breakfast and there is secure off-road parking for overnight guests and customers. On warmer days there is a fantastic rear beer garden that many people like to make the most of. Whether it is a refreshing drink, wholesome meal or a place to stay the night, The Buck Hotel is worth a look.

45 THE DOWNE ARMS

Main Road, Wykeham, Scarborough, North Yorkshire YO13 9QB
Tel: 01723 862471 Fax: 01723 865096
e-mail: info@downearmshotel.co.uk
website: www.downearmshotel.co.uk

You can be sure that a warm welcome awaits you at the **Downe Arms**! This 17th Century former farmhouse, in the picturesque, stone village of Wykeham, is ideally located to discover the gorgeous expanse of the North Yorkshire Moors and Coast. Part of the Dawnay Estates, this traditional country Inn offers you an intimate and historical setting for your special break. A perfect location whether you fancy walking the Cleveland Way along the rugged North Yorkshire coastline, visiting one of the wonderful local heritage sites, golfing on a championship golf course, or riding the steam train from Pickering into Heartbeat country- it's all on their doorstep for you to enjoy (ideal, too, for cyclists, shooters and anglers and a family celebration or function).

The delicious menu can be enjoyed in the relaxed traditional bar, far from the hustle and bustle, or the charming restaurant with its large windows giving lovely views of the village of Wykeham and beyond. In the evening the restaurant is transformed into a cosy venue for an intimate candle-lit supper with friends, family or your special someone. The food is cooked fresh from locally sourced ingredients, and has a great variety. The starter menu, which is available in the bar and restaurant, includes melon and cucumber (a fan of seasonal melon interlaced with cucumber slices and finished with vanilla syrup) and soft French brie (deep fried, on salad leaves with a citrus dressing and finished with cranberry relish). The main menu is brimming with delicious dishes including tenderloin of pork (pork loin steaks pan fried, served with sage gravy & Dauphinoise potatoes) and the "seafarer's favourite" local Whitby scampi (whole tail scampi served with homemade Tartare sauce, hand-cut fries and garden peas.). There is also a delightful little children's menu, and a superb Sunday carvery lunch. Food is served daily 12noon-2pm for lunch and 6pm-9pm for dinner (12noon-6pm for light bites Fri-Sun during the summer).

The Downe Arms has 10 very individual en-suite bedrooms, some with wonderful Georgian windows, others with low beams, all of them offering you a charming, indulgent place to relax and enjoy. All of the rooms offer country elegance and the same level of comfort you would expect from a traditional country Inn. The price for all of these rooms includes a filling breakfast.

47 RYEDALE FOLK MUSEUM

Hutton-le-Hole, North Yorkshire YO62 6UA
Tel: 01751 417367
e-mail: info@ryedalefolkmuseum.co.uk

Ryedale Folk Museum is a wonderful working museum insight into bygone eras. Here you will find the finest collection of thatched buildings in Yorkshire - the rescued and restored houses chart the changes in rural life, from the simplicity of the early Tudor crofter's cottage to the cosy Victorian clutter of the White Cottage.

There were mines and railways in nearby Rosedale, bringing a completely different way of life to the moors - explore the story behind these and the Elizabethan glass furnace and other moorland industries. Rural workers such as tinsmith, wheelwright, blacksmith, saddler, shoemaker and joiner each have a workshop with the tools of their trade on display and regular demonstrations take place including weaving, spinning, woodwork and cane and rushwork. An outstanding collection of tools also records the extraordinary changes in agriculture over the last 300 years, from wooden pitchforks onwards.

In the growing gardens, there are the medicinal herbs of the crofter's garth and the more recent cottage garden flowers, whilst the Victorian vegetable garden contains old varieties of vegetables as they used to be. The working landscape explores the way it was once used and how the way of life has altered it over the years. Farm animals, rare wild flowers and historic crops are sights to be seen here and a project is underway to help conserve the vanishing cornfield flowers. Over 40 varieties are growing here. A gift shop sells a selection of books, maps and souvenirs. Open March to November - ring for details.

48 THE CROWN

Hutton-le-Hole, North Yorkshire YO62 6UA
Tel: 01751 417343
e-mail: thecrownhutton@aol.com

Situated in the historic and popular village of Hutton-Le-Hole, The Crown is the only licensed premises in the village and a magnet for thirsty walkers and tourists. Owners Phil and Sue also own a touring caravan park to the rear of the child-friendly pub, which is open all year round. Ring for details. The Crown is open every session (all day in summer months) and is well known for the good wholesome food served and friendly hospitality. Real ale lovers will like it here with four real ales available – Black Sheep, Theakstons Black Bull, Tetleys and one guest ale.

Garden Centres and Nurseries

www.findsomewhere.co.uk
For people who want to explore the United Kingdom

49 THE FEVERSHAM ARMS INN

Church Houses, Farndale, Kirkbymoorside,
North Yorkshire YO62 7LF
Tel: 01751 433206
e-mail: enquiries@fevershamarmsinn.co.uk
website: www.fevershamarmsinn.co.uk

Surrounded by thousands of acres of open countryside, **The Feversham Arms Inn** is one of the most popular inns in Yorkshire. The former coaching inn is located on an old drovers road and boast beautiful views in and around the isolated village of Church Houses. The inn has been owned by Major Richard Murray and his partner Rachel Armstrong for the past three years.

There is seating for around 100 diners and it is definitely worth a look. There are plenty of dishes to choose from. Starters include duck and vegetable mini spring rolls served on a crisp bed of salad. There is a range of grills and fish dishes on the main menu as well as plenty of traditional favourites such as bangers and mash, lamb shank, homemade beef lasagne and steak and kidney pie. Vegetarians and children are well catered for and for those with a lighter appetite there is a good selection of filled jacket potatoes and sandwiches. It is worth saving room for a dessert as there are plenty of tempting choices to pick from. Banana split, apple pie and sticky toffee pudding are among the options. Three comfortable en-suite rooms are available as well as one self-catering cottage, which sleeps up to four people.

50 PENNY BANK CAFÉ

19 Market Place, Kirkbymoorside,
North Yorkshire YO62 6AA
Tel: 01751 432606
Website: www.pennybankcafe.co.uk

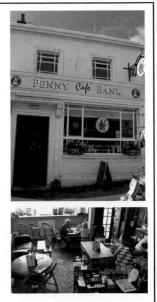

For those who find themselves in the market town of Kirkbymoorside, a visit to Penny Bank Café is a must. This outstanding premises was created in 2006 by Alison Gunton, and along with the help of her team it has become a real magnet for lovers of fine cuisine.

The comprehensive menu offers far more than you would expect to find in a standard café, proving Penny Bank to be rather special indeed. Visitors can expect to sample options such as venison sausage sandwiches, homemade houmous with red peppers, toasted ciabatta with various fillings, salads and much more. The evening menu (available on Friday and Saturday evening) also presents various treats to delight the taste buds, with main courses such as medallions of pork sautéed with carrots, apple and thyme in a cream sauce with vegetables of the season and breast of free range chicken filled with basil butter baked in a puff pastry case and served with vegetables. Due to the popularity of the exceptional food here, it is essential to book during the evenings. Penny Bank Café is open everyday and children are made to feel very welcome, there is even a toy box to keep them entertained.

51 CASTLEGATE CAFÉ

12 Castlegate, Helmsley,
North Yorkshire YO62 5AB
Tel: 01439 772444

A minute's walk from the main square in the town of Helmsley is the **Castlegate Café**. It's small but picturesque entranceway disguises a much larger interior brimming with cosy corners and stylish tea room décor. To the rear of the property a hidden garden can be found, trapping the sun in the summer months for that perfect afternoon tea.

Simon and his wife Louise have been running the café for a number of years, building on Simon's family's traditional tea room trade that has catered for the Helmsley area for over sixty years. Cooking tips and hospitality habits have passed from generation to generation, styling on the motto of serving food 'like Grandma used to cook.' Absolutely everything is homemade from cakes, scones and melt-in-the-mouth pastries to full hot lunches. Main meals include salmon and dill fishcakes, Whitby breaded scampi and homemade cheese and tomato quiche, though the customers' favourite has always been the traditional steak pie. Almost all ingredients are sourced locally, cooked fresh to order.

The café is licensed and also serves a good range of hot and cold drinks for all. The café has good disabled access and toilets. Open daily from 9:30am-4pm, but closed on Mondays in winter months. Cash and cheque only please.

52 DUNCOMBE PARK

Helmsley, North Yorkshire YO62 5EB
Tel: 01439 772625

A girls' school for 60 years, this Baroque mansion built in
1713 is now the family home of Lord & Lady Feversham.
The restored principal rooms are typical of a late 19th
century "grand interior", and the landscaped "green garden" with its temples and terraces, has
been described as 'the supreme masterpiece of the art of the landscape gardener'. The National
Nature Reserve within over 400 acres of rolling Parkland is a delight to explore. End a perfect
day with a visit to the Parkland Centre Tearoom & Shop, taste the delights of homemade food
and browse at your leisure the unusual hand made crafts made in Yorkshire.

53 HELMSLEY WALLED GARDEN

Cleveland Way, Helmsley, North Yorkshire YO62 5AH
Tel: 01439 771427
e-mail info@helmsleywalledgarden.org.uk
website: www.helmsleywalledgarden.org.uk

Helmsley Walled Garden is a 5 acre walled garden built in 1758 and set beneath Helmsley
Castle. The garden produced fruit and vegetables for Duncombe park until it fell into ruin. The
garden fell derelict until 1994 when a charity was established to restore the garden and provide
horticultural therapy. This is a plantsman's garden including 350 varities of Clematis, 52
Yorkshire apples and 34 Victorian vines as well as Victorian glasshouses, a Paeonia Garden, a
dipping well, rainbow border etc. Open daily from April to October. Full wheelchair access.

54 INN AT HAWNBY

Hawnby, Helmsley, North Yorkshire YO62 5QS
Tel: 01439 798202 email: info@innathawnby.co.uk
website: www.innathawnby.co.uk

Set in the heart of the North York Moors National Park, one of
the most beautiful parts of Yorkshire, The Inn at Hawnby is a
welcoming and appealing hotel in a peaceful rural setting
reached via the B1257 from Helmsley. Proud owners Dave and
Kathryn Young have been here since 1999, elevating this
former drover's inn (dating back to the early 1800s) to a fine,
and much awarded, country hotel. Most recent accolades
include the Taste of Yorkshire award and a finalist position for
the Landlady of the Year for 2010/11; The Inn at Hawnby has
also held a Red Rosette for their cuisine for the last two years
– no small accomplishment!

   Their tantalising menu attracts locals and visitors alike, and
can be enjoyed either in the handsome restaurant or in the peaceful country gardens. The
seasonal menu includes dishes such as grilled venison steak with a casserole of butter broad
beans, asparagus and tomato concasse, napped with a light consommé, or slow roasted butternut
squash filled with char-grilled courgette, red onion and sun dried tomato, topped with dressed
rocket and brie. They really go the extra mile here to find the very finest and freshest
ingredients, much coming from local sources; there are also 3 real ales, usually from Yorkshire
breweries. Food is served seven days a week 12noon-2pm and 7pm-9pm.

55 SUN INN

Normanby, York, North Yorkshire YO62 6RH
Tel: 01751 431051

Dating back, in parts, to the 18th century the **Sun Inn** is a delightful find in the hamlet of Normanby, within the North Yorkshire Moors National Park. Harriet Sanders is the leaseholder here and is ably helped by her parents Kay and Howard.

The impressive property attracts plenty of locals and visitors through its doors to sample the real ales on offer and homemade food. Produce from Yorkshire is used where possible and all of the dishes are freshly prepared and cooked to order.

The menu features all the traditional favourites you would expect to find at a quality pub including homemade steak pie and homemade beef lasagne. All of the prices are reasonable and that is a good thing because it means customers are more likely to taste the benefits of the irresistible desserts and puddings.

Food is available 12pm – 3pm and 5pm – 8.30pm on Wednesdays, 12pm – 9pm on Saturdays and 12pm – 7.30pm on Sundays.

The child-friendly inn has a good reputation and if you are visiting North Yorkshire a visit is a must. Disabled access isn't a problem. All major credit cards taken.

56 THE ROYAL OAK COUNTRY INN

Church Street, Nunnington, York, North Yorkshire YO62 5US
Tel: 01439 748271

Sharon has been running **The Royal Oak Country Inn** for the past three years, alongside owners Anita and Ian Hilton and together they do a remarkable job. Found between the pretty market towns of Helmsley and Malton in Nunnington, the inn dates back to the early 18th century when it was once a coaching inn.

The team serve up hearty country food from 12-2pm and 6:30-9pm Tuesday to Saturdays and from 12-2pm and 7-9pm on Sundays. The Inn is also open Bank Holiday Mondays for lunch and afternoon tea. Dishes are created using only the very best in locally sourced Yorkshire produce, ensuring high quality dining in a relaxing and informal environment. Dishes from the weekly changing specials board include Scarborough fish and chips, slow roasted lamb shank in a port and mint sauce, and salmon and root ginger fishcakes. Marion's homemade steak pies are also a popular choice and are what keep many visitors return time and time again. There is a children's menu but the team will endeavour to cook up any child's request providing they have the ingredients. On Sundays a popular roast dinner is added to the menu, when booking is essentail to avoid disappointment at this nice traditional country pub.

A carefully selected and varied wine list accompanies the menu; sourced mainly from family run vineyards. A range of real ales are also on offer including Yorkshire brews Black Sheep and Wold Top. Dogs are welcome.

57 THE BLUE BALL INN

14 Newbiggin, Malton,
North Yorkshire YO17 7JF
Tel: 01653 690692
e-mail: blue.ball.inn@btinternet.com

Located conveniently in the heart of the popular market town of Malton in North Yorkshire you will find the **Blue Ball Inn.** This charming inn once started its life as a farmhouse, dating back to the early 15th century. It retains much of its original warmth and rustic feel, with plenty of nooks and crannies to explore.

Its present owners Christine and Gary have worked hard to keep the spirit of the place alive combining its original features with earthy colours and farmhouse furniture. The couple only took over the venture in March 2010, but have really created a name for themselves amongst the local people who enjoy their personable and friendly attitude to running the place.

Gary previously worked in another trade for many years before giving it up to pursue his dream of running his own pub and restaurant. Following his passion, he went to college to study about food and six years on, he is a reputable professional chef, drawing in the crowds with his rustic creations. Christine's expertise comes from years of working in the hospitality and licensed trade, making her perfectly placed to aid Gary in keeping the bar well stocked and their customers happy. A good selection of wines and spirits are always available, as are the popular real ales; Timothy Taylor Landlord and Tetleys. Guests are welcome to join the team for drinks all day everyday whatever the weather, although the handsome floral baskets in the garden make good viewing in the summer months.

Food is available from Thursday to Tuesday between midday and 9pm. Guests can choose from Gary's popular main menu, or from the ever changing specials board; which showcases the very best in seasonal produce. Main courses range from proper fish and chips in a deliciously crispy beer batter, to rib-eye steak with all the trimmings or half roasted boned duck with orange or cherry sauce. His dishes focus on simple and wholesome English fayre, cooked to the highest standards – which is why such simple dishes are so popular. Other favourites include premium bangers and mash in a fine onion gravy with seasonal vegetables, and slow roasted belly pork. Gary also caters for those with a lighter appetite; offering a good selection of sandwiches and omelettes throughout the day. Each Sunday a handsome roast is available with succulent topside beef being the main attraction. This, as with the majority of Gary's other ingredients, is sourced from within Yorkshire itself.

Children are welcome to dine and can choose from their own menu or order half portions from the main menu. Why not bring them over on the second Tuesday of the month for a hearty dinner followed by a good old sing and dance at the Blue Ball's monthly folk night; perfect for all the family. All major credit cards accepted apart from Diners and Amex.

58 ROYAL OAK

47 Town Street, Old Malton, North Yorkshire YO17 7HB
Tel: 01653 699334

The secret location of this gorgeous hidden gem only enhances its charm, and once you have discovered it you will return again and again! Owned by the very dedicated Marion and Duncan for the last 4 years, the **Royal Oak** has become a hugely popular restaurant with locals and visitors alike (it is always best to book your table in advance, to avoid disappointment). The delicious home-made and locally sourced food, created for you by Marion, is irresistible and the essence of this beautiful county; for the full, warm Yorkshire experience come on a Thursday evening, when they serve home-made speciality pies.

59 EDEN CAMP MODERN HISTORY MUSEUM

Old Malton, Malton, Ryedale, Yorkshire YO17 6SD
Tel: 01653 697777
e-mail: admin@edencamp.co.uk
website: www.edencamp.co.uk

Housed in the grounds of an original Prisoner of War Camp, a visit to **Eden Camp** will allow you to experience the sights, sounds and even the smells of life on both the Home Front and Front Line during World War Two.

The award winning museum also covers the First World War, and the military conflicts around the world in which British Military Forces have been involved since 1945.

A visit to Eden Camp provides both an entertaining and educational day out for all ages. Open 7 days a week, 50 weeks of the year (closed 24th Dec - until the second Monday in January.)

Disabled and dog friendly, free parking and full catering is available on site.

60 HOME FARM HOLIDAY COTTAGES

Slingsby, York, North Yorkshire YO62 4AL
Tel: 01653 628277
e-mail: rachelprest@yahoo.co.uk
website: www.yorkshire-holiday-cottage.co.uk

Really get away from it all at any time of the year in the gorgeous Yorkshire countryside at **Home Farm**, two self-catering cottages nestled in the picturesque village of Slingsby, between Malton and Helmsley. These lovely properties, in fact cleverly converted old farm buildings, are brimming with charm and character, and have been awarded four stars with Gold Award by English Tourism for their impeccably high standards.

The first property, The Arches, sleeps up to four people. The main bedroom is a double with ensuite shower, and there is also a twin room with a separate bathroom perfect size for a family holiday or a romantic break for two. Other facilities include a light and spacious sitting/dining room with patio doors, a well equipped kitchen, and an open fire to get roaring in the colder months. The other cottage, The Stables, is Home Farm's jewel. It is slightly larger than The Arches, sleeping up to six people, and has three bedrooms; one double, one twin, and one single with hideaway bed, and a bathroom and separate shower room. There is also a sitting room with wood burning stove and patio doors leading into a conservatory, a dining room with exposed stone walls and wood beams, a kitchen and a utility room.

Both properties are ground level with excellent access and come with TV, with freeview and DVD player, immersion heater, and ample private parking. Children's bikes and tumble drier are available.

62 THE FLEECE INN
INCORPORATING THE DROVERS REST

9 Westgate, Rillington, North Yorkshire YO17 8LN
Tel: 01944 758464 Fax: 01944 758097
e-mail: info@drovers-rest.co.uk
website: www.drovers-rest.co.uk

The Fleece Inn is a traditional family run pub close to the market town of Malton, on the picturesque route along the A64 towards the North East coast of Scarborough and Filey. The new addition of **The Drovers Rest** restaurant in 2010 has confirmed the family's reputation for superb food and great hospitality, which has put this establishment on the map since they started here in 1999.

Home-cooked is the watchword here, and with over 30 years of experience Chef Mike excels in showcasing exciting English cuisine at its very best, preferring to use nothing but fresh local ingredients and speciality produce provided by their own garden to add his individual twist to the classical pub favourites... just remember to leave room for one of his decadent homemade desserts! Highlight of the week has to be the Sunday Carvery, with one, two or three course options, and choices for children (it is always advised to book to avoid disappointment). The Fleece Inn and Drovers Rest is open Tuesday 4pm-9pm, Wednesday to Saturday 12noon-9pm and Sundays 12noon-6pm.

61 THE MALT SHOVEL

Main Street, Hovingham, Yorkshire YO62 4LF
Tel: 01653 628264
e-mail: info@themaltshovelhovingham.co.uk
website: www.themaltshovelhovingham.co.uk

The Malt Shovel is a fantastic find in the picturesque village of Hovingham. It offers a most friendly service and its traditional atmosphere with good-value food prepared from quality local ingredients all make this establishment one of the most popular in the area. The Malt Shovel is owned & run by two couples who are related, Steve & Julie and Jamie & Vanessa who have been here for almost four years.

It isn't only locals that enjoy it here, many visitors are attracted to this picture postcard pub for its real ales and fine food. Jamie is the professional Chef who has been in the trade for over twenty years. It definitely shows. The food here is delicious and there is a fantastic selection listed on the extensive menu and Specials Boards which change regularly.

Smoked salmon (lightly pan fried smoked salmon with a dill and white wine sauce), brie tartlet (sautéed leek and onion finished with brie in a pastry crust with a seasonal salad), and bruschetta (slice of Mediterranean bread topped with tomato and buffalo mozzarella) are among the reasonably priced starters. Jamie's culinary skills are imaginative and creative and his dishes are cooked to order. A lot of the produce, especially the meat, is sourced locally adding to the quality of the dishes. Main courses include seafood pancakes (pancakes filled with salmon, haddock, scampi, cray fish and prawns in a lobster sauce), medallions of pork (pan fried pork fillet with a bacon, mushroom and red wine sauce),and strips of steak, sweet peppers, tomato and garlic in a red wine sauce served on a bed of rice. It is definitely wise to leave room for a homemade dessert because they are likely to be very hard to resist.

In the summer months Friday nights equal steak nights an in the winter months themed food evenings are often held on Thursday nights. As well as a good place to choose for food lovers, those who enjoy real ales will always be welcomed with a choice of two or three, with Tetleys and Black Sheep the regulars. Customers sitting towards the rear of the property can enjoy views of the rolling Yorkshire countryside.

Food is available between 11.30am and 2pm as well as 5.30pm – 9pm Monday – Saturdays and between 12pm and 2.30pm and 5.30pm – 8pm every Sunday. It is advisable to book at all times to avoid disappointment. Pensioners can get special food deals on Thursday lunch times (phone for details).

63 CROSS KEYS

Thixendale, nr Malton,
North Yorkshire YO17 9TG
Tel: 01377 288272

What started life in the 18th century as a farmhouse is
now the Cross Keys, a delightful one-roomed pub that
enjoys a scenic setting in the heart of the Yorkshire Wolds.
Long-established hosts Paddy, Steve and Mary run this
delightful award-winning gem, offering a warm, cosy
ambience, real ales and wholesome bar meals prepared as
far as possible from local ingredients and served lunchtime
and evening. Paddy and Mary cook a varied selection of
dishes that include burgers, omelettes, chilli con carne,
steak & Guinness pie, pasties and vegetarian specials like
a tasty chestnut casserole. Food is available noon – 2pm
and 6.30 – 9pm Tuesday – Saturday and 12 – 2.30pm and
7pm – 9pm on Sunday. Three real ales are served in the
bar, where a log fire burns in a huge brick hearth. When
the sun shines, picnic benches on the hedge-fringed lawn come into their own.

This is glorious walking country: the Wolds Way passes through the village, and established
walks in the vicinity include one that takes in the deserted village of Wherram Percy. For guests
taking a break in these superb surroundings the Cross Keys has three en suite rooms for B&B - a
double and two twins - in the refurbished old stable block. Thixendale is located a short drive
north of the A166 York-Driffield road (leave at Fridaythorpe)

64 JORVIK VIKING CENTRE

16 Coppergate Walk, York, North Yorkshire YO1 9NT
Tel: 01904 643211

The world famous **JORVIK** centre in York transports visitors
back in time to experience the sights, sounds and - perhaps
most famously - the smells of 10th century York. Over 20 years
of archaeological research led to the new re-creation of
Viking Age York in JORVIK, which re-opened to wide acclaim in
April 2001. The new JORVIK now presents a far broader view
and more detailed depiction of life in the Viking Age.

Visitors to the centre are shown that, in AD975, York was a
bustling commercial centre where 10,000 people lived and
worked. Travelling in state-of-the-art time capsules, visitors
are carried past and through two storey dwellings, enjoying
views over backyards and rooftops, and even glimpsing the
Viking Age equivalent of today's Minster.

February 2002 saw the launch of the new 'Viking Voyagers'
exhibition. Visitors can get the low-down on all aspects of
sea-faring from trading in the Far East and raiding in the
North East, to life on board and the technicalities of
mastering the ocean waves. The year-long exhibition features
hands-on activities, artefacts and new academic research
around the theme of Viking ships and is not to be missed.

65 YORK MINSTER

Deangate, York, Yorkshire YO1 7JA
Tel: 01904 557226/557200
website: www.yorkminster.org.uk

York Minster acts as a beacon welcoming all visitors to the City of York. Built over 250 years, and renowned worldwide as an artistic and architectural masterpiece, it offers a wealth of things to see for people of all ages, and offers thrilling memories for all who visit.

The Minster is much more than a superb building. It is a site where history has been made over the centuries. The Emperor Constantine began his progress to greatness here, and the Roman buildings in which he lived still stand beneath the central tower. St Paulinus baptised the local Saxon King here, and here are buried many of the Archbishops of York, including St William of York.

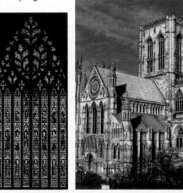

York Minster provides a wealth of history for you to discover. The Minster itself is an architectural masterpiece and a treasure house of stained glass. It is a living community of Christian worship where the sound of choral music has lifted the spirits of visitors and pilgrims for centuries. You can also visit our shop for a range of gifts that will remind you of your visit in years to come.

68 THE YORKSHIRE AIR MUSEUM

Halifax Way, Elvington, York,
North Yorkshire YO41 4AU
Tel: 01904 608595 Fax: 01904 608246

Over the past few years the **Yorkshire Air Museum** has become one of the most fascinating and dynamic Museums of its type in the country. With its unique collection of over 40 internationally recognised aircraft and displays all combined into this historic site, make the Museum a very special place for aviation enthusiasts young and not so young. The aircraft collection covers aviation history from the pioneering 1849 work of the Yorkshire bom Sir George Cayley, recognised internationally as the true "17cither of Aeronautice, to WWII aircraft and modem military jets. The Museum has one of the largest special events calendars in the North.

The excellent displays house internationally recognised artefacts and in the many original buildings you can explore histories on a varied list of related topics. These include Bames Wallis; Air Gunners; Airborne Forces and Home Guard as well as observing aircraft restoration workshops and seeing how wartime life was like in the French Officers' Mess or the Airmen's Billet. The famous NAAFI restaurant is well known for its excellent fare and Museum shop is well stocked for that extra special gift or keepsake. The site is ideal for private functions, corporate events and conferences.

66 MERRICOTE COTTAGES AT VERTIGROW PLANT NURSERY

Malton Road, York, Yorkshire YO32 9TL
Tel: 01904 400256
e-mail: enquiries@merricote-holiday-cottages.co.uk
websites: www.merricote-holiday-cottages.co.uk
or www.vertigrow.co.uk

Located in 8 acres of rural Yorkshire, just 3 miles from York City centre, **Merricote Cottages at Vertigrow Plant Nursery** provide a great place to relax as well as an excellent base for exploring the surrounding area. Awarded 3 stars by the English Tourist Council, the 9 cottages have been furnished and individually decorated to a high standard with meticulous attention to detail. The buildings, standing at the heart of what was once a traditional working farm, have been sympathetically converted to create superb self-catering cottages, each with its own character, along with a detached four-bedroom bungalow. All the accommodation is centrally heated, with modern bathrooms, well-equipped kitchens and comfortable seating areas with TV and Broadband. Other facilities include ample safe parking and a laundry service. Children and pets are very welcome, and the kids, in addition to a secure play area, will find plenty to keep them busy and happy in the vicinity. Cots and high chairs can be provided for toddlers. The warm, welcoming atmosphere generated by the owner and the high standard of accommodation bring guests back to the cottages, which are located off the A64 York to Scarborough road. They are open throughout the year. There is also a 4 bedroom, 3 bathroom house with indoor heated swimming pool set in its own private gardens adjacent to the nursery. As well as a 10 acre wood which is part of the property for walking.

Adjacent to the cottages is the superb Vertigrow Plant Nursery which was created by owner Andrew Williamson some 10 years ago. Throughout the year, Vertigrow stocks more than 1000 varieties of shrubs and perennials and is renowned for its ever-increasing selection of mature trees. These specimens are imported from Europe and New Zealand as well as being sourced from local suppliers.

The stock reflects changes with the different seasons. In the spring and autumn the nursery is awash with colour from bedding plants that are competitively priced and of excellent quality. The nursery offers the service of making up hanging baskets for customers and there are always ready made baskets in stock.

If you visit the nursery in the autumn you will find nearly every type of hedging, fruit tree and soft fruit that you might require. If you can't find the plant you were looking for, the staff will always try to find an alternative or source you one from one of its many suppliers.

67 MURTON PARK

Murton Lane, Murton, York, Yorkshire YO19 5UF
Tel: 01904 489966
website: www.murtonpark.co.uk

Murton Park. is your gateway to the Yorkshire Museum of Farming, Danelaw Dark Age Village, Brigantium Roman Fort, the Tudor Croft and the Home Front Experience. Based just outside York. Education programmes at Murton Park are designed to provide realistic Living History experiences for adults and children both on site and in schools. Murton Park now offers a Celtic Settlement, a Roman Fort, a Dark Age Village, Tudor Experience, the Home Front Experience and Farming Museum all of which are used as large classrooms.

Farming Museum

The Museum opened in 1982 to house a range of exhibits from Burton Constable, collected by East Yorkshire Farm Machinery Preservation Society. The Museum holds a fantastic regional agricultural collection. The collection includes many thousands of objects, photographs and archival material dedicated to the tools and techniques that have produced our 'daily bread for over 250 years. The Livestock Building concentrates on the farming of animals, including sheep, cows, pigs and the uses of heavy horses. This complements the wide variety of rare breeds raised and kept on site.

Roman Fort

Brigantium is a large outdoor classroom cunningly disguised as a Roman auxillary Fort of the 1st Century AD. Designed to take up to 65 children a day as trainee soldiers in the Roman army. Equipped with their uniform, helmet, spear and shield, the young recruits are put through their paces by our centurion.

Dark Age Village

Danelaw Dark Age Village is a unique educational environment that is designed to allow children to become Vikings or Saxons for a day. Costumes are provided and children carry out activities as the villagers of a Dark Ages Settlement. Grinding wheat, weapons training (with blunt, dummy weapons), guard duty, pottery, field and house work are some of the tasks children will undertake. Various visitors arrive to create role play scenarios and on a full day a banquet lunch is included.

Tudor Croft

The Tudor Croft forms the backdrop to a half day of activities for up to 30 children. Whilst in Tudor costume children will learn various skills such as candle dipping, calligraphy and making pomanders. The session is nicely rounded off with a period story told in front of the fire.

The Home Front Experience

The children arrive as evacuees and carry out a range of activities including baking on a ration, taking cover in an air raid and visiting the ARP Warden's observation post. Role play, craft activities and scenarios will be used to create a realistic, unforgettable experience for children. ID cards and evacuation labels will be sent prior to you school visit. An authentic pack lunch is provided.

Derwent Valley Light Railway

The Derwent Valley Light Railway officially opened on the 19th July 1913; it ran for a distance of nearly 16 miles from Layerthorpe Station at York to the village of Cliffe Common near Selby. Although passengers were carried in the early years, this discontinued in 1926 and the railway remained predominantly agricultural throughout the rest of its history. The DVLR was never nationalised and remained very much a "light" railway until its closure on the 30th September 1981. The only section of the railway still in use comprises of the half-mile section within the Museum grounds.

69 THE CROOKED BILLET

Wakefield Road, Saxton, nr Tadcaster,
North Yorkshire LS24 9QN
Tel: 01937 557389
e-mail: pricklypearpubs@btinternet.com

Anthony Hunter took over **The Crooked Billet** in May 2010 and has worked tirelessly since to straighten it out. He has over 18 years in the hospitality trade and has used that experience to renovate the inn, bringing life to the Saxton community once again. Anthony opens for drinks every session and all day on Saturdays when two real ales are on offer alongside a good wine list and selection of spirits. There is room for up to sixty guests within the rustic interior, but on sunnier days many can be seen enjoying summer blooms in the rear beer garden.

Food is available from Monday to Friday between 12-2:30pm and 5-9pm and on weekends from 12-9pm. The menus have been created by local head chef Shane Carling, who is proud to use only locally sourced produce in his cooking. Popular dishes include the Billet's famous giant Yorkshire pudding with a variety of hearty fillings, locally reared meat from the grill, traditional lamb hot pot, seared salmon fillet and fisherman's pie. Vegetarian dishes here include butternut squash, spinach, walnut and Yorkshire blue pie, nut roast, and spiced pumpkin and wild mushroom mezzaluna. A great selection of hot and cold sandwiches and snacks are available for those with smaller appetites.

Anthony also runs the Black Bull at Escrick just a short drive from the Billet, where great food and accommodation is also provided.

71 THE SPOTTED OX INN

Westfield Road, Tockwith,
North Yorkshire YO26 7PY
Tel: 01423 358387
website: www.thespottedox.com

For the last six years owners Ian and Sheila have been running **The Spotted Ox**; a cosy and very popular public house in the pretty village of Tockwith. Their passion for food big in quality and taste has been the driving force behind the business, and has customers coming back time and time again. The menu, which is locally sourced and freshly cooked, is available for lunch and dinner; on Sundays a delicious roast is added, which is very busy so it is always advisable to book your table! Dishes such as large Yorkshire pudding served with Lincolnshire sausage and onions, and lasagne verdi served with a lush side salad grace the main menu; and there is always a brilliant specials board brimming with the best seasonal cuisine.

As well as the food people come to the Spotted Ox for the friendly atmosphere, and the range of real ales which are Cask Marque accredited and include guest ales from local and national breweries, as well as the two regulars Tetleys and Timothy Taylor. There is a lovely hidden beer garden at the rear, and a function room named The Forge which is available for hire, seating up to 80 people. Opening hours are Monday to Friday 12-2.30pm and 5-11pm, Saturday 12-11pm, and Sunday 12-10.30pm.

70 THE LORD COLLINGWOOD

The Green, Upper Poppleton, Yorkshire YO26 6DP
Tel: 01904 794388

This friendly public house is a fantastic discovery in the picturesque village of Upper Poppleton. The Lord Collingwood is just a short drive away from the centre of the historic town of York. Deana Massey is your friendly host here and has personally run the show for the past three years.

She has worked really hard to turn this place around and it is now well-known for its fine food, drink and hospitality. Real ale lovers will be delighted to get the opportunity to sample up to seven real ales. The regular is Ringwood Best and a selection of other real ales, of differing strengths, are always available.

There is a good range of meat and fish dishes for diners to choose from and on Sundays roast dinners are served. Such is the popularity of dining at The Lord Collingwood it is advisable to book on weekends and Sunday lunchtime. This stylish premise is child friendly and is popular with families, couples, locals and visitors.

There is regular entertainment nights here with several quizzes each month including a well attended music quiz held on the first Sunday of each month from 9pm. Any one is welcome to join in and new comers are always welcome. The place has a really friendly atmosphere and Deana is a fantastic host. The food is absolutely superb and is served between 12pm and 2.3pm Tuesday – Saturday and from 6pm – 9pm in the evening. On Sundays food is available between 12pm and 6pm. Food is not served on Mondays (except from on Bank Holidays). There is a varied selection of dishes, made using local Yorkshire produce, and for those who can't make a decision there is a daily specials board offering additional options. Parking is never a problem at The Lord Collingwood because there is good off-road parking here. Disabled access is not a problem. All major credit cards are taken.

If you are local or planning a visit to Yorkshire, The Lord Collingwood is worth a look. It is located in a picture-postcard village and offers the very best in hospitality, food and real ales.

72 THE BAY HORSE INN

York Road, Green Hammerton,
North Yorkshire YO26 8BN
Tel: 01423 330338
e-mail: enquiry@bayhorsegreenhammerton.co.uk
website: www.bayhorsegreenhammerton.co.uk

Between the popular towns of Harrogate and York is the village of Green Hammerton. Nestled within its centre is **The Bay Horse Inn** which has been taking care of its customers for over three hundred years. Formerly a coaching inn, it holds a certain traditional charm befitting its idyllic location.

Owners Stella and Mike with their children Tom and Connie have been here since November 2009 opening every session bar Sunday evenings. Between two and four real ales are on offer at any one time with the well kept Timothy Taylor Landlord and Black Sheep being the regular brews. On Wednesday the family run a popular quiz night from 9:30pm, an easy night out for all.

Food is available Monday to Saturday between 12-2:30pm and 6-9:30pm and on Sundays from 12-3pm. Stella uses as much local produce in her dishes as possible so the menu changes daily based on what's on offer that day. Dishes are displayed on the blackboard and include popular meat dishes like the mighty T-bone steak with all the trimmings, and succulent pork fillet with apple cider sauce. Barbeque chicken, cheesy pasta bake and Whitby scampi are amongst other favourites, all of which are homemade fresh to order.

73 THE SIDINGS HOTEL AND RESTAURANT

Station Lane, Shipton by Beningbrough,
Yorkshire YO30 1BT
Tel: 01904 470221
e-mail: info@sidingshotel.co.uk
website: www.sidingshotel.co.uk

This establishment has got to boast one of the finest settings for dining and accommodation. There are seven superb en-suite guest rooms to be found within luxury refurbished railway coaches. They are full of character and some rooms have fantastic four poster beds, which are ideal for those wanting a romantic weekend away.

The Sidings Hotel and Restaurant was founded in 1985 by an ex-railwayman with a passion and enthusiasm for all things connected with railways. The accommodation is based around five restored Pullman-style railway carriages, so if you are a railway fanatic you are bound to love staying here. The restaurant's conservatory looks directly onto one of the fastest and most impressive stretches of track in the land – the York to Thirsk run. There is even special floodlit viewing area, which is popular with overnight guests, who want to soak up and enjoy the authentic style of this delightful and intriguing hotel.

Sid Monoyiou has owned The Sidings Hotel and Restaurant for four years and is proud about what it has to offer.

The hotel and restaurant is surrounded by open countryside and there are some amazing views to be seen. In this quiet location railway enthusiasts are given the opportunity to thrive in a haven built from a collection of genuine railway artifacts and memorabilia.

The modern restaurant is open to overnight guests and non residents and seats more than 100 people. It offers a wide range of contemporary cuisine, including Italian, Greek and English dishes. Guests can dine surrounded by a wealth of admirable railway memorabilia. Morning coffee, lunch, afternoon tea and individual menus can be created to satisfy individual requirements. Food is served between 12pm and 2.30pm every day and between 5pm and 10pm. (The restaurant often stays open later on weekends).

On Sundays roast dinners are served and they are arguably the finest in Yorkshire.

York is a city full of character and history and those staying at this fine establishment will have plenty to explore like the Cathedral and ancient walls.

Greek themed party nights, fantastic buffet nights and fabulous traditional Sunday lunches are also available. Ring for details. The hotel and restaurant can be hired for weddings, functions, children's parties etc (ring for information). Disabled access is not a problem.

74 THE NEW INN

Howden Road, Barlby, Selby,
North Yorkshire YO8 5JE
Tel: 01757 702349
e-mail: mewinnbarlby@gmail.com

Daryl and Lisa have only just taken over **The New Inn** but have already struck up good business with their locals in the bustling village of Barlby. Opening all day every day, the pair offer up to four real ales to enjoy with John Smiths and Black Sheep being the regular brews. Daryl is a professional chef by trade, and brings his skills to the inn's menu, creating a range of traditional and European dishes using only the best in locally sourced produce. On Sunday lunchtimes he serves a very popular traditional roast, and plans to introduce a summer barbeque in the near future. Aside from this, the main menu operates Tuesday to Saturday 12-8:30pm.

Families and children are more than welcome at all times, and are free to make use of the inn's excellent play area outside in the spacious beer garden. On various weekends, live entertainment is also held; please call for details. At present Daryl and Lisa can only take cash, but credit card facilities will soon be introduced.

75 THE ROYAL OAK INN

Main Street, Hirst Courtney, nr Selby, East Yorkshire YO8 8QT
Tel: 01757 270633

In the picturesque village of Hirst Courtney this impressive premises, **The Royal Oak Inn**, offers the very best a local or visitor could wish for. With quality accommodation, so close to the M62 for a stop-over, a quality caravan park to the rear, plus well kept ales and super food. Found between the A19 and A1041, south of Selby and a very short drive to either J34 or J35 of the M62.

Delicious food is available at all opening times (Thursday – Sunday lunchtimes, and every evening), with various menus to choose from; a delightful range of dishes which are sure to suit all tastes, as well as the daily specials board which is always brimming with the best fresh and seasonal food. Two regular real ales are Tetleys and Black Sheep, but you'll also find the occasional guest ale.

There are 12 upstairs en-suite rooms (2 single, 3 double, and 7 twins), and the tariff includes breakfast. There's a patio for those sunny days, and a pool table for when it's raining! Children are welcome and all major credit cards are taken.

76 LA ANCHOR BAR & PIZZERIA

Main Street, Hensall, East Yorkshire DN14 0QZ
Tel: 01977 663026
website: www.la-anchor.co.uk

Sometimes you find a wonderful establishment in a place you wouldn't expect to- **La Anchor Bar & Pizzeria** is one of those. Situated in the village of Hensall, found north off the A645 between Goole and Knottingley.

This family-run premises oozes class in every department. Manageress Miss Lawra Tangi has recently taken over the business within the family, and has had an influential hand in the complete refurbishment and hard work which has made it one of the destination premises for fine food and surroundings. The interior décor is truly sleek and elegant; a perfect slice of modern Italy, in Yorkshire!

The cosy restaurant looks onto the open kitchen, where you can view your choice of dish being prepared and cooked. The stone bake oven is also in view to enjoy that magical experience of your pizza being cooked. The aroma of the place makes you dream of being on holidays abroad, and the taste is as good, if not better than the smell.

There is a wide range of choice in the menu, from Pasta dishes such as a classic Carbonara (Spaghetti with pancetta, egg, parmesan cheese with cream) and Polpette (Spaghetti with meatballs), to more exquisite dishes with salmon, duck, seabass, and risotto. Homemade pasta dishes include Crab Ravioli and Gnocchi Al Tricolore (cherry tomato, mozzarella, basil in a tomato sauce). In the Antipasti section of the menu, you can expect to find some high quality cuisine, including Calamari Fritti, Carpaccio di Manzo (sliced beef seasoned with garlic and lemon juice finished in olive oil and shredded parmesan), and Funghi Trifolati (Garlic mushroom). There is also, naturally, a big variety of pizzas, which are homemade and as fresh as you will find, with toppings ranging from the classic favourites (Margherita, Hawaiian) to new and inventive flavours (why not try the fiery Diavola, with hot pepperoni, red peppers & chilly oil, or the indulgent Veneto, with chicken, caramelised onion, garlic & butter?).

Fully licensed bar, and an extensive wine list is available, with one to suit just about everyone's palate and pocket! The quality rear garden is perfect for eating out and relaxing on a sunny day, and there's also a children's play area to keep them entertained. Off-road parking is available.

Open every evening except Mondays, from 5.30pm. It is essential to book Friday and Saturday nights and advisable at all other times to avoid disappointment. All major credit cards taken.

77 JUG INN

**Hirst Road, Chapel Haddlesey, Selby,
Yorkshire YO8 8QQ
Tel: 01757 270718
e-mail: info@juginn.com
website: www.juginn.com**

Hidden away in the village of Chapel Haddesley, but just a few yards from the main A19, the **Jug Inn** is a welcoming traditional hostelry complete with authentic beamed ceilings and open fires. Mine hosts at the Jug are business partners Phil and Barry who have had many years of experience in catering industries. The third key player in the enterprise is Head Chef Simon who has established a reputation for serving fine restaurant cuisine at village pub prices! All the steaks and meat products are supplied by a wholesale meat company run by Phil's brother and father, so it's comforting to know that the food being served is of the very highest possible quality! Meals are served from noon until 2pm; and from 5pm to 9pm, Monday to Saturday; and from noon until 8pm on Sundays.

Barry is in charge of the bar and his real ales are very popular, with a choice of 4 different brews, including the two regulars Black Sheep and Tetley Cask Mild.

Outside, there is ample parking and a superb beer garden with plenty of seating and children's play equipment. Go through the 5-barred gate and you are standing on the bank of the River Aire.

78 BLACKSMITHS ARMS

**Oxmoor Lane, Biggin, Leeds LS25 6HJ
Tel: 01977 685353**

Experienced landlord and landlady Jim and Jo Bryan and Jim's brother Andy took over the **Blacksmiths Arms** two years ago, relishing the opportunity to create a traditional destination pub in the heart of the rural village of Biggin. The inn occupies a quiet, scenic location, but is usually popular with a selection of food and ale lovers. Jim and Jo hold traditional values about what a good pub should be, endeavouring to provide a warm and cosy atmosphere for all.

Jim is a professional chef by trade with over twenty years experience which he puts to good use serving food from Monday to Saturday between 12-2:30pm and 5:30-9pm and on Sundays from 12-6pm. There is no set menu as all dishes are devised on a daily basis using the freshest seasonal produce sourced from within the area. Roast dinners are added to the menu on Sundays which are always a popular choice with locals. Booking is heavily recommended at all times to avoid disappointment.

Jo and Jim's brother Andy ensure the bar is fully stocked with up to four well kept ales, alongside an excellent selection of wines and spirits. Jazz evenings are usually held one Thursday a month, offering a chilled out respite from the busy nearby city of Leeds. Please call for details. All credit cards except American Express accepted.

79 THE SWAN HOTEL

1 Low Street, South Milford, West Yorkshire LS25 5AR
Tel: 01977 682783

You will find a warm welcome waiting for you at **The Swan Hotel**; a highly recommended inn situated in the small historical village of South Milford, conveniently close to the motorway routes A1 (M), M1 and M62. A former coaching inn, the hotel dates in parts back to the mid 18th century, and certainly looks historic with the traditional stone and white-washed exterior with black wooden beams. Its long history allegedly includes Dick Turpin, who once stabled his horse Black Bess here, and (much) later a visit from Hollywood bombshell Marilyn Monroe.

The new licensees, Melanie and David, took over here in 2010 and have great plans for the hotel. They are both enthusiastic and brilliantly qualified; David has 10 years experience in the trade under his belt, and Melanie combines high quality hospitality in the air and on the ground in her profession as an airhostess.

The delicious menu, which is served here Monday to Saturday 12noon until 8.30pm (12noon until 5pm on Sundays for the popular carvery), is a delicious and traditional treat. Main dishes include traditional Yorkshire steak and ale (or steak and mushroom) pie, or fish and chips with mushy peas, as well as other favourites like chilli con carne with rice and Nann bread, lasagne with garlic bread, or a selection for burgers (including a veggie alternative). There is also an irresistible selection of steaks from the grill, such as 8oz sirloin, 16oz rump or a gammon steak with egg or pineapple, and a tasty array of starters and deserts to complete your meal. There are also a selection of sandwiches for lunch or a light dinner, and a brilliant children's menu which includes free ice cream! Of course the main event each week here is the Sunday carvery with all the trimmings, which is loved by many in the village and is a must during your stay.

The accommodation here is also a delight, and is available all year round, on a room only or bed & breakfast tariff. Each bright and spacious room is supplied with its own en-suite, kept to the highest standard, and are available in either double or single, suiting all budgets.

80 THE SNUG RESTAURANT

2 Central Buildings, Market Place, Easingwold,
Yorkshire YO61 3AB
Tel: 01347 822316
website: www.thesnugrestaurant.co.uk

This stylish restaurant is a perfect place to dine for couples, friends and family wanting to eat in a cosy and more intimate establishment. **The Snug Restaurant**, which can be found at the heart of Easingwold, has just been extended and is bigger than it seems from the outside. The modern decor and furnishings add to the atmosphere of the restaurant, which is extremely popular for its traditional tasty food.

The dishes, sourced mainly from Yorkshire produce, are all reasonably priced and main courses like smoked chicken Caesar salad, haddock goujons, lasagne and gammon and eggs are just some of the dishes available. The mouth watering desserts can prove very tempting for diners. Sticky toffee pudding, panna cotta and eton mess are among the favourites. For those with a lighter appetite there is a delicious range of sandwiches, toasties, cakes and more. Jason and Anne-Marie Sargent took over the running of The Snug Restaurant, which seats 45 diners, in November 2008 and are welcoming hosts to locals and visitors. The business is really thriving and is generally busy during the day time and evening.Fine English cuisine is served Monday – Saturday 9.45am – 2.15pm and 6pm – 9pm.

82 NEWBURGH PRIORY

Coxwold, York, North Yorkshire HG4 5AE
Tel: 01347 868435
website: www.newburghpriory.co.uk

Newburgh Priory is a large and imposing house near Coxwold, North Yorkshire. Standing on the site of an Augustinian priory, founded in 1145, it is a fine stately home in a superb setting with breathtaking views to the Kilburn White Horse in the distance. The extensive grounds contain a water garden, walled garden topiary yews and woodland walks.

The house was the country seat for the Belassis family in the 16th and 17th century. Originally an Augustinian Priory from 1145 providing priests for the surrounding churches in return for gifts of land and money. It is reputed to be the burial place of Oliver Cromwell whose remains were said to have been brought to Newburgh Priory by his daughter Mary when she married the 2nd viscount.

Newburgh belonged formerly to the Earls of Fauconberg is presently the home of Sir George and Lady Wombwell who open the Priory to visitors for guided tours from April to June.

81 THE WHITE BEAR INN

Main Street, Stillington, Yorkshire YO61 1JU
Tel: 01347 810338

Situated in the picturesque village of Stillington is **The White Bear**. A well run, Traditional Free House Country Pub established as an Inn since 1754. Owned and personally run by Phil & Sue Robinson the friendly hosts are very proud to have owned & been in charge here for the past 15 years & are waiting to welcome you inside to enjoy a relaxing drink or sample some of the excellent Yorkshire feyer.

A wide range of dishes are listed on their a la carte, Prime Time (early bird) & Bar Snack menu's and if that wasn't enough a specials board. Selections with examples such as; Smoked Fish Platter (Salmon, Trout & Mackerel, on a Bed of Crispy Lettuce Drizzled With a Lemon Dressing), Black Pudding Fritters with a Redcurrant & Orange Sauce & Homemade Chicken Liver, Smoked Bacon & Brandy Pate. Those are just some of the starters on offer. Main courses include Fresh Whole Pan-Fried Sea-Bass with Ginger & Spring Onion Chilli Butter or Locally sourced Fillet Steak stuffed with Blue Yorkshire Stilton Wrapped with Smoked Bacon & served with a Green Peppercorn Sauce, as well as Local Game when in Season. As for desert, our landlady Sue makes all, such as; Tangy Lemon Cheese Cake on a Ginger Nut base drizzled with a Raspberry Coulis and an old time favourite of suet Jam Roly Poly. Oh and her Fruit Filled Meringues are just to die for!

Our Traditional Family Service Sunday lunch of hot steaming roast dinners, homemade casseroles, fresh fish & vegetarian option seasonal vegetables prove a popular affair with families who often choose to sit in our restaurant which then leaves our bar open for people to enjoy our 5 real ales for which they have recently been awarded 'Country pub of the Season' by 'York CAMRA'.

For any further details & booking, including restaurant opening times and prices or even an update on the accommodation that they plan to have completed in the summer of 2011.

83 WHITE SWAN

Ampleforth, York,
North Yorkshire YO62 4DA
Tel: 01439 788239
e-mail: swan.ampleforth@virgin.net
website: www.thewhiteswan-
ampleforth.co.uk

One of the finest pubs in North Yorkshire, a visit to The White Swan, nestled in the attractive village of Ampleforth, is a must. Not far from the City of York – renowned for its quaint cobbled streets and one of the most popular tourist areas in the region; The White Swan boasts an extensive menu offering traditional British cuisine served to a high standard. Tried once, you'll certainly be heading back for more. Born in Ampleforth, the owners understand the importance of sourcing produce locally, as much as possible, supporting local farms and businesses in the area.

The food is the star attraction at The White Swan, making it a popular place to go not just for locals but for visitors far and wide. This fantastic mixture of people creates a wonderful atmosphere and allows the visit out to the countryside so much more relaxed and enjoyable. For lunch there is a wide variety of dishes to choose from – if you fancy a light bite maybe the *Crayfish & Parma Ham Salad* may suit, or for something more substantial the *Baked Salmon Supreme with a creamed lobster sauce*. Sunday lunches are always very popular, offering and a la carte menu of *Traditional Roast Topside of Beef, Roast Leg of Pork or Lamb* or delicious alternatives of *Traditional Steak & Ale Pie topped with short crust pasty lid or Breast of Chicken with a leek & bacon sauce* amongst others. All dishes come with generous side dishes at no extra cost. Owner and Head Chef Robert Thompson really shines through in his Evening Menu. Wonderfully created and well thought-out dishes allows many choices for any visitor; *Fillet of Pork Escallops in a sauce of bacon strips, apple & Byland blue cheese; Wild & Forest Mushrooms in cream & brandy sauce served with linguini; Best Quality line caught Fresh Haddock (1-1¼lb) deep- fried with home-made mushy peas & chips* – food which is of exceptional quality and a balance of price that is neither exorbitant or devalues the produce.

The dining area in The White Swan is divided into 4 parts, all situated around a grand central oak bar. The Dining Room bestows a formal elegant aura with crisp white linen on the tables, superb for that special occasion, whereas the lounge area allows for the more informal and relaxed meal with soft furnishings and a large comforting wood burner. The local bar allows for interaction in true community style, and out on the large patio the children can run free in the summer months. The White Swan is open seven days a week, serving food Monday to Sunday 12noon-2pm, Monday to Saturday 6pm-9pm, and Sundays 6pm-8.30pm.

84 FAIRFAX ARMS

Gilling East, York, North Yorkshire YO62 4JH
Tel: 01439 788212
e-mail: info@fairfaxarms.plus.uk
website: www.thefairfaxarms-gilling.co.uk

Nestled in the beautiful Howardian Hills, an Area of Outstanding Natural Beauty, the **Fairfax Arms** is located in the picturesque village of Gilling East. With a lively history as a coaching inn in the 17th century, this Visit Britain four-star rated Inn now offers eleven contemporary en-suite bedrooms, two traditional dining rooms and a spacious lounge and bar. The Fairfax Arms was taken over in May 2009 by Robert Thompson and his wife Gillian, the proud owners of the very successful restaurant, The White Swan, in nearby Ampleforth. As well as serving the same high quality of delicious food as the White Swan,

the Fairfax Arms also offers this perfection and standard in accommodation.

Of the eleven rooms which make up the accommodation within this charming property, there are 6 double and 1 twin rooms situated in the building and 2 family cottages plus a superior suite and a deluxe double that are situated off the courtyard at the rear of the building. Every part of the accommodation has been lovingly styled and decorated in a traditional yet contemporary style, and are very comfortable. All of the rooms are normally booked on a bed and breakfast basis, and there are occasionally special offers on, so you should phone them or have a look at their website and find the best deal for you.

The menu is a delight; focusing on fresh, locally sourced ingredients, it changes through the seasons so you get the freshest tasting dishes. The written menu for lunch and dinner is augmented by a number of blackboard specials. On Sundays, the menu is simply written on the blackboard, so they can make sure it's as seasonal and fresh as possible. There is a special children's menu available for lunch and dinner Mondays to Saturdays (on Sundays, children may request smaller portions from our blackboard menu).

The opening times for meals are, every day, 12:00 till 2:00pm for lunch, and 6:00 to 9:00 pm for dinner. Outside, there is a beer garden set prettily beside the stream, perfect for a drink or meal on warmer days, relaxing with your family or partner. For the festive season, there is a party menu, for parties of 2 up to 35.

85 WOMBWELL ARMS

Wass, North Yorkshire YO61 4BE
Tel: 01347 868280
e-mail: wombwellarms@btconnect.com
website: www.wombwellarms.co.uk

Nestling at the bottom of the Hambleton Hills within the North York Moors National Park is the **Wombwell Arms**. Ian and Eunice Walker are the owners of this privately owned free house that can be found in the delightful village of Wass, between the villages of Coxwold and Ampleforth.

The Wombwell Arms dates back to 1620 and has been an inn since 1645. It is a great place to stay for lovers of fine ale and food. The inn is much bigger inside than you would imagine from the outside. There are two restaurant areas, and two public bars. There is seating for around 60 diners and it is definitely advisable to book to avoid disappointment.

The extensive menu has plenty of choice for diners. There is a good range of traditional dishes as well as seafood, meat and vegetarian options and if you are looking for something a little bit special you could well find it among the weekly specials. Eunice is in charge of the kitchen and her food has become a hit with locals and visitors.

Gressingham duck breast roasted and served with a marmalade liqueur sauce, potatoes and seasonal vegetables; king prawn paella with scallops, chicken and chorizo sausage; and Masham pork and apple sausages served with creamy mash, gravy and seasonal vegetables are among the delicious options.

All of the dishes are freshly prepared on the premises and where possible ingredients are sourced from suppliers in North Yorkshire. Food is served 12pm - 2pm and 6.30pm – 9pm Monday – Thursday, 12pm – 2pm and 6.30pm – 9.30pm on Fridays, 12pm – 2.30pm and 6.30pm – 9.30pm on Saturdays and 12pm – 3pm and 6.30pm – 8.30pm on Sundays.

The business has really gone from strength to strength since the Walkers took over a couple of years ago. It is open every session and all day on Saturdays, which is a bonus for lovers of real ales brewed in Yorkshire. Timothy Taylor Landlord, Theakston Best and Theakston Old Peculier are among the favourites.

There are three comfortable en-suite bedrooms available. All are double rooms and located upstairs. Ring for details.

86 MOUSEMAN VISITOR CENTRE

Kilburn, Yorkshire YO61 4AH
Tel: 01347 868218
website: www.robertthompsons.co.uk

From a single acorn to a finished piece of beautifully hand crafted oak furniture. One man's work from start to finish. A simple ethos established by Robert Thompson – The Mouseman of Kilburn.

In perfect reflection of this, the new **Mouseman Visitor Centre** will take you on an amazing journey through the life and times of the Mouseman from humble beginnings to furniture legend. Visitors to the centre can pass through rooms set in the 1930s that are full of Robert Thompson's own personal furniture made with his own hands and signed with early examples of the carved mouse symbol. Learn all about the Mouseman of Kilburn from our audio-visual display then browse our Gift shop where you can purchase handcrafted items that we sell today.

Robert Thompson, born in 1876 dedicated his life to the craft of carving and joinery in English Oak. He taught himself to use the traditional tools and by 1919 he was experimenting with his own ideas for producing furniture based on the English styles of the 17th Century.

Now the famous mouse symbol, found on every item crafted by Robert Thompson's has an uncertain history. The story told by Robert Thompson himself is that one of his craftsmen remarked that they "We all as poor as church mice" Whereupon Robert carved a mouse on the church screen he was working on. That particular mouse has never been found but it has continued as a trade mark of quality and dedication to craftsmen ever since.

87 LE JARDIN

Number 7, Montpellier Parade, Harrogate HG1 2TJ
Tel: 01423 507323
website: www.lejardin-harrogate.com

Le Jardin is found in a well loved location overlooking the gardens on Montpellier Parade in Harrogate. This attractive bistro is known locally and further afield for serving fine food at excellent value prices. Its' owners Phil and Melanie have been here since December 2006, opening Tuesday to Friday from 11:30-2:30pm, Saturday from 11:30-3pm, on Sundays from 12-3pm, and Tuesday - Saturday from 6pm.

It is the time honoured combination of great food and hospitality that keeps guests coming here, with Phil in the kitchens and Melanie at the front of house. For lunch guests can choose from a wide variety of paninis, salads, sandwiches, jacket potatoes and fuller meals like Whitby scampi, homemade roasted vegetable lasagne and sausages and mash. In the evenings, the bistro menu offers a sumptuous selection with dishes like fresh salmon Florentine, pork loin in mustard and cider apple sauce, fresh fish pie, and oven roasted beef steak in a rich red wine gravy. From 6pm Tuesday-Saturday a set menu is also offered with two courses for £8.75 or three courses for £12.50 per person – a must try option for Auntie Ron's homemade dessert and secret recipe ice cream.

88 ALEXA HOUSE

26 Ripon Road, Harrogate,
North Yorkshire HG1 2JJ
Tel: 01423 501988 Fax: 01423 504086
e-mail: enquires@alexa-house.co.uk
website: www.alexa-house.co.uk

Hands-on proprietors David and Sandra Doherty offer the warmest of welcomes at **Alexa House**, an elegant detached property a short stroll from the International Conference Centre and Harrogate's many visitor attractions. The house was built in 1896 for a renowned art collector and remains late-Victorian in style, with a lovely tiled hallway and grand marble fireplaces. But it also moves with the times, and the 13 en suite guest bedrooms provide all the modern comforts and amenities expected by today's guests. Nine of the rooms are on the first and second floors of the main house, the other four (pets allowed) on the ground floor in converted stable cottages in the courtyard.

David's cooked-to-order breakfast, served in the bright dining room, are definitely worth getting up for, part of the outstanding hospitality that keeps guests coming back to Alexa House. For special occasions flowers, chocolates and champagne can be laid on, and bookings and a taxi arranged for an evening meal in town. Guests can enjoy a drink and plan their days in the lounge or in the garden.

89 MERCER ART GALLERY

Swan Road, Harrogate, North Yorkshire HG1 2SA
Tel: 01423 556188 Fax: 01423 55613

Situated 100 yards from the entrance to the Valley Gardens and Royal Pump Room Museum, the Mercer Art Gallery is home to the district's collection of fine art, which is featured throughout the year as part of an exciting and diverse exhibition programme.

2007 is an exciting year when Harrogate's most famous artist, William Powell Frith, is celebrated with a blockbuster exhibition of works by this great Victorian painter from March to July. This is the first exhibition of his work for over 50 years and the first time over 60 of his paintings, prints and drawings have been brought together.

Other exhibitions include:
Treasures of the Mercer, a chance to see some highlights from the permanent collection; pastel and charcoal drawings by Knaresborough Castle's 2006 artist in residence, Andrew Cheetham; and art from Turkmenistan.

Watch out for special events and activities for families, adults, and children. Open: Tuesday to Saturday and Bank Holiday Monday 10-5, Sunday 2-5.

Admission is free.

90 RIPLEY CASTLE

Estate Office, Ripley, Harrogate,
Yorkshire HG3 3A7
Tel: 01423 770152
website: www.ripleycastle.co.uk

For almost 700 years the Ingilby family has loved their castle and no wonder, given its fabulous treasures, and glorious grounds. The first clue to the magnificence of **Ripley Castle** lies in its impressive 15th Century arched gatehouse at the entrance to its 1,000 acres of land. The estate - which today includes a stately home, complete with paintings and furniture that would grace a royal palace, as well as grounds containing a glorious lake and deer park - has been in the possession of the Ingilby family since the marriage of Sir Thomas Ingilby to Edeline Thweng in 1308.

Ripley Castle's grounds contain some of Britain's largest herbaceous borders, interspersed with fountains and lawns. There are walled gardens that are a pleasure to visit at any time of year, and the National Hyacinth Collection which creates a delightful pastiche of colours and fragrances, especially in early summer. The kitchen gardens, meanwhile, contain rare collections of herbs, spices, fruit trees and vegetables. A walk around the wooded pleasure grounds leads to the lakeside path, where herds of Fallow and Red Deer graze peacefully under ancient oak trees.

92 YE OLDE CHYMIST SHOPPE AND THE LAVENDER ROOMS

16 Market Place, Knaresborough,
North Yorkshire HG5 8AG
Tel: 01423 860555 / 01423 863153
e-mail: maurice_bardon@yahoo.co.uk
website: www.lavenderrooms.co.uk
*   or www.yeoldechymistshoppe.co.uk*

Located at the heart of Knaresborough two superb premises can be found within one olde worlde property. Brothers Maurice and Peter Bardon have owned **Ye Olde Chymist Shoppe** and **The Lavender Rooms** since 2001. Downstairs, Ye Olde Chymist Shoppe draws in locals and visitors with a sweet tooth. There are a variety of products on sale including fine Belgian Chocolates, a range of jams and preserves and fine array of lavender based products from Yorkshire and Norfolk.

Upstairs, the quality, busy and bustling Lavender Rooms seats 38 diners and there are plenty of dishes to choose from including a good range of filled sandwiches, wraps and melts. There are also several hot dishes on the menu as well as soups and cream teas available. The Lavender Rooms is open between 9.30am and 5pm and many people pay a visit to sample the speciality lemon and lavender scones. Home cooking is the main focus here and all dishes are freshly prepares and cooked to order. The tea rooms are child friendly and customers can eat in or take away. There are plenty of tempting homemade cakes by the till – you might find it difficult to decide which one to have. All major credit cards taken.

91 THE GROVES

30 Market Place, Knaresborough,
North Yorkshire HG5 8AG
Tel: 01423 863022
e-mail: seanpedel@aol.com
website:
www.thegrovesknaresborough.com

Centrally located in the pretty town of Knaresborough, which is conveniently nestled between the historic cathedral city of York and the vibrant city of Leeds is a true gem indeed. Open all day, everyday, **The Groves** continues to maintain its popularity with visitors and locals alike, many returning time and time again to sample the quality ale, delicious food and fine accommodation on offer. Welcoming hosts, Sean and Jo have really made their mark on this establishment, and continue to offer a warm welcome to all who cross the threshold.

The exceptional menu (cooked by Sean and Jo) includes homemade favourites such as; cottage pie, steak pie, chicken curry and chilli. There is also a selection of lighter options available such as jacket potatoes, sandwiches and large Yorkshire puddings. The traditional Sunday lunches are also very popular and it is advisable to book in advance. Accompany your meal with a refreshing beverage served by an attentive member of staff, and your dining experience will be one to remember. The bar offers a varied selection of refreshments, including 2 real ales with John Smith Cask the regular.

For those looking to explore the popular town of Knaresborough, The Groves provides the perfect base, boasting four bright and contemporary rooms, many with views over the market place. All rooms are fully equipped with en-suite bathrooms, flat screen televisions, tea and coffee amenities, hair dryers and ironing facilities. Family rooms can be arranged with additional pull out beds or travel cots upon request and the tariff includes a hearty full english breakfast.

Entertainment is also something that The Groves does very well, Thursday evening hosts a quiz night, games night every Sunday from 4pm - Higher or Lower! Every Saturday evening there is a disco/karaoke.

93 MOTHER SHIPTON'S CAVE

Harrogate Road, Knaresborough, Yorkshire HG5 8DD
Tel: 01423 864600 website: www.mothershipton.com

Mother Shipton is England's most famous Prophetess. She lived some 500
years ago during the reigns of King Henry VIII and Queen Elizabeth I. Her Prophetic visions
became known and feared throughout England, with many of them still proving uncannily
accurate today. The Cave, her legendary birthplace is near to the famous, unique, geological
phenomenon - The Petrifying Well. See its magical cascading waters turn items into stone! The
Petrifying Well is England's Oldest Visitor Attraction, first opening its gates in 1630! Mother
Shiptons Cave & The Petrifying Well lie at the heart of the Mother Shipton Estate - a relic of the
Ancient Forest of Knaresborough.

94 THE WATER RAT

24 Bondgate Green, Ripon, North Yorkshire HG4 1QW
Tel: 01765 602251
e-mail: rick@thewaterrat.co.uk
website: www.thewaterrat.co.uk

In an idyllic location on the banks of the river in the city of Ripon
you will find **The Water Rat**. This well loved inn is just a five
minute walk from the city centre in a convenient location for a
beautiful city dinner. Licensee Rick Jones took over here in
February 2007 and was joined by experienced Head Chef Kevan
Lambert in April 2008. Together they offer a dream team of
hospitality and cuisine, evidenced by the high volume of customers
they see each day. Three real ales from local breweries are
available alongside a handsome wine and spirit list. Food is
available between 12-2pm and 6-9pm throughout the week, with a
carvery being held on Sundays from 12 - 2pm and the bar and dinner menu from 5 - 7pm. Owing to
popularity, booking is essential on weekends. Regrettably no food is offered on race days.

The luncheon menu includes a selection of homemade soups, ciabattas, jackets and pub
favourites like steak and ale pie and lasagne with chips. By contrast the dinner menu offers a
small but exquisite selection of English cuisine with braised lamb shoulder, roasted sea bass,
Nidderdale chicken and roasted pepper and Yorkshire Fettle wellington. Each day specials are
displayed on the blackboard, showcasing the freshest produce from the market that day. On the
third Thursday of every month themed food evenings are held, with a winter quiz held from
October to April on Sunday nights from 7pm.

www.findsomewhere.co.uk
For people who want to explore the United Kingdom

Places to Visit

95 NORTON CONYERS HALL AND GARDENS

Norton Conyers, Ripon, Yorkshire HG4 4EQ
Tel: 01765 640333
e-mail: norton.conyers@bronco.co.uk

This charming old house has belonged to the
Graham family since 1624, and is now the home of
Sir James and Lady Graham. Of medieval origins, it
was altered in Stuart times and again in the
eighteenth century. The interior, with its pictures
and furniture, reflects over 380 years of occupation
by the same family.

Charlotte Brontë memorably paid a visit in 1839.
A legend that a mad woman had, some time in the
previous century, been confined in the attics is said to have been her
inspiration for the mad Mrs Rochester in "Jane Eyre", and Norton Conyers is
an original of "Thornfield Hall". The discovery in November 2004 of a
blocked staircase, clearly described in "Jane Eyre", connecting the first floor
with the attics, aroused world-wide interest. Other notable visitors were
Charles I in 1633 and James II and his wife in 1679 (the room and the bed
they traditionally used are on display).

The house is set in a fine park. The large 18th century walled garden has
herbaceous borders flanked by yew hedges, and an Orangery with an
attractive little pool in front of it. There is pick-your-own fruit in season
(please check beforehand), and a small sales area specialises in unusual hardy plants.

96 NEWBY HALL & GARDENS

Skelton, nr Ripon, North Yorkshire HG4 5AE
Tel: 0845 4504068
website: www.newbyhall.com

Newby Hall and Gardens, near Ripon in North Yorkshire, is
one of England's renowned Adam
Houses, and home to spectacular
treasures and antiques as well as 25
acres of stunning landscaped gardens.
Acclaimed as one of the Historic
Houses Association's most visited
properties, Newby Hall has an enviable
position as one of Yorkshire's best-
loved historic properties.

Collections inside Newby Hall itself
include a set of 18th Century Gobelins
tapestries, fine Chippendale furniture, classical statuary and even an unusual selection of
European and Far-Eastern chamber pots!

Newby Hall and Gardens remains a firm favourite with families, gardening enthusiasts and
heritage lovers who come to experience the many attractions this beautiful estate has to offer.

Newby's miniature railway is ever-popular with children and adults alike, and the Adventure
Garden will amuse children for hours. The Sculpture Park takes in many pieces of contemporary
work from a variety of artists, all of which are for sale, while the Woodland Walk is a delightful
stroll through Bragget Wood and the adjacent orchard.

97 THE BLACK BULL INN

6 St James Square, Boroughbridge, North Yorkshire YO51 9AR
Tel: 01423 322413 Fax: 01423 323915

Yorkshire abounds in ancient hostelries but **The Black Bull Inn** in the heart of Boroughbridge is one of the most venerable with a history going back to 1262. For many years it provided hospitality for travellers on the stage coaches running between Thirsk and Harrogate. Inside it has plenty of character and still has lots of traditional features, complemented by modern décor and furnishings.

The child-friendly inn is well known for the quality of the food it serves. There's an extensive bar snacks menu with a choice of dishes ranging through chargrilled dishes to traditional favourites such as haddock and chips, curry and a home-made pie of the day. The regular choice is supplemented by seasonal specials and fresh seafood dishes. If you choose from the à la carte menu, you'll find a tasty dish of king prawn tails and queen scallops amongst the starters; steaks, char grilled dishes, a selection of 'Sizzlers', and dishes such as tenderloin of pork with a pink peppercorn and calvados sauce as main courses. Round off your meal with one of the wonderful desserts - lemon heaven perhaps, or baked jam sponge, dark chocolate truffle torte, or a banoffee meringue roulade. If you prefer a savoury, a selection of English and continental cheeses is available.

To accompany your meal, the bar offers an extensive choice of beverages. Real ale lovers will be in their element with three to choose from - John Smiths, Timothy Taylor Bitter and a rotating guest ale.

The Black Bull offers comfortable accommodation in six well-appointed bedrooms, all with en suite facilities. The very reasonable tariff includes a hearty English breakfast. Ring for details. The inn is popular with people visiting the area and there are plenty of things for holiday-makers and day visitors to do. Within easy reach of the inn are some of Yorkshire's major visitor attractions. The World Heritage Site of Fountains Abbey; the magnificent Studley Royal Gardens, Ripon with its great cathedral; and the spa town of Harrogate are all just a short drive away.

All major credit cards are accepted; there's off road parking; and the inn has good disabled access to the bar and restaurant but the accommodation is upstairs.

Food is served every day from noon until 2pm, (2.30pm on Sunday); and from 6pm to 9pm. Booking a table at weekends is strongly recommended. The inn itself is open from 11am to 11pm.

98 THORPE LODGE B&B

Littlethorpe, Ripon, North Yorkshire HG4 3LU
Tel: 01765 602088 Fax: 01765 602835
e-mail: jowitt@btinternet.com
website: www.thorpelodge.co.uk

Thorpe Lodge is a listed Georgian building in a secluded setting
off the A61 a mile south of Ripon town centre. Set in extensive
grounds at the end of a half-mile driveway, it's a quintessential
informal English country house, with colourful, inviting rooms full
of handsome antiques, interesting pictures and ornaments and
comfortable, homely furnishings. The south-facing Lodge is the
home of Juliet and Tommy Jowitt and their dogs. Juliet has lived
here with her family for more than 30 years; she loves the house,
the garden and the surrounding area and she shares that love with
her guests, who are made to feel like family friends from the
moment they step over the threshold.

The two guest bedrooms are a pure delight – light, roomy,
well-planned, with period furnishings and beautiful décor that reflects Juliet's expertise as an
interior designer. A cooked-to-order breakfast using prime local produce makes an excellent start
to the day, and an evening meal is available with a little notice. The garden, developed by the
owners over more than twenty years, is a wonderful place for a stroll, with a mixture of natural,
country and formal styles. It is full of lovely features, including spectacular borders, a walled rose
garden, a row of tall cypresses, ponds and a hornbeam walk. Guests also have the use of an
outdoor swimming pool in the summer months.

findSOMEWHERE.co.uk
For people who want to explore Britain and Ireland

Specialist Shops

Our easy-to use website contains details and locations of places to stay, places to eat and drink, specialist shops and places of
interest throughout England, Wales, Scotland and Ireland.

Places to Stay:	**Places to Eat and Drink:**	**Places of Interest:**	**Specialist Shops:**	**Gardens:**
Hotels, guest accommodation, bed & breakfast, inns, self-catering accommodation	Restaurants, pubs, inns, cafes, tea rooms	Historic buildings, gardens, art galleries, museums, nature parks, wildlife parks, indoor and outdoor activities	Fashion shops, art and craft shops, gift shops, food and drink shops, antique shops, jewellery shops	Garden centres and retail nurseries

99 THE GRANTLEY ARMS

High Grantley, Ripon, North Yorkshire HG4 3PJ
Tel: 01765 620227
e-mail: vsails2@aol.com
website: www.grantleyarms.com

The Grantley Arms is a real hidden gem in the village of Grantley. It dates back in parts to the mid 17th century and is the ideal oasis for visitors to the area. It can be found situated off the B6265 between Ripon and Pateley Bridge at High Grantley next to the impressive village hall and across the road from the village school.

Valerie and Eric have owned the free house for almost ten years now and are well known in the area for their warm and friendly hospitality. And it isn't just the hospitality here that is of a high standard – it also has a fine reputation for its food and drink.

Two professional chefs are employed in the kitchen and they have a strong focus on using the very best of local produce. The dishes are absolutely divine and a great example of quality fine dining.

Crispy roast duck served with braised red cabbage, potato gnocchi and a campari and orange sauce; pan fried medallions of pork, slow roasted belly pork and a pork, smoked bacon and black pudding roll with crispy crackling and chutney jus are among the delicious main courses available at The Grantley Arms. Starters include chicken liver and mushroom parfait, chilli and lime marinated sardines, and chef's soup of the day.

There are two real ales to sample with Theakstons Best the regular as well as a rotating guest ale. The well-stocked bar has plenty to suit all tastes, from fine wines to beer, spirits and soft drinks.

There is a special menu for lunch time served in the bar between 12pm and 2pm Monday – Saturday. It is extremely popular and it is advisable to book, so that you don't miss out on an opportunity to dine here.

In the spring the exterior of The Grantley Arms is awash with bloom and has a real picture postcard look to it. It is extremely attractive and really draws in visitors and locals to enjoy fine food and drink in a lovely setting.

This free house is definitely a must if you are visiting the area. Its stunning location, fantastic food, ale and hospitality make for a particularly wonderful dining experience.

100 THE BULL INN

Church Street, West Tanfield, Ripon, North Yorkshire HG4 5JQ
Tel: 01677 470678
e-mail: jules_vanveen@hotmail.com
website: www.thebullinnwesttanfield.co.uk

Standing in the delightful village of West
Tanfield, **The Bull Inn** is a charming
former coaching inn. The menu offers
appetising dishes based on the best of
fresh local produce wherever possible.
Owner Jules van Veen arrived here in
the spring of 2008 and has carried out a
complete refurbishment of the premises
while retaining its olde worlde flavour.
The inn in the village, which is perhaps
best known for its impressive Tudor
gatehouse, the Marmion Tower, is close
to the ancient bridge that straddles the
River Ure. Its riverside location attracts
a lot of locals and visitors and a friendly

welcome from Jules and her team waits. The team is
extremely professional and provides a friendly and warm
service.

Food is available every lunchtime and evening, except
Tuesday when the pub is closed and food is served until
4pm on Sundays. Starters include homemade soup of day
served with a fresh bread roll, deep fried brie wedge
with red onion marmalade and tomato, red onion, goat's
cheese and pesto tartlet. Among the varied selection on
the main menu is Theakston's beer battered fish of the
day, chips and pea puree and flame grilled chicken piri
piri and chorizo sausage, chips and salad. For those with
room left for dessert there are plenty of tempting choices
available – sticky toffee pudding and custard, and apple
and autumn berry and custard are among the favourites.

There are real ales on tap and in good weather
customers can enjoy their refreshments in the riverside
garden. There is a fine selection of wines and
champagnes and other refreshments too. Children are
welcome and dogs can be taken into the gardens.

For those who are visiting the area there are five
comfortable en-suite bedrooms available in this gorgeous
pub in the Yorkshire Dales. The rooms are attractively
furnished – four of them are doubles and the fifth is
single. Ring for details.

Games nights and music nights are often held at The
Bull Inn and they are particularly popular with locals and
visitors. A fantastic Beer Festival is held every year on
the last weekend in August. There are real ales on tap
including Black Sheep, Theakston's and one or two guest
ales. Ring for details.

101 FANCY THAT TEA ROOM

8 Market Place, Masham,
North Yorkshire HG4 4EB
Tel: 01765 688161
e-mail: info@fancythattearooms.co.uk
website: www.fancythattearooms.co.uk

It is the smell of home cooking that attracts people to
Fancy That Tea Room. Lovers of homemade food will be
in their element at this popular family run business
located at the heart of the historic town of Masham. It
can be found on one side of the town's main square and
has been owned by the Ebbage family since May 2008.
Jamie is a qualified baker and is helped out by his mum
Susan and Holly.

The home baked cakes are absolutely divine and if you
are after something savoury first there is a fine selection
of freshly prepared filled sandwiches, jacket potatoes,
hot baguettes, toasted sandwiches, and salads.

Whether it is lunch or afternoon tea you are after
Fancy That Tea Room is definitely worth a look. There is room for 25 diners inside and six more
outside.

The child friendly establishment is closed on Thursday, but open every other day between
9.30am and 5pm in the summer and 9.30am and 4.30pm in winter months. There is good access for
disabled customers as well as disabled friendly toilets. Major credit cards taken.

102 THEAKSTON BREWERY & VISITOR CENTRE

Masham, Ripon, North Yorkshire HG4 4YD
Tel: 01765 680000
website: www.theakstons.co.uk

For beer drinkers, the first place to visit in the

Yorkshire Dales is the home of the legendary 'Old
Peculier', the **Theakston Brewery.** Robert Theakston
began brewing 170 years ago at the Black Bull Inn in
1827. Forty eight years later, his son Thomas built the
famous brewery on Masham's Paradise Fields, where it
stands today. Most of the original equipment is still in
use today, and with a trained tour guide, visitors can
follow the entire brewing process, from selecting the
ingredients to filling the casks.

Meet the people behind the beer, ask questions or simply soak up
the atmosphere of the brewer's art. Watch one of only seven brewery
coopers in England crafting the wooden casks that Theakston's still use
for supplying local pubs.

After the tour, visitors are invited to the Visitor Centre Bar, where
they can enjoy real British beer by a roaring log fire. The admission
price includes a complimentary half pint of beer, from a comprehensive
selection of Theakston ales, including Old Peculier and Theakston Cool
Cask - you'll be spoilt for choice.

103 THORP PERROW ARBORETUM, WOODLAND GARDEN AND FALCONRY CENTRE

Thorp Perrow, Bedale, North Yorkshire DL8 2PR
Tel: 01677 425323
website: www.thorpperrow.com

Thorp Perrow Arboretum is one of the finest private collections of trees and shrubs in the country. This 85 acre arboretum is unique to Britain, if not Europe, in that it was the creation of one man, Colonel Sir Leonard Ropner (1895 – 1977) and is now owned and managed by Sir John Ropner.

Situated in the peaceful and unspoilt Yorkshire Dales, not far from the historic town of Bedale, Thorp Perrow is an exciting place to explore offering something for everyone. This tranquil and peaceful haven is home to some of the largest and rarest trees and shrubs in England. A treasure trove of specimen trees and woodland walks.

The Falcons of Thorp Perrow is the ultimate family day out, incorporating the opportunity to learn more about birds of prey and associated wildlife, with the enjoyment of hands on experience for all the family. Combined with the beautiful and historic Arboretum, a full and spectacular day in the Yorkshire countryside is complete. The regular flying demonstrations will not only give the opportunity to witness the breathtaking ability of eagles, falcons, hawks, vultures and owls from all five continents of the world, but also an opportunity to participate.

105 THE WORLD OF JAMES HERRIOTT

23 Kirkgate, Thirsk, North Yorkshire YO7 1PL
Tel: 01845 524234 Fax: 01845 525333
e-mail: wojhemails@hambleton.gov.uk
website: www.worldofjamesherriott.org

Celebrating the world's best-known vet, **The World of James Herriott** opened in the spring of 1999, since when it has welcomed more than 400,000 visitors. The setting is Skeldale House, now a Grade II listed building, where James Herriott lived and worked. The house has been lovingly restored to how it was in the 1940s and 1950s, with many original pieces of furniture donated by the author's family.

Beyond the famous red door, visitors enter the dining room, which doubled as the practice office. Then on to the cosy family room where the vet's favourite music – Bing Crosby – plays. Further down the corridor is the dispensary where he made up the prescriptions and the little surgery where he would treat domestic animals. Skeldale houses the only veterinary science museum in the country and a new interactive surgery and farm. The World of James Herriott moves with the times with audio tapes escorting visitors round the house and a short film of the vet's life story narrated by Christopher Timothy. The garden has also been taken back in time, and other attractions include studio sets from *All Creatures Great and Small*, some 70s cameras and equipment and the original Austin Seven tourer AJO 71. This fascinating, family-friendly place is open throughout the year.

104 BLACK LION BAR AND BISTRO

8 Market Place, Thirsk, North Yorkshire YO7 1LB
Tel: 01845 574302
website: www.blacklionthrisk.co.uk

The Black Lion Bar and Bistro has stood in its handsome location in the centre of Thirsk for many years, but has become incredibly popular over the last two years with the arrival of its current team. Richard Bainbridge and Raymond Dyer are the Lion's owners and business partners, and are ably assisted by Chef Owen Moody and Sara Haigh who manages special events. The team come together from a variety of industries centring around the hospitality trade, combining a wealth of skills and experience to make the Lion the success it is today.

After a full refurbishment, the Lion now sports a wonderful mix of traditional yet chic decor with shades of duck egg blue and patterned china accompanying handsomely upholstered chairs and fine tablecloths. Guests can choose from a variety of dining areas in either bustling or more private dining rooms, with a tranquil courtyard to the rear, also bedecked with tables for the summer months.

Open all day every day apart from Sunday evenings, the Lion offers coffee from 10am until close each day, whilst food is served from 11:30am-5pm Monday to Saturday and 12-5pm on Sundays. All dishes are cooked fresh to order and are created using only the best in local seasonal produce. The sandwich menu offers a range of traditional sandwiches with a bistro twist such as tuna with crème fraiche and spinach, and mature cheddar with homemade chutney; all with a chunky chip option if desired. The lunch menu offers a great selection of light bites from soups to pate, prawn cocktails and cheese boards, to crunchy salads and tasty pasta dishes from simple lasagne to ham and garlic tortellini. The dinner menu also offers a mouth-watering selection of starters, either great on their own or an appetiser to a main meal. Oak smoked salmon and herb crème fraiche, and Portobello mushrooms glazed with Yorkshire blue cheese are just some of the options. Main courses include roasted monkfish bound in prosciutto ham, Veal escalope, and slow cooked lamb Henry. Game lovers will benefit from their own special menu sampling the very best in duck, pigeon, venison, partridge, guinea fowl and rabbit cuisine. Owing to popularity, booking is advised from Thursday to Sunday when tables are quickly filled.

The team are planning to create some contemporary accommodation in the near future to include six double and two single bedrooms, please call for details and bookings.

106 THE ANGEL INN

Long Street, Topcliffe, Thirsk, North Yorkshire YO7 3RW
Tel: 01845 577237 Fax: 01845 578000
e-mail: info@topcliffeangelinn.co.uk
website: www.topcliffeangelinn.co.uk

The Angel Inn stands proudly in the centre of Thirsk, on the corner of Long Street just a short drive from the A1. It's attractive red roof and bay windows speak of the warm décor and welcome that awaits inside.

Kevin Bird and his bar manager Phil Gibbons took over the running of the Angel in February 2009, and have quickly found themselves with a success on their hands. Kevin has over ten years in the trade, with Phil adding a further ten years of expertise as well. Their efficient but friendly style of working has meant that the inn runs like clockwork, typically filled with a happy selection of locals and visitors from further afield who have come to enjoy the homely pub vibe.

Open all day every day, there are up to three real ales on offer with the Yorkshire brew Black Sheep making regular appearances. Drinks can also be enjoyed outside in the inn's pretty beer garden, where a small pond with a Monet style bridge over it provides a good view for spotting the resident fish.

Food is served at the inn from 12-3pm and 5-9pm Monday-Saturday and from 12-3pm and 6-9pm on Sundays. Dishes are created using the best in locally sourced produce and range from pub classics to more exotic fayre displayed on the daily specials board. Popular choices include bangers and mash, chilli burgers, hunter's chicken, steak pie and deep dried cod and chips. Other dishes include rainbow trout, lamb rogan josh, half a roast duck served with a plum sauce and a tender rack of lamb. Owing to popularity, booking is recommended on Saturday nights when the inn can become quite busy.

Saturday nights are also prime booking time for the Angel's function suite which can be adapted to cater for a variety of events including seminars, conferences, birthdays, weddings and anniversary parties. The main suite holds up to 110 people, whilst the resident lounge holds a further 12, and the attractive Garden Room housing up to 40 guests. For added convenience in any event, or as part of a weekend away in Yorkshire, the Angel also offers fifteen en suite guest bedrooms in a variety of sizes to suit individual need. Breakfast is served between 7-9 am, making the perfect start to a day exploring all that Thirsk has to offer.

107 THE WHITE SWAN INN

Danby Lane, Danby Wiske, Northallerton, North Yorkshire DL7 0NQ
Tel: 01609 775131
e-mail: thewhiteswandanbywiske@googlemail.co.uk

The White Swan Inn is very popular with walkers, many who want to explore North Yorkshire by foot. Dating back to the 17th century it has a very traditional feel to it, a lot of character and locals and visitors alike frequent this establishment, which is nestled between the Yorkshire Dales and the North Yorkshire Moors.

Licensees Stephen and Gillian offer a very warm welcome and offer three guest bedrooms. The inn is an ideal place to stay as a base to those wanting to explore the surrounding countryside and the comfortable rooms are available all year round. They have all been recently updated and are all located upstairs. One has an en-suite bathroom. Ring for details. Up to four real ales can be enjoyed at The White Swan Inn, with Black Sheep Ale and brew from the nearby Hambleton Brewery the two regulars.

Stephen and Gillian are looking at introducing food options at the pub too and a menu is likely to be available shortly. Ring for details. The inn is located at the heart of the pretty village of Danby Wiske and is child friendly. Only cash and cheque are accepted here debit card payments will be accepted in the near future.

108 THE BRIDGE HOUSE HOTEL

Catterick Bridge, Richmond, North Yorkshire DL10 7PE
Tel: 01748 818331 Fax: 01748 810910
e-mail: manager@bridgehousehotelcatterick.com
website: www.bridgehousehotelcatterick.com

The Bridge House Hotel is notably one of the most famous properties in Yorkshire. Dating back to the 15th century in parts, it exudes an aura of historic importance and has been beautifully preserved to retain this. It stands in an attractive position opposite the racecourse in Catterick, on the grassy banks of the River Swale, and has a long history of supporting the forces, based nearby at Catterick Garrison. It's conveniently located for both holiday makers and businessmen alike; being within an easy drive of Richmond and the Yorkshire Dales National Park, with the bright lights of Newcastle just further afield.

Tina and Doug Birnie have run the hotel for a number of years and pride themselves on being able to provide high standards in all areas of service from the bar and bistro, to the rooms and function facilities.

Fifteen en suite guest bedrooms are available year round, each traditionally decorated and equipped with all modern facilities. A variety of sizes are available to suit individual need, and all come with a delicious breakfast.

The bar and bistro provide a homely and comfortable dining area with an impressive array of traditional and continental dishes on offer. Head chef Brian offers up a range of menus for any appetite and budget, with countless chicken, beef, fish, pork, lamb and vegetarian dishes to choose from. Popular choices include salmon with an orange and mustard sauce, exotic vegetable stir fry, pork steak with apple and sage sauce, lamb mousaka and chicken fajitas. Brian's speciality is homemade steak and ale pie – however he also serves a delicious range of baguettes, salads and snacks throughout the day. During the week Brian also puts on themed food nights with meal deals on curry and steak nights, not forgetting the popular Sunday carvery from 12-3pm – most often the destination for groups following a day at the races.

The Ballroom Lounge offers a charming space for any function, whether it's for a conference, birthday party or wedding; and can be elegantly styled as such. Brian can provide catering for up to 200 guests, who can enjoy beautiful views of the river and surrounding countryside as they dine.

109 THE LAKESIDE COUNTRY CAFE

North Farm, Ellerton upon Swale, Scorton, Richmond,
North Yorkshire DL10 6AP
Tel: 01748 818382 Fax: 01748 810257
e-mail: enquiries@thelakesidefarmshop.co.uk
website: www.thelakesidefarmshop.co.uk

The Lakeside Country Cafe is an outstanding hidden gem, set in a converted grain store at North Farm, Ellerton between Scorton and Kiplin. Brimming with character and Yorkshire charm, Lakeside is a winning combination of gorgeous country cafe and designer outlet centre, named the Otterburn Mill. It has become amazingly successful since opening its doors in April 2006, the idea of owners Sarah & Graeme; after taking over the pig farm from Graeme's parents in 1998, and then starting a butchery selling their own produce, the couple learnt the need for values customers can't find in their local supermarket. As Graeme puts it, "People want to know where their meat has come from, and they want to be able to identify with the farm and the farmer."

Founded on these values, it is no surprise to find The Lakeside Country Cafe selling a delicious array of home-made food at the finest quality. As Sarah admits "We do serve burgers and chips in the Café, but they are real burgers made by my husband and real chips made in our kitchen from good quality local potatoes". The menu includes a wide selection of mouth watering sandwiches, quiches, filled jacket potatoes, salads, soups, cakes, pies and desserts, as well as daily specials and a selection of roast meats for the popular Sunday lunch. All the meals served are made from scratch with fresh local produce in their country kitchen. The dining area is delightful; light and spacious with widely spaced tables and huge windows, looking out onto the well equipped children's play area with an expanse of farmland behind. In warm weather you can savour their food and the sun at picnic tables on the lovely patio.

Within the same building, on a vast mezzanine floor, is the new **Otterburn Mill**, selling outdoor and leisure clothing, including well known brands such as Berghaus, The North Face, Craghoppers, Bear Grylls clothing, Regatta, Joules and Weird Fish. There is also a dedicated section selling Brasher, Salamon, Merrell and Regatta footwear. Downstairs are two amazing independent businesses. Damsels and Dragonflies is a small WAHM (Work At Home Mum) business which specialises in organic, fair trade, made in the UK, natural, recycled and educational clothes and gifts for your little ones (0 – 5 years). And there is **Quite Contrary**, a small jewellery business run by local designer Pam Bradby, from her home in Brompton-on- Swale; quite gorgeous! Opening hours are, 364 days a year, Monday to Saturday 9.00am - 4.30pm and Sunday 9.00am - 4.00pm (closed Christmas day).

110 KING WILLIAM IV INN

1 Silver Street, Barton, Richmond, North Yorkshire DL10 6LT
Tel: 01325 377256
e-mail: kingwilliamivbarton@yahoo.co.uk

The **King William IV Inn** is located within the pretty village of Barton in North Yorkshire. Though hidden away, it is still within easy reach of the main A1 road close to the Scotch Corner and therefore easily accessible on any day trip through the larger northern towns.

The King William was taken over by Jeffrey Savage in March 2010 with the help of Head Chef Scott Fisher. The pair have much experience in the trade, making this venture a sure success. They open to public all day everyday, endeavouring to serve their local community and visitors from further afield who share their values for good ale, food and company.

Three real ales are on offer at any one time, including the award winning Timothy Taylor Landlord brew. Other ales rotate regularly from local breweries and a good wine and spirit selection is also available.

Food is served daily from 12-2pm and 5-8:30pm from Monday to Saturday. Scott has been a chef for over twenty years in various establishments and has brought a new lease of life to the menu at the King William. He offers guests a taste of Yorkshire with a selection of traditional pub dishes crafted with delicious locally sourced Yorkshire produce, alongside more exotic dishes inspired by the continent. The menu includes dishes like haddock and chips, sirloin steak, pork medallions in a creamy sauce, mince and dumplings and Scott's speciality short crust pastry steak and ale pie. Other favourites include the pizza selection, the oriental platter, and the chorizo stuffed chicken breast. A range of themed food evenings are held throughout the month with regular curry and steak nights, whilst the popular 'Early Bird' menu runs daily between 5-7pm.

The inn itself is traditionally styled, with handsome tiled floor, and stuffed leather benches. With a variety of rooms to choose from, the cosy bar, the bistro styled dining room or the laid back pool room, guests are assured to find a comfy corner. Jeffrey frequently puts on entertainment on the weekends, which he believes brings the community together. Its not just discos and quiz nights here though – although they are popular evenings too – Jeffrey regularly holds charity events and activity days, the most recent of which being a bungee jump! Even when there are no events held, children are easily amused with a great play area in the rear beer garden, also a popular haunt amongst adults in the sunnier weather.

111 THE PANTRY

19 North End, Bedale,
North Yorkshire DL8 1AF
Tel: 01677 424922

The Pantry is a very popular destination for lovers of home cooking. Sophie Mitchell is the owner here and is helped out by her mum Denise, who used to run her own tea rooms close to Knaresborough.

The business is absolutely superb and has built up a fantastic reputation in the area since it opened in October 2009. There is seating for up to 30 people at The Pantry, and it is very often full of people enjoying the home made delicacies on offer. Toasted teacakes, crumpets and freshly baked scones are among the light bights on offer. But if it is something a bit more filling you are after there is a fine selection of lunch time meals including a range of omelettes, filled sandwiches, jacket potatoes and hot muffins. If your favourite isn't on the menu Sophie and Denise will do their best to rustle it up for you if they have the produce.

Children are always welcome here and there is plenty on the menu, which is changed seasonally, to suit all tastes. Perhaps the most popular dish with customers is the home made raspberry meringue.

112 THE BAY HORSE INN

The Green, Crakehall, Bedale, North Yorkshire DL8 1HP
Tel: 01677 422548
website: www.crakehall.org.uk

The Bay Horse Inn, opposite the village green in Crakehall, is frequented by both locals and visitors alike who enjoy the fine brand of hospitality found here. Dianne and John have been running the inn for 17 years and their experience shows. They know what their clientele want and provide it with the good heart and humour that really brings a small inn like this to life. Dianne is well known in the area for making mouth-watering short crust pastry pies amongst other delicious dishes. Three real ales are part of the well stocked bar which opens every session; no food on Mondays.

113 MOUNT GRACE PRIORY

Saddlebridge, Northallerton,
North Yorkshire DL6 3JG
Tel: 01609 883494
website: www.english-heritage.org.uk

In this unusual monastery, the best-preserved priory of the Carthusian order in Britain, you can see how hermit-monks lived 600 years ago. Enjoy the wonderful woodland setting, and take a picnic in the lovely grounds - a haven for wildlife, including bats and the famous 'Priory Stoats'.

114 THE GEORGIAN ROOMS

56 High Street, Old Town, Bridlington,
East Yorkshire YO16 4QA
Tel: 01262 608600 Mobile: 07815672866
e-mail: georgianrooms@btinternet.com
website: www.thegeorgianroomsbridlington.webeden.co.uk

Step into a gracious world of charm, style and elegance at **The Georgian Rooms**, located in the historic heart of Bridlington's quaint old town. The owners Diane, who runs the award winning Georgian Tea Rooms, and her husband Andrew who runs the upstairs antiques business, lovingly and painstakingly restored this gorgeous building, and opened it as The Georgian Rooms in May 2000. Since then it become a popular and important feature of old town Bridlington.

The tea rooms, which are beautifully furnished with antique furniture seat 40 with a further 20 seats in the pretty garden, are renowned for delicious home made food. The freshly made soups and quiches are popular favourites, as well as all the lovely dishes added daily to the specials board, but the real speciality here are the home made puddings; too tempting to resist with a nice cup of tea! Where possible ingredients used in the menu, such as the meat and fish, are locally sourced and used seasonally. The Antique Centre is home to around 45 dealers and offers a wide variety of antiques, craft items, art, vintage clothing and collectables. The Georgian rooms are open seven days a week Monday to Saturday 10am – 5pm and Sunday 10am – 3pm (closed for two weeks over Christmas and New Years).

115 BURLINGTON'S RESTAURANT

91 High Street, Old Town, Bridlington, Yorkshire YO16 4PN
Tel: 01262 400383
e-mail: judyanddavehall@talktalk.net
website: www.burlingtonsrestaurant.net

Husband and wife team Judy and Dave Hall have been opening the doors to **Burlington's Restaurant** for the past twenty years. In that time they have seen their clientele grow and grow and now have themselves a popular and well loved business. Located in the heart of historic Bridlington, the restaurant offers a homely environment with earthy tones and idyllic pictures adorning the walls whilst comfy leather sofas and cushions provide more than enough comfort for a pre-dinner drink.

David is an experienced and talented chef, offering up an a la carte menu and regularly changing specials menu that focuses on combining the best seasonal produce available. Starters include stuffed mushrooms, Parisian pate and Cointreau Melon, whilst mains on offer are roasted duckling, pork fillet with sautéed chorizo, Thai simmered seafood, locally caught sea bass and a traditional steak. Judy will happily real off her homemade dessert menu to complete the perfect meal. Open Tuesday to Saturday evenings from 6:30-9pm and Sunday lunchtime from 12-2pm. The Early Bear Special from 6:30-7:30pm Tuesdays to Fridays also offers two and three course meals at great value for money.

116 SEWERBY HALL AND GARDENS

Church Lane, Sewerby, Bridlington, East Riding of Yorkshire YO15 1EA
Tel: 01262 673769
e-mail: sewerby.hall@eastriding.gov.uk
website: www.eastriding.gov.uk/sewerby/hall

Sewerby Hall is situated 2 miles north of the seaside resort of
Bridlington, on the East Yorkshire coast. The grade I listed
country house is set in 50 acres of landscaped gardens in a cliff
top location on the outskirts of Sewerby village.

The house was built 1714-1720 by John Greame. Bow wings
and a portico were added in 1808-1811. Later additions include
an Orangery and dining room. These days the magnificent
ground floor Orangery and Swinton Rooms provide wonderful settings for civil marriage
ceremonies, concerts & piano recitals, meetings, seminars, educational activities, art workshops
and tea dances. The Amy Johnson Room is given over to Amy Johnson memorabilia in 1959. This
collection was a gift from Amy's father in October 1958, and consists of various souvenirs and
mementoes presented to Amy and her husband, Jim Mollison. Since then, additional material
received from other sources has further enhanced the Amy Johnson Collection.

The Lovely Gardens of Sewerby extend some 50 acres and offer magnificent views over
Bridlington Bay, from Flamborough headland to the north-east, down to Spurn Point looking
south.The gardens are a skilful blend of art and nature, with formal walks, terraces and
contrasting woodland. The magnificent monkey puzzle trees of the pleasure gardens are
reputed to be amongst the oldest in England, and there are many more fine specimen trees over
200 years old.entrepiece to many of the beds.

117 RSPB'S BEMPTON CLIFFS NATURE RESERVE

RSPB Reserve, Bempton Cliffs, Bridlington, East Yorkshire YO15 1JF
Tel: 01912 813366

The chalk cliffs at Bempton form part of England's largest seabird colony
between Flamborough Head and Bempton. Over 200,000 seabirds breed
on the reserve alone. As well as managing reserves such as this the RSPB
also works for the better protection of the marine environment. For
much of the year, the cliffs at Bempton are relatively quiet, but during
the breeding season, between April and August, they are crammed with
birds. The spectacle, noise, activity and smell all contribute to an
overwhelming and memorable experience. As many seabird colonies are
on remote islands Bempton offers a rare opportunity to watch breeding
seabirds at close quarters.

Both puffins and gannets breed at Bempton. About 2,000 pairs of
puffins return to the cliffs to breed and each pair lays a single egg in a
crevice in the rock face. Between May and the end of July they regularly
visit their young with small fish but by August, the young puffins have left
the cliffs to spend the winter on the North Sea. Bempton has the largest mainland gannet colony
(gannetry) in Britain. Over 2,500 pairs nest on the cliffs and can be seen here from January to
November, but are most active between April and August when they are breeding. They will travel
up to 60 miles to find food. Six other species of seabirds nest at Bempton Cliffs. Kittiwakes are
the most numerous, with 45,000 pairs packed onto the cliffs. Guillemots and razorbills also nest
on the narrow cliff ledges. Look out for the distinctive gliding flight of fulmars around the cliffs,
and herring gulls and a few shags also nest on the cliffs.

118 INSPIRATION CAFÉ BAR

59 Market Place, Driffield, East Yorkshire YO25 6AW
Tel: 01377 272323

Situated on the main street in the popular market town of Driffield is Inspiration Café Bar. Proud owners Anne and Nick Jennings and their son Tom opened this popular eatery in 2005 and with the help of right hand lady Liz they have created a friendly vibrant atmosphere where fans regularly meet and enjoy good company.

Fully Licensed and renowned for it's superb coffee, freshly made food includes breakfasts, panini, wraps and sandwiches along with more hearty options such as pasta specials, bacon cheeseburger, bruschetta and delicious afternoon teas.

119 ST QUINTIN ARMS

Main Street, Harpham, nr Driffield
East Yorkshire YO25 4QY
Tel: 01262 490329
website: www.stquintinarms.co.uk

The St Quintin Arms is a lovely little find in the picturesque village of Harpham. Andrew Frost has just taken over the running of the establishment which can be found a mile or so off the main A614 (Driffield – Bridlington Road). The St Quintin Arms has recently been refurbished and the inside areas match the beauty of the excellent gardens. The outside beer garden is popular on sunnier days and with several real ales to choose from (including John Smiths) real ale lovers will be in their element.

A good range of dishes are listed on a printed menu and there are plenty of additional choices on the daily specials board. Around 60 diners can be catered for here and children are welcome in the family room. Food is served between 11am and 2pm and between 6pm and 9pm Monday – Saturday. On Sundays food is served between 11am and 11pm. Three en-suite rooms are available at the St Quintin Arms and apart from the rooms being located upstairs, there is no problems with regards to disabled access.

120 BRADLEY'S BISTRO CAFÉ BAR

13-15 High Street, Market Weighton, Yorkshire YO43 3AQ
Tel: 01430 873240 Fax: 01430 871997
e-mail: bradleys24@btinternet.com

Named after the Market Weighton resident William Bradley whom the *Guinness Book of Records* authenticates as 'England's Tallest Ever Man' at 7ft 9ins, **Bradley's Bistro Café Bar** also sets itself some pretty tall targets in providing quality food in a friendly and relaxed atmosphere. Owned and run by Sharon and Howard Gant since 2008, this town centre venue has become a highly popular eating place.

The extensive menu ranges from Early Starters served until 11.30am, through hot Panini grills, baked potatoes and sandwiches to a selection of light meals and snacks. There are daily home-made specials and a tempting display of home-made cakes, desserts and other treats. Bradley's is open from 8.30am to 4.30pm, Monday to Saturday; and from 11am to 4pm on Sundays when it offers a traditional Sunday lunch with a choice of 2 roasts. Booking for this is essential. The downstairs café can seat 40 diners and there is also seating in the rear garden and on the front patio. For larger parties, there's an upstairs function room which can accommodate up to 70 people. Bradley's is fully licensed and also offers a full take away service.

121 THE YORKWAY MOTEL

Hull Road, Pocklington, York,
East Yorkshire YO42 2NX
Tel: 01759 303071
e-mail: info@yorkway-motel.co.uk
website: www.yorkway-motel.co.uk

Superb accommodation, fine food and a warm welcome await you at The Yorkway Motel, situated on the A1079, a mile from the Market town of Pocklington. Michael and Julia have managed the motel, a former farm house, for the past three years. It is an excellent base when visiting the many attractions in beautiful Yorkshire. Open all year round, The Yorkway Motel has twelve en-suite rooms which vary in size and are all on the ground floor, making them easily accessible. The tariff includes a hearty breakfast which is guaranteed to set you up for the day.

Non residents are very welcome to dine in the Motel Restaurant which is open from 5 to 9p.m. every weekday, 12 to 2.30p.m. and 5 to 9 p.m. Fridays and Saturdays and between 12 and 7 p.m. on Sundays. The a la carte menu offers locally sourced steaks and produce together with homemade pies and puddings.

The Motel has a large car park so off road parking is not a problem, but please note, the Sunday Carvery is extremely popular so it might be as well to book.

122 THE STEER INN

Hull Road, Wilberfoss, York, North Yorkshire YO41 5PF
Tel: 01759 380600
e-mail: reception@thesteerinn.co.uk
website: www.thesteerinn.co.uk

The Steer Inn has recently undergone a major transformation. The impressive building was bought in the summer of 2010. The couple also own the touring caravan park next door – Lynby Caravan Park. The inn is an ideal place to stay for visitors to Yorkshire, with 15 en-suite bedrooms to offer guests. All of the tastefully decorated rooms vary in size and one ground floor room has been specially adapted, with separate access, for disabled guests.

Food here is extremely popular and it is definitely advisable to book at weekends and particularly for the Sunday carvery, which is served between 12 noon and 3.30pm. Monday - Saturday food is served 6pm - 9pm for dinner and the pub is also open for lunches on Saturday from 12 noon until 2pm. The bar, which is open at all times for residents, is well-stocked and Tetleys, John Smiths, Kronenburg and Fosters are all available on draught. There is a function room available to hire (ring for details). All major credit cards taken.

123 THE HALF MOON INN

Main Street, Newton upon Derwent,
Yorkshire YO41 4DB
Tel: 01904 608883
website: www.thehalfmoon-newton.co.uk

Located in the delightful village of Newton on Derwent, just off the A1079 York to Hull road, **The Half Moon Inn** is a picture postcard establishment which has been recently refurbished but has retained its traditional atmosphere with open fires, superb beer garden and a welcoming ambience. A fine display of vintage LP and EP record sleeves in the bar adds to the charm.

Owners Steve and Alexandra Footman took over here in 2007 and have made their inn a magnet for discerning diners. Local chef Richard Treacher has created a small but varied menu based on locally sourced produce. At lunchtime you'll find local pork sausages with a chive mash and gravy along with traditional steak & ale pie, sandwiches and other old favourites. In the evening, amongst the main courses you'll find a 21-day matured sirloin steak, tasty lamb chops and spicy vegetable enchiladas. To accompany your meal, there's a choice of up to 4 real ales, a selection of Belgian beers, and a well-chosen wine list of vintages from around the world. Food is served every evening except Sunday from 6pm to 9pm; and at lunchtimes, Wednesday to Saturday.

124 THE CARPENTERS ARMS

Fangfoss, East Yorkshire YO42 5QG
Tel: 01759 368222

If it is excellent food, real ales and a friendly welcome you want,
that is exactly what awaits you here at The Carpenters Arms.
Real ale lovers will be in their element with John Smiths Cask
the regular and two rotating guest ales – one nationally brewed and one locally brewed. The child-
friendly pub is run by Jon and Emma Szpakowski who have been the leaseholders here for more
than five years. Such is the popularity of the hearty traditional food served it is advisable to book
at all times. Food is served 12pm – 2pm Tuesday – Thursday, 5.30pm – 9pm Monday – Thursday,
12pm – 9pm Friday – Saturday and 12pm – 3pm on Sundays.

125 THE FLEECE INN

47 Main Street, Bishop Wilton, York YO42 1RU
Tel: 01759 368251
e-mail: info@thefleeceinn.co.uk
website: www.thefleeceinn.info

Standing at the heart of the unspoilt village of Bishop
Wilton in the Yorkshire Wolds, **The Fleece Inn** is a fine
old traditional hostelry with a wealth of atmosphere.
Mine hosts are Lisa and Ian Rushworth who arrived here in
the summer of 2010, bringing with them some 15 years of
experience in the hospitality business, mainly in
Yorkshire.

Lisa is an accomplished cook and her menu offers a
very varied range of dishes, all based on local produce
wherever possible. Food is served from noon until 2pm,
and from 6pm to 9pm, Tuesday to Saturday; and from
noon until 3pm on Sundays when there's a choice of
traditional roasts. Meals can be enjoyed either inside, on
the patio or in the beer garden. Real ale lovers will be
pleased to find a choice of 4 different brews - three from

Yorkshire (Black Sheep, John Smith's and Tetley's) plus a rotating locally-brewed guest ale. The
Fleece also offers quality accommodation in 4 en suite rooms set around a courtyard and away
from the main inn. All the rooms are on the ground floor and a hearty breakfast is included in the
tariff.

126 SLEDMERE HOUSE

Sledmere, Driffield, East Yorkshire YO25 3XG
Tel: 01377 236637
website: www.driffield.co.uk

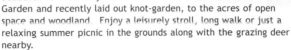

There has been a **manor house** at Sledmere since medieval times. The present house was built in 1751 by Sir Christopher Sykes 2nd Baronet. Sir Christopher employed fellow Yorkshireman Joseph Rose, the most famous English plasterer of his day, to execute the decoration of Sledmere. Rose's magnificent work, unique in his career, and parkland planned by 'Capability Brown', have combined to create one of Yorkshire's hidden treasures.

The gardens and parkland can offer enjoyment for all, from the beautiful 18th Century walled Rose Garden and recently laid out knot-garden, to the acres of open space and woodland. Enjoy a leisurely stroll, long walk or just a relaxing summer picnic in the grounds along with the grazing deer nearby.

When the need for refreshment arises try something different in the Bistro-Café', anything from a light snack to a delicious meal, before you move on to the Exhibition Centre, Waggoners Museum, the village, Monuments and Church. Sledmere's famous pipe organ is played for Visitors – Wednesday, Friday and Sunday 2.00pm – 4.00pm

127 THE POPPY SEED

13 North Bar Within, Beverley, East Yorkshire HU17 8AP
Tel: 01482 871598

Located just down the road from Beverley's medieval gateway, **The Poppy Seed** is an outstanding delicatessen and coffee shop serving quality home-cooked food prepared to the highest standards. It is owned and run by the mother and daughter team of Rita Jones and Kate Johnson who came here in 2001 after some years cooking for weddings at a stately home.

In their ground floor delicatessen you'll find an extensive choice of quiches, patisseries, traditional puddings and picnic 'kits'. The deli items are also served in the two restaurant areas, along with a variety of other dishes. These include a choice of breakfasts, served daily until 11am, an extensive selection of sandwiches and paninis with fillings ranging from rare roast beef to goat's cheese & beetroot; salads and daily specials such as aromatic lamb meatballs. The huge choice of drinks includes a dozen different teas, coffees and iced coffees; pure fruit juices, home-made lemonade, and fresh fruit smoothies and milk shakes.

The Poppy Seed is open from 9am to 5pm, Monday to Saturday, plus Sundays during the season, and is licensed. Rita and Kate are also happy to provide outside catering. "We can cater for any size - from whole quiches to whole parties!"

128 HORNSEA FOLK MUSEUM

11 Newbegin, Hornsea, East Yorkshire HU18 1AB
Tel: 01964 533443

Established in 1978, the excellent **Hornsea Folk Museum** occupies a Grade II listed former farmhouse where successive generations of the Burn family lived for 300 years up until 1952. Their way of life, the personalities and characters who influenced the develop-ment of the town or found fame in other ways, are explored in meticulously restored rooms brimming with furniture, decorations, utensils and tools of the Victorian period. The kitchen, parlour, bedroom, have fascinating displays of authentic contemporary artefacts, and the museum complex also includes a laundry, workshop, blacksmith's shop and a barn stocked with vintage agricultural implements.

129 HARE & HOUNDS

1 North Street, Leven, East Yorkshire HU17 5NF
Tel: 01964 542523
e-mail: andy_gillyon@btconnect.com
website: www.levenhareandhounds.co.uk

Located in the picturesque little village of Leven, a convenient distance from the A165 between Beverley and Bridlington, is the beautiful **Hare & Hounds**; an Inn which dates from the early 19th Century. The owners, who have run the Inn with growing success for the last two years, have 24 years experience in the business; and this is clear to see through the high quality of service and delicious food. The Hare & Hounds has become very popular with visitors to the area and locals alike; being known as the place to go for a home-cooked hearty meal, real ale and friendly hospitality.

The menu, which is made from locally-sourced ingredients and cooked to order, has a tasty traditional flavour which will please all of the family. Favourite dishes include Whitby scampi & chips, with garden or mushy peas, and home-made steak pie topped with short crust pastry served with a choice of potatoes and fresh seasonal vegetables. The menu also includes a great range of vegetarian dishes, cuts of meat from the grill, build your own burgers with your favourite ingredients, and lite bites.

The outside seating is lovely on a sunny day. Food served Tuesday-Saturday 12noon-8pm and Sunday (for lunch) 12noon-5pm.

Garden Centres and Nurseries

www.findSOMEWHERE.co.uk
For people who want to explore the United Kingdom

130 BURTON CONSTABLE HALL

Burton Constable, Hull, Yorkshire HU11 4LN
Tel: 01964 562400
website: www.burtonconstable.com

Burton Constable is a large Elizabethan mansion set in a 300 acre park with nearly 30 rooms open to the public. The interiors of faded splendour are filled with fine furniture, paintings and sculpture, a library of 5,000 books and a remarkable 18th century 'cabinet of curiosities' which contains fossils, natural history specimens and the most important collections of scientific instruments to be found in any country house. Occupied by the Constable family for over 400 years, the house still maintains the atmosphere of a home. The superb 18th and 19th century interiors include a Gallery, Dining and Drawing Rooms, Bedrooms, Chapel and Chinese Room. A total of 30 rooms are open to view and these include some fascinating 'below stairs' areas such as an intriguing Lamp Room.

As part of the exhibition project on Work & Play: Life on The Yorkshire Country House Estate, the skeleton of a sixty-foot long sperm whale has been put on display in the Great Hall at Burton Constable. The Burton Constable Whale was stranded on the Holderness coast in 1825, and the skeleton was brought to the park at Burton Constable where it was put on public display. The Burton Constable Whale was a source of inspiration for the American novelist Hermann Melville and appears in his famous novel: Moby Dick.

Outside the house there are gardens with statues, a delightful orangery ornamented with coade stone, a stable block and wild fowl lakes set in 300 acres of parkland landscaped by 'Capability' Brown in the 1770's.

131 WRYGARTH INN

Station Road, Great Hatfield, Hornsea,
East Yorkshire HU11 4UY
Tel: 01964 533300
website: www.wrygarthinn.co.uk

The picturesque village of Great Hatfield in East
Yorkshire is home to the popular **Wrygarth Inn.** Just a
short drive from Hornsea between the coast road and
the B1243, the inn is conveniently located for those
exploring the Yorkshire coast, although it has become
a destination pub in itself.

Dating back to the 18th century in parts, the inn
manages to retain an old country home regality,
however it underwent a large refurbishment in 2008
when its present owners Ray and Sandra took over.
They worked hard to update both the décor and the
facilities so that guests can now dine and drink in
both comfort and style. Striking colours draw the eye
on feature walls, whilst cosy brown leather
armchairs and quirky nik naks create a truly chilled
out environment.

Open every day apart from Tuesdays, Ray and
Sandra offer up a fine selection of food and drink.
Ale lovers can content themselves with a guest ale
from one of the many Yorkshire Breweries, although
other lagers, wines and spirits are also available.
Food is served from 12-9pm on Mondays and
Wednesday to Saturday, and then from 12-8pm on
Sundays. Ray and Sandra believe that their food is
the reason they see so many repeat customers
through their doors each week. They aim to cater for
all tastes and budgets, with dishes ranging from a
daily carvery to succulent fillet steak or a good old
fashioned homemade steak pie. They also offer a
novel 'Beat the Clock' meal deal where the earlier
you dine the cheaper your meal; here the early bird
really does get the worm. Desserts at the Wrygarth
are not to be missed either, with sumptuous
selections of crème brulees and moist chocolate
fudge cakes made from scratch each day. Children
have their own special menu, although dining is not
the only attraction for children here...

Ray and Sandra operate a small crazy golf course
at the back of the inn, particularly popular
throughout the summer months as well as an indoor
children's play area, conference suite and corner shop . Guests can also pop into the inn's own
shop, selling all essential local and homemade produce from the area, perfect for those staying
nearby. Great for holidaymakers, Great Hatfield is just minutes from the Trans Pennine Trail with
many other areas of Outstanding Natural Beauty close by.

The inn also offers fantastic conference facilities, complete with air conditioning and a variety
of hassle free packages to cater for a variety of business and private functions, please call for
details.

132 GEORGE & DRAGON

1 High Street, Aldbrough, East Yorkshire HU11 4RP
Tel: 01964 527698
e-mail: trclayton@hotmail.com

Situated in the picturesque village of Aldbrough, the **George & Dragon** is a unique find. The premises dates from 1551 and is Grade II listed has, at various times through its long life, been a raucous coaching inn, a post inn, and even at one time a morgue! This fine 16th Century property brimming with history was, until this year, stood for quite some years empty and abandoned. Owners Tom and Lynda clearly saw the potential of such a gorgeous building, in equally breathtaking surroundings, and got to work carefully restoring it back to its former glory as an Inn. And

they haven't disappointed! Since opening, the George & Dragon has gone from strength to strength, and the compliments over the warm hospitality, and love of Lynda's cooking, have rushed in from both locals and visitors.

The accommodation, which is available all year round, is as cosy as you would expect from such a beautiful rustic building. There are two double rooms with en-suite, a spacious family room with en-suite, and one single room with a private bathroom; all lushly decorated and furnished. The prices for all of the rooms include a hearty breakfast, which is helpfully served at flexible times so you needn't miss out on a relaxing lay-in!

The delicious home-made food, which is served everyday, has been the secret to the George & Dragon's amazing success (that, and their real ales!). The inn offers a light lunch menu, and an extensive evening menu, as well as a specials board always full of the most delicious seasonal treats. Dishes include a range of juicy rump steaks, which include Surf & Turf, traditional scampi and chips, and a delicious vegetarian mushroom stroganoff with rice. For lunch you can order sandwiches, Panini's and jacket potatoes with your favourite filling and a fresh side salad or, if you just want a light bite, there are scones and toasted tea cakes which go perfectly with a hot pot of tea or coffee. Most popular is the George & Dragon's Sunday lunch with all the trimmings, which is brilliantly priced for families; it is always advised to book to avoid disappointment. Food is served 12noon-3pm and 5pm-9pm, seven days a week.

133 THE LIGHTHOUSE

Hull Road, Withernsea, East Yorkshire HU19 2DY
Tel: 01964 614834

Withernsea Lighthouse uniquely towers 127 feet above the town. The base of the lighthouse features many exhibits, R.N.L.I., H.M. Coastguard, Ships Bells, models and old photography recording the history of ship wrecks and the Withernsea lifeboats and heroic crews who saved 87 lives between 1862 and 1913 and the history of the Spurn lifeboats. Views from the lamproom are breathtaking, especially after climbing 144 steps. The cafe provides a welcome cup of tea and light refreshments. Souvenirs are on sale.

134 THE DEEP

Hull, Yorkshire HU1 4DP
Tel: 01482 381000
e-mail: info@thedeep.co.uk
website: www.thedeep.co.uk

Welcome to The Deep, one of the most spectacular aquariums in the world. This award-winning Yorkshire family attraction is home to 40 sharks and over 3,500 fish. The dramatic building designed by Sir Terry Farrell is located in Hull on the Humber Estuary, just an hour from York. The Deep is operated as a charity dedicated to increasing enjoyment and understanding of the world's oceans. Behind the scenes a team of dedicated marine biologists care for all of the animals at The Deep as well as carrying out vital research into the marine environment.

It first opened its doors in March 2002 and so far has welcomed over 2 million visitors from the UK and abroad. Using a combination of hands on interactives, audiovisual presentations and living exhibits it tells the story of the worlds oceans. Visitors will be taken on a journey from the beginning of time through the present day oceans to the icy darkness of a futuristic Deep-Sea research lab, Deep Blue one.

www.findSOMEWHERE.co.uk
For people who want to explore the United Kingdom

Places to Stay

135 THE TIGER INN

The Green, North Newbald, East Yorkshire YO43 4SA
Tel: 01430 827759 Mobile: 07896 764108
e-mail: kimberley-tiger@unicombox.co.uk

North Newbald is a delightful small village located just off the A1034 about 4 miles south of Market Weighton. It has a spacious village green and, overlooking it, a fine old hostelry, **The Tiger Inn,** parts of which date back to the 1700s. This is very much a family-run pub with Kimberley, her mother Dee and Kimberley's daughter Jasmin all involved in the enterprise.

The pub is well-known locally for its excellent home-cooked food. Dishes include old pub favourites such as home-made beef & ale pie, cottage pie, and battered "Whale" & chips.

Baguettes, burgers and jacket potatoes are also available. Customers can eat throughout the pub, at picnic tables overlooking the green, or on the patio to the rear. Food is served from noon until 2pm, Tuesday to Sunday; and from 5pm to 8pm, Tuesday to Saturday. A wide choice of beverages is available, including wines by the glass and 3 real ales.

Recently re-decorated and with a new Games Room, The Tiger hosts a Pub quiz on Tuesday evenings and also occasional live music. Children are welcome. Payment is by cash or cheque but there is an ATM on the premises.

136 WARDS HOTEL

Main Road, Gilberdyke, Brough,
East Yorkshire HU15 2SL
Tel/Fax: 01430 440356
e-mail: wardshotel@live.co.uk
website: www.wardshotel.webs.com

One of the best public houses in this area and beyond,
Wards Hotel enjoys a fine reputation for its food, ale
and hospitality. It stands alongside the B1230 in the
village of Gilberdyke, just a short distance from
junction 38 of the M62.

Mine hosts, Andrew and Kelly Hirst, arrived here in
the autumn of 2009, bringing with them some 20 years
experience in the hospitality business. Andrew is a
gifted chef and his menu offers a good selection of
traditional favourites based on locally reared meat and
locally grown vegetables. Yorkshire puddings are
strongly featured, along with Whitby breaded scampi, a
Wards Hotel pie of the day, or fish of the day, chicken
tikka masala and a vegetarian broccoli cheese bake
served with garlic bread. Also available are burgers, sandwiches, jacket potatoes and kids' meals.
The regular menu is supplemented by daily specials. Food is served from 12pm to 7pm, Tuesday to
Saturday. On Sundays, there is a set roast menu offering a selection of roast meats, Monday is
poker night, Tuesday evenings the Curry Club offers a choice of up to 6 curry dishes at very
reasonable prices, Wednesday brings with it sizzling steak night, Thursday is Kelly's £50 quiz night
with a free supper and on Saturday there is a disco/karokee. The hotel also has sky tv.

To accompany your meal, there's an extensive choice of beverages, with a good selection of
wines and whiskeys alike as well as up to 4 real ales with Timothy Taylor Landlord as the regular
brew. The inn is open from 4pm on Monday and then all day throughout the rest of the week;
children are welcome and are kept entertained by the play area. Payment is by cash or cheque
only.

137 THE ROYAL OAK

Holme Road, Portington, Howden,
East Yorkshire DN14 7NA
Tel: 01430 430563

The Royal Oak is found on the main A614 road on the way to Portington, rather than within the village itself. This traditional Yorkshire pub acts as a convenient spot to enjoy a quiet drink or scrumptious meal. Its licensee Neil O'Driscoll has been running it for the past two years, serving hand pulled real ale amongst a good selection of other soft and alcoholic beverages. In the summer months Neil opens from 9am-12 midday for breakfast and then stays open for the rest of the day serving both food and drink. In the winter months however, the inn is open every session and all day on weekends.

The menu at the Royal Oak is devised by Neil's experienced head chef Luke. He creates his dishes using as much fresh locally sourced produce as possible, giving a real Yorkshire taste to the food. Traditional dishes include homemade steak and Martson's smooth ale pie, pan fried liver and bacon, fish and chips and cheesy bangers and mash, not to mention a hearty selection of steaks from the grill. Vegetarians can enjoy dishes like wild mushroom asparagus risotto and lasagne, whilst children have their own menu. All major credit cards taken.

138 JAY JAY'S

11-15 Vicar Lane, Howden, East Yorkshire DN14 7DP
Tel: 01430 432924

Jay Jay's is a superb cafe bar and bistro style live music venue; possibly Howden's best kept secret, tucked in just off of the lively town's main thoroughfare. The slightly traditional red brick exterior, with pretty hanging baskets of blooms, conceals an effortlessly cool and contemporary cafe bar interior; the brainchild of owner Jo. Her concept, to combine hearty home-made food in a relaxed atmosphere, with live music and regular events, has gone down very well in Howden, and Jay Jay's has becoming a bustling "place to be" in the town. The large cosy sofas and friendly staff make this an ideal place to come for a lazy lunch, or come night-time, when the energy goes up a few notches, you can enjoy the delicious food with live entertainment (both local and from further afield) and possibly the nicest crowd of people in town.

Jay Jay's is not just about style (this is not just another trendy wine bar!), and you will find real substance here on the menu. This includes a tantalising selection of home-made tapas, great for a light bite for one or a snack to share; among the tapas dishes are delights such as chorizo in red wine, mixed sea food in a tomato and garlic sauce, and a choice of succulent tiger prawns or chicken with a white wine and garlic sauce. Pizzas are a real favourite here, with a wide selection of tempting toppings, coming fresh from Jay Jay's own stone baked oven. There are also pasta dishes, burgers, chunky homemade chips, and a lovely spread of homemade cakes to choose from; there certainly is something for everyone here! Naturally, all dishes are prepared and cooked on demand, fresh from the kitchen. The next new addition to Jay Jay's will be a beautiful rear courtyard, built from Italian stone, which is certainly going to add to the bar's charm. The cafe bar is open everyday from 12 noon until late, with food being served 12 noon until around 7pm; be aware that it could get busy at the weekends!

139 THE FERRYBOAT INN

Boothferry Bridge, Howden, East Yorkshire DN14 7ED
Tel: 01430 430300 Website: www.theferryboatinn.co.uk

The outstanding and historic **Ferryboat Inn** stands in a picturesque
location, a short drive out of Howden towards Goole. New licensees Ian and Sandra have, in
their short time here, given the Ferryboat a new lease of life, with the winning combination of
their years of experience and excellent hospitality. The menu is a delight; home cooked to
order, and locally sourced where possible. The Sunday Carvery (between 12-3pm) has been a
great hit, as has the Saturday and Sunday breakfasts (7-10am) which are popular with anglers
who fish nearby. The delicious menu is served daily 12noon-9pm. There is plenty of off road
parking, and a lovely patio and beer garden for sunny days.

140 THE YORKSHIRE WATERWAYS MUSEUM

Dutch River Side, Goole, East Yorkshire DN14 5TB
Tel: 01405 768730
website: www.waterwaysmuseum.org.uk

The Yorkshire Waterways Museum offers an extensive collection which tells the story of the
Port of Goole, the transportation of coal, the lives of barge families, and the boat building
tradition of our ancestors. The economic and social purpose of the museum it to be an
attraction and archive for visitors and to offer friendship, dignity and training to disadvantaged
people to enable them to gain the skills and confidence to be economically and socially active.
The emphasis is on team-work organised to meet the expectations of visitors.

Registered in 1995 and extended in 2001. The
Yorkshire Waterways Museum celebrates the
social and economic history of the canal port of
Goole and its associated compartment boats and
hoists, and present day links with the Humber,
Europe and the Yorkshire river and canal
network. More than 7000 documents,
photographs and artefacts comprise a ollection
and archive whose largest object is the working
Tom Pudding tug Wheldale.

The museum plans to improve the heritage
value of the existing collection by conserving and
interpreting large objects which have not yet
been part of the current public displays.

141 HENRY MOORE INSTITUTE

74 The Headrow, Leeds, West Yorkshire LS1 3AH
General Enquiries: 0113 246 7467   Information Line: 0113 234 3158
Fax: 0113 246 1481
website: www.henry-moore-fdn.co.uk

The Henry Moore Institute in Leeds is a unique resource devoted exclusively to sculpture, with a programme comprising exhibitions, collections and research. The centre was established by the Henry Moore foundation as a partnership with Leeds city council in 1982. In 1993 it moved from Leeds city art gallery to the newly converted Henry Moore institute next door.

Whereas the Henry Moore foundation at Moore's home in Perry Green in Hertfordshire devotes its activities exclusively to the work of Henry Moore himself, in Leeds they are concerned with the subject of sculpture in general; both historic and contemporary, and of any nationality. Though some exhibitions may travel from elsewhere, most are generated from within, and draw on research activity or collection development. The content of the collections is substantially British and is designed to represent a cross section of material which all, in different ways, represents and documents sculptural activity.

142 THWAITE MILLS WATERMILL

Thwaite Lane, Leeds, Yorkshire LS10 1RP
Tel: 01132 496453

One of the last remaining examples of a water-powered mill in Britain, **Thwaite Mills** is situated in beautiful riverside surroundings just two miles from Leeds city centre. Visit Thwaite Mills to discover a unique part of Leeds' industrial heritage. Explore the mills and island to discover the importance of water power. Be guided around the mill buildings to see the industrial processes of former years. Marvel at the amazing noises and movements as industrial machines make the mill buildings vibrate.

Have fun at Thwaite Mills on special event days. See 'Scotch Derrick' the steam crane and 'Titan' the historic tractor in action. Look out for the regular train demonstration and 'Steaming Up' days, as well as 'Family Fun Days'. Bring all the family during the school holidays to enjoy the range of outdoor games and Victorian toys available in the paddock.

Enjoy lunch at one of the mills three picnic sites situated on the scenic riverside location. Take a walk around the island to spot the wildlife often seen close to Thwaite Mills, including over 200 species of birds and butterflies. Make the most of the riverside location by exploring part of the 'Trans Pennine Trail' along the River Aire. For the more adventurous, walk from Leeds City Centre south along the river past the Royal Armouries until you reach Thwaite Mills Watermill.

143 HAREWOOD HOUSE

Moor House, Harewood Estate,
Harewood, Leeds,
West Yorkshire LS17 9LQ
Tel: 0113 2181010
e-mail: info@harewood.org
website: www.harewood.org.uk

Designed in 1759 by John Carr, **Harewood House**
is the home of the Queen's cousin, the Earl of
Harewood. His mother, HRH Princess Mary,
Princess Royal lived at Harewood for 35 years
and much of her Royal memorabilia is still displayed.

The House, renowned for its stunning architecture and exquisite Adam interiors, contains a rich
collection of Chippendale furniture, fine porcelain and outstanding art collections from Italian
Renaissance masterpieces and Turner watercolours to contemporary works. The Victorian
kitchen, contains "the best collection of noble household copperware in the country" giving
visitors a glimpse into an essential area of yesteryear's below-stairs life.

The inspiring grounds, enfold gardens which include a restored parterre terrace, oriental rock
garden, walled garden, lakeside and woodland walks, a bird garden and for youngsters, the
thrills and excitement of the adventure playground!

Throughout the season Harewood hosts a number of special events including open air
concerts, theatre performances, craft festivals, car rallies and much more! Harewood House is
easily accessible and is just 20 minutes drive from Leeds City Centre or 45 minutes from York.

144 THE CROWN HOTEL

128 High Street, Boston Spa, nr Wetherby,
West Yorkshire LS23 6PW
Tel: 01937 842006
e-mail: enquiries@bostonspacrown.co.uk
website: www.bostonspacrown.co.uk

Situated in the popular village of Boston Spa, a short drive from
bustling Wetherby and conveniently close to the junction 45 of
the A1 (M), **The Crown Hotel** is the perfect place to call home
while you are on holiday. The food served here in the cosy bar
and restaurant is full of flavour and yet quite unpretentious;
just how owners Theresa and Paul like it!

The traditional Sunday lunch is the cornerstone meal of the
week for many families and couples, and The Crown Hotel will
not disappoint with their extensive Sunday menu, certain to
satisfy everyone's tastes. With dishes such as Chef's
homemade chicken liver pate served with toast & caramelised
onions, roast leg of British pork with apple sauce & stuffing,
and homemade apple pie, who could resist? All food is fresh and cooked to order, and where
possible it is locally sourced. Peruse the specials board for the best seasonal dishes. Food is served
Monday to Saturday 12-2pm and 6-9pm, and Sunday12-3pm.

Being a short drive from York, the horse racing at Wetherby, and many of the most beautiful
and historic sights in the region, this is a perfect place to be your base while holidaying. The six
homely rooms here also have a great tariff which includes breakfast.

145 THE ARABIAN HORSE

Main Street North, Aberford,
North Yorkshire LS25 3AA
Tel: 01132 813312

Quality is the keynote at the **Arabian Horse**, making it a winner not just with the local community but with lovers of good food and good hospitality from many miles around. The pub is equally handsome from the outside and within, where a huge open fire in the beautifully restored 18th century fireplace keeps things cosy even in the coldest months. Since they took over here three years ago, owners Sarah and Andy Ridgeon have made the Arabian Horse a renowned establishment, with the warmth of the welcome and the excellence of Sarah's cooking. Her menu offers both light bites (nachos, chips, chicken strips with a mayonnaise dip) and more hearty familiar favourites, as well a choice of vegetarian main courses and other tempting specials. The delicious traditional roast here on Sundays is not to be missed, and is a real treat for the whole family.

Opening hours for food are Tuesday to Saturday 12pm to 2pm, and the Sunday lunch is served 12pm-4pm. Booking is advisable for all meals. The Arabian Horse stands in the village of Aberford, five miles east of Leeds, and easily reached from the M1 (J47), A1 (J45), A64 or B1217. Cash only.

146 THE LEGGERS

Stable Buildings, Saville Town Wharf,
Mill Street East, Dewsbury,
West Yorkshire WF12 9BD
Tel: 01924 502846

The Leggers was originally a hay loft that stored food for horses in the area that pulled the canal boats on the nearby Dewsbury Canal Basin, but was converted in 1998 into a beautiful inn by John Smithson and the present owner, Gordon Lambert's father. Together the team dedicate themselves to serving both locals and visitors to the pretty town of Dewsbury in their attractive wharf side location.

Opening all day every day, John and Gordon are proud to offer up to six real ales counting Tiger, Rooster and Leeds within their regulars. Real cider and wheat beer is also available on tap alongside a host of fine wines and spirits.

Food is available from 12-8pm each day, cooked fresh to order using the best in local produce. The ever changing menu is displayed on the blackboard, offering great seasonal food throughout the year. Parties of over twelve need to book, but are well accommodated. Guests can dine within the rustic styled interior, or enjoy a spot overlooking the canal basin outside in the summer months. Children welcome up to 8pm.

147 RED HOUSE

Oxford Road, Gomersal, Cleckheaton,
West Yorkshire BD19 4JP
Tel: 01274 335100

This delightful house now looks very much as it would
have done in Charlotte Bronte's time when she used it as
a model for the Briarmains of her novel *Shirley*. **Red
House** was the home of her close friend Mary Taylor and
Charlotte stayed here often. Wander around this wool
merchant's home where each room brings you closer to the 1830s, from the elegant parlour to
the stone-flagged kitchen with its Yorkshire range, jelly moulds and colourful crockery. Then
take a stroll through the re-created 19th century garden with its shaped flower beds and
decorative ironwork; even the plants and shrubs are in keeping with the period.

Explore Charlotte Bronte's Spen Valley connections and her friendships with Mary Taylor and
Ellen Nussey in *The Secret's Out* exhibition in the barn. What did local people say when they
discovered that Charlotte had based some of her characters in *Shirley* on them? And how did
Charlotte, Mary and Ellen react to society's strict view of 'a woman's place'?

Move along to the 20th Century and the *Spen Valley Stories* exhibition in the restored
cartsheds. Relive schooldays, Teddy Boys, dance marathons and street parties through the
pictures and mementoes of local residents. The latest audio technology lets them tell their own
stories while you browse through historical photos on a user-friendly, touchscreen terminal.

And, before you leave, call in to the museum shop. With its period toys, books, gifts and
preserves, you'll be more than tempted to take home a taste of the past!

148 EMPORIO ITALIA

7 Railway Road, Ilkley, West Yorkshire LS29 8HQ
Tel: 01943 430005
e-mail: samwagstaff@hotmail.co.uk
website: www.emporio-italia.co.uk

Owner-chef Luigi brings an authentic taste of Italy to Ilkley in
his **Emporio Italia** just off the main street. Luigi, a fine chef
with many years' experience, is a passionate believer in fresh
home cooking, and the regions, the seasons, the flavours and
the traditions of his homeland all combine in the fine dishes
prepared by the talented team in the kitchen. In surroundings
reminiscent of a neighbourhood *ristorante* in Italy, the menus
provide a wide and tempting variety of meat, poultry, fish and
vegetarian dishes, some of them inspired by Luigi's
grandmother's recipes. The main menu is supplemented by
daily specials that might be anything from lentil soup and
tonno e fagioli to chicken saltimbocca, pepper steak and
Tuscan lamb, as well as a number of pasta dishes. Apart from
the main restaurant menu the *stuzzicheria* offers nibbles of
pasta, cured meats, salads, cheese and olives, and the
salumeria sells a variety of Italian meats and delicatessen items to take away.

The restaurant is open from 10 to 3 and from 7 till late (from 6 Friday and Saturday). Closed
Mondays. No bookings at lunchtime, but reservations are recommended in the evening. A sister
restaurant is at 3a Mill Bridge, Shipton. Tel: 01756 793357.

149 MANOR HOUSE MUSEUM

Castle Yard, Ilkley, West Yorkshire LS29 9DT
Tel: 01943 600066

The Manor House is a very old house dating back to the Middle Ages with later alterations and additions; the Housebody is furnished. It stands within the area of the Roman fort, Olicana, and has on show artefacts excavated locally. Other local history material relates to the expansion of Ilkley starting with the spa in Victorian times. The upper gallery is devoted to temporary exhibitions of mainly fine and decorative art but with some social history. Programme of concerts, lectures and workshops.

150 KORKS WINE BAR AND BRASSERIE

40 Bondgate, Otley, West Yorkshire LS21 1AD
Tel: 01943 462020
e-mail: eat@korks.co.uk
website: www.korks.co.uk

Just two minutes walk from the centre of town in Bondgate lies **Korks Wine Bar and Brasserie**. With a fine reputation for delivering excellent food and hospitality on every visit, it is a popular place to dine and drink. Chris Payne has been running the brasserie for 29 years along with Head Chef Michael Pickard for the past five years. Open from Tuesday to Saturday for drinks until late and serving food from 12-2pm Tues-Sat and 12-2:30pm on Sundays, from 6:30-10pm Tues-Thurs and 6-10pm Fri-Sunday.

All produce is sourced locally and cooked fresh to order. The food is always exquisite with dishes like roasted salmon and fresh crab crust with spicy noodles, king scallops and crayfish risotto, beer braised oxtail roast roots with mash and oyster fritters, slow cooked belly pork with butternut squash puree, award winning bangers and mash and juicy rib eye steaks. Starters, sides and vegetarian dishes are all created with equal care. Proving ever popular is the early bird menu where two or three course can be enjoyed at a very reasonable price. Guests can dine or drink within the bars sleek interior or in the quaint courtyard to the rear, where the sounds of the bar's piano often trickles out to fill the summer air.

152 EAT! IN HORSFORTH

157 New Road Side, Horsforth, West Yorkshire LS18 4DR
Tel: 0113 239 0966

Just one minute from the main Leeds ring road, **Eat! In Horsforth** serves a wide selection of snacks and meals from early in the morning through to lunchtime. George, Judith and Kim offer a great choice for breakfast, and other popular orders run from BLT and roast beef sandwiches to jacket potatoes, burgers, omelettes, salads, scampi and buffet lunches. The staff are always happy to see children, and a high chair is available for tinies. Books and crayons make Saturdays a real treat for youngsters. Most items can be orderd to atke away, and telephone orders are welcome. Service hours are 7am to 2pm Monday to Friday, 8am to 1.30pm Saturday. Close Sunday.

151 THE DROP INN

29 Town Street, Guiseley, West Yorkshire LS20 9DT
Tel: 01943 874967
e-mail: jenny.osborne123@btinternet.com
website: www.thedropinnpub.com

The Drop Inn is found within the quiet town of Guiseley in West Yorkshire. Its old fashioned exterior adorned by hundreds of glorious flowering baskets suggests it's much older than it really is. Although the inn has been in place for hundreds of years, its frontage was knocked down and rebuilt in the 1960's. It has previously been under various names containing the 'Drop' portion of the name but stands today in its simplest and most successful form.

It was taken over two years ago by Jenny, Marc and their daughters Laura, Robyn and Hayley who have given the inn a real lease of life and – according to the locals – given them their beloved pub back. Open from 5pm on Mondays, both sessions on weekdays and all day on weekends the inn is usually fairly busy with a good mix of locals and visitors, owing to Guiseley's convenient halfway location between Bradford, Leeds and the Yorkshire moors and Dales.

The family offer up a good selection of real ales, lagers, spirits and wines; with guest appearances from local breweries each week. Jenny has also ensured that guests always have a great selection of food to choose from, creating a variety of main and snack menus served between 11-2pm and 6-8:30pm Tuesday to Saturday. The main menu offers up a range of starters and salads to include breaded mushrooms, homemade soup, pate, potato wedges, Cajun chicken salad and a traditional Ploughman's. Main courses include a tender steak pie, homemade lasagne, traditional fish and chips, rich tikka masala, homely pasta bake and of course Whitby scampi and chips. Throughout the day a snack menu is also available with a range of filled baguettes and jacket potatoes, alongside all your takeaway favourites such a burgers, curly fries, cheesy chips and snack platters with chicken wings, onion rings and a selection of dips. Although there is always plenty to choose from, Jenny is always happy to cook up something else if you don't fancy anything from the menu and she has the ingredients in the larder. On Sundays between 12-4pm, her traditional carvery is hard to resist with a choice of meats and all the trimmings. Due to levels of demand, Jenny has also introduced her carvery on Wednesdays too, but also offers a range of other pensioner's specials on Tuesdays, Wednesdays and Thursdays.

Every week there is a great range of family entertainment available, with quiz night on Tuesdays from 8:30pm, Jazz nights on the 1st and 3rd Wednesdays of each month, and South African dining on the 1st and 3rd Saturday of each month.

153 COBBLES AND CLAY - THE ART CAFE

60 Main Street, Haworth, West Yorkshire BD22 8DP
Tel: 01535 644218
e-mail: info@cobblesandclay.co.uk
website: www.cobblesandclay.co.uk

Nestled within the pretty town of Howarth, **Cobbles and Clay** opens seven days a week from 9am-5pm. It's known for its unusual combination of delicious cafe catering and a pottery painting workshop, which guests are welcome to try their hand at during their visit. With seating for up to sixty guests both spread throughout the cafe and the charming rear courtyard, everyone's welcome. Guests can choose their own piece of pottery from the gallery and paint it with their own personal design. The team then pop the pot in the kiln to fire the glaze, and you can take your pot home with you or have it posted at no additional cost. Ever popular, guests can buy these sessions as gift vouchers, or perhaps purchase a pre-painted pot created by the talented owner, Jill Ross.

Jill does much more than painting pots however, she also runs the cafe side of the business which focuses on serving scrumptious and healthy food all day long. By using the best in fresh local produce and supporting organic and fair trade alliances Jill aims to remind people how good food should taste. Desserts are all homemade and include a variety of cakes, pastries and scones. The premises is also fully licensed and sells a neat selection of organic wines and beers with additive soft drinks, real dairy milkshakes, smoothies and old fashioned presses. Everything is served on Jill's own painted crockery – what else?!

154 BRONTË PARSONAGE MUSEUM

Haworth, Keighley, West Yorkshire BD22 8DR
Tel: 01535 642323
website: www.bronte.org.uk

Charlotte, Emily and Anne Brontë, were the authors of some of the greatest books in the English language.

Haworth Parsonage was their much loved home and *Jane Eyre*, *Wuthering Heights* and *The Tenant of Wildfell Hall* were all written here.

Set between the unique village of Haworth and the wild moorland beyond, this homely Georgian house still retains the atmosphere of the Brontës time. The rooms they once used daily are filled with the Brontës furniture, clothes and personal possessions.

Here you can marvel at the handwriting in their tiny manuscript books, admire Charlotte's wedding bonnet and imagine meeting Emily's pets from her wonderfully lifelike drawings. Gain an insight into the place and objects that inspired their work.

155 DALESBANK HOLIDAY PARK

Low Lane, Silsden, Keighley, West Yorkshire BD20 9JH
Tel: 01535 653321

Hidden away on the edge of the Yorkshire dales is **Dalesbank Holiday Park**. A true 'gateway to the Dales,' the holiday park is an ideal base for exploring the surrounding areas which include West Yorkshire, Bronte Country, Haworth and the acres of industrial heritage in the wool towns at Skipton and beyond.

The park itself was formerly a working farm, but thirty years ago its owner Meadmore Preston decided to change the farm's fortune and create the holiday park as it's known today. Meadmore himself is a real character and has been working the site for the last 56 years, offering a traditional Yorkshire welcome to all. The park is set in 20 acres of beautiful rolling Yorkshire countryside, and beyond its boundaries are another 100 acres of unspoilt land. Within the park, there are outstanding facilities for bed and breakfast, caravan and camping, with a function room and restaurant/ bar also available.

Dalesbank Lodge is home to the park's bed and breakfast accommodation. It encompasses five family sized rooms, each with an en suite bathroom and shower, and a further selection of rooms sleeping between 3-6 people in a variety of twin style and double rooms. Meadmore also offers one suite fully adapted for disabled customers, also with its own en suite bathroom. Each room is spacious with glorious views across the countryside, being set within the farm's old barn.

The caravan and campsite offers pitches for touring, static and motor homes, with ample winter storage and tent facilities also. The site opens from Easter to October, and encompasses electric hook ups and access to a shower and toilet block. In the summer months the large games area is a hive of activity; families and children playing alike.

Guests of both the bed and breakfast and the campsite are welcomed to use the park's restaurant and bar; 'Meadmore's Restaurant.' It's best known for its Sunday lunch, served from 12-2pm on a bookings only basis. Throughout the rest of the week the menu remains traditional with plenty of classic Yorkshire fayre, all deliciously cooked in a farmhouse style. The bar opens on demand, but is always stocked with a good choice of real ales, lagers, spirits and wines. The Clubhouse is also able to hold functions with up 200 guests, complete with dance floor and traditional catering options, including a magnificent hog roast.

For a real taste of the countryside, and all the friendly charm that goes with it; visit Meadmore and his beloved park.

156 BOLLING HALL MUSEUM

Bolling Hall Road, Bradford, West Yorkshire BD4 7LP
Tel: 01274 723057
website: www.bradfordmuseums.org.uk

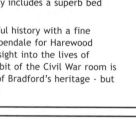

Bolling Hall offers visitors a fascinating journey through
the lives and times of the Bradford families for whom it
provided a home over five hundred years. Situated just a
mile from Bradford city centre and situated in a quiet,
leafy garden, Bolling Hall was for many years the seat of
two important land-owning families, the Bollings and the
Tempests. With parts of the building dating from the
Medieval, Bolling Hall is a rambling mixture of styles with
every nook and cranny packed with history. During the
Civil War the household supported the Royalist cause,
and the house provided a stronghold during the 'siege of

Bradford'. Rooms are furnished and decorated to give an accurate taste of life at different
periods of the house's history, and the fascinating furniture on display includes a superb bed
made for Harewood House by Thomas Chippendale.

Bolling Hall has been furnished in keeping with its long and eventful history with a fine
collection of period furniture, including a bed made by Thomas Chippendale for Harewood
House. Bedrooms are decorated by period, providing a fascinating insight into the lives of
wealthy families of the 16th, 17th and 18th Centuries. A central exhibit of the Civil War room is
Cromwell's death mask. Spend some time exploring a different side of Bradford's heritage - but
watch out for an appearance by the 'White Lady' in the Ghost Room!

157 SHIPLEY GLEN CABLE TRAMWAY

Baildon, Shipley, West Yorkshire BD17 5BN
Tel: 01274 589010
website: www.glentramway.co.uk

The Tramway, built in 1895, is situated near the World Heritage Site of
Saltaire, and the trams trundle up and down the quarter mile long narrow gauge tracks on
Britain's oldest working cable tramway. They run up the wooded hillside, studded with glacial
rocks, to enable visitors to reach the delights of Shipley Glen. The area is a popular visitor
attraction, with pub, cafe, Countryside Centre, small souvenir shop and replica Edwardian shop
which sells many nostalgic items. A museum displays photos and memorabilia of the tramway and
the glen. Open most weekend afternoons throughout the year.

158 SHIBDEN HALL

Lister's Road, Halifax, West Yorkshire HX3 6XG
Tel: 01422 352246 Fax 01422 348440
e-mail shibden.hall@calderdale.gov.uk

For over 300 years this was the Lister's family home, but **Shibden
Hall** itself is even older, built in 1420. Generations have lived
and worked here and today the hall reflects this continual
development. The rooms, ranging from the 17th century to the 20th century, are set out as if
someone has just slipped out for a moment. There is the 17th century barn with its display of
carriages and the Folk Museum that shows how craftsmen worked in the 19th century.

159 BANKFIELD MUSEUM

Akroyd Park Boothtown Road, Halifax HX3 6HG
Tel: 01422 354823
e-mail: bankfield.museum@calderdale.gov.uk

Set in a wonderful Victorian millowner's house, Bankfield has a growing
reputation as a centre for textiles and contemporary craft. With its internationally important
collection of textiles, weird and wonderful objects from around the world, plus commissions by
leading makers and a varied programme of exhibtitions and activities, there is much to see and
enjoy. Don't miss the Toy Gallery; the Duke of Wellington's Regimental Museum and the Marble
Gallery, a new selling space for contemporary craft. Open: Tuesday to Saturday 10am - 5pm.
Sundays 2pm - 5pm Bank Holiday Mondays 10am - 5pm. Free admission.

161 THE OLD SHIP INN

34 Bethel Street, Brighouse,
West Yorkshire HD6 1JN
Tel: 01484 719543
e-mail: enquiries@theoldshipinnbrighouse.co.uk
website: www.theoldshipinnbrighouse.co.uk

Sitting proudly alongside one of Brighouse's main streets lies
the award winning The Old Ship Inn. Formerly known as The
Prince of Wales it was rebuilt in the 1930s keeping the
magnificent black and white facade but renamed The Old Ship
Inn in 2007. Experienced licensees Mark and Katie took over
here in 2008 and are eager to welcome locals and visitors to
enjoy a relaxing drink or freshly cooked meal. It is a haven for
real ale lovers and there are regularly seven real ales to enjoy.
Since Mark and Katie took over at the helm it has gone from
strength to strength and they serve excellent pub food every
day of the week. The menu offers plenty of choice with many
traditional dishes, including cider gammon, homemade fish pie
and beer battered fish and chips with bits. Food is served at
lunch time only, between midday and 2.30pm from Monday to
Saturday and between midday and 4pm on Sunday for
traditional Sunday lunches. A special steak offer is available
every Thursday and there are other deals too (ring for details).
The Old Ship Inn is child friendly and has won numerous
awards in recent years including the Halifax and Calderdale CAMRA Pub of the Year

160 BLAKELEY'S FISH AND CHIP RESTAURANT

1 Canal Street, Brighouse, West Yorkshire HD6 1JR
Tel: 01484 713907
e-mail: blakeleyfishshop@aol.com
website: www.blakeleysofbrighouse.co.uk

Located close to the canal at the heart of Brighouse, Blakeley's Fish and Chip Restaurant is a superb family run establishment waiting to take your order. Gary and Margaret Blakeley and their son Andrew have owned the restaurant since 1987 and it moved to its current location in 2003. They are extremely welcoming and like to make sure that every customer has a positive dining experience.

The manager here is Chris and he will ensure every diner has a pleasant and welcoming experience. The fully licensed restaurant is extremely popular with locals and attracts plenty of visitors through its doors every week. There is seating room for 50 diners inside with further tables outside, which are perfect for alfresco dining in the summer months. A lunch time special is offered between 11am and 3pm Monday - Friday (excluding Bank holidays), which is fish & chips, bread & butter and a tea or coffee. On the printed menu prawn cocktails, chicken goujons and battered garlic mushrooms are among the selection of starters. There is a wide range of fish dishes on the main menu including smoked haddock, sea bream and scampi. For those not keen on fish there are several chicken dishes as well as spicy chilli, spam and a choice of healthy meals such as steamed salmon fillet salad. There is a special menu for younger guests and for those with room left over there are plenty of tempting desserts for those with a sweet tooth. Ice cream sundaes, hot sponge pudding and brandy snap baskets are all reasonably priced. Such is the popularity of Blakeley's Fish and Chip Restaurant it is advisable to book on Wednesdays and Saturdays.

The restaurant's bar is well stocked and there are plenty of beverages and refreshments on sale. Whether it is an alcoholic drink you are after, a cold soft drink or a hot drink you are guaranteed to be looked after by this experienced team. A takeaway service is available from 11am to 9.30pm Monday – Friday, 11am – 8pm on Saturday and 1pm – 5pm on Sunday.

The Blakeley's welcome everyone to dine at their wonderful fish and chip restaurant and it is definitely advisable to check it out should you be looking for somewhere to eat in Brighouse. It has excellent disabled facilities, including wide doors and a disabled toilet. Major credit cards are taken.

162 THE CLOUGH HOUSE INN

129 Clough Inn, Rastrick, West Yorkshire HD6 3QL
Tel: 01484 512120
e-mail: martinbcockram@gmail.com

Dating back to the early 1800s, The Clough House Inn is a handsome old hostelry in the village of Rastrick in the Calder Valley. Martin and Lauren Cockram took over the running of the inn in March 2010, but Martin has been the head chef here for almost four years.

The menu is based on local produce wherever possible and professionally prepared. The choice ranges from a selection of grills, through perennial favourites such as giant beer-battered fish & chips or home-made pies, to lasagne or pan seared lamb's liver & dry cured bacon. Vegetarians are well catered for with choices including sweet potato, aubergine & spinach curry.

Children are unusually well-catered for with a menu that includes a 4oz Gammon steak, a sausage and tomato pasta, and a children's portion of fish and chips - these dishes are also available as smaller plates for smaller appetites!

In addition to the printed menus, which change seasonally, there are always daily specials listed on the blackboard, along with a choice of delicious home-made desserts. At Sunday lunchtime, a choice of roasts is served together with a few favourites from the regular menu.

Food is served every lunchtime and evening except Monday lunchtime unless it's a Bank Holiday. From Tuesday to Saturday, food is available from noon until 2.30pm; and from Monday to Saturday, from 5pm to 8.30pm. On Sundays, food is served from 12 noon until 8pm. Booking at the weekends is strongly recommended.

To accompany your meal, the well-stocked bar offers a wide range of beverages including 3 - 4 real ales – Red Bass is the local's favourite. In good weather, customers can enjoy their refreshments in the beer garden at the rear of the inn or in front of the roaring log fire which is a popular feature on cold days.

This popular hostelry has a pool room and on Sunday evenings hosts a Pub Quiz from 9pm - entry is free, a free supper is served and everyone is welcome.

For those with a lighter appetite there is a good range of hot and cold sandwiches and light bites including salads and 'posh things on toast'.

The inn accepts all major credit cards apart from American Express; there is good disabled access throughout. A visit to The Clough House Inn is a must, even if it's just to see their award winning flower displays!

163 THE DUKE OF YORK

Stainland Road, Stainland, Halifax,
West Yorkshire HX4 9HF
Tel: 01422 370217

Sitting proudly in the minster town of Halifax, originally built as 3 cottages in the mid-1700s, is a true gem indeed. The Duke of York is a spacious and impressive building, with striking décor using a mix of traditional and modern elements, including a stone-built bar, exposed brickwork and walls painted a deep red. The dining area has polished wood floors, stylish seating and floor-to-ceiling windows looking out over the attractive beer garden to the rolling countryside beyond. Attentive hosts Maria and James have been here since 2003, and their enthusiasm and drive has made the venture a great success.

The bar offers plenty of refreshments to accompany a meal, there are up to 4 real ales on tap, as well as the usual bottled beers, wines and soft drinks.

Wholesome home-cooked food is a speciality here. Maria is a creative cook and her dishes, based on top quality produce most of which is sourced locally, have something to cosset every palate. The appetising choices include superb home-made pies (Steak, Ale & Mushroom for example), sausage and mash, fisherman's pie and more. The lunchtime 'lite bite' menu features hearty favourites such as gammon with egg and chips and liver & sausage casserole with mash. Food is served from 6pm to 9pm, Mon and Tues; noon until 2pm, and 6pm to 9pm, Wed to Sat; and from noon until 9pm on Sun.

164 BRANCH ROAD INN

Saddleworth Road, Upper Greetland,
Halifax HX4 8NU
Tel: 01422 310152
e-mail: michael.ramsden@tesco.net
website: www.branchroadinn.com

Located in the pretty village of Upper Greetland, is the immensely popular Branch Road Inn. With over 20 years experience in the trade, professional chef, Michael Ramsden took over as licensee in 2009 and has been offering a warm welcome to all ever since.

The bar offers a selection of refreshments, including 3 real ales, a variety of fine wines, plenty of bottled beers and a selection of soft drinks.

With Michael in charge of the food, the menu offers some real treats. Every dish is home made and uses fresh ingredients from local suppliers. He uses only British beef and for those who are particularly peckish why not try the fabulous 16 oz Rump Steak, with all the trimmings, it is guaranteed to fill. With a regular changing specials board, diners can expect to enjoy a variety of dishes including; mushroom risotto served with side salad, chicken chasseur with new potatoes, and garlic bread and game pie with chips and vegetables.

Food is available Tuesday to Friday noon to 2pm and 5pm to 9pm, Saturday noon to 9pm and Sunday noon to 7pm. During the warmer months diners can enjoy their food outside in the pleasant rear patio. All major credit cards are accepted and children are made very welcome.

165 THE WORKS

12 Hollins Mill Lane, Sowerby Bridge, Halifax   HX6 2QG
Tel: 01422 834821
e-mail: info@theworkssowerbybridge.co.uk
website: www.theworkssowerbybridge.co.uk

'Real ale at it's best' describes The Works at Sowerby Bridge perfectly. Originally an old workshop, **The Works was created by Sara-Jo in 2005** into a lovely big space for people to meet and drink beer. Since that time, it has become so popular it has even been referred to as 'the hub of Sowerby Bridge'. There is no loud music or television which means guests can enjoy a refreshment accompanied by fine conversation with friends.

The bar offers up to 9 real ales and other than 3 Timothy Taylor brews, the rest come from Micro Breweries. Also on offer is The Works very own 'house beer' brewed especially for the establishment by the Phoenix Brewery aptly named 'Works Wonder Bitter'.

'Home cooked food – made with love' is the motto for The Work's menu. The food here is outstanding and uses quality ingredients to create simple, honest dishes that will leave you eager to return. Diners can expect to sample old favourites such as pork pie & peas, slow roasted lamb shank, ploughman's lunch and nachos. There are also more healthy options including grilled halloumi, smoked salmon, honey baked ham and Greek salad. The thick fresh cut sandwiches and baked potatoes are also extremely popular and come with a variety of fillings. For the regulars, a daily specials board offer a choice of 3 tasty dishes meaning there is always something new to enjoy. Food is served Monday to Friday, 12.00 until 2.30pm for lunch and 5pm until 8pm for tea. On Saturday food is served from noon until 5pm and Sundays from 10.30 until 2.30pm. It is advisable to book, especially for parties of 10 or more.

If you are stuck for something to do, The Works provides regular entertainment nights. Monday brings with it 'Phoebes night', Tuesday offers a quiz for all, Wednesday provides 'Gitas curry night' and Thursday winds down with some live acoustic music, the perfect way to welcome the weekend.

The Works is open Monday to Saturday 12:00 to 11pm and Sundays at 10:30 for brunch until 10.30pm (alchohol is served from noon onwards).

166 THE ALMA INN & FRESCO ITALIAN RESTAURANT

Cotton Stones, Sowerby Bridge,
West Yorkshire HX6 4NS
Tel: 01422 823334
e-mail: info@almainn.com
website: www.almainn.com

The Alma Inn and Fresco Italian Restaurant
has been privately owned by David Giffen for
the past 23 years. Customers can indulge in
quality Italian cuisine and popular real ales
including Tetley, Timothy Taylor Landlord and
Timothy Taylor Golden Best.

The Fresco Italian Restaurant is a superb
eatery and is renowned in the area for its tasty
and reasonably priced food. Fresh fish dishes
are a speciality and particular popular with
regular diners and visitors to the area.
Different fishes are purchased each day and in
addition to the main menu there are plenty of
choices on the daily specials board. The fish are
displayed in ice and when selected are cooked
to order.

The restaurant has seating room for 50 diners
and the bar offers space for 50 more. On a nice
day the outside area, which seats 200 people, is
an ideal place to dine and enjoy a refreshing
meal.

Starters include a range of garlic bread, char grilled pork
ribs with Italian BBQ sauce, spicy king prawns with fresh
chilli, onion, peppers and garlic; and shell roasted queen
scallops with fresh herbs, parmesan and parma ham.

There is a good selection of main meals with a choice of
grills, specials, pastas and pizzas. Among the most popular
dishes are seared sirloin steak with sautéed vegetables,
chorizos & red wine jus, pan fried fillet of sea bass with
fennel, lemon & dill, lasagne alla Bolognese and sun blushed
tomato & leek capellini. Vegetarians are well catered for. For
those customers with a lighter appetite snacks can be ordered
from the well stocked bar

The Alma Inn and Fresco Italian Restaurant is child friendly
and set in a spectacular location in the ... of Cotton Stones.

It is open all day, every day. The inn has five en-suite guest rooms, which are all situated
upstairs. The rooms, which are available all year round, vary in size and there is one family room.
Night guests can choose from a 'room only' tariff or B&B rates – and with a good reputation for its
quality cuisine the latter might be wise. A part from the rooms being located upstairs disabled
access is not a problem. All major credit cards taken.

The Alma Inn is one of Yorkshire's finest. It offers superb home-cooked food in its Italian
restaurant, hand-pulled real ales, a vast stock of Belgium beers, luxurious bed and breakfast/hotel
accommodation and dramatic rural views.

167 EL GATO NEGRO TAPAS

1 Oldham Road, Ripponden, Sowerby Bridge, West Yorkshire HX6 4DN
Tel: 01422 823070
e-mail: feedme@elgatonegrotapas.com
website: www.elgatonegrotapas.com

Guests would be forgiven for being surprised to find such a continental, stylish restaurant in the heart of a sleepy West Yorkshire town, but the popularity of **El Gato Negro Tapas** proves that it's a perfect fit.

El Gato is situated right in the centre of Ripponden, on the junction of the A58 and A672, making it ideally suited to both locals and customers from further afield who flock in year round to sample the cuisine from this unusual restaurant. The restaurant is owned by Simon Shaw, a professional chef with an enviable reputation and over thirty years of experience in various high profile restaurants. Five years ago he moved to West Yorkshire and created El Gato to the delight of those living in the area. Many of his regular customers follow him here for a first class meal; tribute to the quality of what he serves.

It is not just the food that's on offer that is in demand here though, the quirky ordering style with 'tick-your-own-menu' options and instructions to smile and enjoy affords diners a laid back and fun experience every time. Service is efficient and faultless creating a high class feel to the restaurant without the airs and graces that put so many off.

Simon closes on Mondays and Tuesdays, but opens lunchtimes on Friday and Saturday from 12-2pm and 12:30-5pm on Sundays, and in the evenings on Wednesdays and Thursdays from 6-9:30pm and Friday and Saturdays from 6-10pm. The menu, which also acts as a funky placemat offers a large variety of mouth-watering tapas dishes, each of which is cooked fresh to order in the kitchen and makes its way to your table as soon as it's ready. Diners can choose from a selection of hams and salamis and tapas meats like Alejandro chorizo with a wood roasted pepper puree, char grilled lamb skewers and crispy belly pork served with roasted scallops. Fish dishes include pan fried squid with black ink rice, Catalan fish stew and roasted hake. The vegetarian dishes are great as an accompaniment or in their own right and include

Syrian lentils, roasted butternut squash with salted almonds, patatas bravas and char grilled baby leeks in a Romesco sauce. A delicious range of bar snacks, breads and cheese dishes are also served alongside the specials board housing various traditional and tapas delicacies. Children are welcome, booking essential at all times.

168 WATERGATE LICENSED TEA ROOM & TEA GARDEN

9 Bridge Gate, Hebden Bridge,
West Yorkshire HX7 8EX
Tel: 01422 842978
e-mail: info@tandcakes.com
website: www.tandcakes.com

Watergate Licensed Tea Room and Tea Garden is one of West Yorkshire's finest tea rooms. It is nestled at the heart of Hebden Bridge and has a fantastic courtyard overlooking the river. It has been family owned and run for the last eight years and is extremely popular with locals and visitor to the area. The tea rooms are owned by Kara and Robert Howard and managed by Stef Thorley. There is a strong focus on quality home cooking with a delicious selection of filled sandwiches, salads, paninis, baguettes, jacket potatoes and breakfasts. As well as the main menu there are always additional tempting choices on the daily specials board. Local produce is used wherever possible at this child friendly establishment. There are plenty of speciality cakes to choose from and the tea room's award winning homemade scones are a mouth watering delight. Hot and cold drinks are served all year round along with all of the other delicacies on offer. It is open every day between 10am and 4.30pm and seats 28 downstairs and, 30 upstairs and a further 30 in the tea garden. Disabled access is not a problem.

169 WHITE LION HOTEL

Bridge Gate, Hebden Bridge,
West Yorkshire HX7 8EX
Tel: 01422 842197
e-mail: enquiries@whitelionhotel.net
website: www.whitelionhotel.net

Dating back to 1657, The White Lion Hotel is a traditional coaching inn, with a warm and friendly atmosphere. The hotel is set in an attractive riverside location in central Hebden Bridge and is well known for excellent food, wines and a wide choice of real cask ales. Steve Howard and Gemma Esders recently took over here and there is a lot to do before they have the place running the way they want it to run. There are ten spacious en-suite bedrooms available and the hotel has become well known for its hearty breakfasts.

The hotel provides an ideal base for visitors to the Calder Valley and Brontë country and is surrounded by history and stunning countryside. The area is very popular with walkers, cyclists, country lovers and those in search of a contrast to a hectic life style.

The hotel is open to residents and non-residents, and fresh home cooked food is served from 12 noon to 9pm every day. The professional chef uses fresh, locally-sourced, produce for all the dishes on the main menu and the specials board changes daily to make the most of fresh seasonal produce.

170 WHITE LION

58 Towngate, Heptonstall, Hebden Bridge, West Yorkshire HX7 7NB
Tel: 01422 842027 / 07833547276
e-mail: whitelion.heptonstall@hotmail.com
website: www.whitelionheptonstall.com

The main street of the ancient village of Heptonstall is still cobbled and it's in this street you'll find the impressive stone-built White Lion. Your friendly host at this popular hostelry is Barry Shaw who was born into the trade. His extensive experience proved useful when Barry took over here in the summer of 2006 as the inn had fallen on hard times.

Happily, he has turned things around, and it is now a popular pub selling quality food. The chef is a professional and his menu is based on locally sourced produce, freshly prepared. You'll find a good choice of pub favourites such as steaks, steak & ale pie, fish and chips and gammon and pineapple along with home-made beef burgers, a vegetarian option, and a home-made Italian lasagne. In addition to the regular menu, there's a daily specials board. On Sundays, traditional roasts are served complete with all the trimmings. Half portions at half the price are available for children. Food is served from noon until 3pm, and from 5pm to 9pm, Wednesday to Friday; from noon until 9pm on Saturday, and from noon until 8pm on Sunday. The inn is also happy to cater for small parties and buffets.

To complement your meal, the bar stocks an extensive range of beverages, including six real ales. The White Lion also has three en-suite guest bedrooms available, two doubles and a twin room. Also available is a four berth static caravan with panoramic views and holiday cottages. Walkers are made welcome as well as dogs (provided they are on a lead).

If you enjoy Irish music, be sure to visit the White Lion on Tuesday evening when there's a regular session. Another good time to visit Heptonstall is Good Friday when the Pace Egging takes place, in Weavers Square. Heptonstall is one of few places where the churchyard has two churches in it. Ted Hughes the poet Laureat used to write poems in the pub. There is a foundation named after him at the top of the village. Sylvia Plath, his lady, is buried in the graveyard, which attracts a lot of tourists from abroad. The coiners (a group of counterfeiters) were committed to York Castle in 1769 and were hung, drawn and quartered before being buried in the graveyard.

Barry has just taken over two other public houses – The Weavers in Luddenden Foot and The Engineers in Sowerby Bridge.

171 THE BLACKSMITHS ARMS

106 Heaton Moor Road, Kirkheaton,
Huddersfield, West Yorkshire HD5 0PH
Tel : 01484 422529

Chris and Verity took over **the Blacksmiths Arms** in May 2010, relishing the opportunity to fulfil an ambition to provide good wholesome food for families of all ages at great value. Chris has over ten years of experience in the catering trade ranging from hotels to county pubs, which compliments Verity's expertise and character front of house.

The quality food offering has gained a following of regular weekly customers especially for the lunch time specials.

Open every day, guests can enjoy a choice of four Yorkshire brewed real ales along with a traditional Yorkshire Fayre menu changed with the seasons and served from 12 to 8 p.m. All the dishes are prepared by the resident chefs from locally sourced produce bursting with flavour. Sunday lunches are extremely popular and booking is recommended.

Guests can enjoy a cosy seat in the character bar and lounge or sit out in the beer garden and enjoy breathtaking views across Castle Hill and the Pennine Chain. Ideally located for many visits across West Yorkshire, the Blacksmiths rural setting allows Chris, Verity and their guests a taste of country living with their very own geese, hens and ducks in the gardens. There is also a small caravan and camping site as featured by the caravan club and available all year round. Please call for more details or to book a pitch.

172 LAST OF THE SUMMER WINE EXHIBITION

30 Huddersfield Road, Holmfirth, West Yorkshire HD9 2JS
Tel: 01484 681408
website: www.wrinkledstocking.co.uk/exhibition

Back in the early 1970s, the sleepy Pennine town of Holmfirth was turned head over heels by the introduction of three rascally men, joined over the years by a mix of equally amusing and varied characters. **Last of the Summer Wine** is the longest-running comedy series on television, with fans all over the Globe, particularly the United States, where they have fallen in love with the gentle charm, Yorkshire humour and rolling countryside.

The dramatic beauty of the Pennine moorlands, featuring quaint villages, dry stone walls and beautiful cottages, is an added bonus to the mischievous antics TV viewers have come to expect from the Summer Wine characters. The late Bill Owen, who played the lovable and famous rogue Compo, described himself as an adopted "Holmfirther", for a time living in the town, and lending his name and support to many local worthy and charitable causes.

He was also heavily involved in the creation and design of the Summer Wine Exhibition in conjunction with local Summer Wine photographer Malcolm Howarth. The BBC supported the venture with props and equipment, and Bill was keen to make sure the Exhibition faithfully represented the programme, and provided an interesting and memorable feature for visitors.

The exhibition was officially opened by Compo on Easter Saturday, 1996, the 25th anniversary of the programme.

173 ROTCHER COFFEE BAR

Rotcher House, Holmfirth, West Yorkshire HD9 2DL
Tel: 01484 685512 e-mail: rotchercoffeebar@aol.com

There are many good reasons to visit Holmfirth – the scenery across
the Holme Valley, the markets, the June Arts Festival and the *Last of
the Summer Wine* connection. For visitors wanting to take a break
from the sightseeing Helen and Dean Hulme extend a warm welcome to one and all at their
Rotcher Coffee Bar. The coffee is excellent, but Rotcher is much more than just a licensed coffee
bar, it's also a great place to relax and enjoy anything from a made-to-order sandwich, a wrap, a
melt or a panini to a salad, a home-made pastry or a hot special such as chilli con carne. Rotcher
is open every day except Christmas Day from 8am to 5pm (from 9am Sunday)

174 PENNY'S PANTRY

39 Bridge Street, Slaithwaite, nr Huddersfield HD7 5JN
Tel: 01484 844646

Wholesome home cooking brings a steady stream of customers to **Penny's
Pantry**, which enjoys an attractive Colne Valley setting by a bridge over
the Huddersfield Narrow Canal. Susan and Jim Pawson brought a wealth of experience when they
took over here in the summer of 2010, and throughout the day they prepare a tempting selection
of tasty snacks and meals, from a variety of breakfast options to sandwiches, lunch dishes,
afternoon teas, cakes and pastries. Hot lunchtime specials might include liver & onions with a red
wine gravy, broccoli & Yorkshire Blue quiche and cod, spinach & cheddar fishcakes. Penny's Pantry
is open from 8.30 to 4.30 Monday to Friday, 8.30 to 5 Saturday, 9 to 5 Sunday.

175 ROSE & CROWN

132 Knowl Road, Golcar, West Yorkshire HD7 4AN
Tel: 01484 460160
website: www.roseandcrown-golcar.co.uk

Situated on a hillside crest above the Colne Valley in
West Yorkshire, is the pleasant village of Golcar. It is
here that you will find a remarkable pub in the **Rose
& Crown**. Attentive hosts Jake and Christine offer a
warm and friendly welcome to all who enter this
vibrant and popular community pub.

Making an appearance in the CAMRA good beer
guide, the bar offers a choice array of Cask
conditioned real ales & keg beers, plus a fine and
varied selection of cool premium largers and bottled
beers, along with all the latest designer and
traditional ciders, wines & spirits, whilst also
stocking the occasional and popular guest beer.

For those who love a traditional roast dinner, the Rose & Crown is the place to head to on
Sunday. Available between 12 – 3pm there are also a number of optional dishes for those who
don't fancy a roast.

There is a weekly Quiz Night held every Thursday from 9.30pm and all are welcome. All major
credit cards are accepted and children are made very welcome.

176 THE HORSE AND GROOM WAKEFIELD

3, Horse Race End, Heath Common Wakefield WF1 5SG
Tel: 01924 373377 e-mail: pub@horseandgroomwakefield.com
website: www.horseandgroomwakefield.com
Facebook: Horse and Groom Wakefield

The rural setting of Heath Common just outside Wakefield is home to the
Horse and Groom pub. Taken over by Graham and Stuart in June 2010, this pub has been given a
new lease of life bringing in people from the surrounding areas as well as those passing by. The
pub hosts events and entertainment, fundraising activities, darts, dominoes and pool and offers
real ales and ciders along with traditional humble pub food. Each Sunday the pub serves a
traditional Sunday roast from 12noon to 5pm. At this public house you can be sure of a warm
welcome and a beautiful view across the Heath.

177 NOSTELL PRIORY

Nostell, Wakefield, Yorkshire WF4 1QE
Tel: 01924 863892
website: www.nationaltrust.org.uk

Nostell Priory takes its name from the 12th century Augustinian
Priory dedicated to Saint Oswald. Now in its place is the 18th
century house built by James Paine and Robert Adam for Sir
Rowland Winn in 1733. The house has been the home of the Winn
family for the last 350 years. The house is home to over 100
pieces of Thomas Chippendale furniture, but other treasures
include works by Pieter Brueghel the Younger and Angelica
Kauffman. The house is surrounded by nearly 350 acres of
parkland. Enjoy a lakeside walk with stunning wild flower
collections throughout the year or visit the rose garden
beautifully set behind the stableblock. Whatever the season, the
19th century parkland is open to all; come and see parkland
restoration as it happens. Wander around and enjoy sumptuous views of the magnificent mature
trees, lush restored wildflower meadows and the peacefully grazing cattle. Wildlife, ranging
from oxeye daisies to kestrels, are to be found at every turn throughout the estate.

The garden comes alive from March onwards, with radiant carpets of glorious spring flowers.
Winding round the two lakes are a series of spectacular tree lined rhododendron walks, passing
through the 18th Century Menagerie Gardens and pleasure grounds. The scented delights of the
Rose Garden are a feast for the senses, and the inspiring midsummer magnificence of the white
climbing iceberg rose, covering over 130 metres of wall is a sight to behold.

178 BRIDGE INN

Altofts Lane, Whitwood, Castleford, West Yorkshire WF10 5PZ
Tel: 01977 519696 Fax: 01977 519686
e-mail: bridgeinn51@btconnect.com
website: www.bridgeinnhotel.com

A warm welcome awaits you at the **Bridge Inn**; a magnificent establishment which provides the
perfect setting for a quick drink, light
meal, evening out, or a relaxing over
night stay. The owners Norma and Geoff,
who have been here since 2006, have the
passion and experience (they have been
running their own public houses since
1984!) which has been the driving force
behind the Bridge Inn's success. Quality
and style are the order of the day, and
you will find the both in ready abundance
here. There is a relaxed and elegant
mixture of the traditional and the modern
throughout the decor, with comfortable
leather seating and wooden furnishings
set against the rustic exposed stone
walling and wooden beamed ceilings.

The extensive menus provide something for everyone,
and whatever the occasion. At the bar you can have a
brilliant informal drink with friends or family, along with
everything from light bites and bits to share to full meals.
The speciality sandwiches, which include topside of beef
& fried onions and hot fresh haddock, served in ciabatta
bread or baguette with chips, are a particular delight;
washed down with a draught or glass of wine from the
bar. Children are also well catered for, with a menu of
selected mains and deserts to satisfy even the fussiest
taste buds! For a more formal atmosphere the dining area
is perfect, and is soon bustling with people when there is
the delicious Carvery or one of the Bridge Inn's renowned
speciality nights. Most popular is the simply divine
romantic meals for two, served every Friday and Saturday
night 6pm until 10pm, which contains four fine dining
course and a bottle of wine, all for £30. The mains
include a choice of fillet steak with a stilton glaze,
chicken bon femme, grilled sea bass, or lamb rump steak;
and naturally with all the trimmings, followed by deserts
and coffee. All food is freshly and skilfully prepared on
the premises.

There are 16 quality en-suite guest rooms at the Bridge
Inn, housed adjacent to the main building and away from
the hubbub of inn. Of these there are four twin rooms,
ten doubles and two very spacious family rooms, all of
which have been newly decorated in the inn's tyle of
understated elegance. These are available all year round,
the tariff for which includes a hearty full English
breakfast in the morning, and all rooms include all of the
amenities you will need.

179 THE RISING SUN AND PALM COURT
ITALIAN/SPANISH RISTORANTE AND PIZZERIA

Whitwood Common Lane, Whitwood, Castleford, West Yorkshire WF10 5PT
Tel: 01977 554766
e-mail: rising_sun@btconnect.com
website: www.risingsunandpalmcourt.co.uk

The pleasant village of Whitwood in Castleford in West Yorkshire is home to an eclectic and unusual bar and restaurant known as **The Rising Sun and Palm Court Italian/Spanish Ristorante and Pizzeria**. It is owned by the marvellous Maureen Madeley, who has been successfully running the business for the past thirteen years. In that time she has perfected the art of combining everyone's favourite food in two distinct but adjacent restaurants.

The Rising Sun caters for those who prefer a traditional English menu in a true English pub atmosphere. Its attractive frontage sports bursting blooms of summer flowers, a handsome traditional red slated roof and original oak beams. Inside it affords its diners time honoured décor with sumptuous collections of fabrics and cosy corners in which to relax. Many tables sit within the pretty bay windows that overlook the street, providing ample space for people watching. A day time and early bird menu operates from 12-6:30pm on weekdays alongside a full evening a la carte menu offering everything from homemade soup of the day to traditional steak and ale pie or a mammoth mixed grill made with locally reared meat. Early bird choices include fisherman's pie, a traditional Yorkshire roast and a liver and sausage casserole. Each Thursday night a special themed food night is held ranging from steak or fish nights to American, pies and Mexican nights.

If it's a taste of the exotic that's wanted however, Palm Court, the Rising Sun's sister restaurant, provides the very best in Italian and Spanish cuisine. It operates a great value for money tapas menu, with a selection of lunch and dinner menus also available sampling traditional continental dishes from melt-in-the-mouth pastas, succulent meats and hand tossed pizzas. Diners can choose a seat in the Mediterranean themed dining room flush with white tablecloths, large palms and mood lighting or take a seat in the rear garden terrace acting as West Yorkshire's very own slice of sun kissed Spain.

Maureen is also able to provide a range of entertainment for functions, children's parties and bank holidays with specials offers for everyone. On the last Sunday of every month a popular Jazz night is held where guests can indulge a bottle of wine whilst being serenaded for just £26 per couple for dinner and wine. Please call for details. Booking is heavily recommended for both restaurants on weekends.

180 THE BOAT PUB AND RESTAURANT

Main Street, Allerton Bywater, Castleford,
West Yorkshire WF10 2BX
Tel: 01977 552646
e-mail: richardjuliafreddie@btinternet.com
website: www.theboatallertonbywater.co.uk

The Boat Pub & Restaurant enjoys a superb setting right
beside the River Aire with picnic tables placed overlooking
the water. The hosts at this fine old traditional inn are
Richard and Julia Wilson who took over here in early 2007 and
recently refurbished the dining area to a high standard. The
couple has made the pub a place that's well worth seeking
out - and not just for the lovely location.

Good food is a priority here and the menu offers an
appetising choice of dishes, which are prepared and cooked
by head chef Tracey and her team. Starters range from a traditional Prawn Cocktail to Goats
Cheese Bruschetta. Main courses include perennial favourites such as Steak & Ale Pie or Fish &
Chips as well as a good choice of steaks and poultry, pasta and vegetarian dishes. Food is served
from 12 noon – 2.30pm and 5.30pm until 9pm Thursday to Saturday; from 5.30pm – 9pm on
Wednesday and 12 noon until 4pm on Sunday, when a choice of roasts replaces the regular menu.

Real ale devotees will be happy - there are several real ales on offer, which are usually from
the Osset Brewery, Leeds Brewery and Skipton Brewery.

181 THE GOLDEN LION HOTEL

1 The Square, Ferrybridge,
West Yorkshire WF11 8ND
Tel: 01977 673527

A warm welcome is assured to all at **The Golden Lion Hotel** which
stands in a glorious spot alongside the River Aire in Ferrybridge.
Over the last nine months its facilities and décor have undergone
a stylish update under the control of new owners Nigel and Donna.
This energetic couple have given a new lease of life to the hotel;
offering fine drink, entertainment and accommodation throughout
the week.

Guests have a choice between nine comfortable upstairs rooms,
five of which have full en suite facilities. Each room is stylishly
decorated with all modern conveniences, making every stay here
an easy one. Its convenient location to Pontefract racecourse and
a selection of golf courses and colourful market towns creates the
perfect opportunity for a short break away for families or couples.

During the evenings there is also plenty to do with a great selection of entertainment
throughout the week. On Thursdays and Saturdays from 9pm Nigel and Donna offer Bingo, quizzes
and their own version of 'Play Your Cards Right,' whilst on Fridays and Saturdays from 7:30pm
guests are invited to try out their karaoke skills. On Wednesday nights it's Poker night from 8pm,
with all abilities welcome. On Sundays the hotel holds a popular carvery from 12-3pm offering a
choice of meats and vegetarian options. Cash only please.

182 PONTEFRACT CASTLE

Castle Chain, Pontefract, Yorkshire WF8 1QH
Tel: 01977 723440
website: www.wakefield.gov.uk

In the Middle Ages, **Pontefract Castle** was one of the most important
fortresses in the country. It became a royal castle in 1399, upon
the accession of Henry Bolinbroke to the throne. Richard II subsequently died in the castle the
following year after being one of many important prisoners to lodge there. During the English
Civil War it was held by the King's supporters throughout three sieges, but as a result, after
1649, it was largely demolished. The remains of the castle, and the underground magazine
chamber, are open to visitors. There is also a working blacksmith on site.

184 THE GARDENERS ARMS

101 High Street, Crigglestone,
West Yorkshire WF4 3EF
Tel: 01924 249545

The Gardeners Arms in Crigglestone was in a sorry state
until its current owner Frank Sherlock took over in May
2010. With over thirty years experience in the licensing
trade, Frank knew he could turn the fortune of the inn
around and in doing so gave the village its local pub back.
After much renovation and the updating of facilities in all
areas, Frank has brought back booming trade and a sense
of community. He now opens all day every day offering
four real ales to his customers alongside a healthy
selection of wines, spirits and lagers.

Food is available between 12:30-3:30pm Thursday to
Saturday and from 12:30-4pm on Sundays when a popular
roast is served cooked to order. The main menu uses local
produce to create good old fashioned Yorkshire fayre
available between 12:30-3:30pm Thursday to Saturday and
from 12:30-4:30pm on Sundays when a hearty Sunday
roast is served. In warmer weather guests can enjoy
Frank's patio now sporting a flash TV and pool table for entertainment. Live entertainment is also
held most weekends with a regular karaoke slot on Sunday nights. Frank is also able to provide a
function room for hire, with or without catering, please call for details.

www.findsomewhere.co.uk
For people who want to explore the United Kingdom

Places to Stay

183 THE ARMS AT UPTON

High Street, Upton, West Yorkshire WF9 1HG
Tel: 01977 650495

The popular village of Upton between Doncaster and Pontefract is home to **The Arms At Upton,** a well loved, family orientated inn known for its great hospitality and fantastic facilities. The inn is run by Kelvin and Avril, who took over the Arms just eighteen months ago. It's the couples' first venture into the hospitality trade but their locals say they are naturals, bringing a breeziness and charm to the inn that it has never had before.

The pair open from 4pm Mondays and Tuesdays, and from midday Wednesday through to Sunday. Kelvin always ensures that there is at least one real ale to sample from a local brewery, alongside a host of other lagers, spirits and wines. Drinks can be enjoyed within the contemporary interior, or in the summer sun of the inn's rear beer garden.

Guests can sample a delicious range of food each day with the help of head chef Clive. Catering for the family market, Clive creates his menu using as much locally sourced produce as possible, all cooked fresh to order. His dishes include succulent steak pie, lasagne, fish and chips, juicy rump steak, chicken tikka massala, pasta bake, chilli and Cajun chicken and chips along with all your other pub favourites, salads and snacks. Food is served between 4-8pm Mondays and Tuesdays and from 12-8pm Wednesday to Saturday with a well attended carvery on Sundays from 12-3pm.

Clive also offers several party buffets available in partnership with the inns contemporary function room which can hold up to 200 guests. Its neutral but stylish décor allows guests to put their own stamp on the room depending on the event; whether it's a birthday party, engagement party, wake or private dinner. The room has its own big screen projector, on which guests can upload their own photos to bring a real sense of personality to the event.

Kelvin and Avril also offer three upstairs en suite guest bedrooms which are available all year round. Ideal for families, the rooms offer all mod cons in a safe environment, with a hearty breakfast thrown in.

Families can also enjoy the inn's weekly entertainment; consisting of a popular quiz night on Thursdays and karaoke on certain weekends, please ring for details.

185 THE BREWERS PRIDE & MILLERS BAR & RESTAURANT

Low Mill Road, Healey Road, Ossett, West Yorkshire WF5 8ND
Tel: 01924 273865
e-mail: sally@brewers-pride.co.uk
website: www.brewers-pride.co.uk

Troud to be Independent" says the sign outside **The Brewers Pride** in Ossett. This is indeed a truly independent free house with "real ales, real fires and real food". Attentive hosts, Sally and Jon, arrived here in 1998 and have established a glowing reputation for the quality food, well-kept ales and entertainment that is provided here.

The food here is second to none and with starters such as seafood roulade, salmon, haddock and chive fishcakes and creamy garlic mushrooms, diners will be spoilt for choice. For the main course, there's a choice of steak and ale pie, farmhouse Cumberland sausages, chicken and chorizo tagliatelle, as well as fresh fish dishes and a variety of vegetarian options. At lunchtime, from noon until 3pm, Monday to Saturday, a choice of light snacks is also available. Food is also served from 7pm to 9pm, Tuesday to Thursday. On Wednesday evenings, there's an alternating themed menu - Fish Night, Pie Night and Curry Night. The bar stocks no fewer than 9 authentic brews. Red Lion Ales are brewed locally and are supplemented by an ever-changing choice of guest ales. In good weather, beverages can be enjoyed in the pleasant beer garden which also has a smoking area.

Recently completed and already extremely popular is the **Millers Bar & Restaurant** which is located to the rear of the pub. Diners can expect a great selection of continental beers (both on draught and by the bottle) and delicious wines.

The cosy restaurant has a traditional 'feel' with exposed oak purlins and roof trusses, hand-fired bricks, oak sash windows and a traditional cast iron stove set in original fireplace. Combine this with more contemporary furniture, table dressing and lighting makes it simply one of the finest places to eat out locally.

The menu at Millers is exceptional; moules marinieres, garlic scented toasted ciabatta with fresh parsley and pan seared scallops, fresh pea puree with crispy parma ham are just two of the delicious options available. Main courses include Yorkshire lamb rump, served pink with truffle oil mash, mint and rosemary jus with redcurrant tartlet and crispy sinned sea bass fillets, sauté pak choi, saffron potato with sweet soy glaze. Those with a sweet tooth will not be disappointed either, white chocolate cheesecake, Yorkshire strawberry & almond tart and dark chocolate torte offer a perfect way to finish off a meal.

186 BISHOPS' HOUSE

Norton Lees Lane, Sheffield, Yorkshire S8 9BE
Tel: 0114 278 2600
website: www.sheffieldgalleries.org.uk

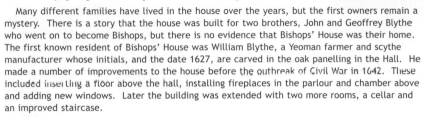

Bishops' House is the best preserved timber-framed house in Sheffield. It was built around 1500 and is tucked away at the top of Meersbrook Park. Bishops' House typifies the development of the smaller English domestic house in the 16th and 17th centuries. Inside, the house retains many of its original features and looks just as it would have done in the 17th century, giving a tantalising flavour of Stuart England.

Many different families have lived in the house over the years, but the first owners remain a mystery. There is a story that the house was built for two brothers, John and Geoffrey Blythe who went on to become Bishops, but there is no evidence that Bishops' House was their home. The first known resident of Bishops' House was William Blythe, a Yeoman farmer and scythe manufacturer whose initials, and the date 1627, are carved in the oak panelling in the Hall. He made a number of improvements to the house before the outbreak of Civil War in 1642. These included inserting a floor above the hall, installing fireplaces in the parlour and chamber above and adding new windows. Later the building was extended with two more rooms, a cellar and an improved staircase.

The last Blythe to live in Bishops' House was Samuel. After he died in 1753 his son sold the house to William Shore. The house was then let to a tenant farmer and his labourer and the building was divided into two self-contained dwellings. In 1886 the property passed to the Corporation (now Sheffield City Council) and until 1974 Recreation Department employees lived in the house. In 1976 Bishops' House was restored and opened as a museum.

187 SHEFFIELD BOTANICAL GARDENS

Clarkhouse Road, Sheffield, Yorkshire S10 2LN
Tel: 01142 676496
website: www.sbg.co.uk

This 19-acre site is a green haven within our busy city and has recently undergone a major restoration programme. Originally laid out in 1836, the Gardens are listed by English Heritage as a Grade II site and contain a number of listed buildings, including the stunning glass pavilions. The restoration programme reinstated much of the original Victorian design, whilst rejuvenating the plant collections and adapting the Gardens for modern-day needs.

188 THE ROYAL OAK

44 High Street, Beighton, Sheffield, South Yorkshire S20 1EA
Tel: 0114 2697410

Located at the heart of Beighton, **The Royal Oak** gives a warm welcome to customers all day every day. The child-friendly pub is run by Denise and Ian Dyett and their daughter Trudi who took over here at the beginning of July 2010. It is their first venture into the licensing trade and they are gradually building up a fantastic reputation in the area.

Delicious homemade food is freshly prepared and cooked by Denise and Trudi. The menu is littered with traditional favourites including homemade meat pie, homemade lasagne, homemade cottage pie and homemade broccoli and cauliflower bake. Food is served Monday – Thursday between 2pm and 7pm, Friday – Saturday between 12pm and 7pm and 12pm – 4pm on Sundays.

There is plenty of entertainment put on at The Royal Oak throughout the week and it is always bustling with friendly locals and visitors to the area. Live music is available on Saturday evenings and there is a good range of other entertainment on week day evenings including karaoke, bingo and poker.

189 THE BEEHIVE

16 Union Street, Harthill, Sheffield,
South Yorkshire S26 7YH
Tel: 01909 770205   Fax: 01909 774819
e-mail: info@thebeehiveharthill.co.uk
website: www.thebeehiveharthill.co.uk

Well renowned for its excellent food and well kept ales, **The Beehive** is a quality public house located in the delightful village of Harthill. It is a family-run establishment with owners Jim and Hilary in charge for the past 16 years. Their daughter Emma has been the manager of the pub since February 2010.

Outstanding homemade meals are served Tuesday – Saturday (the pub is closed on Mondays). There are plenty of typical traditional English pub dishes to choose from. Traditional fish and chips, beef lasagne and ham & eggs are among the choices. Vegetarians are well looked after with several suitable dishes to select from including mushroom stroganoff, stilton and vegetable crumble, and vegetable stir fry. There are plenty of starters, grills and salads on the menu and all of the dishes are of high quality, locally sourced, and reasonably priced.

The Beehive has a very good reputation and many customers return time and time again. Every Tuesday there is a quiz from 9.30pm and there is a function room that can be hired out, which has room for up to 70 people. Children are very much welcomed at The Beehive up until 9pm. Dogs welcome. Good off road parking.

190 THE ROYAL HOTEL

Main Road, Dungworth, Sheffield,
South Yorkshire S6 6HF
Tel: 0114 285 1213
e-mail: joanne@royalhotel-dungworth.co.uk
website: www.royalhotel-dungworth.co.uk

Set on the edge of the Peak District, high on the moors northwest of Sheffield but only a 20-minute drive from the centre of the city and Meadow Hall shopping centre, the **Royal Hotel** is a welcoming family-run public house. Its location makes it the ideal place for people visiting the area or for those that want to stay longer but not wanting to stay in the hustle bustle of a city. The hotel was built around 1813 and retains much of its original character. It is divided into 3 areas, all with open fires. There is the snug which overlooks the beautiful countryside, a spacious lounge at the front of the pub; also at the front of the pub there is a separate room ideal for families.

A major attraction at the Royal is Dave and Joanne's quality home-made food - just try one of Dave's Royal pies, known the world over! Vegetarian and children's meals are also available, along with freshly prepared sandwiches. The royal also offers three pristine en-suite bedrooms in their own annex over looking the wonderful countryside.

193 CAFE OASIS

8 Rother Court, Parkgate, Rotherham,
South Yorkshire S62 6DR
Tel: 01709 522254

Cafe Oasis has only been open since August 2006 after the previous owners shut it down for eight weeks. Susan and Scott Foster took over the cafe recently and have been welcoming customers through their doors gladly since opening. It's their first venture into this type of business together and they have gone into it with gusto, opening every day apart from bank holidays. They are currently opening each day from 7am-2pm, but will be extending their hours as their first year in trade wears on. Business is soon picking up under their leadership serving freshly prepared food to eat in or takeaway every day of the week.

Susan and Scott's extensive menu covers an impressive range of dishes from hot and cold sandwiches, filled jacket potatoes, salads and toasties. An all day breakfast menu also operates alongside a lunchtime menu, with a variety of burgers, pies and pasta dishes all in regular or large portions. All dishes are created with ingredients sourced from local suppliers and all the special dishes are homemade before guests in the cafe's large open plan kitchen.

The cafe also offers a wide variety of soft drinks including cans, energy drinks, juices and homemade milkshakes, alongside a selection of lighter snacks and tasty treats like flapjacks, yoghurts and fruit. All of these can also be added to takeaway orders, which are all able to take

191 PLOUGH INN

New Road, Low Bradfield, South Yorkshire S6 6HW
Tel: 0114 285 1280
e-mail: ploughinn2@btconnect.com
website: www.the-plough-inn.com

The award-winning Plough Inn can be found in a picturesque and scenic location at the heart of the Peak District National Park in the village of Low Bradfield. This attractive and impressive pub has plenty of character and many locals and visitors flock here to indulge in delicious home cooked food. The Plough Inn is run by Chris and Mandy Davies and the experienced couple have personally run it for almost four years. At least four real ales are available here, one of which is brewed especially for the pub – Farmers Plough. Another regular is the locally brewed Farmers Blonde - both of these are brewed by the local Bradfield Brewery. There are also two rotating guest ales served, coming mainly from northern breweries. All of the homemade dishes are cooked fresh to order. The extensive menu has plenty to offer hungry diners and the quality of the grub is evident after the pub won monthly awards for the Sheffield area from CAMRA in July 2008 and again in February 2010. Starters such as breaded camembert with cranberry sauce, prawn cocktail, and mini vegetable spring rolls and sweet chilli dip are listed on the reasonably priced menu. Main meals include a good range of meat and vegetarian options including traditional favourites like roast beef and Yorkshire pudding, homemade pie of the day, homemade cottage pie, beef lasagne Verdi and lamb's liver in onion gravy. Broccoli, potato and cream cheese bake, vegetable curry served with rice and naan bread, and creamy peppered mushrooms served with rice and garlic bread are among the vegetarian alternatives. Healthy salad options are listed as well as selections for those with a lighter appetite. Filled sandwiches and toasties are popular with lunchtime diners. For those customers with room left for dessert, the menu does not disappoint. Treacle sponge, lemon meringue pie, blackcurrant cheesecake and chocolate junkyard are some of the favourites. Food is served between midday and 2.30pm Monday – Saturdays, 12 until 7pm on Sundays, and 5.30pm – 8.30pm Wednesday – Saturday. The Plough is open all day every day except Monday when the times are 12 - 3pm and 6pm - 9pm. The beer garden is extremely well-used on warmer days and there is a large off-road car park. It is advisable to book at all times and essential on weekends because of the number of people that flock to this well liked and child friendly community hub. Disabled access is not a problem.

192 THE STRINES INN

Bradfield Dale, Sheffield, South Yorkshire S6 6JE
Tel: 01142 851247
e-mail: bruce@thestines@tiscali.co.uk

Despite being located on Sheffield's border, **The Strines Inn** could be a world away. Nestled amongst breathtaking moorland scenery it is one of many local landmarks within the Peak District National Park. Originally a manor house, it was built in 1275 for the Worrall family, although most of the present day structure is 16th century. After becoming an inn in 1771 when John Morton leased the property from the Worrall's, it got its name from an olde English word meaning 'the meeting of water,' quite appropriate as it stands in an unrivalled location overlooking the Strines reservoir.

In the height of summer the inn attracts hundreds of visitors on a daily basis. The glorious sunshine and stunning views perfectly compliment the excellent food and drink available. For those with children there is an enclosed play area outside where youngsters are free to play to their hearts content. Outside also is an area for peacocks, geese and chickens who never tire of seeing friendly faces. None of the inn's charm is lost during the winter months however, as its three open fires create a warm and comfortable atmosphere to help forget about the dreary weather. Regardless of the time of year the inn makes for a wonderful day out.

Bruce Howarth remains the owner of the inn, and licensee to the well stocked bar which houses an impressive selection of aged spirits, wines and real ales. The inn is well known also for its restaurant, serving traditional English fayre throughout the day. Light bites and starters range from giant homemade Yorkshire puddings, game and port pate, to various filled paninis, jacket potatoes and sandwiches. Main meals encompass a handsome choice with plenty of Yorkshire country classics including a hearty roast

dinner encased in a Yorkshire pudding, homemade pie, mammoth mixed grill, liver and onions and a tender 10 oz rump steak cooked to your liking. Other favourites include lasagne, a traditional Ploughman's and the Strines cheeseburger. Children can benefit from their own menu, all cooked with the same fresh local produce as the rest of the menu.

Should guests want to extend their stay in their visit to Bradfield Dale, Bruce offers three stunning en suite guest bedrooms. In a style that befits the inn's character and history well, each room is decadently furnished with a four poster bed, and dining tables for two where breakfast can be enjoyed whilst overlooking the reservoir. Rooms also come with chaise lounges, screened baths and open stoves, adding true atmosphere to a cosy night in. Please call for details.

194 SOUTH YORKSHIRE TRANSPORT MUSEUM

Waddington Way, Aldwarke, Rotherham, South Yorkshire S65 3SH
Tel: 0114 255 3010
website: www.sytm.co.uk

The new Museum - now called the **South Yorkshire Transport Museum** - is situated just off the A6123 on Waddington Way at Aldwarke. On open days the Museum is open to visitors from 12 noon to about 5 p.m. (the last admission is at 4 p.m.). There is ample car parking on site. Whenever possible we will run a frequent vintage shuttle bus from the bus lay-by at ASDA direct to the Museum. Otherwise it's about a 20 minute walk to the Museum.

195 ELSECAR HERITAGE CENTRE

Wath Road, Elsecar, Barnsley, South Yorkshire S74 8HJ
Tel: 01226 740203
e-mail: elsecarheritagecentre@Barnsley.gov.uk
website: www.Barnsley.gov.uk/leisure

The Elsecar Heritage Centre nestles within the beautiful South Yorkshire countryside and dates from the early 1800's when it was originally owned by the local Earls Fitzwilliam as their main industrial workshops, producing everything needed for their industrial empire. Many of the buildings and facilities have been restored and preserved, with many being used again as workshops for local crafts people, from traditional printers, woodwork shop, to more delicate crafts such as jewellery making and flower arranging.

As well as a large selection of Craft Workshops, the Centre also has an Antiques Centre, a Bottle Museum, 'Playmania' children's activity centre, the Elsecar Preservation Group Steam Railway Line and the world famous Newcomen Beam Engine, the only remaining Beam Engine in its original location. Our on-site 'Brambles Tea-rooms' can provide light refreshments to a full and varied menu of main meals throughout the day.

The Heritage Centre also holds regular special events within its multi-purpose exhibition hall all year round, from concerts, antique fairs, championship dog shows, and natural health festivals to even Japanese Koi Fish shows.

196 ELEPHANT & CASTLE BAR & RESTAURANT

Tingle Bridge Lane, Hemingfield, Barnsley,
South Yorkshire S73 0NT
Tel: 01226 755986
e-mail: elephantandcastle@live.co.uk

Elephant and Castle Bar and Restaurant is located within the town of Hemingfield near the Heritage Centre. It's owned and run by the delightful Watson family, who took over the property in July this year. Patricia and Adrian's family orientated business style is evident in everything they do, and they have provided Hemingfield with another great place to eat out for young and old.

Situated on the waterfront, the restaurant's enviable location sees many repeat visitors who can enjoy its tranquil rear garden in the summer months when its own water feature becomes a highlight, complete with great play area for the kids. The Watson's open all day every day serving a mixture of wines, spirits and real ales. They serve food throughout the day with breakfast between 10am-12pm, lunch from 12-3pm, cold sandwiches from 3-5pm and evening meals in the atmospheric candlelit restaurant from 5-9:30pm.

Guests can choose from the main menu or specials board which regular houses dishes like smoked haddock and spring onion fishcakes, chicken sizzlers served fajita style, and pork tenderloin with a thyme and pepper crust. Themed food evenings are held on weeknights with pie night on Tuesdays, steak nights on Wednesday, curry and a pint night on Thursday and fish and chip night on Fridays. On Sundays a traditional roast is added to the menu, always a popular choice amongst the locals. Cash or cheque only please.

197 OLD MOOR WETLANDS CENTRE RSPB

Pontefract Road, Wombwell, Barnsley, South Yorkshire S73 0YF
Tel: 01226 751593
website: www.rspb.org.uk

There are five hides out on the **Old Moor Wetlands Centre RSPB** reserve and one overlooking the bird-feeding garden. There are two viewing platforms in the pond and picnic area. Two easy-going trails give excellent views of wildlife on the reserve. Follow the trail around the ponds and picnic area to see wildflower meadows and a variety of birds and insects, or take the trail to the hides, where you can get closer to wildlife in a variety of different habitats. Both trails are suitable for wheelchairs and pushchairs and are less than one mile in length.

Spend time in the hides and you may be rewarded with an unforgettable kingfisher encounter. Listen for their shrill, piping calls and then watch for the flash of blue and orange. You may be luck enough to find a Little Owl perched in a tree or on a fencepost. They become very active at dusk and you may hear their shrill calls. Huge numbers of lapwings gather in winter. If a bird of prey, such as a peregrine, is in the area, they take to the air in a vast wheeling mass. Look among the black and white of the lapwing flocks for the golden glow of the Golden plovers. Several thousand spend winter here. Tree sparrows can be seen at the bird feeding alongside the commoner birds. Listen for their short and sharp 'tek' calls as the fly in and out.

198 THE HUNTSMAN

136 - 138 Manchester Road, Thurlstone, Sheffield,
South Yorkshire S36 9QW
Tel: 01226 764892
e-mail: enquiry@thehuntsmanthurlstone.co.uk
website: www.thehuntsmanthurlstone.co.uk

The Huntsman is a good old-fashioned pub, located adjacent
to the A628 in Thurlston, a short drive South West of
Penistone. This fine, award-winning public house dates in part
back to the 17th Century, and appear not to have aged a day
so soaked is it in local charm and spirit. The father and
daughter team Andy and Ruth who took over in 2009, have
been very successful; no doubt partly due to it being Andy's
local for some 20 years! It has already become renowned for
the fantastic range of real ales, which include regulars
Timothy Taylor Landlord, Black Sheep and Tetleys traditional,
and a rotating selection of three which Andy sources from
proper Yorkshire breweries within a 25 mile radius; why not ask for a little taster when you visit?

The food is, as you can imagine, a fresh hearty affair, with delicious locally sourced produce
used where possible. Sunday afternoons are most popular with local families with the traditional
lunch menu, and there are other special nights (such as curry or chilli) held regularly which are
worth watching out for. Food is served Monday to Friday 6pm - 11pm, Saturdays 5pm - 11pm and
Sundays noon - 10.30pm. Well behaved dogs and children are always welcome!

199 CANNON HALL MUSEUM

Cawthorne, Barnsley, South Yorkshire S75 4AT
Tel: 01226 790270
e-mail: cannonhall@barnsley.gov.uk

Set in 70 acres of historic parkland and gardens, **Cannon Hall
Museum** provides an idyllic and tranquil setting for a day out.
For two hundred years Cannon Hall was home to the Spencer-
Stanhope family. From the 1760s the architect John Carr of
York was commissioned to extend and alter the house while
the designer Richard Woods was hired to landscape the park
and gardens. Over forty varieties of pear trees still grow in the
historic walled garden, as well as peaches and nectarines. The
famed Cannon Hall vine grows in one of the greenhouses. The
park provides an ideal setting for a picnic, outdoor activities
and games. Cannon Hall was sold by the family in the early
1950s to Barnsley Council and was first opened as a museum in
1957. The Hall now contains collections of furniture, paintings, glassware and pottery, much of
which is displayed in period settings. It also houses 'Charge', the Regimental Museum of the
13th/18th Hussars (QMO).

The Victorian Kitchen Cafe near the gardens is open each weekend and during the school
holidays for home-made light refreshments in the traditional setting of the original kitchens and
Servant's Hall. The Museum also has a shop stocking a range of greetings cards, local history
books, confectionery and giftware. Off the A635 Barnsley to Huddersfield Road. Easy access from
junctions 37 or 38 of the M1.

200 CUSWORTH HALL (MUSEUM OF SOUTH YORKSHIRE LIFE)

Cusworth Lane, Doncaster, South Yorkshire DN5 7TU
Tel: 01302 782342 website: www.doncaster.gov.uk

Cusworth Hall is an imposing 18th century country house set in
extensive landscaped parklands. It houses the Museum of South Yorkshire Life which illustrates
the changing home, work and social life of people and communities across the region in the last
250 years. There is access to the ground floor of the museum via a wheelchair lift. The public
toilets in the East Wing contain facilities for people with disabilities.There is a regular
programme of seasonal events as well as a series of temporary exhibitions.

201 CUSWORTH HALL TEA ROOM

Cusworth Lane, Cusworth, Doncaster, South Yorkshire DN5 7TU
Tel: 01302 390959
website: www.cusworthhalltearoom.co.uk

Cusworth Hall Tea Room is found within the old stable block
of Cusworth Hall. In keeping with the hall's traditional
features it has cobblestone floors and a working fire;
affording its guests a truly charming environment in which to
enjoy morning coffee, a light lunch or afternoon tea.

Owner Kay has been running the tearoom for the past eight
years and has a sturdy reputation as the area's best cook and
finest chocolatier. Each day she uses only the freshest local
ingredients to cook up her dishes, which range from breakfast bites,
sandwiches and baguettes, to cakes, pastries and scones. A daily specials
board offers homemade specials whilst the cake display is constantly
changing to offer treacle sponge, ginger cake, carrot cake, flapjacks and
much more. The tearooms themselves are open seven days a week from
10am-4pm, however Kay also offers a buffet service for private functions
in the evenings where she gets to demonstrate real culinary flare with
dishes like melt-in-the-mouth goat's cheese tarts and sautéed tarragon
chicken.

For those with a devilishly sweet tooth, Kay also offers the ultimate in
indulgent experiences; chocolate workshops. Anyone can book a session,
but they are proving particularly popular as gift ideas and hen parties who work away to make
their own chocolates for wedding favours. Please call for details. Cash and cheque only please.

Garden Centres and Nurseries

www.findsomewhere.co.uk
For people who want to explore the United Kingdom

202 MARR LODGE

Barnsley Road, Marr, Doncaster, South Yorkshire DN5 7AX
Tel: 01302 390355

Conveniently located close to junction 37 of the A1(M) on the A635 going towards Barnsley, **Marr Lodge** stands in its own grounds with a large and peaceful beer garden at the rear. Simon and Hazel Denton recently took over this fine establishment, which offers an extensive menu of traditional home-cooked food based on the best, locally-sourced produce. All the meat used here is British and wherever possible is acquired from South Yorkshire farmers.

Two professional chefs are employed here. The extensive menu has plenty to offer. Starter dishes include home-made soup, mushrooms served in a smooth creamy garlic sauce accompanied by hot buttered toast, cheesy nachos; and spring roles.

Among the main courses served are hunters chicken, homemade steak and ale pie, whole-tail breaded scampi, large battered cod and homemade beef lasagne. Vegetarian options include mushroom, broccoli and stilton bake, veggie burger, and vegetable lasagne.

In addition to the regular menu, from Monday to Friday lunchtime specials are available from noon until 2.30pm. These include dishes such as liver & onions, roast of the day, cold meat salad and shepherd's pie. For desserts, how about a treacle sponge pudding, apple crumble or ice cream?

The child-friendly Marr Lodge has a well-stocked bar that always has one or two real ales on tap, with Black Sheep as the regular brew. The Lodge also has a separate dining room which is available to hire for functions.

Food is served from noon until 9pm, Monday to Saturday; and from noon until 7pm on Sunday. From Monday to Saturday, a Carvery is also available from noon until 3pm, on Saturday evenings from 6pm to 9pm, and on Sunday from noon "till it's gone!". Because of the popularity of the food served here, booking is strongly advised, especially on Sundays.

All major credit cards are accepted; there is good disabled access throughout; and ample off road parking.

203 SCARBOROUGH ARMS

Sunderland Street, Tickhill, Doncaster, South Yorkshire DN11 9QJ
Tel: 01302 742977

Just eight miles south of Doncaster lies the town of Tickhill. This historical town owes its place in history to William the Conqueror who gave much of the estate surrounding Tickhill to Roger de Busli, one of the most powerful Norman magnates to accompany him to England. The castle he built there played a part in many historical events including the base for Prince John when usurping his brother Richard I in the 12th century. Today the ruins make an atmospheric day trip for visitors of any age, but is sometimes usurped itself by the town being the hometown of the Top Gear star Jeremy Clarkson.

It's also the hometown of the **Scarborough Arms**, a handsome ivy covered establishment, known for its range of real ales and excellent hospitality. It's owned and run by Stephen and Rosemarie Walters who have been at the Scarborough for four years. They open all day every day and offer their guests a choice of up to five real ales. Regular brews include Abbot Ale, Spitfire and John Smith's Cask. Two brews are kept on rotation from both local and national breweries ensuring that there is always something new to try. During bank holidays beer festivals are also held at the Scarborough, adding over thirty new ales to the mix. As there is no food served at the Scarborough, the focus is on providing the best. Stephen and Rosemarie have won awards for their ales, and also stock a fine variety of wines and spirits. The wood panelled bar provides an atmospheric watering hole with beautiful brass topped barrels converted into tables and old fashioned pub pews for seats. A large beer garden to the rear of the inn also provides a handsome setting for an afternoon drink, particularly in the summer months when the flowers are in bloom. Entertainment at the inn includes a quiz from 9:30pm on Mondays and a music themed quiz on Thursdays at the same time.

Stephen and Rosemarie also offer upstairs accommodation throughout the year. There are three twin rooms and one double room to choose from, each of which has full en suite facilities. The rooms are elegantly decorated in a variety of cool creams and duck egg blues with splashes of chocolate woven throughout. Each room commands good views across the surrounding area, bringing a country feel to rather contemporary accommodation. Breakfast is served to each room in a continental fashion. Cash and cheque only please.

204 THE SHIP

Gainsborough Road, Bawtry near Doncaster, South Yorkshire DN10 6HT
Tel: 01302 710129/710235
e-mail: davewallis@theship-bawtry.com
website: www.theship-bawtry.com

Just two hundred yards from the centre of Bawtry lies the **Ship Inn**. A few short years ago this attractive property was an average village inn with a somewhat lack lustre appeal. Today it stands vibrant and alive; a real hub of activity for the locals and visitors from further afield who frequent it.

The Ship was taken over three years ago by Dave and Mandy Wallis, who have an extensive background in the hospitality trade. They make a fantastically charismatic team who have forged a true bond with the area and its inhabitants and intend on taking over another inn called the Blacksmith's Arms in Everton soon where guest accommodation is available. The Ship's interior is reminiscent of an old country house with fine brass fixtures and polished woods, testament to the hard work that has been put into restoring it.

Dave and Mandy open every session, serving a fine selection of wines and spirits and show dedication to the real ale trade, keeping four cask marque approved ales rotating throughout the year. Each September they hold a beer festival complete with live music and an outside bar. The inn's beer garden comfortably offers guests an outdoor space with attractive hanging baskets to brighten it up on greyer days.

Food is available between 12-9pm Monday to Saturday from 12-9pm and from 12-5pm on Sundays. Dave began his career as a professional chef in 1972 and has built up an impressive reputation throughout Yorkshire and its neighbouring counties. Owing to popularity, booking is recommended – or as one newspaper review cleverly put it 'don't miss the boat with food this good.' Guests can choose from a small printed menu or the specials board which offers a selection of more creative dishes made using the best seasonal produce available. There is plenty of choice on the menu, with something for every taste and budget. All dishes are reasonably priced, cooked fresh to order each day. Guests can choose from a selection of filled sandwiches and baguettes, jacket potatoes, succulent grills, fish dishes and traditional pies. The Sunday lunch is something of a speciality, with additional pie, fish and vegetarian options. Guests can also opt for a two or three course Sunday lunch with a selection of homemade hot and cold puddings to round off the meal.

205 THE GARDEN ROOM

High Street, Braithwell, Rotherham,
South Yorkshire S66 7AL
Tel: 01709 790790

'Daytime Dining'

People come from all over South Yorkshire and beyond to enjoy fresh homemade food in a happy, relaxed atmosphere at **The Garden Room**, which is run by Gina and Stuart Moore and their cheerful, hardworking team.

The restaurant is located in the village of Braithwell, a short drive south from Doncaster and east of Rotherham, and just five minutes from Junction 1 of the M18. In the heart of the village, it occupies old farm buildings on the farm where Gina was born. The aim of Stuart, a chef of 20 years' standing, is to provide customers with good-quality home-cooked food using local, fresh ingredients cooked simply and served in a relaxed and friendly environment. The success of that ambition is a large and loyal clientele and accolades from all over the region.

The small kitchen produces an amazing variety of dishes to cater for a wide range of tastes and appetites; some dishes are British stalwarts, while others take their inspiration from the Mediterranean and beyond. The breakfast menu, available from 10 to 11.30, offers a variety of combinations, from dry-cured bacons sandwiches and several ways with eggs. From 11.45 the options comprise salads, sandwiches and 'Heartier Options'. Sandwiches are made to order in white or granary bread, on ciabatta or in tortilla wraps, fillings can be cold – honey-roast ham, tuna with spring onions and mayonnaise – or hot – succulent steak, bacon & brie melt. All the sandwiches are accompanied by a beetroot compote and a salad garnish, thus providing a tasty, satisfying quick lunch. Interesting speciality salads include chicken & pancetta and sirloin steak with cashew nuts, chilli, spring onions and an oriental dressing. 'Heartier Options' run from onion & manchego tart to four-herb pasta and Friday's fish & chips whos accolades have been discussed on the local BBC radio station. For those with a sweeter tooth, all-day goodies include Danish pastries, and a fantastic selection of homemade cakes including our famous lemon meringue and carrot cake.

To drink, the Garden room offers everything from teas and coffees to fruit juices and wines by glass or bottle – and champagne to push the boat out for a special occasion. The restaurant has seats for 40 inside and a similar number outside in the patio garden. Awarded best restaurant for couples and friends in the area. Dogs are also welcome outside. The Garden Room is open from 10am to 4.30pm (last orders by 3.30. Closed Mondays except Bank Holidays.

206 CONISBROUGH CASTLE & VISITOR CENTRE

Castle Hill, Conisbrough, Doncaster, South Yorkshire DN12 3BU
Tel: 01709 863329
website: www.conisbroughcastle.org.uk

Conisbrough Castle has been standing guard over the Dearne valley for nearly 850 years and is now open for families to enjoy all year round. Built in 1180 by Hamelin Plantagenet, one of England's most influential noblemen, this castle has weathered the centuries in remarkable condition, helped by an ambitious reconstruction project which has added new floors and a roof to the splendid circular tower.

The fame of this landmark has been spread worldwide thanks to Sir Walter Scott's classic novel Ivanhoe, from where the name of the present managing agent The Ivanhoe Trust arises. The Trust employs specialist guides who run spectacular medieval re-enactments, take educational and leisure tours, and strive to bring eight centuries to history of life for the new millennium.

The castle tearooms, in the former custodian's cottage, also feature an exhibition of old photographs of the area donated by the local heritage society.

Open from 10am until 5pm April – end September and until 4pm October – end March. Last admission is 40 minutes before closing.

207 BRODSWORTH HALL AND GARDENS

Brodsworth, nr Doncaster, South Yorkshire DN5 7XJ
Tel: 01302 722598
website: www.english-heritage.org.uk

One of England's most complete Victorian country houses, **Brodsworth Hall** was opened to the public in 1995 following a major programme of restoration and conservation by English Heritage. Charles Sabine Augustus Thellusson inherited the Brodsworth estate, together with a considerable fortune, in 1859 and decided to commission a new mansion to replace the old 18th century house. Built in the Italianate style and then decorated and furnished in the opulent fashion of the 1860's, much of the original scheme survives to this day. Rich decorative schemes and finishes are found throughout the house and the halls form an elegant setting for a succession of bright white marble statues, many of which came from the Dublin International Exhibition of 1865. English Heritage decided to conserve rather than restore the interior, retaining the original furnishings and finishes, so preserving the patina that only time and family use can bring. Hence Brodsworth today is the story of a once brashly opulent house now having grown comfortably old and inviting to all.

The gardens complemented the house when laid out in the 1860's and are now well on their way to being restored to their appearance at the time of their maturity. Beyond the terrace and croquet lawns, bordered by clipped evergreen shrubs, lies the formal flower garden now superbly laid out with spring and summer bedding appropriate to the period. Beyond can be found the romantic quarry garden, an enchantment of paths, bridges and vistas, with its newly resorted rock garden and fern dell.

TOURIST INFORMATION CENTRES

Aysgarth Falls

Aysgarth Falls National Park Centre, Aysgarth Falls,
Leyburn, North Yorkshire DL8 3TH

e-mail: aysgarth@ytbtic.co.uk

Tel: 01969 662910

Barnsley

Central Library, Shambles Street, Barnsley,
South Yorkshire S70 2JF

e-mail: barnsley@ytbtic.co.uk

Tel: 01226 206757

Beverley

34 Butcher Row, Beverley, East Yorkshire HU17 0AB

e-mail: beverley.tic@vhey.co.uk

Tel: 0844 811 2070

Bradford

City Hall, Centenary Square, Bradford,
West Yorkshire BD1 1HY

e-mail: bradford.vic@bradford.gov.uk

Tel: 01274 433678

Bridlington

25 Prince Street, Bridlington,
East Riding of Yorkshire YO15 2NP

e-mail: visitrealyorkshire.co.uk

Tel: 01262 673474

Danby

The Moors Centre, Danby Lodge, Lodge Lane, Danby,
Whitby, North Yorkshire YO21 2NB

e-mail: moorscentre@northyorkmoors-npa.gov.uk

Tel: 01439 772737

Doncaster

38-40 High Street, Doncaster, South Yorkshire DN1 1DE

e-mail: tourist.information@doncaster.gov.uk

Tel: 01302 734309

Filey

The Evron Centre, John Street, Filey,
North Yorkshire YO14 9DW

e-mail: fileytic@scarborough.gov.uk

Tel: 01723 383637

Grassington

National Park Centre, Colvend, Hebden Road,
Grassington, North Yorkshire BD23 5LB

e-mail: grassington@ytbtic.co.uk

Tel: 01756 752774

Halifax

Piece Hall, Halifax, West Yorkshire HX1 1RE

e-mail: halifax@ytbtic.co.uk

Tel: 01422 368725

Harrogate

Royal Baths, Crescent Road, Harrogate,
North Yorkshire, HG1 2RR

e-mail: tic@harrogate.gov.uk

Tel: 0845 389 3223

Hawes

Dales Countryside Museum, Station Yard, Hawes,
North Yorkshire,DL8 3NT

e-mail: hawes@ytbtic.co.uk

Tel: 01969 666210

Haworth

2/4 West Lane, Haworth, Near Keighley,
West Yorkshire, BD22 8EF

e-mail: haworth.vic@bradford.gov.uk

Tel: 01535 642329

Hebden Bridge

Visitor and Canal Centre, New Road, Hebden Bridge,
West Yorkshire, HX7 8AF

e-mail: hebdenbridge@ytbtic.co.uk

Tel: 01422 843831

TOURIST INFORMATION CENTRES

Helmsley

The Visitor Centre, Helmsley Castle, Castlegate,
North Yorkshire, YO62 5AB

e-mail: helmsley.tic@english-heritage.org.uk

Tel: 01439 770173

Holmfirth

49-51 Huddersfield Road, Holmfirth,
West Yorkshire HD9 3JP

e-mail: holmfirth.tic@kirklees.gov.uk

Tel: 01484 222444

Hornsea

120 Newbegin, Hornsea, Yorkshire HU18 1PB

e-mail: hornsea.tic@eastriding.gov.uk

Tel: 01964 536404

Horton-in-Ribblesdale

Pen-y-ghent Cafe, Horton-in-Ribblesdale, Settle,
North Yorkshire BD24 0HE

e-mail: mail@pen-y-ghentcafe.co.uk

Tel: 01729 860333

Hull

1 Paragon Street, Hull, East Yorkshire HU1 3NA

e-mail: tourist.information@hullcc.gov.uk

Tel: 01482 223559

Humber Bridge

North Bank Viewing Area, Ferriby Road, Hessle,
East Yorkshire HU13 OLN

e-mail: humberbridge.tic@vhey.co.uk

Tel: 0844 811 2070

Ilkley

Town Hall, Station Rd, Ilkley, West Yorkshire LS29 8HB

e-mail: ilkley.vic@bradford.gov.uk

Tel: 01943 602319

Ingleton

The Community Centre Car Park, Ingleton,
North Yorkshire LA6 3HG

e-mail: ingleton@ytbtic.co.uk

Tel: 015242 41049

Knaresborough

9 Castle Courtyard, Market Place, Knaresborough,
North Yorkshire HG5 8AE

e-mail: kntic@harrogate.gov.uk

Tel: 0845 389 0177

Leeds

Leeds Visitor Centre, PO Box 244, The Arcade,
City Station, Leeds, West Yorkshire LS1 1PL

e-mail: tourinfo@leeds.gov.uk

Tel: 0113 242 5242

Leeming Bar

The Yorkshire Maid, The Great North Road, Leeming
Bar, Bedale, North Yorkshire DL8 1DT

e-mail: leeming@ytbtic.co.uk

Tel: 01677 424262

Leyburn

4 Central Chambers, Railway Street, Leyburn,
North Yorkshire DL8 5BB

e-mail: Leyburntic@Richmondshire.gov.uk

Tel: 01748 828747

Malham

National Park Centre, Malham, Skipton,
North Yorkshire BD23 4DA

e-mail: malham@ytbtic.co.uk

Tel: 01969 652380

Malton

Malton Museum, Market Place, Malton,
Yorkshire YO17 7LP

e-mail: maltontic@btconnect.com

Tel: 01653 600048

TOURIST INFORMATION CENTRES

Otley

Otley Library & Tourist Information, Nelson Street, Otley, West Yorkshire LS21 1EZ

e-mail: otleytic@leedslearning.net

Tel: 0113 247 7707

Pateley Bridge

18 High Street, Pateley Bridge, North Yorkshire HG3 5AW

e-mail: pbtic@harrogate.gov.uk

Tel: 0845 389 0179

Pickering

Ropery House, The Ropery, Pickering, North Yorkshire YO18 8DY

e-mail: pickering@ytbtic.co.uk

Tel: 01751 473791

Reeth

Hudson House, The Green Reeth, Richmond, North Yorkshire DL11 6TB

e-mail: reeth@ytbtic.co.uk

Tel: 01748 884059

Richmond

Friary Gardens, Victoria Road, Richmond, North Yorkshire DL10 4AJ

e-mail: Richmondtic@Richmondshire.gov.uk

Tel: 01748 828742

Ripon

Minster Road, Ripon, North Yorkshire HG4 1QT

e-mail: ripontic@harrogate.gov.uk

Tel: 0845 389 0178

Rotherham

40 Bridgegate, Rotherham, South Yorkshire S60 1PQ

e-mail: tic@rotherham.gov.uk

Tel: 01709 835904

Scarborough

Brunswick Shopping Centre, Westborough, Scarborough, North Yorkshire YO11 1UE

e-mail: tourismbureau@scarborough.gov.uk

Tel: 01723 383636

Scarborough Harbourside

Harbourside TIC, Sandside, Scarborough, North Yorkshire YO11 1PP

e-mail: harboursidetic@scarborough.gov.uk

Tel: 01723 383636

Selby

Visitor Information Centre, 52 Micklegate, Selby, North Yorkshire YO8 4EQ

e-mail: selby@ytbtic.co.uk

Tel: 0845 0349543

Settle

Town Hall, Cheapside, Settle, North Yorkshire BD24 9EJ

e-mail: settle@ytbtic.co.uk

Tel: 01729 825192

Sheffield

Visitor Information Point, 14 Norfolk Row, Sheffield, Yorkshire S1 2PA

e-mail: visitor@sheffield.gov.uk

Tel: 0114 2211900

Skipton

35 Coach Street, Skipton, North Yorkshire BD23 1LQ

e-mail: skipton@ytbtic.co.uk

Tel: 01756 792809

Sutton Bank

Sutton Bank Visitor Centre, Sutton Bank, Thirsk, North Yorkshire YO7 2EH

e-mail: suttonbank@ytbtic.co.uk

Tel: 01845 597426

TOURIST INFORMATION CENTRES

Thirsk

Thirsk, 49 Market Place, Thirsk,
North Yorkshire YO7 1HA
e-mail: thirsktic@hambleton.gov.uk
Tel: 01845 522755

Todmorden

15 Burnley Road, Todmorden, West Yorkshire OL14 7BU
e-mail: todmorden@ytbtic.co.uk
Tel: 01706 818181

Wakefield

9 The Bull Ring, Wakefield, West Yorkshire WF1 1HB
e-mail: tic@wakefield.gov.uk
Tel: 0845 601 8353

Wetherby

Wetherby Library & Tourist Info. Centre, 17 Westgate,
Wetherby, West Yorkshire LS22 6LL
e-mail: wetherbytic@leedslearning.net
Tel: 01937 582151

Whitby

Langborne Road, Whitby, North Yorkshire YO21 1YN
e-mail: whitbytic@scarborough.gov.uk
Tel: 01723 383636

Withernsea

Withernsea Lighthouse Museum, Hull Road,
Withernsea, Yorkshire HU19 2DY
e-mail: info@vhey.co.uk
Tel: 0844 8112070

York

1 Museum Street, York, North Yorkshire YO1 7HB
e-mail: info@visityork.org
Tel: 01904 550099

IMAGE COPYRIGHT HOLDERS

COPYRIGHT HOLDERS ARE AS FOLLOWS:

IMAGE COPYRIGHT HOLDERS

ORDER FORM

To order any of our publications just fill in the payment details below and complete the order form. For orders of less than 4 copies please add £1 per book for postage and packing. Orders over 4 copies are P & P free.

Please Complete Either:

I enclose a cheque for £ [_____] made payable to Travel Publishing Ltd

Or:

CARD NO: [_____]   EXPIRY DATE: [_____]

SIGNATURE: [_____]

NAME: [_____]

ADDRESS: [_____]

TEL NO: [_____]

Please either send, telephone, fax or e-mail your order to:

Travel Publishing Ltd, Airport Business Centre, 10 Thornbury Road, Estover, Plymouth PL6 7PP
Tel: 01752 697280   Fax: 01752 697299 e-mail: info@travelpublishing.co.uk

	PRICE	QUANTITY		PRICE	QUANTITY
HIDDEN PLACES REGIONAL TITLES			**COUNTRY LIVING RURAL GUIDES**		
Cornwall	£8.99	....	East Anglia	£10.99	....
Devon	£8.99	....	Heart of England	£10.99	....
Dorset, Hants & Isle of Wight	£8.99	....	Ireland	£11.99	....
East Anglia	£8.99	....	North East of England	£10.99	....
Lake District & Cumbria	£8.99	....	North West of England	£10.99	....
Lancashire & Cheshire	£8.99	....	Scotland	£11.99	....
Northumberland & Durham	£8.99	....	South of England	£10.99	....
Peak District and Derbyshire	£8.99	....	South East of England	£10.99	....
Yorkshire	£8.99	....	Wales	£11.99	....
HIDDEN PLACES NATIONAL TITLES			West Country	£10.99	....
England	£11.99	....			
Ireland	£11.99	....			
Scotland	£11.99	....			
Wales	£11.99	....	**TOTAL QUANTITY**	[_____]	
OTHER TITLES					
Off The Motorway	£11.99	....	**TOTAL VALUE**	[_____]	
Garden Centres and Nurseries of Britain	£11.99	....			

READER REACTION FORM

The *Travel Publishing* research team would like to receive readers' comments on any visitor attractions or places reviewed in the book and also recommendations for suitable entries to be included in the next edition. This will help ensure that the *Hidden Places series of Travel Guides* continues to provide its readers with useful information on the more interesting, unusual or unique features of each attraction or place ensuring that their visit to the local area is an enjoyable and stimulating experience. To provide your comments or recommendations would you please complete the forms below and overleaf as indicated and send to:

The Research Department, Travel Publishing Ltd, Airport Business Centre, 10 Thornbury Road, Estover, Plymouth PL6 7PP

YOUR NAME:

YOUR ADDRESS:

YOUR TEL NO:

Please tick as appropriate: COMMENTS   RECOMMENDATION

ESTABLISHMENT:

ADDRESS:

TEL NO:

CONTACT NAME:

PLEASE COMPLETE FORM OVERLEAF

READER REACTION FORM

COMMENT OR REASON FOR RECOMMENDATION:

....

....

....

....

....

....

....

....

....

....

....

....

....

....

....

READER REACTION FORM

The *Travel Publishing* research team would like to receive readers' comments on any visitor attractions or places reviewed in the book and also recommendations for suitable entries to be included in the next edition. This will help ensure that the *Hidden Places series of Travel Guides* continues to provide its readers with useful information on the more interesting, unusual or unique features of each attraction or place ensuring that their visit to the local area is an enjoyable and stimulating experience. To provide your comments or recommendations would you please complete the forms below and overleaf as indicated and send to:

The Research Department, Travel Publishing Ltd, Airport Business Centre, 10 Thornbury Road, Estover, Plymouth PL6 7PP

YOUR NAME:

YOUR ADDRESS:

YOUR TEL NO:

Please tick as appropriate: COMMENTS ☐   RECOMMENDATION ☐

ESTABLISHMENT:

ADDRESS:

TEL NO:

CONTACT NAME:

PLEASE COMPLETE FORM OVERLEAF

READER REACTION FORM

COMMENT OR REASON FOR RECOMMENDATION:

READER REACTION FORM

The *Travel Publishing* research team would like to receive readers' comments on any visitor attractions or places reviewed in the book and also recommendations for suitable entries to be included in the next edition. This will help ensure that the *Hidden Places series of Travel Guides* continues to provide its readers with useful information on the more interesting, unusual or unique features of each attraction or place ensuring that their visit to the local area is an enjoyable and stimulating experience. To provide your comments or recommendations would you please complete the forms below and overleaf as indicated and send to:

The Research Department, Travel Publishing Ltd, Airport Business Centre, 10 Thornbury Road, Estover, Plymouth PL6 7PP

YOUR NAME:

YOUR ADDRESS:

YOUR TEL NO:

Please tick as appropriate: COMMENTS ☐   RECOMMENDATION ☐

ESTABLISHMENT:

ADDRESS:

TEL NO:

CONTACT NAME:

PLEASE COMPLETE FORM OVERLEAF

READER REACTION FORM

COMMENT OR REASON FOR RECOMMENDATION:

INDEX OF TOWNS, VILLAGES AND PLACES OF INTEREST

INDEX OF TOWNS, VILLAGES AND PLACES OF INTEREST

INDEX OF TOWNS, VILLAGES AND PLACES OF INTEREST

INDEX OF TOWNS, VILLAGES AND PLACES OF INTEREST

INDEX OF TOWNS, VILLAGES AND PLACES OF INTEREST

INDEX OF TOWNS, VILLAGES AND PLACES OF INTEREST

INDEX OF TOWNS, VILLAGES AND PLACES OF INTEREST

ADVERTISERS

ADVERTISERS

ADVERTISERS

PLACES OF INTEREST

331

ADVERTISERS